William Warburton

The Divine Legation of Moses Demonstrated

Vol. 4

William Warburton

The Divine Legation of Moses Demonstrated
Vol. 4

ISBN/EAN: 9783337779917

Printed in Europe, USA, Canada, Australia, Japan

Cover: Foto ©Lupo / pixelio.de

More available books at **www.hansebooks.com**

THE

DIVINE LEGATION

O F

MOSES

DEMONSTRATED,

IN NINE BOOKS.

The FOURTH EDITION, Corrected and Enlarged.

BY
WILLIAM, Lord Bishop of GLOUCESTER.

VOL. IV.

LONDON,
Printed for A. MILLAR, and J. and R. TONSON,
in the Strand. MDCCLXV.

CONTENTS

TO THE

FOURTH VOLUME.

A *nature*

CONTENTS.

CONTENTS.

S E C T. V.

S E C T. VI.

THE
DIVINE LEGATION
OF
M O S E S
DEMONSTRATED.

BOOK IV.

SECT. VI.

I COME, at length, to my fecond propofition: which if, by this time, the Reader fhould have forgotten, he may be eafily excufed. It is this, *That the Jewifh people were extremely fond of Egyptian manners, and did frequently fall into Egyptian fuperftitions: and that many of the laws given to them by the miniftry of Mofes, were inftituted, partly in compliance to their prejudices, and partly in oppofition to thofe fuperftitions.*

The firft part of this propofition,—*the people's fondnefs for, and frequent lapfe into, Egyptian fuperftitions,* — needs not many words to evince. The thing, as we fhall fee hereafter, being fo natural

in itſelf; and, as we ſhall now ſee, ſo fully recorded in holy Scripture.

THE time was now come for the deliverance of
the choſen People from their Egyptian bondage:
For now VICE and IDOLATRY were arrived at their
height; the former (as St. Paul tells us) by means
of the latter; for *as they did not like to retain
God in their knowledge, God gave them over to a
reprobate mind, to do thoſe things which are not convenient; being filled with all unrighteouſneſs*, &c[a].
The two moſt populous regions at that time in
the world were CANAAN and EGYPT : The firſt
diſtinguiſhed from all other by its *violence and
unnatural crimes*; the latter by its *ſuperſtitions and
idolatries*.   It concerned God's moral government
that a ſpeedy check ſhould be put to both; the inhabitants of theſe two places being now ripe for
divine vengeance.   And as the Inſtruments he employed to puniſh their preſent enormities were deſigned for a barrier againſt future, the Iſraelites
went out of Egypt with a *high hand*, which deſo-
lated their haughty tyrants; and were led into the
poſſeſſion of the land of Canaan, whoſe inhabitants
they were utterly to exterminate.   The diſpenſation of this Providence appears admirable, both in
the time and in the modes of the puniſhment.
VICE and IDOLATRY had now (as I ſaid) filled up
their meaſure.   EGYPT, the capital of falſe Religion, being likewiſe the nurſery of arts and ſciences,
was preſerved from total deſtruction for the ſake of
civil life and poliſhed manners, which were to
derive their ſource from thence: But the CA-
NAANITES were to be utterly exterminated, to vindicate the honour of humanity, and to put a ſtop

[a] ROM. i. 28.

to a spreading contagion which changed the reasonable Nature into brutal.

Now it was that God, remembering his Covenant with Abraham, was pleased to appoint his People, then groaning under their bondage, a Leader and Deliverer. But so great was their degeneracy, and so sensible was Moses of its effects, in their ignorance of, or alienation from the true God, that he would willingly have declined the office: And when absolutely commanded to undertake it, he desired however that God would let him know by what name he would be called, when the people should ask the *name* of the God of their fathers.—*And Moses said unto* God, *Behold when I come unto the children of Israel, and say unto them, The* God *of your fathers hath sent me unto you; and they shall say unto me,* what is his Name? *what shall I say unto them*[b]? Here we see a people not only lost to all knowledge of the Unity, (for the asking for a *name* necessarily implied their opinion of a plurality) but likewise possessed with the very spirit of Egyptian idolatry. *The religion of* names, as we have shewn[c], was a matter of great consequence in Egypt. It was one of their essential superstitions: it was one of their native inventions: and the first of them which they communicated to the Greeks. Thus when Hagar, the handmaid of Sarai, who was an Egyptian woman, saw the angel of God in the wilderness, the text tells us[d], *She called the name of the Lord that spake unto her,* Elroi, *the God of vision, or the visible God:* that is, according to the established custom of Egypt, she gave him a name of *honour:* not merely a name of *distinc-*

---

[b] Exod. iii. 13.   [c] Page 254, *& seq.*   [d] Gen. xvi. 13.

tion;

tion; for fuch, all nations had (who worfhiped local tutelary deities) before their communication with Egypt [e]. But, after that, (as appears from the place of Herodotus quoted above, concerning the Pelafgi) they decorated their Gods with diftinguifhed Titles, indicative of their fpecific office and attributes. A NAME was fo peculiar an adjunct to a local tutelary Deity, that we fee by a paffage quoted by Lactantius from the fpurious books of Trifmegift, (which however abounded with Egyptian notions and fuperftitions) that the one fupreme God had no *name* or title of diftinction [f]. Zachariah evidently alluding to thefe notions, when he prophefies of the worfhip of the fupreme God,

---

[e] In the hiftory of the acts of Hezekiah, king of Judah, it is faid, that, " He removed the high places, and brake the " images, and cut down the groves, and brake in pieces the " brafen ferpent that Mofes had made: for unto thofe days the " children of Ifrael did burn incenfe to it: and he called it " NEHUSHTAN." [2 KINGS xviii. 4.] The hiftorian's care to record the *name* which the king gave to the brafen ferpent, when he paffed fentence upon it, will appear odd to thofe who do not reflect upon what hath been faid, about the fuperftition of NAMES. But that will fhew us the propriety of the obfervation. This idol, like the reft, had doubtlefs, its *name of honour*, alluding to its fanative attributes. Good Hezekiah, therefore, in contempt of its title of deification, called it NEHUSHTAN, which fignifies A THING OF BRASS. And it was not out of feafon either to nickname it then, or to convey the mockery to pofterity: For the NAME of a demolifhed God, like the fhade of a deceafed Hero, ftill walked about, and was ready to prompt men to mifchief.

[f] Hic fcripfit libros — in quibus majeftatem fummi ac fingularis dei afferit, iifdemque nominibus appellat, quibus nos, DEUM & PATREM. Ac ne quis NOMEN eju requireret, ANΩNYMON effe dixit; eo quod nominis proprietate non egeat, ob ipfam fcilicet unitatem. Ipfius hæc verba funt, ὁ δὲ Θεὸς ἕϊς; ὁ δὲ εἷς ὀνόματος ἡ προσδιᾶται; ἔςι γὰρ ὁ ὢν ἀνώνυμος. Deo igitur nomen non eft, quia folus eft: nec opus eft proprio vocabulo, nifi cum difcrimen exigit multitudo, ut unamquamque perfonam fua nota et appellatione defignes. *Div. Inf.* l. i. c. 6.

unmixed

unmixed with idolatry, fays, *In that day shall there be one Lord, and* HIS NAME ONE [g]; that is, only bearing the fimple title of LORD : and, as in the words of Lactantius below, *ac ne quis* NOMEN *ejus requireret,* ANΩNYMON *esse dixit* ; *eo quod nominis* PROPRIETATE *non egeat, ob ipsam scilicet* UNITATEM. Out of indulgence therefore to this weaknefs, GOD was pleafed to give himfelf a NAME. *And God said unto* MOSES, I AM THAT I AM: *And he said, Thus shalt thou say unto the children of Israel,* I AM *hath sent me unto you*[h]. Where we may obferve (according to the conftant method of divine Wifdom, when it condefcends to the prejudices of men) how, in the very inftance of indulgence to their fuperftition, he gives a corrective of it. — The *Religion of names* arofe from an idolatrous polytheifm; and the NAME here given, implying *eternity* and *self-exiftence,* directly oppofeth that fuperftition.

This compliance with the *Religion of names* was a new indulgence to the prejudices of this people, as is evident from the following words: *And* GOD *spake unto Mofes, and said unto him, I am the Lord: and I appeared unto Abraham, unto Ifaac, and unto Jacob, by the* NAME OF GOD ALMIGHTY, *but by my* NAME JEHOVAH *was I not known to them*[i]. That is, as the GOD of Abraham, I before condefcended to have *a Name of diftinction :* but now, in compliance to another prejudice, I condefcend to have *a Name of honour.* This feems to be the true interpretation of this very difficult text, about which the commentators are fo much embarraffed. For the word *Jehovah,* whofe name is here faid to be unknown to the Patriarchs, frequently occurr-

---

[g] Ch. xiv. ver. 9.   [h] EXOD. iii. 14.   [i] EXOD. vi. 3.

ing in the book of Genefis, had furnifhed Unbelievers with a pretext that the fame perfon could
not be author of the two books of Genefis and
Exodus. But Ignorance and Scepticifm, which
fet Infidelity on work, generally bring it to fhame.
They miftook the true fenfe of the text. The
affertion is not, that the word *Jehovah* was not
ufed in the patriarchal language ; but that the
name *Jehovah*, as a title of honour, (whereby a
new *idea* was affixed to an old *word*) was unknown
to them. Thus, in a parallel inftance, we fay
rightly, that the King's supremacy was unknown
to the Englifh Conftitution till the time of Henry
VIII. tho' the word was in ufe, and even applied
to the chief Magiftrate, (indeed in a different
and more fimple fenfe) long before.

The common folution of this difficulty is as
ridiculous as it is falfe. You fhall have it in the
words of a very ingenious Writer.—" The word
" Jehovah fignifies the being unchangeable in his
" refolutions, and confequently the being infinitely
" faithful in performing his promifes. In this
" fenfe, the word is employed in the paffage of
" Exodus now under examination. So that
" when God fays, *by my name Jehovah was I not
" known to them*, this fignifies,—" as one faithful
" to fulfil my promifes, was I not known to them."
" i. e. I had not then fullfilled the promife which
" I had made to them, of bringing their pofterity
" out of Egypt, and giving them the land of Ca-
" naan [k]." By which interpretation, the Almighty

---

[k] — il fignifie *l'etre immuable dans fes refolutions*, et par con-
fequent *l'etre infiniment fidelle dans fes promeffes*, et c'eft dans
cette acception que ce nom eft emploié dans le paffage de
l'Exode, que nous examinons. Qu' ainfi quand Dieu dit, *Je
ne*

mighty is made to tell the Israelites that he was not known to their forefathers as the God who had redeemed their posterity from Egypt, before they had any posterity to redeem. A marvellous revelation, and, without doubt, much wanted. To return.

MOSES however appears still unwilling to accept this Commission ; and presumes to tell GOD, plainly, *Behold they will not believe me, nor hearken to my voice : for they will say, The Lord hath not appeared unto thee* [1]. But could this be said or thought by a People, who, groaning in the bitterest servitude, had a message from GOD, of a long promised deliverance, at the very time that, according to the prediction, the promise was to be fulfilled, if they had kept him and his dispensations in memory ? When this objection is removed, Moses hath yet another; and that is, his inability for the office of an ORATOR. This too is answered. And when he is now driven from all his subterfuges, he with much passion declines the whole employment, and cries out, *O my* GOD, *send I pray thee by the hand of him whom thou wilt send* [m]. This justly provokes GOD's displeasure : and thereon, he finally complies. From all this backwardness, (and the cause of it could be no other than what is here assigned ; for MOSES, as appears by the former part of his history [n], was

ne leur ai point esté connu en mon nom de Jehovah, cela signifie, *Je ne me suis point fait connoitre, comme fidelle à remplir mes promesses,* c'est a dire, JE N'AI PAS ENCORE REMPLI LA PROMISSE, *qui je leur avois faite, de retirer de l'Egypte leur posterité, et de lui donner la terre de Chanaan.* — M. Astruc. *Conjectures sur le livre de la Genese,* p. 305. He says very truly, that, in this solution, he had no other part to perform, *qu' suivre la foule des Commentateurs tant Chretiens que Juifs.* p. 301.

[1] Chap. iv. ver. 1.   [m] Chap. iv. ver. 3.   [n] EXOD. hap. ii. ver. 12.

forward and zealous enough to promote the welfare of his brethren) we muſt needs conclude, that he thought the recovery of this People from Egyptian superstitions to be altogether deſperate. And, humanly ſpeaking, he did not judge amiſs; as may be ſeen from a ſuccinct account of their behaviour during the whole time God was working this amazing Deliverance.

For now Moſes and Aaron diſcharge their miſſage; and having confirmed it by ſigns and wonders, the *People believed:* but it was ſuch a belief, as men have of a new and unexpected matter, well atteſted.—*They bow the head* too, *and worſhip* [o]; but it appears to be a thing they had not been lately accuſtomed to. And how little true ſenſe they had of God's promiſes and viſitation is ſeen from their murmuring and deſponding [p] when things did not immediately ſucceed to their wiſhes; though Moſes, as from God, had told them before-hand, that Pharaoh would prove cruel and *hard-hearted*; and would defer their liberty to the very laſt diſtreſs [q]. And at length, when that time came, and God had ordered them to purify themſelves from all the *idolatries* of Egypt, ſo prodigiouſly attached were they to theſe follies, that they diſobeyed his command even at the very eve of their deliverance [r]. A thing althogether incredible,

[o] Exod. iv. 31. [p] Chap. v. ver. 21. [q] Chap. iii. ver. 19, 20, 21.

[r] A learned writer [Mr. Fourmont — *Reflexions Critiques ſur les Hiſtoires de anciens Peuples*] hath followed a ſyſtem which very well accounts for this unconquerable propenſity to Egyptian ſuperſtitions. He ſuppoſeth that the Egyptian, and conſequently the Jewiſh idolatry, conſiſted in the worſhip of the dead Patriarchs, Abraham, Iſaac, and Jacob, &c. The miſchief is,

dible, but that we have GOD's own word for it, by the prophet Ezekiel: *In the day* (says he) *that I lifted up mine hand unto them to bring them forth of the land of Egypt, into a land that I had spied for them flowing with milk and honey, which is the glory of all lands: Then said I unto them, Cast ye away every man the abominations of his eyes, and defile not yourselves with the idols of Egypt: I am the Lord your* GOD *But they rebelled against me, and would not hearken unto me: they did not every man cast away the abominations of their eyes, neither did they forsake the idols of. Egypt: Then I said, I will pour out my fury upon them, to accomplish my anger against them in the midst of the land of Egypt. But I wrought for my name's sake, that it should not be polluted before the heathen, amongst whom they were, in whose sight I made myself known unto them, in bringing them forth out of the land of Egypt:*

is, that this should have the common luck of so many other learned Systems, to have all Antiquity obstinately bent against it. Not more so, however, than its Author is against Antiquity, as the reader may see by the instance I am about to give him. Mr. Fourmont, in consequence of his system, having taken it into his head, that Cronos, in Sanchoniatho, was ABRAHAM; notwithstanding that fragment tells us, that Cronos rebelled against his father, and cut off his privities; buried his brother alive, and murdered his own son and daughter; that he was an idolater; and a propagator of idolatry, by consecrating several of his own family; that he gave away the kingdom of Athens to the Goddess Athena; and the kingdom of Egypt to the God Taaut; notwithstanding all this, so foreign and inconsistent with the history of Abraham, yet, because the same fragment says, that Cronos, in the time of a plague, sacrificed his only son to appease the shade of his murdered father; and circumcised himself and his whole army; on the strength of this, and two or three cold, fanciful etymologies, this great Critic cries out, *Nier q'il s'agisse ici du seul Abraham, c'est être* AVEUGLE D'ESPRIT, ET D'UN AVUGLEMENT IRREMEDIABLE. Liv. ii. sect. 3. §. 3. ——

Wherefore

Wherefore I caused them to go forth out of the land of Egypt, and brought them into the wilderness [s].

From all this it appears, that their *Cry, by reason of their bondage, which came up unto* GOD, was not for such a deliverance as was promised to their forefathers, to be *brought up out of Egypt*; but for such a one as might enable them to live at ease, amongst their *flesh-pots*, in it.

But now they are delivered: and, by a series of miracles performed in their behalf, got quite clear of the power of Pharaoh. Yet on every little distress, *Let us return to Egypt*, was still the cry. Thus, immediately after their deliverance at the Red-Sea, on so common an accident, as meeting with *bitter waters* in their rout, they were presently at their *What shall we drink* [t]? And no sooner had a miracle removed this distress, and they gotten into the barren wilderness, but they were, again, at their *What shall we eat* [u]? Not that indeed they feared to die either of hunger or of thirst; for they found the hand of GOD was still ready to supply their wants; all but their capital want, to return again into EGYPT; and these pretences were only a less indecent cover to their designs: which yet, on occasion, they were not ashamed to throw off, as where they say to Moses, when frightened by the pursuit of the Egyptians at the Red-Sea, *Is not this the word that we did tell thee in Egypt, Let us alone that we may serve the Egyptians* [x]. And again, *Would to God, we had died by the hand of the Lord in the land of Egypt, when we sat by the flesh-pots and did eat bread to the full* [y]. That is, in

---

[s] EZEK. xx. 6. *& seq.*   [t] EXOD. xv. 24.   [u] Chap. xvi. ver. 2.   [x] Chap. xiv. ver. 12.   [y] EXOD. xvi. 3.

plain

plain terms, " Would we had died with our bre-
" thren the Egyptians." For they here allude to
the *destruction* of the *first-born*, when the destroying angel (which was more than they deserved)
passed over the habitations of Israel.

But they have now both flesh and bread, when
they cry out the second time for water: and even
while, again, at their *Why hast thou brought us up
out of Egypt* [z], a rock, less impenetrable than their
hearts, is made to pour out a stream so large that
the water run down like rivers [a] : yet all the effect
it seemed to have upon them was only to put them
more in mind of *the way of Egypt, and the*
WATERS *of Sibor* [b].

Nay even after their receiving the LAW, on their
free and solemn acceptance of *Jehovah* for their
GOD and KING, and their being confecrated anew,
as it were, for his peculiar People, Mofes only
happening to stay a little longer in the Mount
than they expected, They fairly took the occasion of projecting a scheme, and, to say the truth,
no bad one, of returning back into Egypt. They
went to Aaron; and pretending they never hoped
to see Mofes again, desired another Leader. But
they would have one in the mode of Egypt; an
Image, or visible representative of GOD, *to go before them* [c]. Aaron complies, and makes them a
GOLDEN CALF, in conformity to the superstition
of Egypt; whose great God Ofiris was worshiped
under that representation [d]; and, for greater holi-
ness too, out of the jewels of the Egyptians. In

---

[z] Chap. xvii. ver. 3.   [a] Ps. lxxviii. 16.   [b] JER.
ii. 18.   [c] EXOD. xxxii. 1.

[d] Ὁ ΜΟΣΧΟΣ οὗτος, ὁ ΑΠΙΣ καλούμενος. *Herodot.* l. iii. 28.

this

this fo horrid an impiety to the God of their fathers, their fecret drift [e], if we may believe St. Stephen, was this; they wanted to get back into Egypt; and while the Calf, fo much adored in that country, went before them, they could return with an atonement and reconciliation in their hands. And doubtlefs their worthy Mediator, being made all of facred, Egyptian metal, would have been confecrated in one of their temples, under the title of osiris redvctor. But Mofes's fudden appearance broke all their meafures; and the ringleaders of the defign were punifhed as they deferved.

At length, after numberlefs follies and perverfities, they are brought, through God's patience and long-fuffering, to the end of all their travels, to the promifed place of reft, which is juft opening to receive them; When, on the report of the cowardly explorers of the Land, they relapfe again into their old delirium, *Wherefore hath the Lord brought us unto this land, to fall by the fword, that our wives and our children fhould be a prey? were it not better for us to return into Egypt? And they faid one to another, Let us make a captain, and let us return into Egypt* [f]. This fo provoked the Almighty, that he condemned that Generation to be worn away in the Wildernefs. How they fpent their time there, the prophet Amos will inform us, *Have ye offered unto me* (fays God) *any facrifices and offerings in the Wildernefs, forty years, O houfe of Ifrael* [g]?

---

[e] — " To whom our fathers would not obey, but thruft him " from them, and in their hearts turned back again into Egypt, " faying unto Aaron, Make us Gods to go before us," &c. Acts vii. 39, 40.

[f] Numb. xiv. 3, 4.   [g] Am. v. 25.

In

In a word, this unwillingness to leave Egypt, and this impatience to return thither, are convincing proofs of their fondness for its customs and superstitions.   When I consider this, I seem more inclined than the generality even of sober Critics to excuse the false accounts of the Pagan writers concerning the Exodus; who concur in representing the Jews as expelled or forcibly driven out of Egypt; For so indeed they were.   The mistake was only about their driver.   The Pagans supposed him to be the King of Egypt; when indeed it was the GOD of Israel himself, by the ministry of Moses.

Let us view them next, in possession of the PROMISED LAND.   A land *flowing with milk and honey, the glory of all lands.*   One would expect now their longing after Egypt should have entirely ceased. And so without doubt it would, had it arose only from the *flesh-pots*; but it had a deeper root; it was the spiritual luxury of Egypt, their *superstitions,* with which the Israelites were so debauched. And therefore no wonder they should still continue slaves to their appetite.   Thus the prophet Ezekiel, *Neither* LEFT *she her whoredoms brought from Egypt* [h]. So that after all GOD's mercies conferred upon them in putting them in possession of the land of Canaan, Joshua is, at last, forced to leave them with this fruitless admonition: *Now therefore fear the Lord, and serve him in sincerity and in truth, and* PUT AWAY *the Gods which your fathers served on the other side of the flood and in* EGYPT [i].   It is true, we are told that *the people served the Lord all the days of Joshua, and all the days of the elders that outlived Joshua, who had seen all the great works of the Lord*

[h] EZEK. xxiii. 8.   [i] JOS. xxiv. 14.

that

that he did for Israel[k]. But, out of fight out of mind. It is then added—*And there arose another generation after them, which knew not the Lord, nor yet the works which he had done for Israel*—*And they forsook the Lord God of their fathers, which brought them out of the land of Egypt, and followed other Gods, of the Gods of the people that were round about them*[l]. And in this ftate they continued throughout the whole adminiftration of their Judges; except, when, from time to time, they were awakened into repentance by the feverity of God's judgments; which yet were no fooner pafs'd, than they fell back again into their old lethargy, a forgetfulnefs of his mercies.

Nor did their fondnefs for Egypt at all abate when they came under the iron rod of their Kings; the Magiftrate they had fo rebellioufly demanded; and who, as they pretended, was to fet all things right. On the contrary, this folly grew ftill more inflamed; and inftead of one Calf they would have two. Which Ezekiel hints at, where he fays; *Yet fhe* MULTIPLIED *her whoredoms in calling to remembrance the days of her youth wherein fhe had played the harlot in Egypt*[m]. And fo favourite a fuperftition were the Calves of Dan and Beth-el, that they ftill kept their ground againft all thofe general Reformations which divers of their better fort of Kings had made, to purge the land of Ifrael from idolatries. It is true, their extreme fondnefs for Egyptian fuperftition was not the only caufe of this inveterate adherence to their Calves. There were two others:

They flattered themfelves that this fpecific idolatry was not altogether fo grofs an affront to the

---

[k] Judges ii. 7.　[l] Judges ii. 10—12.　[m] Ezek. xxiii. 19.

God

God of their fathers as many of the rest. Other of their idolatries consisted in worshiping Strange Gods in conjunction with the God of Israel; this of the calves, only in worshiping the God of Israel in an idolatrous manner: as appears from the history of their erection. *And Jeroboam* [n] *said in his heart, Now shall the kingdom return to the house of David: if this people go up to do sacrifice in the house of the Lord at Jerusalem, then shall the heart of this people turn again unto their lord, even unto Rehoboam King of Judah, and they shall kill me, and go again to Rehoboam King of Judah. Whereupon the King took counsel, and made two* calves *of gold, and said unto them, It is too much for you to go up to Jerusalem, Behold thy Gods, O Israel, which brought thee up out of the land of Egypt. And he set the one in Beth-el, and the other put he in Dan* [o].—— *It is too much for you* (says he) *to go up to Jerusalem.* Who were the men disposed *to go up?* None surely but the worshipers of the God of Israel. Consequently the calves, here offered to save them a journey, must needs be given as the representatives of that God. And if these were so, then certainly the calf *in Horeb:* since, at their several consecrations, the very same proclamation was made of all three: *Behold thy* Gods, *O Israel, which brought thee up out of the land of Egypt.*

The other cause of the perpetual adherence of the Kingdom of Israel to their Golden Calves was their being erected for a prevention of reunion with the Kingdom of Judah. *If this people* (says

---

[n] It is to be observed of this Jeroboam, that he had sojourned in Egypt, as a refugee, during the latter part of the reign of Solomon, 1 Kings xi. 40.

[o] 1 Kings xii. 26. & seq.

the

the politic contriver) *go up to do facrifice in the houfe of the Lord at Jerufalem, then fhall the heart of this people turn again unto their lord, even unto Rehoboam king of Judah.* The fucceeding kings, therefore, we may be fure, were as careful in preferving them, as He was in putting them up. So that, good or bad, the character common to them all was, that *he departed not from the fins of Jeroboam the fon of Nebat, who made Ifrael to fin*; namely in worfhiping the Calves in Dan and Beth-el. And thofe of them who appeared moft zealous for the Law of God, and utterly exterminated the idolatry of Baal, yet connived at leaft, at this political worfhip of the CALVES.—*Thus Jehu deftroyed Baal out of Ifrael. Howbeit from the fins of Jeroboam the fon of Nebat who made Ifrael to fin, Jehu departed not, to wit, the golden* CALVES *that were in Beth-el, and that were in Dan* [P].

But the Ifraelites had now contracted all the fashionable habits of Egypt. We are affured that it has been long peculiar to the Egyptian fuperftition for every city of that empire to have its own tutelary God, befides thofe which were worfhiped in common: But now Jeremiah tells us the people of Judah bore a part with them in this extravagance: *Where are thy Gods that thou haft made thee? Let them arife, if they can fave thee in the time of thy trouble:* FOR ACCORDING TO THE NUMBER OF THY CITIES, ARE THY GODS, O JUDAH [q].

And by the time that the fins of this wretched People were ripe for the punifhment of their approaching Captivity, they had polluted themfelves with all kind of *Egyptian abominations:* as appears

[P] 2 KINGS X. 28, *&feq.*   [q] Chap. ii. ver. 28.

from

from the famous VISIONS of EZEKIEL, where their three capital idolatries are so graphically described. The Prophet represents himself as brought, in a vision, to Jerusalem : and, at *the door of the inner gate that looked towards the north,* he saw *the seat of the* IMAGE OF JEALOUSY *which provoketh to jealousy* [r]. Here, by the noblest stretch of an inspired imagination, he calls this *seat* of their idolatries, the *seat of the Image of Jealousy,* whom he personifies, and the more to catch the attention of this corrupt people, converts into an *Idol*; THE IMAGE OF JEALOUSY *which provoketh to jealousy,* as if he had said, God, in his wrath, hath given you one idol more, to avenge himself of all the rest. After this sublime prelude, the prophet proceeds to the various scenery of the inspired Vision.

I. The first of their capital idolatries is described in this manner : *And he brought me to the door of the court, and when I looked, behold a* HOLE IN THE WALL. *Then said he unto me, Son of man, dig now in the wall : and when I had digged in the wall, behold a* DOOR. *And he said unto me, Go in, and behold the wicked abominations that they do here. So I went in and saw, and behold* EVERY FORM OF CREEPING THINGS, AND ABOMINABLE BEASTS, *and all the idols of the house of Israel* POURTRAYED UPON THE WALL ROUND ABOUT. *And there stood before them seventy men of the ancients of the house of Israel, and in the midst of them stood Jaazaniah the son of Shaphan, with every man his censer in his hand, and a thick cloud of incense went up. Then said he unto me, Son of man, hast thou seen what the ancients of the house of Israel do* IN THE DARK, *every man in the* CHAMBERS OF HIS IMAGERY ? [s].

---

[r] EZEK. viii. 3.　　[s] EZEK. viii. 6, *& seq.*

1. The firſt inference I draw from theſe words is, That the Superſtition here deſcribed was EGYPTIAN. This appears from its objects being the Gods peculiar to Egypt: *every form of creeping things and abominable beaſts*; which, in another place, the ſame prophet calls, with great propriety and elegance, the *abominations of the eyes* of the Iſraelites [1].

2. The ſecond inference is, That they contain a very lively and circumſtantial deſcription of the ſo celebrated MYSTERIES OF ISIS AND OSIRIS. For 1. The rites are repreſented as performed in a ſecret ſubterraneous place. *And when I looked, behold a* HOLE *in the wall; Then ſaid he unto me, Son of man, dig now in the wall: and when I had digged in the wall, behold a* DOOR. *And he ſaid unto me, Go in—Haſt thou ſeen what the Ancients of the houſe of Iſrael do in the* DARK? This ſecret place was, as the Prophet tells us, in the Temple. And ſuch kind of places, for this uſe, the Egyptians had in their Temples, as we learn from a ſimilitude of Plutarch's: *Like the diſpoſition* (ſays he) *and ordonance of their Temples; which, in one place, enlarge and extend themſelves into long wings, and fair and open iſles; in another, ſink into dark and ſecret ſubterranean Veſtries, like the Adyta of the Thebans* [u]: which Tacitus deſcribes in theſe words—atque alibi anguſtiæ, et profunda altitudo, nullis inquirentium ſpaciis pene-

----

[1] EZEK. xx. 7, 8. This ſhews *brute-worſhip* in *Egypt* to have been vaſtly extenſive at the *Exodus*; the time the prophet is here ſpeaking of.

[u] Ὡς —— ἅ τε τῶν Ναῶν διαβάσεις, πῆ μὲν ἀνειμένων εἰς αἴθρα κỳ δρόμους ὑπαιθρίους κỳ καθαρὰς, πῆ δὲ κρυπῆὰ κỳ σκότια καὶα γῆς χρόνων τολιτήρια Θηέαίοις ἐοικότα κỳ σηκοῖς. —— Περὶ Ισ. κỳ Οσ. p. 639. *Steph. ed.*

trabilis."

trabilis *.*" 2. These rites are celebrated by the Sanhedrim, or the elders of *Israel: And there stood before them seventy men of the ancients of the house of Israel.* Now it hath been shewn in the Account of the Mysteries, that none but princes, rulers, and the wisest of the people, were admitted to their more secret celebrations. 3. The paintings and imagery, on the walls of this subterraneous apartment, answer exactly to the descriptions the ancients have given us of the mystic cells of the Egyptians *.* *Behold every form of creeping things and abominable beasts, and all the idols of the house of Israel pourtrayed upon the wall round about.* So Ammianus Marcellinus — " Sunt et " syringes subterranei quidam et flexuosi secessus, " quos, ut fertur, periti, rituum vetustorum — " penitus operosis digestos fodinis, per loca diversa " struxerunt: *et excisis parietibus volucrum ferarumque genera multa sculpserunt, quas hieroglyphicas literas appellarunt* *.*" There is a famous antique monument, once a consecrated utensil in the rites of Isis and Osiris, and now well known to the curious by the name of the Isiac or Bembine Tables ; on which (as appears by the order of the several compartiments) is pourtrayed all the imagery that adorned the walls of the *Mystic Cell.* Now if one were to describe the engravings on that table, one could not find juster or more emphatic terms than those which the Prophet here employs.

---

* Ann. xi. c. 62.

y Thus described by a learned Antiquary, Adyta Ægyptiorum, in quibus sacerdotes sacra operari, ritusque et cæremonias suas exercere solebant, *subterranea loca erant,* singulari quodam artificio ita constructa, ut nihil non mysteriosi in iis occurreret. *Muri ex omni parte pleni tum hieroglyphicis picturis, tum sculpturis* ———— Kircher.

z Lib. xxii. c. 15.

3. The

3. The third inference I would draw from this vifion is, that the Egyptian fuperftition was that to which the Ifraelites were more particularly addicted. And thus much I gather from the following words, *Behold every form of creeping things and abominable beafts, and* ALL THE IDOLS OF THE HOUSE OF ISRAEL, *pourtrayed upon the wall round about.* I have fhewn this to be a defcription of an Egyptian myftic cell: which certainly was adorned only with Egyptian Gods: and yet thofe Gods are here called, by way of diftinction, *all the idols of the houfe of Ifrael:* which feems plainly to infer this People's more particular addiction to them. But the words, *houfe of Ifrael,* being ufed in a vifion defcribing the idolatries of the *houfe of Judah,* I take it for granted, that in this indefinite number of *All the idols of the houfe of Ifrael,* were eminently included thofe two prime idols of the *houfe of Ifrael,* the calves of Dan and Beth-el. And the rather, for that I find the original Calves held a diftinguifh-ed ftation in the paintings of the Myftic Cell; as the reader may fee by cafting his eye upon the Bem-bine Table. And this, by the way, will lead us to the reafon of Jeroboam's erecting two Calves. For they were, we fee, worfhiped in pairs by the Egyptians, as reprefenting Ifis and Ofiris. And what is remarkable, the Calves were *male* and *fe-male,* as appears from 2 Kings, c. x. ver. 29. compared with Hofea c. x. ver. 5. where in one place the mafculine, and in the other the feminine term is employed. But tho' the Egyptian Gods are thus by way of eminence, called the *idols of the houfe of Ifrael,* yet other idols they had befides Egyptian; and of thofe good ftore, as we fhall now fee.

For this prophetic vifion is employed in defcri-bing the three mafter-fuperftitions of this unhappy people,

people, the EGYPTIAN, the PHENICIAN, and the PERSIAN.

II. The Egyptian we have seen. The PHENI-CIAN follows in thefe words : *He faid alfo unto me, Turn thee yet again, and thou fhalt fee greater abo-minations that they do. Then he brought me to the gate of the Lord's houfe which was towards the* NORTH, *and behold there fat* WOMEN WEEPING FOR TAMMUZ* [a].

III. The PERSIAN fuperftition is next defcribed in this manner: *Then he faid unto me, Haft thou feen this, O fon of man? Turn thee yet again, and thou fhalt fee greater abominations than thefe. And he brought me into the inner court of the Lord's houfe, and behold at the door of the temple of the Lord, between the porch and the altar, were about five and twenty men with their backs towards the temple of the Lord, and* THEIR FACES TOWARDS THE EAST, AND THEY WORSHIPED THE SUN TO-WARDS THE EAST [b].

1. It is to be obferved, that when the Prophet is bid to turn from the Egyptian to the Phenician rites, he is then faid to look towards the *north*; which was the fituation of Phenicia with regard to Jerufalem: confequently, he before ftood *fouthward*, the fituation of Egypt, with regard to the fame place. And when, from thence, he is bid to turn into the inner court of the Lord's houfe, to fee the Perfian rites, this was *eaft*, the fituation of Perfia. With fuch exactnefs is the reprefentation of the whole Vifion conducted.

---

[a] EZEK. viii. 13, *& feq.*   [b] EZEK. viii. 15, *& feq.*

2. Again,

2. Again, as the myſterious rites of Egypt are ſaid, agreeably to their uſage, to be held in ſecret, by their ELDERS AND RULERS only: ſo the Phenician rites, for the ſame reaſon, are ſhewn as they were celebrated by the PEOPLE, in open day. And the Perſian worſhip of the ſun, which was performed by the Magi, is here ſaid to be obſerved by the PRIESTS alone, *five and twenty men with their faces towards the eaſt.*

Theſe three capital Superſtitions, the Prophet, again, diſtinctly objects to them, in a following chapter. *Thou haſt alſo committed fornication with the* EGYPTIANS *thy neighbours, great of fleſh*[c]; *and haſt increaſed thy whoredoms to provoke me to anger. Thou haſt played the whore alſo with the* ASSYRIANS, *becauſe thou waſt unſatiable: yea thou haſt played the harlot with them, and yet couldſt not be ſatisfied. Thou haſt moreover multiplied thy fornication in the land of* CANAAN *unto Chaldea, and yet thou waſt not ſatisfied herewith*[d].

And when that miſerable Remnant, who, on the taking of Jeruſalem by Nebuchadnezzar, had eſcaped the fate of their enſlaved countrymen, were promiſed ſafety and ſecurity, if they would ſtay in Judea; they ſaid, *No, but we will go into the land*

---

[c] Fornication, adultery, whoredom, are the conſtant figures under which the Holy Spirit repreſents the idolatries of the Iſraelites: conſequently, by this character of the *Egyptians being great of fleſh*, and in another place, that *their fleſh was as the fleſh of aſſes, and their iſſue like the iſſue of horſes*, EZEK. xxiii. 20. we are given to underſtand that Egypt was the grand origin and incentive of idolatry, and the propagator of it amongſt the reſt of mankind: which greatly confirms our general poſition concerning the antiquity of this Empire.

[d] EZEK. xvi. 26, *& ſ.q.*

of EGYPT, *where we shall see no war, nor hear the sound of the trumpet, nor have hunger of bread, and there will we dwell*[c].

Thus we see what a surprizing fondness this infatuated people had for Egypt, and how entirely they were seized and possessed with its superstitions. Which the more I confider, the more I am confirmed in the truth of Scripture-history, (so opposite to Sir Isaac Newton's Egyptian Chronology) that Egypt was, at the egression of the Israelites, a great and powerful empire. For nothing so much attaches a people to any particular Constitution, or mode of Government, as the high opinion of its power, wealth, and felicity; these being ever supposed the joint product of its RELIGION and CIVIL POLICY.

II. Having thus proved the first part of the Proposition, *That the* Jewish *people were extremely fond of Egyptian manners, and did frequently fall into Egyptian superstitions,* I come now to the second; *That many of the Laws given to them by the ministry of* Moses *were instituted partly in compliance to their prejudices, and partly in opposition to those and to the like superstitions.* But to set what I have to say in support of this second part of the Proposition in a fair light, it may be proper just to state and explain the ENDS of the Ritual Law. Its first and principal, was to guard the chosen people from the contagion of IDOLATRY: a second, and very important end, was to prepare them for the reception of the MESSIAH. The first required that the Ritual Law should be OBJECTIVE to the Pagan superstitions; and the second, that it should be

[c] JEREM. xlii. 14.

TYPICAL

TYPICAL of their great Deliverer. Now the coin-
cidencies of thefe two ends, not being fufficiently
adverted to, hath been the principal occafion of
that obftinate averfion to the truth here advanced,
That much of the Ritual was given, PARTLY *in compliance to the People's prejudices, and* PARTLY *in oppofition to Egyptian fuperftitions :* Thefe men thinking the falfhood of the Propofition fufficiently
proved in fhewing the Ritual to be *typical*; as if
the one end excluded the other : whereas we fee
they were very confiftent ; and hereafter fhall fee,
that their concurrency affords one of the nobleft
proofs of the divinity of its original.

And now, to go on with our fubject : The
intelligent reader cannot but perceive, that the
giving a RITUAL in oppofition to Egyptian fuperftition, was a neceffary confequence of the People's
propenfity towards it. For a people fo prejudiced,
and who were to be dealt with as free and accountable Agents, could not poffibly be kept feparate
from other nations, and pure from foreign idolatries,
any otherwife than by giving them laws IN OPPO-
SITION to thofe fuperftitions. But fuch being the
corrupt ftate of man's Will as ever to revolt againft
what directly oppofeth its prejudices, wife Governors, when under the neceffity of giving fuch Laws,
have, in order to break and evade the force of
human perverfity, always intermixed them with
others which eluded the perverfity, by flattering
the prejudice ; where the indulgence could not be
fo abufed as to occafion the evil which the *laws of
oppofition* were defigned to prevent[f]. And in this
manner it was that our infpired Lawgiver acted with

---

[f] See this reafoning inforced, and explained more at large in
the proof of the next propofition.

his

his people, if we will believe JESUS himſelf, where
ſpeaking of a certain poſitive inſtitution, he ſays,
Moſes for the HARDNESS OF YOUR HEARTS *wrote you
this precept* [z]. Plainly intimating their manners to
be ſuch, that, had not Moſes indulged them in
ſome things, they would have revolted againſt all [h].
It follows therefore, that Moſes's giving Laws to
the Iſraelites, *in compliance* to theſe their prejudices,
was a natural and neceſſary conſequence of Laws
given *in oppoſition* to them. Thus far from the
nature of the thing.

Matter of fact confirms this reaſoning. We
find in the Law a ſurprizing relation and reſemblance between Jewiſh and Egyptian rites, in circumſtances both *oppoſite* and *ſimilar.* But the
learned SPENCER hath fully exhauſted this ſubject, in his excellent work, *De legibus Hebræorum
ritualibus & earum rationibus*; and thereby done
great ſervice to divine revelation: For the RITUAL
LAW, when thus explained, is ſeen to be an Inſtitution of the moſt beautiful and ſublime contrivance. Which, without its CAUSES, (no where
to be found but in the road of this theory) muſt lie
for ever open to the ſcorn and contempt of Libertines and Unbelievers. This noble work is no other
than a paraphraſe and comment on the third part
of a famous treatiſe called *More Nevochim*, of the
Rabbi MOSES MAIMONIDES: of whom only to
ſay (as is his common Encomium) that *he was the
firſt of the Rabbins who left off trifling*, is a poor

[z] MARK x. 5. and MAT. xix. 8.

[h] 'This is ſtill farther ſeen from God's being pleaſed to be
conſidered by them as a *local tutelary Deity:* which, when we
come to that point, we ſhall ſhew, was the prevailing ſuperſtition of thoſe times.

and invidious commendation. Thither I refer the impartial reader; relying on his juſtice to believe that I mean to charge myſelf with no more of Spencer's opinions than what directly tend to the proof of this part of my Propoſition, by ſhewing That there is a great and ſurprizing relation and reſemblance between the Jewiſh and Egyptian rites, in circumſtances both *oppoſite* and *ſimilar.*

I aſk nothing unreaſonable of the reader, when I deſire him to admit of this as proved; ſince the learned HERMAN WITSIUS in a book profeſſedly written to confute the hypotheſis of Maimonides and Spencer, confeſſes the fact in the fulleſt and ampleſt manner [1].

What is it then (a ſtranger to Controverſy would be apt to inquire) which this learned man addreſſes himſelf, in a large quarto volume, to confute? It is the plain and natural conſequence of this reſemblance, namely, That *the Jewiſh Ritual was given partly in compliance to the People's prejudices, and*

---

[1] *Ita autem commodiſſime me proceſſurum exiſtimo, ſi primo longa exemplorum inductione ex doctiſſimorum virorum mente, et eorum plerumque verbis, demonſtravero,* MAGNAM ATQUE MIRANDAM PLANE CONVENIENTIAM IN RELIGIONIS NEGOTIO VETERES INTER ÆGYPTIOS ATQUE HEBRÆOS ESSE. *Quæ cum* ſortuita *eſſe non poſſit, neceſſe eſt ut vel* Ægyptii *ſua ab* Hebræis, *vel ex adverſo* Hebræi *ſua ab* Ægyptiis *habeant.* And again, *Porro, ſi, levato antiquitatis obſcurioris velo, gentium omnium ritus oculis vigilantibus intueamur,* Ægyptios & Hebræos, PRÆ OMNIBUS ALIIS *moribus* SIMILLIMOS *fuiſſe comperiemus. Neque hoc* Kircherum *ſefellit, cujus hæc ſunt verba :* Hebræi *tantam habent ad ritus, ſacrificia, cærimonias, ſacras diſciplinas* Ægyptiorum *affinitatem, ut vel* Ægyptios hebraizantes, *vel* Hebræos *ægyptizantes* fuiſſe, *plane mihi perſuadeam.—Sed quid verbis opus eſt? in rem præſentem veniamus,* [Ægyptiaca, p. 4.] And ſo he goes on to tranſcribe, from Spencer and Marſham, all the eminent particulars of that reſemblance.

partly

partly in opposition to Egyptian superstitions; the Proposition we undertake to prove. Witsius thinks, or is rather willing to think, that the Egyptian Ritual was invented in imitation of the Jewish. For the reader sees, that both sides are agreed in this, *That either the Jews borrowed from the Egyptians, or the Egyptians from the Jews*; so strong is the resemblance which forces this confession from them.

Now, the only plausible support of Witsius's party being a thing taken for granted, viz. that the rites and customs of the Egyptians as delivered by the Greeks, were of much later original than these writers assign to them; and my discourse on the ANTIQUITIES OF EGYPT, in the preceding section, proving it to be entirely groundless, the latter part of the proposition, *viz, That many of the laws given to the Jews, by the ministry of Moses, were instituted partly in compliance to their prejudices, and partly in opposition to Egyptian superstitions*, is sufficiently proved.

But to let nothing that hath the appearance of an argument remain unanswered, I shall, in as few words as may be, examine this opinion, That *the Egyptians borrowed from the Israelites*; regarding both Nations in that very light in which holy Scripture hath placed them. The periods then in which this must needs be supposed to have happened, are one or other of these. 1. The time of Abraham's residence in Egypt. 2.—of Joseph's government. 3.—of the slavery of his, and his brethren's descendants: or 4. Any indefinite time after their egression from Egypt.

Now not to insist on the utter improbability of a potent nation's borrowing its religious Rites from

from a private Family, or from a People they held
in flavery, I anfwer, that of thefe four periods,
the three firft are befide the queftion. For the
charaĉteriſtic refemblance infifted on, is that which
we find between the Egyptian ritual, and what is
properly called MOSEICAL. And let it not be faid,
that we are unable to diftinguifh the Rites which
were purely LEGAL from fuch as were PATRI-
ARCHAL [k]: for Mofes, to add the greater force

and

---

[k] Yet this evafive reafoning a fyftematic writer, who has therefore often fallen in our way, would feem to infinuate in an argument defigned to make fhort work with Spencer's learned
volumes. His words are thefe — " It is remarkable that fome
" learned writers, and Dr. Spencer in particular, have imagined,
" that the refemblance between the ancient heathen Religions,
" and the *ancient Religion which was inſtituted by* GOD, was in
" many refpeĉts fo great, that they thought that GOD *was*
" *pleaſed to inſtitute the one in imitation of the other*. This con-
" clufion is indeed a very wrong one, and it is the grand miftake
" which runs through all the works of the very learned author
" laft mentioned." " The ancient heathen Religions do indeed
" in many particulars agree with the inftitutions and appoint-
" ments of that Religion, *which was appointed to* Abraham *and*
" *to his family, and which was afterwards revived by* Mofes ;
" not that thefe were derived from thofe of the heathen nations,
" but much more evidently the heathen religions were copied
" from them ; for there is, I think, ONE OBSERVATION, which,
" as far as I have had opportunity to apply it, will fully anfwer
" every particular that Dr. Spencer has offered, and that is this ;
" He is able to produce no one ceremony or ufage, praĉtifed
" both *in the religion of* Abraham *or* Mofes, and in that of the
" heathen nations, but that it may be proved, that it was ufed
" by *Abraham* or *Moſes*, or by fome other of the true worfhipers
" of GOD earlier than by any of the heathen nations." *Sacred
and Prof. Hiſt. Conneĉted*, vol. i. 2d ed. p. 316, 317. This
writer, we fee, feems here to fuppofe a palpable falfhood ;
which is, that there is an impalpable difference between the
moſaic and *patriarchal* Religions. But this was not the principal reafon of my quoting fo long a paffage. It was to confider
his ONE OBSERVATION, which is to do fuch wonders. Now
I cannot find that it amounts to any more than this : That the
Bible, in which is contained the account of the Jewifh Reli-

gion,

and efficacy to the whole of his Inſtitution, hath
been careful to record each ſpecific Rite which was
properly Patriarchal.

Thus,

gion, is a much older book than any other that pretends to give
account of the national Religions of Paganiſm.   But how this
diſcredits Dr. Spencer's opinion I cannot underſtand.   I can eaſily
ſee, indeed, the advantage this learned writer would have had
over it, had their been any ancient books which delivered the
origin of Gentile religions in the ſame circumſtantial manner that
the Bible delivers this of the *Jewiſh*; and that, on a proper
application of this ONE OBSERVATION, it appeared that Dr.
Spencer, with all his labour, *was able to produce no one ceremony
or uſage practiſed both in true and falſe religion, but that it might
be proved it was uſed firſt in the true.*   But as things ſtand at preſent, what is it this learned writer would be at?   The Bible is,
by far, the oldeſt book in the world.   It records the hiſtory of
a Religion given by GOD to a people who had been long held
in a ſtate of ſlavery by a great and powerful empire.   The ancient hiſtorians, in their accounts of the religious rites and manners of that monarchy, deliver many which have a ſurpriſing
relation to the Jewiſh ritual; and theſe rites, theſe manners,
were, they tell us, as old as the monarchy.   Thus ſtands the evidence on the preſent ſtate of things.   So that it appears, if, by,
it may be proved, the learned writer means to confine his proof
to contemporary evidence, he only tells us what the reader
knew before, *viz.* That the Bible is the oldeſt book in the
world.   But if by, *it may be proved,* he means proved by ſuch
arguments as the nature of the thing will admit, then he tells us
what the reader knows now to be falſe.   Sir Iſaac Newton hath
given us much the ſame kind of paralogiſm in his account of
the original of letters.   *There is no inſtance,* ſays he, *of letters
for writing down ſounds being in uſe before the days of David in
any other nation beſides the poſterity of Abraham.* [*Chron.* p. 209.]
So that what hath been ſaid above in anſwer to the other, will
ſerve equally againſt this.   I would only remark, that the learned writer ſeems to have borrowed his ONE OBSERVATION
from a chapter of Witſius's *Ægyptiaca,* thus intitled, *Nullius
Hiſtorici ſufficienti Teſtimonio probari poſſe, ea quæ in Religione
laudabilia ſunt apud Ægyptios, quam apud Hebræos antiquiora
fuiſſe,* l. iii. c. 1. to which, what I have here ſaid is, I think,
a full anſwer. — The learned writer will forgive me, if, before
I leave this paſſage, I take notice of an expreſſion which ſeems
to reflect on that good man, and ſincere believer, Dr. Spencer;
but

Thus, tho' Moſes enjoined CIRCUMCISION, he hath been careful to record the patriarchal inſtitution of it with all its circumſtances — *Moſes gave unto you circumciſion (not becauſe it is of Moſes, but of the fathers)* ſays JESUS [1]. So again, where he inſtitutes

but I ſuppoſe not deſignedly, becauſe it ſeems a mere inaccuracy. The words are theſe: *They thought* [i. e. Dr. *Spencer* and others] *that* GOD *was pleaſed to inſtitute the one in imitation of the others.* Now this neither Dr. Spencer nor any believer ever thought. They might indeed ſuppoſe that he *inſtituted one in reference to the other*, i. e. that part of its Rites were in direct oppoſition to the cuſtoms of the idolaters; and part, out of regard to the people's prejudices, in conformity to ſuch of their cuſtoms as could not be abuſed to ſurperſtition. But this is a very different thing from *inſtituting one religion in imitation of another*. As no believer could ſuppoſe GOD did this; ſo neither, I will add, could any unbeliever. For this opinion, *That the jewiſh religion was inſtituted in imitation of the heathen*, is what induces the unbeliever to conclude, that GOD was not its author.

[1] JOHN vii. 22. The parentheſis ſeems odd enough. It may not therefore be unſeaſonable to explain the admirable reaſoning of our divine Maſter on this occaſion. JESUS, being charged by the Jews as a tranſgreſſor of the law of Moſes, for having cured a man on the ſabbath-day, thus expoſtulates with his accuſers. "Moſes therefore gave unto you circumciſion, "not becauſe it is of Moſes, but of the Fathers, [οὐχ ὅτι ἐκ τῦ "Μωσέως, ἀλλ' ἐκ τῶν πατέρων] and ye on the ſabbath day cir"cumciſe a man. If a man on the ſabbath-day receive circum"ciſion, that the law of Moſes ſhould not be broken, are ye "angry at me, becauſe I have made a man every whit whole "on the ſabbath-day?" That is, "Moſes enjoined you to obſerve the Rite of Circumciſion, and to perform it on the eighth day: but if this day happen to be on the ſabbath, you interrupt its holy reſt by performing the Rite upon this day, becauſe you will not break the law of Moſes, which marked out a day certain for this work of charity. Are you therefore angry at me for performing a work of equal charity on the ſabbathday? But you will aſk, why was it ſo ordered by the Law, that either the precept for Circumciſion, or that for the ſabbaticalreſt, muſt needs be frequently tranſgreſſed. I anſwer, that tho' Moſes, as I ſaid, gave you Circumciſion, yet the Rite was not

tutes the Jewish sabbath of rest, he records the patriarchal observance of it, in these words:—*In six days the Lord made heaven and earth, &c. and rested the seventh day, wherefore the Lord blessed the sabbath day and hallowed it* [m].

The

originally of Moses, but of the Fathers. Now the Fathers enjoined it to be performed on the eighth day ; Moses enjoined the seventh day should be a day of rest; consequently the day of rest and the day of Circumcision must needs frequently fall together. Moses found Circumcision instituted by a previous covenant which his *law could not disannul* [*]. But had he originally instituted both, 'tis probable he would have contrived that the two Laws should not have interfered." — This I take to be the sense of that very important parenthesis, *not because it is of Moses, but of the Fathers.*

[m] EXOD. chap. xx. ver. 11. —— No one ever yet mistook *Circumcision* for a natural duty ; while it has been esteemed a kind of impiety to deny the *sabbath* to be in that number. There are two circumstances attending this latter institution, which have misled the Sabbatarians in judging of its nature.

1. The first is, *that* which this positive institution and a natural duty hold in common, namely, the setting apart a certain portion of our time for the service of Religion. — Natural reason tells us, that that Being, who gave us all, requires a constant expression of our gratitude for the blessings he has bestowed, which cannot be paid without some expence of time : and this time must first be set apart before it can be used. But things of very different natures, may hold some things in common.

2. The second circumstance is this, that Moses, the better to impress upon the minds of his People the observance of the sabbath, acquaints them with the early institution of it ; that it was enjoined by God himself, on his finishing the work of creation. But these Sabbatarians do not consider, that it is not the time when a command was given, nor even the author who gave it, that discover the class to which it belongs, but its *nature* as discoverable by human reason. And the sabbath is as much a positive institution when given by God to Adam and his posterity, as when given by Moses, the messenger of God,

* See GAL. iii. 17.

to

The laſt period then only remains to be conſidered, namely, from the Egreſſion. Now at
that

to the Iſraelites and to their poſterity. To judge otherwiſe, is
reducing all God's commands to one and the ſame ſpecies.

Having thus far cleared the way, I proceed to ſhew that the
Jewiſh ſabbath is a mere poſitive inſtitution,

1. From the account the Prophet Ezekiel gives of it — *More-*
ever alſo I gave them my SABBATH, *to be a* SIGN *between me and*
them *. A *ſign* of what? A ſign of a *covenant*. And ſo was
circumciſion called by God himſelf — *And ye ſhall circumciſe the*
fleſh of your fore-ſkin, and it ſhall be a TOKEN [or *ſign*] OF THE
COVENANT *between me and you* †. Now nothing but a Rite
by inſtitution of a POSITIVE LAW, could ſerve for a *ſign* or
token of a covenant between God and a particular ſelected People; for beſides it's uſe for a *remembrance* of the covenant, it
was to ſerve them as a *partition-wall* to ſeparate them from
other nations: And this a Rite by poſitive inſtitution might well
do, tho' uſed before by ſome other people, or even borrowed
from them. But a natural duty has no capacity of being thus
employed: becauſe a practice obſerved by *all* nations, would
obliterate every tract of a ſign or token of a covenant made with
one. Indeed, where the Covenant is with the whole race of mankind, and ſo, the *ſign of the covenant* is to ſerve only for a *remem-*
brance, there, the ſign may be either a *moral duty* or a *natural*
phænomenon. This latter was the caſe in GOD's promiſe or covenant, not to deſtroy the earth any more by water. Here the Almighty, with equal marks of wiſdom, made a natural and beautiful phenomenon, ſeen over the whole habitable earth, the *token* of
that covenant. *And* GOD *ſaid, This is the* TOKEN OF THE COVE-
NANT. *I do* SET *my bow in the cloud, and it ſhall be for a token of*
a Covenant between me and the earth, GEN. ix. 12, 13. Yet it is
wonderful to conſider how this matter has been miſtaken. Perhaps the word, *ſet*, did not a little contribute to it: the expreſſion being underſtood abſolutely; when it ſhould have been taken
in the relative ſenſe, of *ſet for a token*. And in this ſenſe, and
only in this ſenſe, the *bow* was then FIRST *ſet in the cloud*. However, Dr. Burnet of the Charterhouſe, who had a viſionary
theory to ſupport, which made it neceſſary for him to maintain

---

* Chap. xx. ver. 12.   † GEN. chap. xvii. ver. 11.

that time and from thence-forward, we say, the
Egyptians would not borrow of the Israelites, for
these

that the phenomenon of the Rain-bow did not exist before the
flood, endeavours to countenance that fancy from the passage
above, by such a kind of reasoning as this, " That, had there
been a Rain-bow before the flood, it could not have been properly used as a *token* of GOD's *Covenant*, that he would no more
drown the earth, because, being a common appearance, it would
give no extraordinary assurance of security." And to this
reasoning Tindal, the author of *Christianity as old as the Creation,*
alludes, *Perhaps* (says he) *the not knowing the natural cause of
the rain-bow, occasioned that account we have in Genesis of its
institution,* page 228, 229. Its *institution!* The expression is
excellent. GOD's appointing the rain-bow to be a *token* or
memorial, *for perpetual generations,* of his covenant with mankind, is called, *his institution of the rain-bow.* But ill expres-
·sion is the homage to nonsense, for the privilege of Freethinking. However, his words shew, he took it for granted that
Moses represents GOD as then FIRST *setting his bow in the clouds.*
And it is the reasoning which we are at present concerned with.
Now this, we say, is founded in gross ignorance of the nature
of *simple* compacts and promises ; in which, the *only security* for
performance is the known good faith of the Promiser. But, in
the case before us, the most novel or most supernatural appearance
could add nothing to their assurance, which arose from the evidence of GOD's veracity. As, on the contrary, had the children
of Noah been ignorant of this attribute of the Deity, such an
extraordinary phenomenon could have given no assurance at all.
For what then served the rain-bow ? For the wise purpose so well
expressed by the sacred writer, for THE TOKEN OF THE COVE-
NANT. That is, for a memorial or remembrance of it throughout all generations. A method of universal practice in the contracts of all civilized nations. Indeed, had this remnant of the
human race been made acquainted with GOD's Covenant or promise by a third person, and in a common way, there had then
been occasion to accompany it with some extraordinary or supernatural appearance. But for what ? Not to give credit to GOD's
veracity; but to the veracity of the messenger who brought his
Will. Now GOD revealed this promise *immediately* to the children of Noah. But here lies the mistake: Our Deists have put
themselves in the place of those Patriarchs, when a much lower
belonged to them ; and, the promise being revealed to them only
by a third hand, and in a common way, they refuse to believe
it, because not accompanied with a miracle. In the mean time
they forget the condition of the Patriarchs when this covenant

thefe two plain and convincing reafons.   1. They'
held the Ifraelites in the greateft contempt, and
abhor-

was made with them; filled with terror and aftonifhment at
the paft, and with the molt difquieting apprehenfions of a future Deluge, they needed fome fuperior affurance to allay their
fears. Had not that been the cafe, a particular Covenant
had not been made with them ; and had their pofterity all along
continued in the fame condition, we may certainly conclude,
from the uniformity of GOD's dealings with mankind, that he
would, from time to time, have renewed this Covenant, in the
way it was firft given ; or have fecured the truth of the tradition by a fupernatural appearance. But thofe fears foon wore
out: and Pofterity, in a little time, became no more concerned
in this particular promife, than in all the other inftances of divine
goodnefs to mankind. But *Mofes*, as this great philofopher
cqncludes, *had no knowledge of the natural caufe of the rain-
bow.* It may be fo: becaufe I know of no ufe that knowledge
would have been to his Miffion. But he was acquainted with
the *moral caufe*, and the *effects* too, of COVENANTS, which
was more to the purpofe of his office and character ; and which
this freethinking DOCTOR OF LAWS fhould not have been fo ignorant of.

2. But fecondly, if the Jewifh Prophets can not convince
our Sabbatarians, that the mofaic day of reft was *a pofitive inftitution*; yet methinks the exprefs words of Jefus might, who
told the Sabbatarians of that time, the Pharifees, That *the Sabbath was made for man, and not man for the Sabbath.* Mark 11.
27. Now were the obfervation of the Sabbath a natural duty,
it is certain, *man was made for the Sabbath*, the end of his creation being for the obfervance of the MORAL LAW, — the worfhip of the Deity, Temperance and Juftice: nor can we by
natural light conceive any other end. On the contrary, all pofitive inftitutions, *were made for man*, for the better direction of his
conduct in certain fituations of life; the obfervance of which is
therefore to be regulated on the end for which they were inftituted : for (contrary to the nature of moral duties) the obfervance of them may, in fome circumftances, become hurtful to
man, for whofe benefit they were inftituted ; and whenever this
is the cafe, God and nature grant a difpenfation.

3. Thirdly, the primitive Chriftians, on the authority of this
plain declaration of their bleffed Mafter, treated the Sabbath as
a pofitive Law, by changing the day dedicated to the fervice of
Religion

abhorrence, as SHEPHERDS, SLAVES, and ENEMIES, men who had brought a total devastation on their Country: and had embraced a Religion whose Ritual daily treated the Gods of Ægypt with the utmost ignominy and despite [1]. But people never borrow their religious Rites from those towards whom they stand in such inveterate distance. 2. It was part of the Religion of the old Egyptians to borrow from none [m]: most certainly, not from the Jews. This is the account we have, of their natural disposition, from those Ancients who have treated of their manners. While, on the other hand, we are assured from infallible authority that the Israelites, of the time of Moses, were in the very extreme of a contrary humour, and were for BORROWING all they could lay their hands on. This is so notorious, that I was surprised to find the learned Witsius attempt to prove, that the *Egyptians were greatly inclined to borrowing* [n] : but much more

---

Religion from the seventh to the first day, and thus abolished *one* positive Law, THE SABBATH instituted in memory of the *Creation*, and, by the authority of the Church, erected another, properly called THE LORD'S DAY, in memory of the Redemption.

[1] See Spencer, *De Leg. Heb. Rit.* vol. i. p. 296.

[m] — *Ægyptii detestari videntur quicquid* οἱ γονεῖς ἢ παρέδειξαν, *parentes non commonstrarunt,* Witsii *Ægyptiaca*, p. 6. — Πλείοισι δὲ χρεώμενοι νόμοισι, ἄλλοι οὐδένα ἐπικλίωσι τοῖσι. *Herodot.* l. ii. c. 78. — Ἑλληνικοῖσι δὲ νομαίοισι φεύγουσι χρᾶσθαι· τὸ δὲ σύμπαν εἰπεῖν, μηδ' ΑΛΛΩΝ ΜΗΔΑΜΑ ΜΗΔΑΜΩΝ ἀνθρώπων νομαίοισι. οἱ μὲν νῦν ἄλλοι Αἰγύπλιοι οὕτω τοῦτο φυλάσσουσι. c. 91.

[n] His words are these : *Magna quidem laterum contentione reclamat Doctissimus* Spencerus, *prorsusque incredibile esse contendit. considerato gentis utriusque genio; ut ab* Hebræis Ægyptii *in suam tam multa religionem adsciverint. At quod ipsi incredibile videtur, id mihi, post alios eruditione atque judicio clarissimos, perquam*

probabile

more furprifed with his arguments; which are thefe.
1. Clemens Alex. fays, that it was the custom of
the Barbarians, and particularly the Egyptians, to
honour their legiflators and benefactors as Gods.
2. Diodorus Siculus confirms this account,
where he fays, that the Egyptians were the moft
grateful of all mankind to their benefactors. And
3. The fame hiftorian tells us, that when Egypt
was become a province to Perfia, the Egyptians
deified Darius, while yet alive; which honour they
never had done to any other king°.—This is the
whole of his evidence to prove the Egyptian genius
fo greatly inclined to foreign Rites. Nor fhould I
have expofed the nakednefs of this learned and
honeft man, either in this place or in any other,
but for the ufe which hath been made of his authority; of which more hereafter. But Witfius,
and thofe in his way of thinking, when they talk
of the Egyptians' borrowing Hebrew rites, feem

---

probabile eft: IPSO ÆGYPTIORUM ID SUADENTE GENIO.
*In eo quippe præftantiffimi Auctores confentiunt, folitos fuiffe Æ-
gyptios maxima eos exiftimatione profequi, quos fapientia atque vir-
tute excellentiores cernerent, & a quibus fe ingentibus beneficiis af-
fectos effe meminerant: adeo quidem ut ejufmodi mortales, non de-
functos folum, fed & fuperftites, pro Diis haberent.* Lib. iii. c. 12.
p. 262.

° Clemens Alexandrinus clarum effe dicit, *Barbaros eximie
femper honoraffe fuos legumlatores & præceptores Deos ipfos appel-
lantes.* — Inter Barbaros autem cum maxime id præftiterint
Ægyptii. *Qui etiam genus Ægyptium diligentiffime illos in Deos
retulit.* Affentitur Diodorus; *Ægyptios denique fupra cæteros
Mortales quicquid bene de ipfis meretur grata mente profequi af-
firmant.* — Neque popularibus modo fuis atque indigenis ——
fed Peregrinis —— Facit huc Darii Perfarum regis exemplum,
quod Diodori iterum verbis exponam. *Laudem Darius legibus
Ægyptiorum animum appuliffe dicitur* — *Nam cum Sacerdotibus
Ægypti familiaritatem iniit,* &c. —— *Propterea tantum honoris
confecutus eft, ut fuperftes adhuc Divi appellationem quod nulli regum
aliorum contigit, promeruerit.* Lib. iii. c. 12. p. 263.

to

to have entertained a wrong idea of that highly poli-
cied People. It was not in ancient Egypt, as in
ancient Greece, where every private man, who
had travelled for it, found himself at liberty to set
up what *lying vanity* he pleased. For in that wary
Monarchy, Religion was in the hand of the magistrate, and under the inspection of the Public: so
that no *private* novelties could be introduced, had
the people been as much disposed, as they were
indeed averse, to innovations; and that any *public*
ones would be made, by rites borrowed from the
Hebrews, is, as we have shewn above, highly
improbable.

Hitherto I have endeavoured to discredit this
proposition, *(that the Egyptians borrowed of the
Israelites)* from the nature of the thing. I shall
now shew the falshood of it, from the infallible testimony of God himself: who upbraiding the Israelites with their borrowing idolatrous
Rites of all their neighbours, expresses himself in
this manner, by the prophet Ezekiel: *The contrary
is in thee from other Women,* WHEREAS NONE FOL-
LOWETH THEE TO COMMIT WHOREDOMS: *and
in that thou givest a reward, and no reward is given
to thee, therefore thou art contrary* [p]. The intelligent reader perceives that the plain meaning of
the metaphor is this, *Ye Jews are contrary to all
other nations: you are fond of borrowing their Rites,
while none of them care to borrow yours.* But this remarkable fact, had it not been so expresly delivered,
might easily have been collected from the whole
course of sacred history. The reason will be accounted for hereafter. At present I shall only need
to observe, that by the words, *Whereas none fol-*

---

[p] EZEK. xvi. 34.

loweth

loweth thee to commit whoredoms, is not meant,
that no particular Gentile ever embraced the Jewish
religion; but, that no Gentile people took in any
of its Rites into their own national Worship.   That
this is the true sense of the passage, appears from
hence, 1. The idolatry of the COMMUNITY of
Israel is here spoken of: and this, as will be shewn
in the next book, did not consist in renouncing the
Religion of Moses, but in polluting it with idolatrous mixtures.   2. The embracing the Jewish religion, and renouncing idolatry could not, in figurative propriety, be called *committing whoredom*,
tho' polluting the Jewish Rites, by taking them
into their own superstitions, gives elegance to the
figure thus applied.

The Reader, perhaps, may wonder how men
can stand out against such kind of evidence.   It is
not, I will assure him, from the abundance of argument on the other side; or from their not seeing
the force on this; but from a pious, and therefore
very excusable, apprehension of danger to the
Divinity of the Law, if it should be once granted
that any of the Ceremonial part was given *in compliance to the people's prejudices.*   Of which imaginary danger lord Bolingbroke hath availed himself,
. to calumniate the Law, for a COMPLIANCE too evident to be denied.

The apprehension therefore of this consequence
being that which makes Believers so unwilling to
own, and Deists, against the very genius of their infidelity, so ready to embrace an evident truth; I
seem to come in opportunely to set both parties
right: while I shew, in support of my THIRD PRO-.
POSITION, that the consequence is groundless; and
that the fears and hopes built upon this supposed
compliance,

compliance, are vain and fantaſtic; which I venture to predict, will ever be the iſſue of ſuch fears and hopes as ariſe only from the Religioniſt's honeſt adherence to *common ſenſe* and to the *word of God.*

II.

OUR THIRD PROPOSITION is, That *Moſes's Egyptian learning, and the Laws he inſtituted in compliance to the People's prejudices, and in oppoſition to Egyptian ſuperſtitions, are no reaſonable objection to the divinity of his miſſion.*

The firſt part of the Propoſition concerns Moſes's *Egyptian wiſdom.* Let us previouſly conſider what that was. MOSES (ſays the holy martyr Stephen) WAS LEARNED IN ALL THE WISDOM OF THE EGYPTIANS, *and mighty in words and deeds* [p]. Now where the WISDOM of a Nation is ſpoken of, that which is characteriſtic of the Nation muſt needs be meant: where the *wiſdom* of a particular man, that which is peculiar to his quality and profeſſion. St. Stephen, in this place, ſpeaks of both. In both, therefore, he muſt needs mean CIVIL or POLITICAL wiſdom; becauſe, for that (as we have ſhewn) the Egyptian nation was principally diſtinguiſhed: and in that, conſiſted the eminence of character of one who had a royal adoption, was bred up at court, and became at length the Leader and Lawgiver of a numerous People. More than this,—St. Stephen is here ſpeaking of him under this public character, and therefore he muſt be neceſſarily underſtood to mean, that *Moſes was conſummate in the ſcience of Legiſlation.* The words indeed are, ALL *the learning of the Egyptians.*

¶ ACTS vii 22.

But

But every good logician knows, that where the
thing fpoken of refers to fome particular ufe (as
here, Mofes's LEARNING, to his CONDUCTING the
Ifraelites out of Egypt) the particle ALL does not
mean *all of every kind*, but *all the parts of one kind*.
In this reftrained fenfe, it is frequently ufed in the
facred Writings. Thus, in the Gofpel of St. John,
JESUS fays, *When he, the fpirit of truth, is come, he
will guide you into* ALL *truth*ʳ. But further, the
concluding part of the character, — *and mighty in*
WORDS *and* DEEDS, will not eafily fuffer the foregoing part to admit of any other interpretation;
ἦν δὲ δυνατὸς ἐν ΛΟΓΟΙΣ ϰ̓ ἐν ΕΡΓΟΙΣ. This was
the precife character of the ANCIENT CHIEF: who
leading a free and willing People, needed the arts
of peace, fuch as PERSUASION and LAW-MAKING,
the ΛΟΓΟΙ; and the arts of war, fuch as CONDUCT
and COURAGE, the ΕΡΓΑ in the text. Hence it is,
that Jefus, who was *The prophet like unto Mofes*,
the Legiflator of the *new* covenant as the other
was of the *old*, and the Conductor of our fpiritual
warfare, is characterifed in the fame words, δυνατὸς
ἐν ΕΡΓΩ ϰ̓ ΛΟΓΩ ἐναντίον τῶ ΘΕΟΥ ϰ̓ παντὸς τῶ λαῶˢ.
—*A prophet, mighty in* DEED *and* WORD, *before* GOD
and all the PEOPLE. This *wifdom*, therefore, in
which Mofes was faid to be fo verfed, we conclude
was the τὸ πραγματικὸν τῆς φιλοσοφίας, in contradiftinction to the τὸ Ξεωρητικόν. Hence may be feen the
impertinence of thofe long inquiries, which, on occafion of thefe words, men have run into, concerning the ftate of the fpeculative and mechanic arts
of Egypt, at this period.

This being the WISDOM, for which Mofes is here
celebrated, the Deift hafti'y concluded, *that there-*

ʳ JOHN xvi. 13.   ˢ LUKE xxiv. 19.

fore the establishment of the Jewish Policy was the sole contrivance of Moses himself: He did not reflect, that a fundamental truth (which, he will not venture to dispute any more than the Believer) stands very much in the way of his conclusion; namely, *That* GOD, *in the moral government of the world, never does that in an extraordinary way which can be equally well effected in an ordinary.*

In the Separation of the Israelites, a civil Policy and a national Religion were to be established, and incorporated with one another, by God himself. For that end, he appointed an under-agent, or instrument: who, in this work of Legislation, was either to understand the government of a People, and so, be capable of comprehending the general plan delivered to him by GOD, for the erection of this extraordinary Policy: or else he was not to understand the government of a People, and so, GOD himself, in the execution of his plan, was, at every step, to interfere, and direct the ignorance and inability of his Agent. Now, as this perpetual interposition might be spared by the choice of an able Leader, we conclude, on the maxim laid down, that GOD would certainly employ such an one in the execution of his purpose.

There was yet another, and that no slight expediency, in such a Leader. The Israelites were a stubborn People, now first forming into Civil government; greatly licentious; and the more so, for their just coming out of a state of slavery. Had Moses therefore been so unequal to his designation, as to need GOD's direction at every turn, to set him right, he would soon have lost the authority requisite for keeping an unruly multitude in awe; and have sunk into such contempt amongst

amongſt them, as muſt have retarded their deſigned eſtabliſhment.

But it will be ſaid, " if there wanted ſo able a Chief at the firſt ſetting up of a THEOCRACY, there would ſtill be the ſame want, though not in an equal degree, during the whole continuance of that divine form of government." It is likely there would, becauſe I find, GOD did make a proper proviſion for it; firſt in the erection of the SCHOOLS OF THE PROPHETS: and afterwards, in the eſtabliſhment of the GREAT SANHEDRIM, which ſucceeded them. But ſacred hiſtory mentioning theſe *Schools of the prophets*, and the aſſembly of the *Seventy elders*, only occaſionally, the accounts we have of both are very ſhort and imperfect. Which is the reaſon why interpreters, who have not well weighed the cauſes of that occaſional mention, have ſuffered themſelves to be greatly miſled by the Rabbins.

I. The moſt particular account we have of the *Schools of the prophets* is in the firſt book of Samuel, and on this occaſion: David, in his eſcape from the rage of Saul, fled to his protector, Samuel, who then preſided over a *School of the prophets*, at Naioth in Ramah[t]. When this was told to Saul, he ſent meſſengers in purſuit of him[u]. And, on the ill ſucceſs of their errand, went afterwards himſelf[x]. But as it was the intent of the hiſtorian, in this mention of the *Schools of the Prophets*, only to acquaint us with the effect they had on Saul and his meſſengers, when the ſpirit of GOD came upon them, we have only a partial view of theſe Collegiate bodies, that is, a view of them while at

---

[t] 1 SAM. xix. 18.   [u] Ver. 21.   [x] Ver. 23.

their

their DEVOTIONS only, and not at their STUDIES.
For Saul and his messengers coming when the Society was *prophesying* [y], or at divine worship, the
spirit of GOD fell upon them, and they *prophesied*
also. And thus the *Chal. Par.* understands *prophesying*, as did the apostolic writers, who use the
word in the same sense, of adoring.God, and singing praises unto him. For we may well suppose
these Societies began and ended all their daily
studies with this holy exercise.

But from hence, writers of contrary parties have
fallen into the same strange and absurd opinion;
while they imagined that, because these *Schools*
were indeed nurseries of the Prophets, that therefore they were places of instruction for I don't
know what kind of ART OF PROPHESY. Spinoza
borrowed this senseless fancy from the Rabbins, and
hath delivered it down to his followers [z]; from
whence they conclude that PROPHESY was amongst
the mechanic arts of the Hebrews. But an inquirer of either common sense or common honesty
would have seen it was a College for the study of
the Jewish Law only; and, as such, naturally and
properly, a seminary of *Prophets*. For those who
were most knowing as well as zealous in the Law,
were surely the most fit to convey GOD's commands
to his People.

y Ver. 20.

z The author of the *Grounds and Reasons of the Christian Religion* says — " They [the Pagans] learnt the art [divination]
" in schools, or under discipline, as the Jews did *prophesying* in
" the *Schools* and *Colleges of the Prophets* [For which *Wheatly's*
" *Schools of the Prophets* is quoted] where the learned Dodwell
" says, the candidates for prophecy were taught the rules of
" divination practised by the Pagans, who were skilled therein,
" and in possession of the art long before them." P. 28.

This

This account of the nature of the *Schools of the prophets* helps to fhew us how it became a proverb in Ifrael, Is SAUL ALSO AMONGST THE PRO-PHETS[a]? which, I apprehend, has been commonly miftaken. The proverb was ufed to exprefs a thing unlooked for and unlikely. But furely the *fpirit of God* falling occafionally on their fupreme Magiftrate, at a time when it was fo plentifully beftowed on private men, could be no fuch unex-pected matter to the people; who knew too, that even Idolaters and Gentiles had partaken of it, while concerned in matters which related to their Oeconomy. But more than this, They could not be ignorant that the *fpirit of God* had ufually made its abode with Saul; as appears from the following words of the facred hiftorian, *But the fpirit of the Lord departed from Saul, and an evil fpirit from the Lord troubled him* [b]. From all this I conclude that the people's furprife, which occafioned this pro-verb, was not becaufe they heard the *fpirit of God* had fallen upon him; but for a very diffe-rent reafon, which I fhall now endeavour to ex-plain.

SAUL, with many great qualities, both of a public man and a private, and in no refpect an unable Chief, was yet fo poorly prejudiced in favour of the human Policies of the neighbouring Nations, as to become impioufly cold and neg-

---

[a] 1 SAM. xix. 24.

[b] 1 SAM. xvi. 14. — Dr. Mead, in his *Medica Sacra*, cap. iii. p. 25. obferves that *what is faid of the fpirit of the Lord is not to be underftood literally.* He did not reflect that the Vice-gerent of the Theocracy is here fpoken of. Otherwife furely, he could not but acknowledge that if there was any fuch thing as the SPIRIT OF THE LORD exifting in that adminiftration, it muft needs refide in the fupreme Magiftrate.

ligent

ligent in the support and advancement of the LAW
OF GOD; tho' raised to regal power from a low
and obscure condition, for this very purpose.   He
was, in a word, a mere Politician, without the
least zeal or love for the divine Constitution of his
Country.   This was his great, and no wonder it
should prove, his unpardonable crime.   For his
folly had reduced things · to that extremity,
that either He must fall, or the Law.   Now,
this pagan turn of mind was no secret to the
People.   When, therefore, they were told that
he had sent frequent messengers to the supreme
School of the prophets, where zeal for the Law was
so eminently professed; and had afterwards gone
himself thither, and entered with divine raptures
and extasy, into their devotions; they received this
extraordinary news with all the wonder and amaze-
ment it deserved.   And, in the height of their
surprise, they cried out, *Is Saul also amongst the pro-*
phets? i. e. Is Saul, who, throughout his whole
reign, hath so much slighted and contemned the
Law, and would conduct all his actions by the mere
rules of human Policy, is he, at length become
studious of and zealous for the *Law of God?* And
the *miracle*, of such a change in a Politician,
brought it into a proverb before the mistake was
found out.

   This matter will receive farther light from what
we are told, in the same story, concerning DAVID.
A man of so opposite a character, with regard to
his sentiments of the Law, that it appears to have
been for this difference only that he was decreed
by GOD to succeed the other, in his kingdom.
Now David, the story tells us, sojourned for some
time in this School. — *So David fled and escaped,*
and came to Samuel at Ramah, and told him all that
Saul

Saul had done to him, and HE AND SAMUEL WENT
AND DWELT IN NAIOTH [c]. And here it was, as
we may reasonably conclude, that he so greatly
cultivated and improved his natural disposition
of love and zeal for the Law, as to merit that
most glorious of all titles, THE MAN AFTER GOD'S
OWN HEART; for, till now, his way of life had
been very distant from accomplishments of this
nature; his childhood and youth were spent in the
country; and his early manhood in camps and
courts [d]. But it is of importance to the cause of
truth

[c] I SAM. xvi. 18.

[d] There is a difficulty in the history of *David*, in which SPI-
NOZA much exults, as it supports him in his impious undertaking on Sacred Scripture. It is this, In the xvith chap.
of the first book of Samuel, we find David sent for to Court,
to sooth Saul's melancholy with his harp. On his arrival, he
gave so much satisfaction, that the distempered Monarch sent to
his father to desire he might *stand before him*, ver. 22. that is,
remain in his service. David hath leave; and becomes Saul's
Armour-bearer, [ver. 21.] Yet in the very next chapter, viz.
the xviith (which relates an incursion of the Philistines, and the
defiance of Goliah) when David goes to Saul for leave to accept
the challenge, neither the king, nor the captain of his host
know any thing of their champion or of his lineage. This is
the difficulty, and a great one it is. But it would soon
become none, in the usual way Critics have of removing
difficulties, which is by supposing, that whatever occasions
them, is *an interpolation*; and some blind manuscript is always at hand to support the blinder Criticism. But had more
time been employed in the study of the *nature of Scripture History*, and somewhat less in *collations* of manuscripts, those would
have found a nearer way to the wood, who now, cannot see
wood for trees. In a word, the true solution seems to be this:
David's adventure with Goliah was prior in time to his solacing
Saul with his music. Which latter story is given by way of anticipation in chap. xvi. but very properly and naturally. For
there, the historian having related at large, how GOD had rejected Saul, and anointed David, goes on, as it was a matter
of highest moment in a RELIGIOUS HISTORY, to inform us of
the effects both of one and the other; though we are not to sup-

pose

truth to know, that this CHARACTER was not given
him for his PRIVATE morals, but his PUBLIC; his
zeal

pose them, the instantaneous effects. The effect of Saul's rejection was, he tells us, the departure of GOD's spirit from him,
and his being troubled with an evil spirit, [ver. 14.] this leads
him, naturally, to speak of the effect of David's election,
namely, his being endowed with many divine graces; for
Saul's malady was only to be alleviated by David's skill on the
harp. When the historian had, in this very judicious manner,
anticipated the story, he returns from the 14th to the 23d verse of
the xvith chap. to the order of time, in the beginning of the xviith
chapter. So that the true chronology of this part of David's life
stands thus: He is anointed by Samuel,—he carries provisions to
his brethren, incamped against the Philistines, in the valley of
Elah, — he fights and overcomes Goliah, — is received into the
king's court, — contracts a friendship with Jonathan, — incurs
Saul's jealousy,—retires home to his father,—is, after some time,
sent for back to court, to sooth Saul's melancholy with his harp
—proves successful, and is made his armour-bearer,—and, again,
excites Saul's jealousy, who endeavours to smite him with his
javelin. This whole history is to be found between the first verse
of the 16th, and the tenth of the xviiith chapter. Within this,
is the anticipation above-mentioned, beginning at the fourteenth
verse of the xvith chapter, and ending at the twenty-third
verse. Which anticipated history, in order of time, comes in
between the 9th and 10th ver. of the xviiith chapter, where,
indeed, the breach is apparent. For in the 9th verse it is said,
And Saul eyed David from that day forward. He had just
began, as the text tells us, to entertain a jealousy of David
from the women's saying in their songs, *Saul hath slain his
thousands, and David his ten thousands.* " — *From that day*
" *forward Saul eyed David,*" *i. e.* watched over his conduct.
Yet, in the very next verse, it says, *And it came to pass on the*
MORROW, *that the evil spirit from* GOD *came upon Saul — And
David played with his hand — And Saul cast the javelin.* This
could never be on the *morrow* of that day on which he first
began to entertain a jealousy; for the text says, *from that day
forward* he began to watch over his conduct, to find whether his jealousy was well grounded. Here then is the
breach, between which, in order of time, comes in the relation of the evil spirit's falling upon Saul; his sending for
David from his father's house, &c. For when Saul began first,
on account of the songs of the women, to grow jealous of
David, and to watch his behaviour, David, uneasy in his situa-
tion,

zeal for the advancement of the glory of the THE-
OCRACY.   This is 'feen from the firft mention of
                                            him

tion, afked leave to retire: which we may fuppofe was eafily
granted.   He is fent for again to court: Saul again grows
jealous: but the caufe, we are now told, was different: *And
Saul was afraid of David*, BECAUSE *the Lord was* WITH HIM,
and was DEPARTED FROM SAUL, ver. 12.   This plainly fhews,
that the departing of GOD's fpirit from Saul was after the conqueft of Goliah: confequently, that all between ver. 14 and 23
of the xvith chapter is an anticipation, and, in order of time,
comes in between ver. 9 and 10 of the xviiith chapter, where
there is a great breach difcoverable by the disjointed parts of
diftant time.   Thus the main difficulty is mafter'd.   But there
is another near as ftubborn, which this folution likewife removes.
When David is recommended by the courtiers for the cure of
Saul's diforder, he is reprefented as a *mighty valiant man, a
man of war and prudent in matters, and that the Lord was with
him*, chap. xvi. 18. *i. e.* a foldier well verfed in affairs, and
fuccefsful in his undertakings.   Accordingly he is fent for;
and preferred to a place which required valour, ftrength, and
experience; he is made Saul's *armour-bearer.*   Yet when afterwards, according to the common chronology, he comes to
fight Goliah, he proves a raw unexperienced ftripling, unufed
to arms, and unable to bear them; and, as fuch, defpifed by
the Giant.   I will not mifpend the reader's time, in reckoning
up the ftrange and forced fenfes the critics have put upon thefe
two paffages, to make them confiftent; but only obferve,
that this reformation of the chronology, renders all clear and
eafy.   David had vanquifhed the Philiftine; was become a favourite of the people; and, on that account, the objeft of
Saul's jealoufy; to avoid the ill effects of which, he prudently
retired.   During this recefs, Saul was feized with his diforder.
His fervants fuppofed it might be alleviated by mufic; Saul
confents to the remedy, and orders an artift to be fought for.
They were acquainted with David's fkill on the harp, and
likewife with Saul's indifpofition towards him.   It was a de-
licate point, which required addrefs; and therefore they recommend him in this artful manner, — *The fon of Jeffe is cunning in playing, and a mighty valiant man, and a man of war, and
prudent in matters, and a comely perfon:* —That is, " as you moft
have one conftantly in attendance, both at court, and in your
military expeditions, to be always at hand on occafion, the fon
of Jeffe will become both ftations well: he will ftrengthen your
camp, and adorn your court; for he is a tried fo'dier, and of a
                                            graceful

him under this appellation, by Samuel, who tells Saul— *But now thy kingdom shall not continue.* —

The

graceful presence. You have nothing to fear from his ambition, for you saw with what prudence he went into voluntary banishment, when his popularity had incurred your displeasure."—Accordingly Saul is prevailed on: David is sent for, and succeeds with his music. This dissipates all former umbrage; and, as one that was to be ever in attendance, he is made his *armour-bearer.* This sunshine continued, till David's great successes again awakened Saul's jealousy; and then the lifted javelin was, as usual, to strike off all court-payments. Thus we see how these difficulties are cleared up, and what light is thrown upon the whole history by the supposition of an anticipation in the latter part of the xvith chapter, an anticipation the most natural, proper, and necessary for the purpose of the historian. The only reason I can conceive of its lying so long unobserved is, that, in the xviith chap. ver. 15. it is said, *But David went, and returned from Saul, to feed his father's sheep at Beth-lehem.* Now this being when the Israelites were incamped in Elah against the Philistines, and after the relation of his going to court to sooth Saul's troubled spirit with his music, seems to fix the date of his standing before Saul in quality of musician, in the order of time in which it is related. But the words, *David went and returned from Saul,* seem not to be rightly understood; they do not mean, David left Saul's Court where he had resided, but that he left Saul's Camp to which he had been summoned. The case was this: A sudden invasion of the Philistines had penetrated to Shochoh, *which belonged to Judah.* Now on such occasions, there always went out a general summons for all able to bear arms, to meet at an appointed rendezvous; where a choice being made of those most fit for service, the rest were sent back again to their several homes. To such a rendezvous, all the tribes at this time assembled. Amongst the men of Beth-lehem, came Jesse and his eight sons; the three eldest were enrolled into the troops, and the rest sent home again. But of these, David is only particularly named; as the history related particularly to him. *Now David was the son of that Ephrathite of Bethlehem-Judah, whose name was Jesse, and he had eight sons: and the man went amongst men for an old man in the days of Saul. And the three eldest sons of Jesse went and followed Saul to the battle.—And David was the youngest, and the three eldest followed Saul. But David went, and returned from Saul, to feed his father's sheep at Beth-lehem,* i. e. he was dismissed by the captains of the host, as too young for

The Lord hath fought him A MAN AFTER HIS OWN
HEART, *and the Lord hath commanded him to be
Captain over his People* ᶜ.   And again, God himſelf
ſays, *I have choſen Jeruſalem that my name might be
there, and have choſen* DAVID *to be over my people
Iſrael* ᵈ.   Here David's vicegerency, we ſee, is repreſented to be as neceſſary to the ſupport of the
Œconomy, as God's peculiar reſidence in Jeruſalem.   Conformably to theſe ideas it was, that
Hoſea, propheſying of the reſtoration of the Jews,
makes the God of Iſrael and his Vicegerent inſeparable parts of the Œconomy. — *Afterwards ſhall
the children of Iſrael return, and ſeek the* LORD *their*
GOD *and* DAVID *their* KING ᵉ, i. e. they ſhall have

ſervice. And in theſe ſentiments, we find, they continued,
when he returned with a meſſage from his father to the camp.
— I have only to add, that this way of anticipation is very
frequent with this ſacred hiſtorian. — In the xviiith chap. ver.
11. it is ſaid, *And Saul caſt the javelin; for he ſaid, I will
ſmite David even to the wall with it: and David avoided out of
his preſence* TWICE.   But one of theſe times relates to a ſecond
caſting of the javelin a conſiderable time after the firſt, here
ſpoken of, which is recorded in chap. xix. 10.   So again the
hiſtorian telling us in the xth chapter, how Saul, when he
was firſt anointed by Samuel, propheſied amongſt the Prophets,
ſays, *And it came to paſs, when all that knew him beforetime ſaw,
that behold, he propheſied among the prophets, then the people ſaid
one to another, What is this that is come unto the ſon of Kiſh?
Is Saul alſo among the prophets? — Therefore it became a proverb,
Is Saul alſo among the prophets?* ver. 11, 12.   But it is evident,
that the original of the proverb, was his ſecond propheſying
amongſt the prophets at *Naioth*, recorded chap. xix. both for
the reaſons given above, and for theſe: 1. Saul was not at this
time known to the people, and 2. The original of the proverb
is ſaid to ariſe from this ſecond propheſying, ver. 24.   Therefore the account of the proverb in the tenth chapter is given by
way of anticipation.

ᶜ 1 SAM. xiii. 14.   ᵈ 2 CHRON. vi. 6.   ᵉ HOS. iii. 5.

the

the fame zeal for the difpenfation which king David had; and on account of which they fhall honour his memory.   Now if we would but feek for the reafon of this pre-eminence, in David's *public*, not in his *private* character, we fhould fee it afforded no occafion of fcandal[e].   His zeal for the Law was conftantly the fame; as is manifeft by this diftinguifhing circumftance, that he never fell into Idolatry.   But the phrafe itfelf of *a man after God's own heart*, is beft explained in the cafe of Samuel.   ELI the prophet was rejected, and SAMUEL put in his place juft in the fame manner that DAVID fuperfeded SAUL.   On this occafion, when God's purpofe was denounced to Eli, we find it exprefled in the fame manner, *And I will raife me up a faithful prieft*, THAT SHALL DO ACCORDING TO THAT WHICH IS IN MINE HEART[f].   What was then *in God's heart?* (to fpeak in the language of humanity) the context tells us, *The eftablifhment of his Difpenfation.*   Thus, we fee, *the man after God's own heart*, is the man who feconds God's views in the fupport of the Theocracy.   No other virtue was here in queftion.   Tho' in an indefinite way

---

[e] A malignant and very dull buffoon, who appears to have had little idea of this matter, and lefs inclination to be better inftructed, lately publifhed a large and virulent invective againft the perfonal character of DAVID; his pretended provocation was as extraordinary; it was a pulpet parallel; of which he ironically complains, as injurious to a modern character of great name, who is complimented with a likenefs to the King of Ifrael.   He was anfwered as he deferved. — But, if Divines think they can manage infidel cavils by the aid of fums and fyftems, inftead of ftudying to acquaint themfelves with the nature and genius of the Jewifh difpenfation, as it lies in the Bible, unbelievers will have little to apprehend, how bad foever be the caufe which a low vanity has put them upon fupporting.

[f] 1 SAM. ii. 35.

of fpeaking, where the fubject is only the general relation of man to God, no one can, indeed, be called a *man after God's own heart*, but he who ufes his beft endeavours to imitate God's purity as far as miferable humanity will allow, in the uniform practice of every virtue.

By this time, therefore, I prefume the ferious Reader will be difpofed to take for juft what it is worth, that refined obfervation of the noble author of the Characteriftics, where he fays, " It is not " poffible, by the *mufe's art* to make that royal " Hero appear amiable in human eyes, who found " fuch favour in the eye of Heaven. Such are " mere human hearts, that they can hardly find the " leaft fympathy with that ONLY ONE which had " the character of being after the pattern of the " Almighty [g]."——His lordfhip feems willing to make any thing *the teft of truth*, but that only which has a claim to it, RIGHT REASON. Sometime this *teft* is RIDICULE; here, it is the ART OF POETRY — *it is not poffible* (fays he) *for the mufe's art to make that royal Hero appear amiable in human eyes*. Therefore, becaufe DAVID was not a character to be managed by the Poet, for the Hero of a fiction, he was not a fit inftrument in the hands of God, to fupport a Theocracy : and having nothing amiable in the eyes of our noble Critic, there could be nothing in him to make him acceptable to his Maker. But when claffical criticifm goes beyond its bounds, it is liable to be bewildered : as here, The noble Author affures us that David was the only man *characterifed*, to be AFTER GOD's OWN HEART, whereas we fee the very fame character is

[g] *Advice to an Author*, Sect. 3d. vol. 1.

given

given of Samuel; and both honoured with this glorious appellation for the same reason.

II. As for the GREAT SANHEDRIM, it seems to have been established after the failure of Prophecy. And concerning the members of this body, the Rabbins tell us, there was a tradition, that they were bound to be skilled in all sciences [h]. So far is certain, that they extended their jurisdiction to the judging of doctrines and opinions as appears by their deputation to JESUS, to know by what authority he did his great works. And as the address of our blessed Saviour on this occasion deserves well to be illustrated, I shall set down the occurrence as it is recorded by St. Matthew: — " When he was " come into the temple, the chief priests and the " elders of the people came unto him as he was " teaching, and said, By what authority dost thou " these things? And who gave thee this autho- " rity? And JESUS answered and said unto them, " I also will ask you one thing, which if you tell " me, I in like wise will tell you by what autho- " rity I do these things. The baptism of *John*, " whence was it? from heaven, or of men? And " they reasoned with themselves saying, If we shall " say from heaven, he will say unto us, Why did " ye not then believe him? But if we shall say of " men, we fear the people, for all hold *John* as a " prophet. And they answered JESUS and said, " We cannot tell. And he said unto them, Nei- " ther tell I you by what authority I do these " things [i]." We are not to suppose this to be a captious evasion of a question made by those whose authority he did not acknowledge. On the

h See Smith's *Select Discourses*, p. 258.   i Chap. **xxi.** ver. 23, *& seq.*

contrary, it was a direct reply to an acknowledged jurifdiction (as Jesus was obedient to all
the inftitutions of his country) convincing them
that the queftion needed not, even on the principles
of that jurifdiction, any precife anfwer. They fent
to him to know the authority on which he acted.
He afks them whether they had yet determined of
John's: they fay, they had not. Then replies
Jesus, " I need not tell you my authority; fince
the Sanhedrim's not having yet determined of
John's, fhews fuch a determination unneceffary; or
at leaft, fince (both by John's account and mine)
he is reprefented as the fore-runner of my miffion,
it is fit to begin with his pretenfions firft." The
addrefs and reafoning of this reply are truly
divine.

The foregoing obfervations concerning this
method of divine wifdom, in the eftablifhment of
the Jewifh Theocracy, will be much fupported,
if we contraft it with that which Providence was
pleafed to take in the propagation of Chriftianity.

The bleffed Jesus came down to teach mankind
a fpiritual Religion, the object of each individual
as fuch ; and offered to their acceptance on the fole
force of its own evidence. The Propagators of
this religion had no need to be endowed with world-
ly authority or learning; for here was no Body of
men to be conducted; nor no civil Policy or government to be erected or adminiftred. Had
Jesus, on the contrary, made choice of the Great
and Learned for this employment, they had
difcredited their own fuccefs. It might have
been then objected, that the Gofpel had made its
way by the aid of human power or fophiftry. To
preferve,

preferve, therefore, the fplendour of its evidence unfullied, the meaneft and moft illiterate of a barbarous people were made choice of for the inftruments of GOD's laft great Revelation to mankind: armed with no other power but of Miracles, and that only for the credence of their miffion ; and with no other wifdom but of Truth, and that only to be propofed freely to the underftandings of Particulars.   St. Paul, who had fathomed the myfterious depths of divine wifdom under each Œconomy, was fo penetrated with the view of this laft Difpenfation, that he breaks out into this rapturous and triumphant exclamation, *Where is the Wife ? Where is the Scribe? Where is the Difputer of this world ? Hath not God made foolifh the wifdom of this world* [k] *?*

But further, Divine wifdom fo wonderfully contrived, that the inability and ignorance of the Propagators of Chriftianity were as ufeful to the advancement of this Religion, as the authority and wifdom of the Leader of the Jews were for the eftablifhment of theirs.

I fhall only give one inftance out of many which will occur to an attentive reader of the Evangelic hiftory.

When JESUS had chofen thefe mean and weak inftruments of his power, he fuffered them to continue in their national prejudices concerning his Character; the nature of his kingdom; and the extent of his jurifdiction; as the fole human means of keeping them attached to his fervice, not only during the courfe of their attendance on his miniftry,

[k] 1 COR. i. 20.

but

but for some time after his resurrection, and the
descent of the Holy Ghost upon them; that Power which was to *lead them into all truth*; but by
just and equal steps. Let us see the use of this, in
the following circumstance: From the order of the
whole of God's Dispensation to mankind, as laid
down in Scripture, we learn, that the offer of the
Gospel was to be first fairly made to the Jews;
and then afterwards to the Gentiles. Now when,
soon after the ascension of our Lord, the Church
was forced, by the persecution of the Synagogue,
to leave Judea, and to disperse itself through all
the regions round about; had the Apostles, on this
dispersion, been fully instructed in the design of God
to call the Gentiles into his church, resentment for
their ill usage within Judea, and the small prospect
of better success amongst those who were without,
which they of Jerusalem had prejudiced against
the Gospel, would naturally have disposed them to
turn immediately to the Gentiles. By which means
God's purpose, without a supernatural force upon
their minds, had been defeated; as so great a part
of the Jews would not have had the Gospel *first
preached unto them*. But now, pushed on by this
commodious prejudice, that the benefits belonged
properly to the race of Abraham, they directly
addressed themselves to their brethren of the *dispersion*: where meeting with the same ill success, their
sense of the desperate condition of the house of
Israel would now begin to abate that prejudice in
their favour. And then came the time to inlighten
them in this matter, without putting too great a
force upon their minds; which is not God's way of
acting with free agents. Accordingly, his purpose
of calling the Gentiles into the Church was now
clearly revealed to Peter at Joppa; and a proper
subject, wherewith to begin this great work, was
ready provided for him.

But

But though ignorance in the Propagator of a divine truth amongst particulars, may serve to these important ends, yet to shew still plainer how pernicious this inability would be wherever a Society is concerned, as in the establishment of the Jewish Religion, I shall produce an occasional example even in the Christian.

For when now so great numbers of the Gentiles were converted to CHRIST, that it became necessary to form them into a Church: that is, a religious Society; which of course hath its Policy as well as the Civil; so hurtful was ignorance in its governing members, that divers of them, though graced with many gifts of the holy Spirit, caused such disorders in their assemblies as required all the abilites of the LEARNED APOSTLE to reform and regulate. And then it was, and for this purpose, that PAUL, the proper Apostle of the Gentiles[1], was, in an extraordinary manner, called in, to conduct, by his learning and abilities, and with the assistance of his companion LUKE, a learned man also, this part of GOD's purpose to its completion. The rest were properly Apostles of the Jews; which people having a religious Society already formed, the converts from thence had a kind of rule to go by, which served them for their present occasions; and therefore these needed no great talents of parts or learning; nor had they any. But a new Society was to be formed amongst the Gentile converts; and this required an able conductor; and such an one they had in Paul. But will any one say that his learning afforded an objection against the divinity of his mission? We con-

---

[1] *The gospel of the uncircumcision was committed unto me, as the gospel of the circumcision was unto* Peter. GAL. ii. 7.

clude

clude therefore, that none can arife from the abilities, natural and acquired, of the great jewifh
Lawgiver. The point to be proved.

II. We come now to the fecond part of the Propofition, *That the Laws inftituted in compliance to
the People's prejudices, and in oppofition to Egyptian
fuperftitions, are no reafonable objection to the divinity of the Jewifh Religion.* That moft of thefe
Laws were given in *oppofition* to Egyptian fuperftitions, believers feem not unwilling to allow; as
apprehending no confequence from fuch a con-
ceffion that will give them trouble. The thing
which ftartles them is the fuppofition that fome of
thefe Laws were given in *compliance* to the Jewifh
prejudices; becaufe infidels have inforced this circumftance to the difcredit of Mofes's pretenfions.
To fatisfy believers therefore, I fhall fhew, " that
the Laws in *compliance* were a confequence of the
Laws in *oppofition.*" And, to reconcile them to
both forts, I fhall attempt to prove, from the
double confideration of their NECESSITY and FIT-
NESS, that the inftitution of fuch Laws is no
reafonable objection to the divinity of their original.

I. If God did indeed interfere in the concerns of
this People, it will, I fuppofe, be eafily granted,
that his purpofe was to feparate them from the
contagion of that univerfal idolatry, which had
now overfpread the whole earth; and to which,
efpecially to the EGYPTIAN, they were moft inve-
terately prone.

There were two ways, in the hand of God, for
effecting this feparation: either to overrule the
Will; and this required only the exercife of his
power:

power : or, by leaving the Will at liberty, to coun-
terwork the paſſions; and this required the exerciſe
of his WISDOM.

Now, as all the declared purpoſes of this ſeparation ſhew, that GOD acted with the Iſraelities as
MORAL AGENTS, we muſt needs conclude, notwithſtanding the peculiar favour by which they were
elected, and the extraordinary providence by which
they were conducted, that yet, amidſt all this diſ-
play and blaze of almighty Power, the WILL ever
remained free and uncontrolled.   This not only
appears from the nature of the thing, but from the
whole hiſtory of their reduction out of Egypt.
To give only one inſtance: Moſes tells us, that
GOD led the Iſraelites into the land of Canaan, not
by the direct way of the Philiſtines, leſt the ſight of
danger, in an expedition againſt a ſtrong and war-
like People, ſhould make them chuſe to return to
Egypt, and ſeek for refuge in their ſlavery : But
he led them about, by the way of the Wilderneſs,
to inure them by degrees to fatigue and hardſhips;
the beſt foundation of military prowefs [m].   And
when GOD, to puniſh them for their cowardice, on
the report of the faithleſs explorers of the land,
had decreed that that generation ſhould be worn
away in the Wilderneſs [n], the wiſe policy of this
ſentence was as conſpicuous as the juſtice of it.

If then the Wills of this people were to be left
free, and their minds influenced only by working
on their paſſions, it is evident, that GOD, when he
became their Lawgiver, would act by the ſame
policy in uſe amongſt human Lawgivers for re-
ſtraining the vicious inclinations of the People.

[m] EXOD. xiii. 17.   [n] NUMB. xiii. and xiv.

The

The fame, I fay, in kind, though differing infinitely in degree. For all People, whether conducted on divine or human meafures, having the fame nature, the fame liberty of Will, and the fame terreftrial fituation, muft needs require the fame mode of guidance. And, in fact, we find the Jewifh to be indeed conftituted like other Civil governments, with regard to the integral parts of a Political fociety.

According to all human conception therefore, we fee no way left to keep fuch a People, thus feparated, free from the contagion of idolatry, but,

First, by fevere penal Laws againft idolaters,

And, Secondly, by framing a multifarious Ritual, whofe whole direction, looking contrary to the forbidden fuperftitions, would, by degrees, wear out the prefent fondnefs for them; and at length bring on an habitual averfion to them. This is the way of wife Lawgivers; who, in order to keep the Will from revolting, forbear to do every thing by direct force and fear of punifhment; but employ, where they can, the gentler methods of reftraint.

Thirdly, but as even in the practice of this gentler method, when the paffions and prejudices run high, a direct and profeffed oppofition will be apt to irritate and inflame them; therefore it will be further neceffary, in order to break and elude their violence, to turn mens fondnefs for the forbidden practice into a harmlefs channel; and by indulging them in thofe cuftoms, which they could not well abufe to fuperftition, enable the more

fevere

severe and opposite institutions to perform their work. Such, for instance, might be the *lighting up of lamps* in religious Worship : which practice Clemens Alexandrinus assures us came first from the Egyptians[o]: nor would Witsius himself venture to deny it[p]. But, for the same reason, we conclude that the *brazen serpent* was no imitation of an Egyptian practice, as Sir. J. Marsham would persuade us; because we see how easily it might, and did suffer abuse. Which conclusion, not only our principle leads us to make, but matter of fact enables us to prove[q].

Such a conduct therefore as this, where the Will is left free, appears to be NECESSARY.

II. Let us see next whether it were FIT, that is, Whether it agreed with the wisdom, dignity, and purity of GOD.

1. His WISDOM indeed is the Attribute peculiarly manifested in this method of government ; and certainly, with as great lustre as we should have seen his POWER, had it been his good pleasure to have over-ruled the Will. To give an instance only in one particular, most liable to the ridicule of unbelievers ; I mean, in that part of the Jewish Institute which concerns *clean* and *unclean* meats ; and descends to so low and minute a detail, that men, ignorant of the nature and end of this re-

---

[o] Αἰγύπτιοι λύχνας καίειν πρῶτοι κατέδειξαν. *Strom.* l. i. p. 306.

[p] Earum [lucernarum] prima ad religionem accensio, utrum Hebræis debeatur, an Ægyptiis, haud facile dixero. *Ægypt.* p. 190.

[q] See above.

gulation,

gulation, have, on its apparent *unfitnefs* to engage the concern of God, concluded againft the divine original of the Law. But would they reflect, that the purpofe of feparating one People from the contagion of univerfal idolatry, and this, in order to facilitate a ftill greater good, was a defign not unworthy the Governor of the Univerfe, they would fee this part of the Jewifh Inftitution in a different light : They would fee the brighteft marks of divine wifdom in an injunction which took away the very grounds of all commerce with foreign Nations. For thofe who can' neither eat nor drink together, are never likely to become intimate. This will open to us the admirable method of divine Providence in Peter's *vifion*. The time was now come that the Apoftle fhould be inftructed in God's purpofe of calling the Gentiles into the Church: At the hour of repaft, therefore, he had a fcenical reprefentation of all kind of meats, *clean* and *unclean*; of which he was bid to take and eat indifferently and without diftinction'. The primary defign of this vifion, as appears by the context, was to inform him that the *partition-wall* was now broken down, and that the Gentiles were to be received into the church of Christ. But befides its figurative meaning, it had a literal; and fignified, that the diftinction of meats, as well as of men, was now to be abolifhed. And how neceffary fuch an information was, when he was about to go upon his miffion to the Gentiles, and was to conciliate their benevolence and goodwill, I have obferved above. But altho' this was the principal caufe of the diftinction of meats into clean and unclean, yet another was certainly for the prefervation of health. This inftitution was

---

' Acts x. 10, *& feq.*

of neceffity to be obferved in the firft cafe, to fecure the great object of a *feparation :* and in the fecond cafe, (which is no trivial mark of the wifdom of the Inftitutor) it might be fafely and commodi-oufly obferved by a People thus *feparated,* who were confequently to be for ever confined within the limits of one country.   And here the abfur-dity of this part of Mahometanifm evidently be-trays itfelf.   Mahomet would needs imitate the Law of Mofes, as in other things, fo in this, *the diftinction of meats, clean and unclean*; without con-fidering that in a Religion formed for conqueft, whofe followers were to inhabit Regions of the moft different and contrary qualities, the food which in one climate was hurtful or nutritive, in another changed its properties to their contraries. But to fhew ftill more clearly the difference be-tween Inftitutions formed at hazard, and thofe by divine appointment, we may obferve, that when Judaifm arrived at its completion in Chriftianity, the followers of which were the inhabitants of all Climes, the diftinction between meats clean and unclean was abolifhed ; which, at the fame time, ferving other great ends explained above, fhew the Difpenfation, (in the courfe of which thefe feveral changes of the Oeconomy took place) to be really Divine.

2. As to the DIGNITY and Majefty of GOD, that, furely, does not fuffer, in his not interfering with his power, to force the Will, but permitting it to be drawn and inclined by thofe *cords of a man,* his natural motives.   The dignity of any Being con-fifts in obferving a conformity between his actions, and his quality, or ftation.   Now it pleafed the GOD of heaven to take upon himfelf the office of fu-preme Magiftrate of the Jewifh Republic.   But it

is

is (as we have ſhewn) the part of a wiſe Magiſtrate
to reſtrain a People, devoted to any particular ſuperſtition, by a Ritual directly *oppoſite* in the general to that ſuperſtition; and yet *ſimilar* in ſuch
particular practices as could not be abuſed or per-
verted: becauſe compliance with the popular prejudices in things indifferent, naturally eludes the
force of their propenſity to things evil. In this
wiſe Policy therefore, the dignity of the GOD of
heaven was not impaired.

3. Nor is his PURITY any more affected by this
ſuppoſed conduct. The Rites, in queſtion, are
owned to be, in themſelves, indifferent: and good
or evil only as they are directed to a true or falſe
object.

If it be ſaid " that their carnal nature, or weari-
ſome multiplicity, or ſcrupulous obſervance, render them unworthy of the purity and ſpiritual nature of GOD:" To Believers, I reply, that this objection holds equally againſt theſe Rites in whatever
view they themſelves are wont to regard them:—
To Unbelievers; that they forget, or do not underſtand GOD's primary end, in the inſtitution
of the Jewiſh Ritual; which was, to preſerve the
people from the contagion of theſe idolatrous practices with which they were ſurrounded. But nothing could be ſo effectual to this purpoſe, as ſuch a
Ritual. And ſince the continual proneneſs of that
People to idolatry hath been ſhewn to ariſe from
the inveterate prejudice of *intercommunity of worſhip*, nothing could be ſo effectual as the extreme
minuteneſs of their Ritual.

If it be ſaid, " that the former abuſe of theſe
indulged Rites, to an abominable ſuperſtition had
made

made them unfit to be employed in the service of
the God of purity:" I reply, that there is nothing in the nature of things, to make them *unfit.*
That a material substance, materially soiled, stained
and infected, is unfit to approach and be joined to
one of great cleanness and purity, is not to be denied. But let us not mistake words for things; and
draw a metaphysical conclusion from a metaphorical expression. The soil and stain, in the case before us, is altogether figurative, that is, unreal.
And in truth, the very objection is taken from the
command of this very Law, to abstain from things
polluted by idolatry: But we now understand, that
the reason of its so severely forbidding the use of
some things that had been abused to superstition,
was the very same with its indulging the use of
others which had been equally abused; namely, to
compass, by the best, though different yet concord-
ing means, that one great end, *the* EXTIRPATION OF
IDOLATRY. Notwithstanding this, the Law concerning things polluted, like many other of the
Jewish observances, hath occasionally been adopted
by different Sects in the Christian church. Thus
our PURITANS, who seem to have had their name
from the subject in debate, quarrelled with
the established use of the cross in baptism, the
surplice, and the posture of communicating, because they had been abused to the support of
popish superstition [s]. I chuse this instance, that
the Men whom I am arguing against, may see the
issue of their objection; and that They, from whom

---

[s] There were no sort of men more averse to the system here
defended of Jewish customs borrowed from Egypt, than those
Puritans. Yet when they could serve a turn by adopting it,
they made no scruple of so doing. Thus, in order to disgrace
the *surplice,* they venture to say, in the *Declaration of the Minis-
ters of London,* published 1566. That *the surplice, or white linnen garment, came from the* EGYPTIANS *into the Jewish church.*

the inſtance is taken, may be ſhewn the unreaſon-
ableneſs of their ſeparation ; as far at leaſt as it was
occaſioned on account of ceremonies.

If, laſtly, it be ſaid, " that theſe Rites, which
once had been, might be again, abuſed to ſuperſtition ; and were therefore *unfit* to be employed in
this new ſervice ;" I reply, that this is a miſtake.
For 1. We go on the ſuppoſition, that the
Jews were indulged in no practices capable of
being ſo abuſed.   2. That tho' they might in themſelves be ſubject to abuſe, yet they carried their corrective with them ; which was, firſt, their being intermixed with a vaſt number of other Rites directly
oppoſite to all idolatrous practice ; and ſecondly,
their making part of a burdenſome multifarious
Worſhip, which would keep the people ſo conſtantly employed, as to afford them neither time nor
occaſion, from the cauſe in queſtion, of falling
into foreign idolatries.

But how can I hope to be heard in defence of
this conduct of the God of Iſrael, when even the
believing part of thoſe whom I oppoſe, ſeem
to pay ſo little attention to the reaſoning of
Jesus himſelf ; who has admirably illuſtrated and
vindicated the wiſdom of this conduct, in the familiar parable of *new cloth in old garments*, and *new
wine in old bottles* ': which, though given in anſwer to a particular queſtion, was intended to in-
ſtruct us in this general truth, That it is the way

' *And he ſpake alſo a parable unto them, No man putteth a
piece of a new garment upon an old : if otherwiſe, then both the
new maketh a rent, and the piece that was taken out of the new,
agreeth not with the old.   And no man putteth new wine into old
bottles, elſe the new wine will burſt the bottles, and be ſpilled, and
the bottles ſhall periſh.*   Luke v. 36.

of God to accommodate his Inftitutions to the ftate, the condition, and contracted habits, of his creatures.

But as this notion hath been condemned ex cathedra[u]; and the *Ægyptiaca* of HERMAN WITSIUS recommended to the clergy, *as a diftinct and folid confutation* of *Spencer's book, de legibus Hebræorum ritualibus,* I fhall examine what that learned Foreigner hath to fay againft it. All Witfius's reafoning on this point is to be found in the fourteenth chapter of his third book; which I fhall endeavour to pick out, and fet in the faireft light.

1. His firft argument is, " that it is a difhonouring of GOD, who has the hearts of men in his power, and can turn them as he pleafes, to conceive of him as ftanding in need of the tricks of crafty Politicians; not but, he confeffes, that GOD deals with men as reafonable creatures, and attains his end by fit and adequate means; and, in the choice of thefe means, manifefts a wifdom perfectly admirable." Yet, for all this, he fays, " we cannot, without the higheft contumely, prefume to compare the facred Policy of Heaven with the arts and fhifts of the beggarly politics of this world[x]."
—All

---

[u] *Waterland's charge to the clergy of Middlefex.*

[x] Verum enimvero quantamcunque hæc civilis prudentiæ fpeciem habeant, præter Dei verbum cuncta dicuntur, & humani commenta funt ingenii, divini numinis majeftate haud fatis digna. Nimirum cauti catique in feculo morta'es Deum ex fua metiuntur indole: arcanafque imperandi artes, & vaframenta politicorum, quæ vix terra probet, cœlo locant. Quafi vero in populo fibi formando firmandoque iis aftutiarum ambagibus indigeat is, qui, mortalium corda in manu fua habens, ea, quorfum vult, flectit. Non nego equidem Deum cum ho-

—All I find here is only mifreprefentation. Spencer never compared the wifdom of God, in the inftitution of the Jewifh republic, to the *tricks* and *fhifts* of politicians; but to their *legitimate arts* of Government, conducted on the rules of ftrict morality. And if, as this writer owns, God *dealt with the Ifraelites as reafonable creatures, and attained his end by fit and adequate means*, he muft needs ufe a wifdom the fame in kind, though vaftly different in degree, with what we call human policy. But indeed, he feems reconciled to the thing: it is the name only which he diflikes. If his followers fay otherwife, I defire they would explain, in fome intelligible manner, their idea of that *wifdom*, in God's civil government of a people, which is not founded in the exercife of almighty power, and is yet different in kind from what we call, Policy.

2. His fecond argument is, " That, as God erected a new Republic, it was his will that it fhould *appear* new to the Ifraelites. Its ftructure was not to be patched up out of the rubbifh of the Canaanitifh or Egyptian Rites, but was formed according to the model brought down from heaven, and fhewn to Mofes in the mount. Nor was it left to the people to do the leaft thing in religious matters, on their own head. All was determinately ordered, even to the moft minute circumftance; which was fo bound upon them, that they could not do, or omit, any the leaft thing contrary to the Law, without becoming liable to immediate punifh-

minibus, uti cum creaturis rationalibus, agentem, media adhibere iis perfuadendis idonea, inque eorum mediorum delectu fapientiam oftendere prorfus admirabilem. Attamen Dei fanctiffima ifta fapientia cum politicorum aftibus ac vafritie comparari fine infigni illius contumelia non poteft. *p.* 282.

ment.

ment ʸ."——If, by this NEWNESS of the Jewish
Republic, be meant, that it was different in many
fundamental circumstances from all other civil policies, so as to vindicate itself to its divine Author,
I not only agree with him, but, which is more
than he and his recommender could do, have proved it.   But this sense makes nothing to the point
in question.   If by NEWNESS be meant, that it
had nothing in common with any of the neighbouring Institutions ; To make this credible, he should
have proved that GOD gave them new *hearts,* new
natures, and a new *world,* along with their new
Government.   There is the same ambiguity in what
he says of the *appearance* of newness to the Israelites.   For it may signify either that the Institution
appeared so new as to be seen to come from GOD ;
or that it appeared so new as not to resemble, in any
of its parts, the Institutions of men.   The first is
true, but not to the purpose : the latter is to the purpose, but not true.——From the fact, of the Law's
coming down entire from heaven, he concludes that
the genius and prejudices of the Israelites were not
at all consulted : From the same fact, I conclude,
that they were consulted : which of us has concluded right is left to the judgment of the public.
Let me only observe, That ignorant men may
compose, and have composed Laws in all things
opposite to the bent and genius of a people ; and

ʸ Uti revera novam moliebatur rempublicam, ita et novam,
qualis erat, videri eam Israelitis voluit. Quippe cujus forma
sive species, non ex rituum ruderibus Canaaniticorum aut
Ægyptiacorum efficta, sed cœlitus delapsa, Mosi primum in
sacro monstrata monte erat, ut ad illud instar cuncta in Israële
componerentur. Neque permissum esse populo voluit ut in
religionis negotio vel tantillum suo ageret arbitratu. Omnia
determinavit ipse, ad minutissimas usque circumstantias ; quibus
ita eos alligavit, ut non sine præsentaneo vitæ discrimine quicquam vel omittere vel aliter agere potuerint. *p.* 282, 283.

they

they have been obeyed accordingly. But, when divine wifdom frames an Inftitution, we may be fure that no fuch folecifm as that of *putting new wine into old bottles* will ever be committed.—*But the people were not confulted even in the leaft thing that concerned religious matters.* How is this to be reconciled with their free choice of GOD for their King; and with his indulgence of their impious clamours afterwards for a Vicegerent or another king? This furely *concerned religious matters*, and very capitally too, in a Policy where both the Societies were perfectly incorporated.—*But every thing was determined even to the moft minute circumftances, and to be obferved under the fevereft penalties.* What this makes for his point, I fee not. But this I fee, that, if indeed there were that indulgence in the Law which I contend for, thefe two circumftances of *minute prefcription*, and *fevere penalties*, muft needs attend it: and for this plain reafon; Men, when indulged in their prejudices, are very apt to tranfgrefs the bounds of that indulgence; it is therefore neceffary that thofe bounds fhould be minutely marked out, and the tranfgreffion of them feverely punifhed.

3. His third argument is—" That no religious Rites, formerly ufed by the Ifraelites, on their own head, were, after the giving of the law, PERMITTED, out of regard to habitude; but all things PRESCRIBED and COMMANDED: and this fo precifely, that it was unlawful to deviate a finger's breadth either to the right hand or to the left[z]."—This in-

---

[z] Nec uli in religione ritus fuerunt, ab Ifraëlitis olim fine numine ufurpati, quibus propter affuetudinem ut in pofterum quoque uterentur lege lata *permifit*: fed præfcripta *juffaque* funt omnia. Et quidem ita diftinéte, ut nec tranfverfum digitum dextrorfum aut finiftrorfum declinare fas fuerit, DEUT. v. p. 283.

deed

deed is an observation which I cannot reconcile to the learned writer's usual candour and ingenuity. He is writing against Spencer's system: and here he brings an argument against it, which he saw in Spencer's book had been brought against Grotius (who was in that system) and which Spencer answers in defence of Grotius. Therefore, as this answer will serve in defence of Spencer himself against Witsius, I shall give it at the bottom of the page[a]. For the rest, I apprehend all the force of this third argument to lie only in a quibble on the equivocal use of the word PERMISSION, which signifies either a *tacit connivance,* or *legal allowance.* Now Spencer used the word in this latter sense[b].

But

---

[a] Testium meorum agmen claudit Grotius——Authoris verba sunt hæc : " *Sicut fines sacrificiorum diversi sunt, — ita et* " *ritus, qui aut ab Hebræis ad alias gentes venere, aut, quod* " *credibilius est, a Syris & Ægyptiis usurpati, correcti sunt ab* " *Hebræis, & ab aliis gentibus sine ea emendatione usurpati.*" Hic in Grotium paulo animosius insurgit auctor nuperus : " nam *hoc,* ait ille, *cum impietate et absurditate conjunctum est.* " Quid ita? *Num enim,* respondet ille, *Deum sanctissima sua* " *instituta, quæ ipse prolixe sancivit, et conscribi in religiosam* " *observationem, per inspirationem numinis sui, voluit credemus* " *ab idolatria Syrorum & Ægyptiorum mutuo sumpsisse? Neque* " *ea pro libitu Ebræi assumpserunt, aut assumpta emendarunt, sed* " *omnia & singula divinitus in lege præscripta sunt, et juxta* " *ejus normam exactissime observari debuerunt.*" At opinio Grotii multo solidior est, quam ut mucrone tam obtuso confodi possit. Non enim asserit ille, vel sanus quispiam, Hebræos ritum ullum a gentibus, pro libitu suo, sumplisse, vel sumptum pro ingenio suo correxisse. Id unum sub locutione figurata, contendit Grotius, Deum nempe ritus aliquos, usu veteri confirmatos (emendatos tamen, et ignem quasi purgatorium passos) a gentibus accepisse, et Hebræis usurpandos tradidisse ; ne populus ille, rituum ethnicorum amore præceps, ad cultum et superstitionem Gentilium rueret, ni more plurimum veteri cultum præstare concederetur. *De leg. Heb. rit. vol.* ii. *p.* 748, 749.

[b] For, with regard to *every thing's being exactly prescribed ; from which direction it was not lawful to make the least devia-*

F 4   *tion,*

But *permiſſion*, in this ſenſe, is very conſiſtent with *every thing's being expreſsly preſcribed and commanded in the law.*

4. His fourth argument proceeds thus,—" But farther, God neither *permitted*, nor *commanded*, that the Iſraelites ſhould worſhip him after the pagan mode of worſhip. For it had been the ſame

tion, Spencer acknowledges this as fully as Witſius himſelf. " Nihil enim cultum divinum ſpectans verbis obſcuris aut in-" certi ſenſus a Moſe traditum, nil cæco vel præcipiti zelo, ni-" hil prurienti Judæorum ingenio, vel naturæ humanæ rerum " novarum in ſacris avidæ, relictum fuit. Nempe lex de mi-" nimis pleriſque curavit. Ipſi arcæ annuli, &c." *De Leg. Rit. Heb.* l. 1. c. 10. ſect. 5. And it is remarkable, that he employs this very circumſtance, with great weight as well as ingenuity, to inforce the oppoſite concluſion; namely, that God admitted ſome rites in uſe amongſt the Gentile nations in compliance to the people's prejudices. ―― Ipſe ritus Moſaïcos inſtituendi modus huic ſententiæ non parum præſidii præbet. Deus enim non tantum eorum materiam, ſed et locum, tempus, ipſum etiam corporis ſitum quandoque quo præſtari debebant, aliaſque minoris notæ circumſtantias, accurate præſcripſit. Et poſtquam Deus minimas quaſque circumſtantias rituum ſingulorum tradidiſſet, præcepto cautum eſt, *Deut.* iv. 2. ne quid e ceremoniis nempe vetitis iis adderetur; aut quicquam e ceremoniis nempe præceptis adimeretur. Nemo vero qui judicio valet, opinari poteſt Deum horum rituum minutias accurate adeo præſcripſiſſe, ex ullo quo ipſe eorum amore vel deſiderio tangebatur. A ratione multo minus abeſt, gentium et Hebræorum ritus haud paucos (ſi materiam eorum vel ſubſtantiam ſpectemus) proximam inter ſe ſimilitudinem et affinitatem habuiſſe, ideoque lege curatum fuiſſe, ne eodem modo peragerentur, ſed ut circumſtantiis quibuſdam peculiaribus et a Deo præſcriptis ab invicem diſcernerentur. Nam Iſraëlitæ ritus ſuos omnes e Dei præſcripto peragentes, ſe in Jehovæ [non dei alicujus ethnici] honorem ſacra ſua præſtare teſtarentur; et ratio temporum exegit, ut cultus Deo præſtitus quandam ἰδιότητα retineret, nec ad ritus gentium nimis accedere, vel ab iis pluſquam par erat abire videretur. Moſis ætate res in loco tam lubrico et ancipiti ſitæ ſunt, quod ſumma tantum ſapientia limites eos definire norat, quos ultra citrave non potuit conſiſtere Dei veri cultus. Lib. iii. cap. 2. ſect. 1.

thing

thing to GOD not to be worshiped at all, as to be worshiped by Rites used in the service of Demons. And Moses teaches us that the Laws of God were very different from what Spencer imagined; as appears from DEUT. xii. 30, 31, 32. and from LEV. xviii. 2, 3, 4. Here the reason given of forbidding the vanities of Egypt, is, that Jehovah, who brought them out from amongst that people, will, from henceforth, allow no farther communication with Egypt. Small appearance of any indulgence. And hence indeed it is, that most of the ritual Laws are directly levelled against the Egyptian, Zabian, and Canaanitish superstitions, as Maimonides confesseth [c]."——As to what this learned man says, that we may as well not worship GOD at all as worship him by Rites which have been employed in Paganism, we have already overturned the foundation of that fanatical assertion. It is true, the argument labours a little in the hands of SPENCER and MAIMONIDES; while they suppose the Devil himself to be the principal Architect of pagan Superstition: for to believe that GOD

[c] Porio nec *permisit*, nec *jussit* Deus, ut eo se modo Israelitæ colerent, quo modo Deos suos colebant Gentiles; veritus scilicet ne per veteres istas vanitates Dæmoni cultum deferrent, si minus Deo licuisset. Nam et inanis ille metus erat: quum Deo propemodum perinde sit, sive quis Dæmoni cultum deferat, sive per vanitates aliquas veteres Deo cultum deferre præsumat. Et longe aliter Deum instituisse Moses docet, DEUT. xiii. 30, 31, 32. at e LEVIT. xviii. 2, 3. 4. Audin', *Spencere*, qua ratione ab ægyptiacis vanitatibus ad suorum observantiam præceptorum Israëlitas Deus avocet? Eo id facit nomine, quod ipse Jehova et Deus ipsorum sit, qui ex Ægypto eos eripiens nihil posthac cum Ægyptiorum vanitatibus commune habere voluit. Hoc profecto non est, id quod tu dicis, allicere eos per umbratiles veterum Ægypti rituum reliquias. Atque hinc factum est ut plurima Deus legibus suis ritualibus inseruerit, Ægyptiorum, Zabiorum, Canaanæorum institutis ἐκ παραλλήλου opposita.——Cujus rei varia a nobis exempla alibi allata sunt. *p.* 283, 284.

would

would employ any Rites introduced by this evil Spirit is indeed of somewhat hard digeſtion. But that writer, who conceives them to be the inventions of ſuperſtitious and deſigning men only, hath none of this difficulty to encounter. As for the obſervation, that *moſt of the ritual Laws were leveled againſt idolatrous ſuperſtition*, we are ſo far from ſeeing any inconſiſtency between this truth and that other, " that ſome of thoſe *ritual Laws* did indulge the people in ſuch habituated practices, as could not be abuſed to ſuperſtition," that, on the contrary, we ſee a neceſſary connexion between them. For if ſevere Laws were given to a people againſt ſuperſtitions, to which they were violently bent, it would be very proper to indulge them in ſome of their favourite habits, ſo far forth as ſafely they could be indulged, in order to break the violence of the reſt, and to give the body of oppoſed Laws a fuller liberty of working their effect. And if they had Laws likewiſe given them in indulgence, it would be neceſſary to accompany ſuch Laws with the moſt ſevere prohibitions of idolatrous practice, and of the leaſt deviation from a tittle of the Inſtitute. In a word, Laws in direct *oppoſition*, and Laws in *conformity* or compliance, had equally, as we ſay, the ſame tendency, and jointly concurred to promote the ſame end ; namely, the preſervation of the Iſraelites from idolatry [d].

---

[d] I cannot therefore agree with Mr. Whiſton in the high value he ſets upon a paſſage of Manetho— *This* (ſays he) *is a very valuable teſtimony of Manetho's, that the laws of Oſarſiph or Moſes were not in compliance with, but in oppoſition to, the cuſtoms of the Egyptians.* Tranſlat. of Joſephus, p. 993. However tho' this fairy treaſure vaniſh, it is ſome comfort that we do not want it.

5. His

5. His fifth argument runs thus.—" Indulgence was so far from being the end of the Law, that the Ritual was given as a most heavy yoke, to subdue and conquer the ferocity of that stiffnecked people, GAL. iv. 1, 2, 3. COL. ii. 21 ᵉ."—By this one would imagine, his adversaries had contended for such a kind of indulgence as arose out of GOD's fondness for a chosen People ; when indeed, they suppose it to be only such an indulgence as tended the more effectually and expeditiously to subdue and conquer the ferocity of their savage tempers :

> *Quos optimus*
> *Fallere & effugere est triumphus.*

If therefore, *that* were the END of the Law which Witsius himself contends for, we may be assured that this indulgence was one of the MEANS. But the principal and more general *means* being Laws in direct opposition, this justified the character the Apostle gives of the Jewish Ritual, in the two places urged against us.

6. His sixth argument is,—" That the intent of the Law was to separate the Israelites, by a partition-wall, as it were, from all other people ; which, by its diversity, might set them at a distance from idolaters, and create an aversion to idolatry ᶠ."——As to the first effect of the diversity

---

ᵉ Id sibi primum in rituum jussione propositum habuit Deus, ut laboriosis istis exercitiis *ferociam* populi indomitam, veluti *difficillimo jugo, subigeret,* GAL. iv. 1, 2, 3. COL. ii. 21. *p.* 286.

ᶠ Deinde hæc quoque Dei in rituum jussione intentio fuit, ut eorum observantia, veluti *pariete intergerino,* eos à gentium communione longe semoveret, EPH. ii. 14, 15.—Quum autem
legem

fity of the Jewifh Law, the keeping the people diftinct; if the learned writer would thereby infinuate
(which is indeed to his point) that this diftinction
could be kept up only while the Jews and other
nations had no fimilar Rites; it could never, even
by the means he himfelf prefcribes, be long kept up
at all. For if the Jews were not indulged in the
imitation of any pagan Rites, the Pagans might indulge themfelves in the imitation of the Jewifh: as
indeed they are fuppofed to have done in the practice
of CIRCUMCISION: and fo this *partition-wall*, if
only built of this untempered mortar of Witfius's
providing, would foon tumble of itfelf. But
the very cafe here given fhews no neceffity for ALL
the laws to be in oppofition, in order to fecure a
feparation; the Jews being as effectually feparated
from all their neighbours when moft of them ufed
the rite of *circumcifion*, as when thefe Jews practifed it without a rival. And the reafon is this;
CIRCUMCISION was not given to Abraham and
to his race as a mark of diftinction and feparation
from all other people, but, what its conftant ufe
made it only fit for, a ftanding memorial of the covenant between GOD and Abraham. *And ye
fhall circumcife* (fays GOD) *the flefh of your fore-
fkin, and it fhall be a* TOKEN OF THE COVENANT
between me and you, GEN. xvii. 11. But though it
was not given as a mark of feparation, yet it effectually anfwered that purpofe: for it preferved the
memory, or was the *token*, of a covenant, which
neceffarily kept them feparate and diftinct from the
reft of mankind. As to the other effect of this di-
verfity of the Jewifh Law, namely the creating an

legem præceptorum in ritibus *inimicitias* Apoftolus vocat, hoc inter
cætera innuit, fuiffe eam fymbolum atque inftrumentum divifionis
atque odii inter Ifraelem & gentes. *p.* 287, 288.

averfion

averfion to the Rites of all other nations; in this,
the learned writer hath betrayed his ignorance of
human nature. For we always find a more inveterate hatred and averfion, between people of differing Religions where feveral things are alike, than
where every thing is diametrically oppofite; of
which a plain caufe might be found in the nature
of man, whofe heart is fo much corrupted by his
paffions. So that the retaining fome innocent Egyptian practices, all accompanied with their provifio-
nal oppofites, would naturally make the Jews more
averfe to Egypt, than if they had differed in every
individual circumftance.

7. His laft argument concludes thus,—" The
ceremonies of the Jewifh Ritual were types and
fhadows of heavenly things: It is therefore highly improbable that GOD fhould chufe the impious
and diabolic Sacra of Egypt, and the mummery of
Magic practices, for the fhadows of fuch holy and
fpiritual matters [g]." Thus he ends, as he begun,
with hard words and foft arguments. No one ever
pretended to fay that fuch kinds of practices were
fuffered or imitated in the Jewifh Ritual. All the
indulgence fuppofed, is of fome harmlefs Rite or
innocent Ornament, fuch as the *lighting up of Lamps,*
or wearing a Linnen garment. And let me afk,
whether thefe things, though done, as we fuppofe,
in conformity to an Egyptian practice, were more
unfit to be made a type or fhadow of heavenly
things, than the erection *of an altar without fteps;*

[g] Denique & hic cærimoniarum fcopus fuit, ut *rerum fpirita-*
alium figuræ atque *umbræ* effent, & exftaret in iis artificiofa
pictura Chrifti, ac gratiæ per ipfum impetrandæ—Non eft autem probabile, Deum ex impiis Ægyptiorum ac diabolicis facris,
ex veteribus vanitatibus, ex magicæ artis imitamentis, picturas
feciffe rerum fpiritualium atque cœleftium. *l.* 289).

done,

done, as they will allow, in direct oppofition to Pagan practice. But it will be fhewn under the next head, that the fuppofition that the Jewifh Ritual was framed, partly in compliance to the people's prejudices, and partly in oppofition to idolatrous fuperftitions, and, at the fame time, typical of a future Difpenfation, tends greatly to raife and enlarge our ideas of the divine Wifdom.

But it is ftrange, that fuch a writer as Witsius (whatever we may think of the admirers of his argument) fhould not fee, that the character given of the RITUAL LAW by God himfelf did not imply that it had a mixture at leaft of no better ftuff than Egyptian and other Pagan practices.

God, by the prophet Ezekiel, upbraiding the Ifraelites with their perverfity and difobedience, from the time of their going out of Egypt to their entrance into the land of Canaan, fpeaks to them in this manner.—

Ver. 1. " And it came to pafs, in the feventh " year, in the fifth month, the tenth day of " the month, that certain of the elders of Ifrael " came to inquire of the Lord, and fat before " me.

2. " Then came the word of the Lord unto " me faying.

3. " Son of man, fpeak unto the elders of If- " rael, and fay unto them, Thus faith the Lord " God, Are ye come to inquire of me? as I live, " faith the Lord God, I will not be inquired of by " you.

6

. 4. " Wilt

4. " Wilt thou judge them, son of man, wilt
" thou judge them? cause them to know the abo-
" minations of their fathers:

5. " And say unto them, Thus saith the Lord
" God, in the day when I chose Israel, and lifted
" up mine hand unto the seed of the house of Ja-
" cob, and made myself known unto them in the
" land of Egypt, when I lifted up mine hand unto
" them, saying I am the Lord your God.

6. " In the day that I lifted up mine hand unto
" them to bring them forth of the land of Egypt,
" into a land that I had espied for them, flowing
" with milk and honey, which is the glory of all
" lands:

7. " Then said I unto them, Cast ye away every
" man the abominations of his eyes, and defile
" not your selves with the idols of Egypt: I am
" the Lord your God.

8. " But they rebelled against me, and would
" not hearken unto me: they did not every man
" cast away the abominations of their eyes, neither
" did they forsake the idols of Egypt: Then I
" said, I will pour out my fury upon them, to
" accomplish my anger against them in the midst
" of the land of Egypt.

9. " But I wrought for my name's sake, that it
" should not be polluted before the heathen, a-
" mong whom they were, in whose sight I made
" myself known unto them, in bringing them
" forth out of the land of Egypt.

10. " Where-

10. " Wherefore I caufed them to go forth out
" of the land of Egypt, and brought them into
" the wildernefs.

11. " And I gave them my ftatutes, and fhew-
" ed them my judgments, which if a man do, he
" fhall even live in them.

12. " Moreover alfo, I gave them, my fabbaths,
" to be a fign between me and them, that they
" might know that I am the Lord that fanctify
" them.

13. " But the houfe of Ifrael rebelled againft
" me in the wildernefs: they walked not in my
" ftatutes, and they defpifed my judgments,
" which if a man do, he fhall even live in them;
" and my fabbaths they greatly polluted : then I
" faid I would pour out my fury upon them in
" the wildernefs to confume them.

14. " But I wrought for my name's fake, that
" it fhould not be polluted before the heathen, in
" whofe fight I brought them out.

15. " Yet alfo I lifted up my hand unto them
" in the wildernefs, that I would not bring them
" into the land which I had given them, flowing
" with milk and honey, which is the glory of all
" lands : '

16. " Becaufe they defpifed my judgments,
" and walked not in my ftatutes, but polluted my
" fabbaths : for their heart went after their idols.

17. " Never-

17. " Nevertheless, mine eye spared them from
" destroying them, neither did I make an end of
" them in the wildernefs.

18. " But I said unto their children in the wil-
" dernefs, Walk ye not in the ftatutes of your fa-
" thers, neither obferve their judgments, nor de-
" file yourfelves with their idols.

19. " I am the Lord your God; walk in my
" ftatutes, and keep my judgments, and do them:

20. " And hallow my fabbaths, and they fhall
" be a fign between me and you, that ye may
" know that I am the Lord your God.

21. " Notwithftanding the children rebelled
" againft me: they walked not in my ftatutes,
" neither kept my judgments to do them, which
" if a man do, he fhall even live in them; they
" polluted my fabbaths: then I faid I would pour
" out my fury upon them, to accomplifh my anger
" againft them in the wildernefs.

22. " Neverthelefs, I withdrew mine hand, and
" wrought for my names fake, that it fhould not
" be polluted in the fight of the heathen, in whofe
" fight I brought them forth.

23. " I lifted up mine hand unto them alfo in
" the wildernefs, that I would fcatter them among
" the heathen, and difperfe them through the
" countries.

24. " Becaufe they had not executed my judg-
" ments, but had defpifed my ftatutes, and had
" polluted my fabbaths, and their eyes were after
" their fathers idols.

25. " Wherefore I gave them also sta-
" tutes that were not good, and judg-
" ments whereby they should not live.

26. " And I polluted them in their own gifts, in
" that they caufed to pafs thro' the fire all that
" openeth the womb, that I might make them
" defolate, to the end that they might know that
" I am the Lord [h]."

Could the Prophet have poffibly given a plainer
or more graphical defcription of the character and
genius of the ritual law, than in thofe laft
words? Yet to fuit it to theologic purpofes,
Syftem-makers have endeavoured, in their ufual
manner, *to interpret it away*, as if it only fignified God's fuffering the Ifraelites to fall into idolatry. Now if it were not indulged to thefe men
to make ufe of any arms they can catch hold of,
one fhould be a little fcandalized to find that they
had borrowed this forced interpretation from the
Rabbins; who holding their Law to be perfect,
and of eternal obligation, were indeed much concerned to remove this opprobrium from it. Kim-
chi is recorded for his dexterity in giving it this
meaning: tho' done with much more caution than
the chriftian writers who took it from him. He
fuppofed that the *ftatutes not good* were the Tributes
impofed on the Ifraelites while in fubjection to
their pagan neighbours. And this takes off fomething from the unnatural violence of the expreffion, of giving statutes, when underftood only
to fignify the permiffion of abufing their free-will,
when they fell into idolatry.

Now, becaufe the right explanation and proper
inforcement of this famous paffage will, befides its

[h] Chap. xx. ver. 1. to 26. inclufive.

ufe

use in the present argument, serve for many considerable purposes, in the sequel of this work, it
may not be time misspent to expose this spurious
pilfered interpretation.   And, as the last inforcer
of it, and the most satisfied with his exploit, the late
Author of the *Connexions between sacred and profane
history*, takes the honour of it to himself, I shall
examine his reasoning at large.

Dr. Spencer, and (I suppose) every capable
judge before him, understood the *statutes and judgments* in the eleventh verse to signify the MORAL
law; and the *statutes and judgments* in the twenty-
fifth verse, to signify the RITUAL.   But Dr.
Shuckford, who always takes a singular pleasure in
carping at that faithful Servant of Common-sense,
directs the defence of his borrowed novelty, against
the great Author of *the Reasons of the Ritual Law*, in
the following manner.———" The persons spoken
of, who had the *statutes given* to them, which were
not good, were not that generation of men to whom
the *whole Law* was given, but their children or
posterity.   To this posterity, God made no addi-
tions to his laws; the whole being completed in
the time of their forefathers.   Therefore all he
GAVE to them of *statutes not good* was the PERMIS-
SION of falling into the pagan idolatries round
about[1]."   This, I believe, his followers will confess
to be his argument, tho' represented in fewer words,
yet with greater force: for a perplexed combination
of needless repetitions, which fill two or three large
pages, have much weakened and obscured his reasoning.

However it concludes in these very terms.   "And
" thus it must be undeniably plain, that the Pro-

[1] Con. v. p. 159—161.

" phet

" phet could not, by the *statutes not good* mean
" any part of the Ritual law: for the whole Law
" was given to the fathers of thofe whom the Pro-
" phet now fpeaks of; but *thefe statutes* were
" not given to the fathers, but to the defcendants.
" If we go on, and compare the narrative of the
" Prophet with the hiftory of the Ifraelites, we
" fhall fee further, that the *statutes and judgments*
" *not good* are fo far from being any part of Mo-
" fes's law, that they were not *given* earlier than
" the times of the Judges [k];" *i. e,* the Ifraelites
then fell into the idolatries, here called (as this
learned interpreter will have it) *statutes and judgments* GIVEN.

And now, to canvafs a little this decifive argument ———— THUS (fays he) *it muft be undeniably
plain*———*Thus!* that is, Grant him his premiffes,
and the conclufion follows.   Without doubt.   But
the whole context fhews that his premiffes are falfe.

Firft then let it be obferved, that the occafion of
the Prophecy, in the xxth chapter of Ezekiel, was
this,—The Jews, by certain of their Elders, had,
as was ufual in their diftreffes, recourfe to the God
of Ifrael for direction and affiftance, [ver. 1.]
On this we are informed, [ver. 3.] that the word
of the Lord came to Ezekiel, bidding him tell
thefe Elders, that GOD would not be inquired of
by them: for that their continued rebellions,
from their coming out of Egypt, to that time,
had made them unworthy of his patronage and
protection.   Their idolatries are then recapitulat-
ed, and divided into three periods.   The FIRST,
from GOD's meffage to them while in Egypt, to
their entrance into the promifed land.—*Thus faith*

---

[k] P. 161.

the

the Lord God, In the day when I chose Israel, and lifted up mine hand unto the seed of Jacob, and made myself known unto them in the land of Egypt, &c. and so on, from the fifth to the twenty-sixth verse inclusively. The SECOND period contains all the time from their taking possession of the land of Canaan, to their present condition when this prophecy was delivered.—*Therefore, son of man, speak unto the house of Israel, and say unto them, Thus saith the Lord God, Yet in this your fathers have blasphemed me, in that they have committed a trespass against me. For* WHEN I HAD BROUGHT THEM INTO THE LAND, *for the which I lifted up mine hand to give it to them, then they saw every high hill,* &c. and so on, from the twenty-seventh to the thirty-second verse inclusively. The TRIRD period concerns the iniquities, and the consequent punishment of the present generation, which had now applied to him in their distresses.— *As I live, saith the Lord God, surely with a mighty hand, and with a stretched out arm, and with fury poured out,* WILL I RULE OVER YOU, &c. And this is the subject of what we find between the thirty-third and the forty-fourth verse, inclusively.

This short, but exact analysis of the Prophecy, is more than sufficient to overturn Dr. Shuckford's system, founded on a distinction between the *fathers* and the *children* in the eighteenth verse, (which is within the first period) as if the *fathers* related to what happened in the wilderness, and the *children,* to what happened under the judges; whereas common sense is sufficient to convince us, that the whole is confined to the two generations, between the exodus from Egypt and the entrance into Canaan.

But the confutation of a foolish system, dishonourable indeed to Scripture, is the least of my con⸱

cern⸱

cern. Such things will die of themselves. My point, in delivering the truths of God as they lie in his Word, is to illustrate the amazing wisdom of that Dispensation to which they belong. Let me observe therefore, as a matter of much greater moment, that this distinction, which the text hath made between the FATHERS and the CHILDREN, in the first period, during their abode in the wilderness, affords us a very noble instance of that divine *mercy* which extends to *thousands*.

The Prophet thus represents the fact. When God brought his chosen people out of Egypt, *he gave them his statutes and shewed them his judgments, which if a man do, he shall live in them. Moreover also he gave them his sabbaths, to be a sign between him and them* [l]. That is, he gave them the *moral* law of the Decalogue, in which there was one *positive* institution [m], and no more; but this one, absolutely necessary as *the token of a covenant*, to be a perpetual memorial of it, and, by that means, to preserve them a select people, unmixed with the nations. What followed so gracious and generous a dispensation to the house of Israel? Why, *they rebelled against him in the wilderness: they walked not in his statutes, and they despised his judgments, and his Sabbaths they greatly polluted* [n]. On which, he threatened *to pour out his fury upon them in the wilderness, and consume them* [o]. But, in regard to his own glory, lest the Heathen, before whom he brought them out of Egypt, should blaspheme, he thought fit to spare them [p]. Yet so far punished that generation, as never to suffer them to come into the land of Canaan [q]. Their *children* he spared, that the race might not be consumed as he had first threatened [r]. And hoping better things of them

---

[l] Ver. 11, 12.   [m] The Sabbath.   [n] Ver. 13.
[o] Ver. 15.   [p] Ver. 14.   [q] Ver. 16.   [r] Ver. 17.

than

than of their Fathers, he said *to them in the wilder-nefs, Walk ye not in the ftatutes of your fathers, nei-ther obferve their judgments, nor defile yourfelves with their idols.   Walk in my ftatutes, and keep my judg-ments and do them : and hallow my Sabbaths, and they fhall be a fign between me and you*'.   Here we fee, the Children, or immediate progeny, were again offered, as their fole rule of government, what had been given to, and had been violated by their Fa-thers ; namely, the moral law of the Decalogue, and the pofitive inftitution of the Sabbath.   Well, and how did they behave themfelves on this occa-fion ?   Juft as their fathers had done before them. —*Notwithftanding* [the repetition of this offered grace] *the Children rebelled againft me, they walked not in my ftatutes, they polluted my Sabbaths*'—What followed ? The fame denunciation which had hung over the Fathers, utter deftruction *in the wilder-nefs* ".   However, mercy again prevails over judg-ment ; and the fame reafon for which he fpared their Fathers inclines him to fpare them ; left his *name fhould be polluted in the fight of the heathen* ˣ. However due punifhment attended their tranfgref-fions, as it had done their Fathers'.   Their Fathers left their bones in the wildernefs : but this perverfe race being pardoned, as a People, and ftill poffeffed of the privilege of a felect and chofen Nation, were neither to be fcattered amongft the Heathen, nor to be confined for ever in the wildernefs : Almighty Wifdom therefore ordained that their punifhment fhould be fuch, as fhould continue them, even againft their Wills, a feparated race, in poffeffion of the land of Canaan.   What this punifhment was, the following words declare.—*Becaufe they had not executed my judgments, but had defpifed my ftatutes,*

ˢ Ver. 18, 19, 20.   ᵗ Ver. 21.   ᵘ Ver. 21.
ˣ Ver. 22.

*and had polluted my Sabbaths, and their eyes were after
their fathers idols, Wherefore* I GAVE THEM ALSO
STATUTES THAT WERE NOT GOOD, AND JUDG-
MENTS WHEREBY THEY SHOULD NOT LIVE[y]. That
is, becaufe they had violated my FIRST fyftem of
laws, the DECALOGUE, I added to them [I GAVE
THEM ALSO, words which imply the giving as a
fupplement] my SECOND fyftem, the RITUAL
LAW; very aptly characterifed (when fet in oppofition to the MORAL LAW) by *ftatutes that were not
good, and by judgments whereby they fhould not live.*

What is here obferved, opens to us the admirable reafons of both punifhments: and why there
was a forbearance, or a fecond trial, before the
yoke of the Ordinances was impofed.   For we muft
never forget, that the God of Ifrael tranfacted with
his people according to the mode of human Governors.   Let this be kept in mind, and we fhall
fee the admirable progrefs of the Difpenfation. God
brought the *Fathers* out of Egypt, to put them in
poffeffion of the land of Canaan.   He gave them
the MORAL LAW to diftinguifh them for the worfhipers of the true God: And he gave them
the POSITIVE LAW of the Sabbath to diftinguifh
them for God's peculiar people.   Thefe *Fathers*
proving perverfe and rebellious, their punifhment was death in the wildernefs, and exclufion
from that good land which was referved for their
Children.   But then thefe *Children*, in that very
Wildernefs, the fcene of their Fathers' crime and
calamity, fell into the fame tranfgreffions.   What
was now to be done? It was plain, fo inveterate
an evil could be only checked or fubdued by the
curb of fome fevere Inftitution.   A fevere Inftitution was prepared; and the RITUAL LAW was

[y] Ver. 24, 25.

eftablifhed,

established.   For the first offence, the punishment was *personal:* but when a repetition shewed it to be inbred, and, like the Leprosy, sticking to the whole race, the punishment was properly changed to *national.*

How clear, how coherent, is every thing, as here explained! How consonant to reason! How full of divine wisdom ! Yet, in defiance of Scripture and Common-sense (which have a closer connexion than the Enemies of religion suspect, or than the common advocates of it dare venture to maintain) comes a Doctor, and tells us, that these *Children in the Wilderness* of the time of Moses, were *Children of the land of Canaan* in the time of the Judges; and that the *statutes given* which were *not good*, were pagan idolatries, *not given*, but *suffered*; indeed not *suffered*; because severely, and almost always immediately punished.

What misled our Doctor (whose *Connexions*, by what we have seen, appear to be little better than a *chain* of errors) seems to have been this, The *Ritual law* was given during the life of the *Fathers*, and soon after their transgression mentioned in the 13th ver. of this Prophecy.   So he could not conceive how the Prophet should mean that this Law was given to the *Children.* But he did not consider, that the proper punishment of the *Fathers* was extinction in the wilderness : the proper punishment of the *Children*, who were reserved to possess the holy land, was the infliction of the RITUAL LAW.

The Dr. however, notwithstanding all his complacency in this his adopted system, yet appears conscious of its want of strength; for he owns that an objection may be made to it from the following words of the Prophecy.——*But I said unto their*
Children

Children IN THE WILDERNES, *Walk ye not in the
statutes of your Fathers—walk in my statutes—and
hallow my Sabbath* [z].   And again, of these *Children
— then I said I would pour out my fury upon them
to accomplish mine anger against* them IN THE
WILDERNESS [a].   And again,—*I lifted up my hand
unto them also* IN THE WILDERNESS [b].   " Here
" (says the learned Doctor) the prophet may SEEM
" TO HINT, that God's anger against the Children
" was *while they were in the wilderness* [c]."

May seem to hint!   The Dr. must be immoder-
ately fond of precise expression when he esteems
this to be no more than a *hint* or doubtful intimation.

But MOSES having omitted to tell us, that these
Children did indeed play these pranks *in the Wilderness,* he will not take a later Prophet's word for
it. *As Moses* (says the Doctor) *wrote before Ezekiel
prophesied ; his prophesy could not alter facts.*   It will
be more than the Doctor deserves, if the Freethinker
neglects to reply, that both the Prophet, and the
Doctor here *seem to hint*; the former, *that God's
anger against the Children was while they were in the
wilderness*; the latter, that Moses and Ezekiel contradict one another.   But to let this pass.—*Prophesy*
he says, *could not alter facts*; by which he means
that Prophesy, any more than the author of Prophesy, could not make that to be undone which was
already done.   Who ever thought it could? But
might not Ezekiel's Prophesy explain facts, and
relate them too, which a former Prophet had omitted?   However Ezekiel is not the only one who
informs us of this fact.   AMOS upbraids these

z Ver. 18, 19, 20.   a Ver. 21.   b Ver. 23.
c P. 169.

sojourners

sojourners *in the wilderness* with a still more general apostacy. " Have ye offered unto me sacrifices " and offerings IN THE WILDERNESS forty years, " O house of Israel? But ye have born the taber- " nacle of your Moloch and Chiun, your images, " the Star of your God, which ye made to your " selves [d]." Now if the Israelites committed ido- latry all the time they sojourned in the Wilder- ness, the crime necessarily included the CHILDREN with the *Fathers*.

The Doctor's second expedient to evade the determinate evidence of the text is as ridiculous as the first is extravagant. The text says,—*I will pour out my fury upon them to accomplish mine anger against them* IN THE WILDERNESS.—" These " words, *in the wilderness*, (says the acute Exposi- " tor) do not hint the place where the *anger* was " to be *accomplished*, but rather refer to *anger*, and " suggest the *anger* to be, as if we might almost " say in English, THE WILDERNESS-ANGER [e]".—If the Doctor's Rhetoric is to be enriched with this new phrase, I think his Logic should not be denied the benefit of a like acquisition, of which it will have frequent use, and that is, WILDERNESS-REA- SONING. And so much for this learned solution.

But the absurdity of supposing, with these men, that the words, *I gave them also statutes that were not good, and judgments whereby they should not live,* might signify, their *taking* (without *giving*) *Baal and Ashteroth for their Gods* [f], is best exposed by the Prophet himself, as his words lie in the text. Consider then the case of these Rebels. God's first intention, (as in the other case of their Fathers' rebellion) is represented to be the renouncing them

---

[d] Chap. v. 25, 26.   [e] P. 171.   [f] P. 163.

for his people, and scattering them amongst the nations. *Then I said I would pour out my fury upon them to accomplish my anger against them in the wilderness* [g]. But his mercy prevails.—*Nevertheless I withdrew mine hand, and wrought for my names sake, that it should not be polluted in the sight of the Heathen, in whose sight I brought them forth* [h]. In these two verses, we see, that the punishment intended, and the mercy shewn, are delivered in general; without the circumstances of the punishment, or the conditions of the mercy. The three following verses, in the mode of the eastern composition, which delights in repetition, informs us more particularly of these *circumstances*, which were DISPERSION, &c. and of these *conditions*, which were the imposition of a *Ritual Law*.—*I lifted up my hand unto them also in the wilderness, that I would* SCATTER THEM *amongst the heathen, and* DISPERSE THEM *thro' the countries; because they had not executed my judgments, but had despised my statutes, and had polluted my Sabbaths, and their eyes were after their Fathers' idols* [i]. Here, the intended punishment is explained specifically, that is, with its circumstances.—The mercy follows; and the terms, on which it was bestowed, are likewise explained.—*Wherefore I gave them also Statutes that were* NOT GOOD, *and Judgments whereby they should* NOT LIVE [k]. And now the beggarly shifts of the new interpretation appear in all their nakedness. Whatever is meant by *statutes not good*, the end of giving them, we see, was to preserve them a peculiar people to the Lord; for the punishment of dispersion was remitted to them. But if by *statutes not good* be meant the permitting them to fall into Idolatries, God is absurdly represented as decreeing an *end*; (the keeping his people feparate) and at the fame time providing *means* to defeat it : For every lapfe into idolatry was a ftep to their difperfion and *utter confumption*, by abforbing them into the Nations. We muft needs conclude therefore, that, by STA-TUTES NOT GOOD is meant the RITUAL LAW, the only means of attaining that end of mercy, The preferving them a feparate people.

Who now can chufe but fmile to hear our learned Expofitor quoting thefe words of the book of Judges,—*The* CHILDREN *of Ifrael did evil in the fight of the Lord, and followed other Gods of the Gods of the people, that were round about them, and pro-voked the Lord to anger and ferved Baal, and Afhte-roth*[l]; and then gravely adding, — " So that here " the fcene opens which Ezekiel alludes to; and " accordingly, what Ezekiel mentions as the pu-" nifhment of thefe wickedneffes began now to " come upon them[m]."

However, it muft be owned, that if words alone could fhake the folidity of the interpretation, I have here given, thefe which immediately follow the contefted paffage of *ftatutes not good*, would be enough to alarm us — *And I polluted them* (fays the text) *in their own gifts, in that they caufed to pafs thro' the fire all that openeth the womb, that I might make them defolate, to the end that they might know that I am the Lord*[n]. The common interpretation of which is this, " I permitted them to fall into that " wicked inhumanity, whereby they were pollut-" ed and contaminated, in making their Children " to pafs through the fire to Moloch, in order to " root them out and utterly to deftroy them."

---

[l] Cap. ii. ver. 11, 12, 13.   [m] P. 163.   [n] Ver. 26. -

Dr.

Dr. Spencer (who follows the general fenfe of
the prophefy which I have here explained and fupported) appeared but too fenfible how much this
text ftood in his way.   He endeavours therefore to
fhew, that " it relates to God's rejecting the firft
" born of the Ifraelites from the priefthood, and
" appointing the tribe of Levi to the facred office
" in their ftead:" and that, therefore, the verfe
fhould be rendred thus, *I pronounced them polluted
in their gifts*, [i. e. unfit to offer me any oblation]
in that I paffed by all that openeth the womb [i. e.
the firft-born] *in order to humble them that they
might know that I am the Lord*.   And this rendering may be the right, for any thing Dr. Shuckford
has to oppofe to the contrary° ; the main of which
is, what has been already confuted ; (or rather,
what the very terms, in which the affertion is advanced, do themfelves confute) namely, that *the
Children in the wildernefs* were not the immediate
iffue of thofe who died *in the wildernefs*, but a remote pofterity.   As for his hebrew criticifm, that
the word *maas*, and not *nabar*, would probably
have been ufed by the Prophet, if *rejecting from the
priefthood* had been the fenfe intended by him P;
this is the flendereft of all reafoning, even tho' it had
been applied to a Rhetorician by profeffion, and in
a language very copious, and perfectly well underftood : How evanid is it therefore, when applied
to a Prophet under the impulfe of infpiration, and
fpeaking in the moft fcanty of all languages ; the
fmall knowledge of which is to be got from one
fingle volume of no large bulk, and conveyed in a
mode of writing fubject to perpetual equivocations
and ambiguities!   From the mifchiefs of which,
God in his good providence preferved us by the

Septuagent Translation, made while the Hebrew was a living language, and afterwards authenticated by the recognition of the inspired writers of the New Testament.

However the truth is, that this explanation of the learned Spencer must appear forced, even tho' we had no better to oppose to it : But when there is a better at hand, which not only takes off all the countenance which this 26th verse affords to Dr. Shuckford's interpretation of *Statutes not good*, but so exactly quadrates with the sense, here given, that it completes and perfects the narrative, we shall be no longer frighted with its formidable look.

To understand then what it aims at, we must consider the context as it has been explained above. The 21st and 22d verses (it hath been shewn) contain God's purposes of *judgment* and of *mercy* in general. The 23d, 24th and 25th explain in what the intended *judgment* would have consisted, and how the prevailing *mercy* was qualified. The Israelites were to be pardoned; but to be kept under, by the yoke of a ritual Law, described only in general by the title of *statutes not good*. The 26th verse opens the matter still further, and explains the nature and genius of that yoke, together with its effects, both salutary and baleful. The *salutary*, as it was a barrier to idolatry, the most enormous species of which was that of *causing their children to pass through the fire to Moloch :* the *baleful*, as it brought on their *desolation* when they became deprived of the Temple-worship. But to be more particular.—*I polluted them in their own gifts.* By *gifts* I understand that homage, (universally expressed, in the ancient world, by Rites
of

of facrifice) which a People owed to their God. And how were thefe *gifts polluted?* By a multifarious Ritual, which being oppofed to the idolatries; of the Nations, was prefcribed in reference to thofe idolatries; and, confequently, was incumbered with a thoufand Ceremonies, refpecting the choice of the animal; the qualities and purifications of the Sacrificers; and the direction and efficacy of each fpecific Offering. This account of their *pollution*, by fuch a Ritual, exactly anfwers to the character given of that Ritual, [*Statutes not good, &c.*] in the text in queftion. Then follows the reafon of God's thus *polluting them in their own gifts—in that* [or, becaufe that] *they caufed to pafs thro' the fire all that openeth the womb*—i. e. the *polluting* Ritual was impofed as a PUNISHMENT FOR, as well as BARRIER TO their idolatries; characterifed under this moft enormous and horrid of them all, the caufing of their children *to pafs thro' the fire to Moloch.* Then follows the humiliating circumftance of this ritual yoke,—*that I might make them defolate,* i. e. that they fhould, even from the nature of that Ritual, be deprived, when they moft wanted it, of their neareft intercourfe with their God and King. A real ftate of *defolation!* To underftand which, we are to confider, that at the time this Prophefy was delivered, the Jews, by their accumulated iniquities were accelerating, what doubtlefs the Prophet had then in his eye, their punifhment of the feventy years Captivity. Now, by the peculiar Conftitution of the ritual Law, their Religion became, as it were, local; it being unlawful to offer facrifice but in the temple of Jerufalem only. So that when they were led captive into a foreign land, the moft folemn and effential intercourfe between God and them, (*the morning and evening Sacrifice*) was entirely cut off: and thus, by means of the ritual Law they were emphatically

said

said to be *made desolate*. The verse concludes in telling us, for what end this punishment was inflicted—*that they might know that I am the Lord.* How would this appear from the premisses? Very evidently. For if, while they were in Captivity, they were under an interdict, and their Religion in a state of Suspension, and yet that they were to continue God's select people, (for the scope of the whole Prophesy is to shew, that, notwithstanding all their provocations, God still *worked for his names sake*) then, in order to be restored to their Religion, they were to be reinstated in their own Land: which work, Prophesy always describes as the utmost manifestation of God's power. Their redemption from the *Assyrian* captivity particularly, being frequently compared, by the Prophets, to that of the *Egyptian*. From hence therefore all men *might know* and collect, that the God of Israel *was the Lord.*

This famous text then, we see, may be thus aptly paraphrased —— *And I polluted them in their own gifts, in that they caused to pass thro' the fire all that openeth the womb, that I might make them desolate, to the end that they might know that I am the Lord.* i. e. " I loaded the religious Worship due to me, as their God and King, with a number of operose Ceremonies, to punish their past and to oppose to their future, idolatries; the most abominable of which was their making their children to pass through the fire to Moloch: And further, that I might have the Ceremonial Law always at hand as an instrument for still more severe punishments, when the full measure of their iniquities should bring them into Captivity in a strange land, I so contrived, by the very constitution of their Religion, that it should then remain

under an interdict, and all stated intercourse be cut
off between me and them: From which evil, would
necessarily arise this advantage, an occasion to
manifest my power to the Gentiles, in bringing my
People again, after a due time of penance, into
their own land."

Here we see, the text, thus expounded, connects and compleats the whole narrative, concerning the imposition of the ritual Law, and its nature and consequences, from the 21st to the 26th
verse inclusively: and opens the history of it by
due degrees, which the most just and elegant com-
positions require. We are first informed of the
threatened judgment, and of the prevailing mercy
in general:—we are then told the specific nature of
that judgment, and the circumstance attending
the accorded mercy;—and lastly, the Prophet explains the nature and genius of that attendant circumstance; together with its adverse as well as
benignant effects.

I have now deprived the Connecter of all
his arguments but one, for this strange interpretation of *Statutes not good*; and that one is, " That
the worshipers of *Baal* and *Ashteroth*, in the book
of Judges, and the slaves to *statutes not good*
in the prophet Ezekiel, having the common name
of Children, must needs be the same individuals:" But this I make a conscience of taking
from him.

Yet such confidence has the learned person in
his goodly exposition, that he concludes his reasoning against the obvious sense of the Prophesy,
in this extraordinary manner — " Dr. Spencer
" imagined, this text alone was sufficient to sup-
" port

" port his hypothesis: but I cannot but think, if
" what has been offered be fairly considered, NO
" HONEST WRITER can ever cite it again for that
" purpose [q]."

What is Dr. Spencer's hypothesis? Just this and
no other, that *Moses gave the ritual Law to the Jews
because of the hardness of their hearts* [r]; the very
Hypothesis of Jesus Christ himself.

But the CONNECTER thinks, that, *if what he
has offered be fairly considered,* NO HONEST WRITER
can ever cite it again for that purpose. This smells
strong of the Bigot.   One can hardly think one's
self in the closet of a learned and sober Divine; but
rather in some wild Conventicle of Methodists or
Hutchinsonians; whose criticisms are all Revelations: which, tho' you cannot embrace but at the
expence of COMMON SENSE, you are not allowed
to question without renouncing COMMON HO-
NESTY.

I have *fairly considered* (as the *Connecter* expects
his Reader should do) *what he has offered against
Dr. Spencer's hypothesis*; and if there be any truth
in the conclusions of human reason, I think a writer may go on very advantageously, as well as with
a good conscience, to defend *that Hypothesis.*   How
such a writer shall be qualified by Bigots, is another
point.   Many an HONEST MAN, I am persuaded,
will still adhere to Dr. *Shuckford's hypothesis*; and
with the same good faith, with which he himself
supported it: for tho' his charity will not allow
that title to those who dissent from him, yet God
forbid, that I should not give it to Him.

[q] Page 167.   [r] MATT. chap. xix. ver. 8.

But

But it is now time to proceed to the *third period* of THIS Prophefy. For the principal defign of this work is to vindicate and illuftrate facred Scripture, tho' in my progrefs I be ftill obliged, from time to time, to ftop a little, while I remove the moft material obftructions which lie in my way.

This Prophefy hitherto contains a declaration of the various punifhments inflicted on the rebellious Ifraelites, from the time of Mofes's miffion, to the preaching of Ezekiel. We have fhewn that their punifhment in the firft period, was *death in the wildernefs:* their punifhment in the fecond period, was *the faftening on their necks the yoke of the ritual Law.*

Their punifhment in the *third period* is now to be confidered: and we fhall fee that it confifted in rendering the yoke of the ritual Law ftill more galling, by withdrawing from them that EXTRAORDINARY PROVIDENCE, which once rewarded the ftudious obfervers of it, with many temporal bleffings. The punifhment was dreadful: and fuch, indeed, the Prophet defcribes it to have been. But we may be affured, their crimes deferved it, as having rifen in proportion with it; and this likewife, he tells us, was the cafe. . Their idolatries were at firft, and fo, for fome time they continued to be, the mixing Pagan worfhip with the worfhip of the God of Ifrael. But tho' they had fo often fmarted for this folly, they were yet fo befotted with the Gods of the nations, *the ftocks and ftones of the high places,* that their laft progrefs in impiety was the project of cafting off the God of Ifrael entirely, at leaft as their TUTELAR God, and of mixing themfelves amongft the Nations. They had experienced, that the *God of Ifrael* was a JEALOUS GOD,

GOD, who would not share his glory with another; and they hoped to avoid his wrath by renouncing their Covenant with him, and leaving him at liberty to chuse another people. To such a degree of impiety and madness was this devoted Nation arrived, when Ezekiel prophesied at the eve of their approaching Captivity. All this will be made plain, by what follows.

We have seen their behaviour in the two former periods; in EGYPT, and in the WILDERNESS. The third begins with a description of their Manners when they had taken possession of the land of CANAAN.

Ver. 27. " Son of man, speak unto the house
" of Israel, and say unto them, Thus saith the
" Lord God, yet in this, your fathers have blaf-
" phemed me, in that they have committed a tref-
" pafs againft me.

28. " For when I had brought them into the
" land, for the which I lifted up my hand to give
" it to them, then they faw every high hill, and
" all the thick trees, and they offered there their
" facrifices, and there they prefented the provoca-
" tion of their offering."

This was their continual practice, even to the delivery of this Prophefy; at which time, their enormities were come to the height, we juft mentioned; to contrive in their hearts to renounce the God of Ifrael, altogether. But being furrounded with calamites, and a powerful enemy at their door, they were willing to procure a prefent relief from him, whom they had fo much offended; tho' at this very inftant, they were projecting to offend

H 3   ftill

ftill more. The fingular impudence of this conduct was, apparently, the immediate occafion of
this famous Prophefy ; as we fhall now fee.

Ver. 30. " Wherefore fay unto the houfe of
" Ifrael, Thus faith the Lord God, Are ye pol-
" luted after the manner of your fathers ? and
" commit ye whoredoms after their abominations ?

31. " For when ye offer your gifts, when ye
" make your fons to pafs through the fire, ye pol-
" lute your felves with all your idols EVEN TO
" THIS DAY. And fhall I be enquired of by you,
" O houfe of Ifrael ? As I live, faith the Lord
" God, I will not be enquired of by you."

That this recourfe to the God of their Fathers
was only a momentary impulfe, arifing from their
preffing neceffities, is evident from what immediately follows; the mention of that fpecific
crime which brought upon them the punifhment
annexed to the third period.—

Ver. 32. " AND THAT WHICH COMETH INTO
" YOUR MIND SHALL NOT BE AT ALL, THAT YE
" SAY, WE WILL BE AS THE HEATHEN, AS THE
" FAMILIES OF THE COUNTRIES, TO SERVE WOOD
" AND STONE.

33. " As I live faith the Lord God, Surely with
" a mighty hand, and with a ftretched out arm,
" AND WITH FURY POURED OUT, WILL I RULE
" OVER YOU.

34. " AND I WILL BRING YOU OUT FROM THE
" PEOPLE, AND WILL GATHER YOU OUT OF THE
" COUNTRIES WHEREIN YE ARE SCATTERED, with
a mighty

" a mighty hand, and with a ftretched out arm,
" AND WITH FURY POURED OUT.

35. " And I will bring you into the WILDERNESS
" OF THE PEOPLE, and there will I plead with you
" face to face.

36. " Like as I pleaded with your fathers in the
" *wildernefs* of the land of Egypt, fo will I plead
" with you face to face."

By all this it appears, that the Jews of this time
were little anxious to *avoid* their approaching
Captivity, denounced and threatened by all their
Prophets.   What they wanted was a light and eafy
fervitude, which might enable them to mingle
with, and at laft, to be loft amongft the Nations;
like the ten Tribes which had gone before them.
Againft the vilenefs of thefe hopes is this part of
the Prophefy directed.   God affures them, he will
bring them out of the *Affyrian* Captivity, as he
had done out of the *Egyptian*; but not in mercy,
as that deliverance was procured, but in judgment,
and *with fury poured out.*   And as he had brought
their Fathers into the *wildernefs of the land* of Egypt,
fo would he bring them into the WILDERNESS OF
THE PEOPLE, that is, the land of Canaan, which
they would find, on their return to it, was become defart and uninhabited; and therefore elegantly called, the *wildernefs of the people.* But
what now was to be their reception, on their
fecond poffeffion of the promifed Land? a very
different welcome from the firft.   God indeed
leads them here again with a *mighty hand and a
ftretched out arm*; and it was to take poffeffion; but
not, as at firft, of a *land flowing with milk and
honey,* but of a prifon, a houfe of correction where

they

they were to paſs under the rod, and to remain in bonds.

37. " AND I WILL CAUSE YOU (ſays God) TO
" PASS UNDER THE ROD, AND I WILL BRING
" YOU INTO THE BOND OF THE COVENANT."

Words which ſtrongly and elegantly expreſs ſubjection to a ritual Law, after the extraordinary Providence, which ſo much alleviated the yoke of it, was withdrawn : And we find it withdrawn ſoon after their return from the Captivity.—But, the Propheſy, carrying on the compariſon to the Egyptian deliverance, adds—

Ver. 38. " And I will purge out from amongſt
" you, the Rebels, and them that tranſgreſs againſt
" me : I will bring them forth out of the country
" where they ſojourn, and they ſhall not enter into
" the land of Iſrael."

Theſe *Rebels*, like their FATHERS *in the wilderneſs*, were indeed to be brought out of Captivity, but were never to enjoy the promiſed Land; and the reſt, like the CHILDREN *in the wilderneſs*, were to have the yoke of the ritual Law ſtill made more galling. And thus the COMPARISON is compleated.

Theſe were the three different puniſhments inflicted in theſe three different periods. The firſt PERSONAL ; the ſecond and the third, NATIONAL ; only the third made heavier than the ſecond, in proportion to their accumulated offences.

But as, in the height of God's vengeance on the ſins of this wretched people, the diſtant proſpect always terminated in a mercy ; So, with a mercy, and

and a promife of better times, the whole of this prophetic Scene is clofed; in order that the NA-TION to which it is addreffed, fhould, however criminal they were, not be left in an utter ftate of defperation, but be afforded fome fhadow of repofe, in the profpect of future peace and tranquillity. For now, turning again to thefe *temporary Inquirers* after God, the Prophefy addreffes them, in this manner,

Ver. 39. " As for you, O houfe of Ifrael, thus " faith the Lord God, Go ye, ferve ye every one " his idols, and hereafter alfo, if ye will not hear-" ken unto me: But pollute you my holy name no " more with your gifts, and with your idols."

As much as to fay, Go on no longer in this divided worfhip; halt no more between two opinions; if Baal be your God, ferve him; if the God of Ifrael, then ferve him only. The reafon follows.

Ver. 40.—43. " *For in mine holy mountain—there* " *fhall all the houfe of Ifrael—ferve me. There will* " *I accept them, and there will I require your offerings* " *—with all your holy things——and there fhall ye re-* " *member your ways, and all your doings wherein ye* " *have been defiled,* AND YE SHALL LOTHE YOUR-" SELVES IN YOUR OWN SIGHT."—i. e. " For then, a new order of things fhall commence. My people, after their return from the Captivity, fhall be as averfe to idolatry, as till then they were prone and difpofed to it: and the memory of their former follies fhall *make them lothe themfelves* in their own fight." And this, indeed, was the fact, as we learn by their whole hiftory, from their reftoration to their own Land, quite down to the prefent hour.

The

The idea of MERCY is naturally attached to that of repentance and reformation; and with MERCY the Prophefy concludes.

Ver. 44. " *And ye fhall know that I am the Lord* " *when I have wrought with you for my name's fake;* " *not according to your wicked ways, nor according to* " *your corrupt doings, O ye houfe of Ifrael, faith the* " *Lord God.*"

The Reader hath now a full explanation of the whole Prophecy: whereby he may underftand how juftly it hath required its eminent celebrity. Its general fubject being no lefs than the Fate and Fortunes of the jewifh Republic: of which the feveral parts are fo important; fo judicioufly chofen, fo elegantly difpofed, and fo nobly enounced, that we fee the divinity of the original, in every ftep we take.

But to return to the peculiar purpofe of this Comment. Which is given to fhew, that God himfelf has delivered the ritual Law of the Jews, under the character of *Statutes that were not good, and Judgments, whereby they fhould not live* '.

The

' That very able interpreter of Scripture, father Houbigant, underftands thefe words of the Prophet as fpoken of the *Jewifh Law.* " Itaque in præceptis *non bonis* intelligendæ veniunt " ejufmodi leges quæ ad pœnam propofitæ erant, non ad " mercedem; quales erant leges de fuppliciis, de aquis ab " uxore fufpectæ pudicitiæ bibendis, de leprofis ab hominum " cœtu arcendis, et aliæ quædam, quæ ab irato Legiflatore " proficifci videbantur." *In loc.* This learned perfon was too well verfed in the ftyle of Scripture, in the fubject of the Prophefy, and in the hiftory of the Jews, to imagine, when God fpeaks in the character of Legiflator, of *giving Statutes and Judgments*, that he meant the general permiffion of divine Providence to fuffer a people to fall into a number of fenfe-

lefs

The uſe I would make of it againſt WITSIUS, with whom I have been concerned, is to ſhew, that, if ſuch be the genius of the ritual Law, it is no wonder it ſhould have, in its compoſition, an alloy of no better materials, than Egyptian and other pagan Ceremonies; cleanſed indeed and refined from their immoralities and ſuperſtitions: And converſely, that a compoſition of ſuch an alloy was very aptly characteriſed by *Statutes not good, and Judgments whereby they could not live.*

Thus having before ſeen what little force there was in Witſius's arguments, and now underſtanding how little reaſon he had to be ſo tenacious of his opinion, the reader may think he ſcarce merited the diſtinction of being recommended to a learned Body as the very bulwark of the faith, in this matter. But let what will become of his arguments, he deſerves honour for a much better thing than orthodox diſputation: I mean, for an honeſt turn of mind averſe to imputing odious deſigns to his adverſaries, or dangerous conſequences to their opinions [1].

On

leſs and idolatrous practices. Indeed, a little to ſoften the character given of *Statutes not good*, he ſuppoſes they were thus qualified on account of their being *penal Laws:* and ſo makes what I underſtand to be a repreſentation of the moral genius of the ritual Law in general, only the phyſical quality of ſome particular Rites. But the very words of the Propheſy evince that a Body of laws was meant; and the character of the Speaker ſhews, that the ſubject is of *moral,* not of *phyſical* good and evil.

[1] Speaking of MARSHAM and SPENCER, he ſays: In omnium nunc fere eruditorum manibus verſatur Nobiliſſimi Viri Johannis Marſhami CANON CHRONICUS. Opus quantivis pretii; quod uti Authori ſuo multa lectione, accurata meditatione, plurimiſque lucubrationibus ſtetit, ita Lectori per ſalebroſos obſcuriſſimæ

On the whole then, we conclude, both againſt
DEIST and BELIEVER, that the Ritual Law's
being

riſſimæ Antiquitatis receſſus viam non paullo faciliorem expe-
ditioremque effecit. Sed ut in humanis rebus nihil omni ex
parte beatum eſſe ſolet, ita nec pulcherrimo huic corpori ſuos
deeſſe nævos videas — Eandem ſententiam magno nuper animo
atque apparatu tuitus eſt Johannes Spencerus in Diſſertatione
de Urim & Thummim. Ubi ita vir doctiſſimus inſtituit, &c. —
Multa a viris doctiſſimis congeſta ſunt, quibus huic ſuæ aſſertioni
fidem faciant. Ea autem quum plurimum reconditæ contineant
eruditionis, non videntur Clariſſimi Authores ſua laude, uti nec
ſtudioſi lectores jucunditate atque utilitate, quæ exinde percipi
poteſt, fraudandi eſſe. — Super omnibus denique ἐπίχεισιν meam
ſubjungam, eo argumentorum robore quod ſuſcepti negotii
ratio patitur firmandam. Nequaquam ea mente ut doctiſſimorum virorum laboribus detraham; ſed ut me & Lectores meos
in inveſtiganda veritate exerceam, ſit forte detur curva corrigere
& egregio inſperſos abſtergere corpore nævos, p. 1—4. This
candour was the more extraordinary, as Sir J. Marſham had
given but too many marks of diſaffection to revealed Religion.
And though that great and good man Dr. Spencer was entirely
free from all reaſonable ſuſpicion of this kind; yet, it muſt be
owned, that too intent on a favourite argument, he was apt to
expreſs himſelf ſomewhat crudely. He had a bright and vigorous imagination, which, now and then, got the better of his
judgment; and the integrity of his heart made him careleſs in
giving it the reins; ſometimes in a dangerous road. Thus, for
inſtance, in his fine diſcourſe *concerning Prodigies,* ſpeaking of
a certain quality in the ſoul, which, as he ſays, makes it *greatly
impreſſive to the perſuaſion of parallels, equalities, ſimilitudes, in
the frame and government of the world,* he goes on in this
ſtrange manner, " This general temper of the ſoul eaſily in-
" clines it to believe great and mighty changes in ſtates,
" uſher'd with the ſolemnity of ſome mighty and analogous
" changes in nature, and that all terrible evils are prefac'd or
" attended with ſome prodigious and amazing alterations in
" the creation — Hence, perhaps, it is that we generally find
" great troubles and judgments on earth deſcribed eſpecially
" by perſons *ecſtatical, Prophets and Poets* (whoſe ſpeeches
" uſually rather follow the eaſy ſenſe of the ſoul than the rigid
" truth of things) by all the examples of horror and confuſion
" in the frame of the creation. The prophet David deſcribes
" GOD's going out to judgment thus," &c. p. 71, 72. 2d ed.
Dr. Spencer ſeems to have been miſled in this philoſophic ſolution

being made in reference to Egyptian superstition is no reasonable objection to the divinity of its original.

But the Deist may object, "That though indeed, when the Israelites were once deeply infected with that superstition, such a ritual might be necessary to stop and cure a growing evil; yet as the remedy was so multiplex, burdensome, and slavish, and therefore not in itself eligible, how happened it, that GOD, who had this family under his immediate and peculiar care, should suffer them to contract an infection which required so inconvenient and impure a remedy?

I have been so accustomed to find the strongest objections of infidelity end in the stronger recommendation of revealed Religion, that I have never been backward, either to produce what they have said, when they write their best, or to imagine what they would say, if they knew how to write better. To

tion by a greater Master, who however, talks still more grosly of what he seems to have understood as little. " In matters of " faith and religion (says lord Verulam) we raise our imagina- " tion above our reason : which is the cause why Religion " sought ever access to the mind by similitudes, types, para- " bles, visions, dreams." *Adv. of learning*, b. 2d. The serious christian reader cannot but be offended at this injurious representation of the holy Prophets. Such remarks as these are altogether unworthy these two excellent men. It is false in fact that Prophetic figures were enthusiastic or fantastic visions raised by, and then represented to, the imagination. I have shewn that the images, which the Prophets employed, composed the common phraseology of their times; 'and were employed by them because this figurative language was well understood, and still better relished by the People. [See p. 111. of this vol.] — But is it therefore fitting that such writers should be treated, by every dirty scribbler, as Libertines, Deists, and secret propagators of Infidelity, for inadvertencies, which a man like the candid Witsius would only call *Nævi in pulcherrimo corpore ?*

this

this therefore I reply, That the promiſe God had made to Abraham, to give his poſterity the land of Canaan, could not be performed till that Family was grown ſtrong enough to take and keep poſſeſſion of it. In the mean time, therefore, they were neceſſitated to reſide amongſt idolaters. And we have ſeen, altho' they reſided unmixed, how violent a propenſity they ever had to join themſelves to the gentile Nations, and to practiſe their Manners. God, therefore, in his infinite wiſdom brought them into Egypt, and kept them there during this period; the only place were they could remain, for ſo long a time, ſafe and unconfounded with the natives; the ancient Egyptians being, by numerous inſtitutions, forbidden all fellowſhip with ſtrangers; and bearing beſides, a particular averſion to the profeſſion ᵘ of this Family. Thus we ſee, that the natural diſpoſition of the Iſraelites, which, in Egypt, occaſioned their ſuperſtitions; and in conſequence, the neceſſity of a burthenſome Ritual, would, in any other Country, have abſorbed them in Gentiliſm and confounded them with Idolaters. From this objection, therefore, nothing comes but a new occaſion to adore the footſteps of eternal Wiſdom in his Diſpenſations to his choſen People.

III.

The laſt propoſition is, *That the very circumſtances of Moſes's Egyptian learning, and the Laws inſtituted in compliance to the people's prejudices, and in oppoſition to Egyptian ſuperſtitions, are a ſtrong confirmation of the divinity of his miſſion.*

Egypt was the great School of legiſlation for the reſt of Mankind. And ſo revered were her

---

ᵘ The profeſſion of Shepherds.

oracular

oracular dictates, that foreign Lawgivers, who went thither for inftruction, never ventured to deviate from thofe fundamental principles of Government which fhe prefcribed. In RELIGION, particularly, which always made a part of civil Policy, they fo clofely adhered to Egyptian maxims, that Pofterity, as we have feen, were deceived into an opinion that the greek Lawgivers had received their very Gods from thence.

What therefore muft we think had been the cafe of a Native of Egypt; bred up, from his infancy in Egyptian wifdom, and, at length, become a member of their Legiflative body? would fuch a man, when going to frame a civil Policy and Religion (though we fuppofe nothing of that natural affection, which the beft and wifeft men have ever borne for their own country inftitutions) be at all inclined to deviate from its fundamental principles of Government?

Yet here we have in Mofes, according to our Adverfaries' account of him, a mere human Lawgiver, come frefh out of the Schools of Egypt, to reduce a turbulent People into Society, acting on fundamental principles of Religion and Policy directly oppofite to all the maxims of Egyptian Wifdom.

One of the chief of which, in the RELIGIOUS POLICY of Egypt, was, That the government of the World had, by the fupreme Ruler of the univerfe, been committed into the hands of fubordinate, local, tutelary Deities; amongft whom the feveral Regions of the earth were fhared out and divided: that thefe were the true and proper objects of all public and popular Religion; and that the

5   know-

knowledge of the ONE TRUE GOD, the Creator of all things, was highly dangerous to be communicated to the People; but was to be secreted, and shut up in their MYSTERIES; and in them, to be revealed only occasionally, and to a few; and those few, the wise, the learned, and ruling part of mankind [x]. Now, in plain defiance and contempt of this most venerable Principle, our Egyptian Lawgiver rejects these doctrines of inferior Deities, as impostures, and *lying vanities*; and boldly and openly preaches up to the People, the belief of the ONE TRUE GOD, the Creator, as the sole object of the Religion of all mankind [y].

Another

---

[x] See an account of these MYSTERIES in the first volume.

[y] Let me here observe how this very circumstance, in Moses's conduct, acquits him of all suspicion of that kind of FRAUD so much in use amongst the best human Lawgivers of Antiquity. The Mosaic Dispensation had been treated by our Freethinkers with great liberties. It was therefore offered by the late learned and ingenious Dr. Middleton, as a means to rescue it from their contempt, and to solve the difficulties which attend it, without hurting the authority whereon it stands, to suppose SOME DEGREE OF FICTION in certain cases, in the Mosaic writings. And this he endeavoured to make credible, from the practice of the ancient Lawgivers. Now I think this supposition neither true nor probable. 1. If we consider what it was that induced the ancient Lawgivers to employ *fiction*, we shall find it arose, in part, from their false pretences to a divine Mission; and, in part, from the imaginary necessity of propagating Polytheism. As to the first, Moses's pretensions to a divine mission are here allowed. And it is notorious that he preached up the one true GOD, the Creator, in opposition to all kinds of Polytheism. No occasion therefore remained for the use of *fiction*. And we can hardly think he would employ it without occasion. What we have then to shew is, that the only cause why the ancient sages employed *fiction* (besides the support of a false mission) was to hide the absurdities of Polytheism. This indeed hath been already done for other purposes, in several places of this Work: So that I shall here confine myself to one single proof. Macrobius assures us, that the ancient sages did not admit the fabulous

in

Another fundamental maxim, in the RELIGIOUS
POLICY of Egypt, was to propagate, by every kind
of

in all their difputations ; but in thofe only which related to the
SOUL, to the HEAVENLY BODIES, and to the HERO-GODS.
Sciendum eft tamen non in omnem difputationem philofophos
admittere *fabulofo* vel *licita*, fed his uti folent cum vel de animâ,
vel de AERIIS' ÆTHERIISVE POTESTATIBUS, vel de CETERIS
DIS loquuntur. [in Som. Scrip. l. i. c. 2.] On the contrary,
when they difcourfed of the FIRST CAUSE, then every thing was
delivered exactly agreeable to truth.   Ceterum cum ad SUM-
MUM ET PRINCIPEM OMNIUM DEUM — tractatus fe audet
attollere — NIHIL FABULOSUM penitus attingunt. [*id. ib.*]
The reafon of their ufing *fiction* or fable, in treating of their
falfe Gods, was to hide the abfurdities attendant on their Worfhip ; a Worfhip thought to be neceffary.   Hence, as hath been
fhewn elfewhere, [vol. i. of the Div. Leg. b. iii. fect. 6.] they
were led from the *abfurdity* and the *neceffity* together, to conclude *that utility, and not truth, was the end of Religion* ; and
from another miftake there mentioned, *that utility and truth do
not coincide*.   From thefe two principles neceffarily arofe a third,
that it was expedient and lawful to deceive for the Public good.
And, on this laft, was founded the practice of *fiction* above-
mentioned.   Now the whole Religion of Mofes being eftablifhed on that very doctrine, in the handling of which the ancient
Sages neither needed nor ufed *fiction* ; and at the fame time
directly oppofing that very fuperftition, for the fake of which,
the *fiction* was employed ; we conclude, with certainty, that
Mofes employed NO DEGREE OF FICTION in the compofition or
in the propagation of the Jewifh Religion.   But 2. That which
he had no occafion to ufe, we think it impoffible he fhould ufe,
if his pretenfions were (as is here allowed) real.   We have, indeed, in order to difplay the wifdom of GOD's Difpenfation, endeavoured to fhew that he employed, in the contrivance of it,
all thofe arts (though in an infinitely more perfect degree) which
human Lawgivers are wont to ufe, in the legitimate exercife of
civil Government : for that, without forcing the Will, no other
method was fufficient to accomplifh the end defigned.   But
this, we prefume, is as different from *fiction* as truth is from
falfhood.   Thus far, we think, GOD, in his difpenfations to
men, would chufe to do, rather than to force the Will.   But
could we fuppofe a People, favoured with a divine Revelation,
fo abfurdly circumftanced as to be incapable of being worked
upon by common means, without the ufe of *fome degree of
fiction*, we fhould then conclude GOD would rather chufe mira-

of method, the doctrine of A FUTURE STATE OF REWARDS AND PUNISHMENTS; as the neceſſary ſupport of all Religion and Government. Here again, our Law-giver, (no Deiſt can tell why[z]) forſakes all his own principles; intentionally rejects a ſupport, which was as really beneficial to mankind, in all his intereſts, as the other notion, of inferior Deities, was but thought to be; intirely omits to mention it in his Inſtitutes of Law and Religion; and is ſtudiouſly ſilent in all thoſe particulars which lead to the propagation of it[a]. But of this, more at large, in the ſixth volume.

Again,

---

culouſly to over-rule the Will: becauſe we conceive *divine Revelation* with *human fiction* to be a mixture of things utterly incompatible; that their can be no alliance between GOD and Belial; nor any union between the Spirit of Truth, and the Father of Lies.

[z] See *a view of L. Bolingbroke's Philoſophy: Let.* IVth.

[a] " Suppoſe (ſays Dr. Stebbing) a Deiſt ſhould alledge that " the Iſraelites learned this doctrine in Egypt where Moſes him- " ſelf alſo might have learnt it, *How would you prove the con-* " *trary?*" Examination, p. 33—4.

Should a *Deiſt alledge this,* as making any thing *againſt* my argument, or *for* his own cauſe, I ſhould ſay he knew as little either of one or the other as Dr. Stebbing himſelf does: For my argument being addreſſed to the Deiſt, ſuppoſes that Moſes and the Iſraelites might have learnt the doctrine in Egypt; and on that ſuppoſition, defies them to find a reaſon, excluſive of the *extraordinary Providence,* why Moſes did not make ſo uſeful and neceſſary a doctrine, (in favour of which his People were much prejudiced) the Sanction of his Laws. Their acquaintance with the doctrine in Egypt, I ſuppoſed: This acquaintance my argument required me to ſuppoſe: and yet this Anſwerer of my Book knew ſo little of its contents as to aſk, How I WOULD PROVE THE CONTRARY? If the learned Doctor had any pertinent drift in this queſtion, you can diſcover it only by ſuppoſing him to go upon this ridiculous aſſumption, that what the Jews once learned they could never
either

Again, it was of the CIVIL POLICY of Egypt to prefer an hereditary despotic Monarchy to all other forms of Government: Moses, on the contrary, erects a THEOCRACY on the free choice of the people; to be administered Aristocratically.

Add to all this, that his deviation from the Policy of Egypt was encountering the strongest prejudices of his People; who were violently carried away to all the customs and superstitions of that Policy.

And now let an ingenuous Deist weigh these instances, with many more that will easily occur to him, and then fairly tell us his sentiments. Let him try, if he can think it was at all likely, that Moses, a mere human Lawgiver, a Native of Egypt, and learned in all its political Wisdom, should, in the formation of a Civil policy, for such a People as he undertook to govern, act directly contrary to all the fundamental principles in which he had been instructed?

I. To this perhaps it may be said,—" That Moses well understood the folly and falshood of inferior GODS :—that he did not believe the doctrine of a future state of rewards and punishments;—— that he was too honest to employ fraud:—that his love to his People made him indisposed to an hereditary despotic Monarchy:—and that the theologic principles of Egypt led him to the invention of a THEOCRACY." To all this, I answer,

---

either *unlearn* or forget, and therefore if they had learned the doctrine of a future state in Egypt, they could not be so ignorant of it as, I say, they were. But to clear up his conceptions in this matter he may have recourse, if he pleases, to the latter division of the fifth Sect. of the fifth Book, of the *Div. Leg.*

1. As to *his seeing the falshood of inferior Gods.* —So did many other of the old Lawgivers, inftructed in Egyptian policy; yet, being taught to think Polytheifm ufeful to Society, they did not, for all that, the lefs cultivate their abominable idolatry.

2. As to *his not believing a future ftate, and his honefty in not teaching what he did not believe.*— Such Objectors forget that they have already made him a fraudulent impoftor, in his pretenfion to a divine employment. Now if the end of civil Government made him fraudulent in that inftance, it would hardly fuffer him to be fcrupulous in this; even allowing the extravagance of this fancy, that he *did not believe* a future ftate; becaufe, as hath been proved at large[b], the propagation of this doctrine is, and was always believed to be, the firmeft fupport of civil government: But of this more at large, hereafter.

3. With regard to *his concern for the happinefs of his people;*—I will readily allow this to be very confiftent with Heroic or Legiflative fraud. But this happinefs the ancient Lawgivers thought beft procured by the Egyptian mode of Government. And indeed they had EXPERIENCE, the beft guide in public matters. For the excellent education which the Egyptians gave their Kings, in training them up to the love of the Public, and high veneration for the Laws, prevented the ufual abufe of power; and gave to that people the longeft and moft uninterrupted courfe of profperity that any Nation ever enjoyed[c]. It is no wonder therefore, that

---

[b] See the firft volume.

[c] This was the character it bore even fo late as the time of Jeremiah, who tells us, that the rebellious Ifraelites, frightened

as

that this should make MONARCHY, (as it did) the first favourite form of Government, in all places civilized by the aid of Egypt.

4. But, *the theologic principles of Egypt led Moses to the invention of a* THEOCRACY.—Without doubt those principles, as we shall see hereafter, occasioned its easy reception amongst the Hebrews. But there is one circumstance in the case that shews its invention must have been of GOD, and not of Moses. For the ground of its easy reception was the notion of local tutelary Deities. But this notion, Moses, in preaching up the doctrine of the one true GOD, entirely took away. This, indeed, on a supposition of a DIVINE LEGATION, has all the marks of admirable wisdom ; but supposing it to be Moses's own contrivance, we see nothing but inconsistency and absurdity. He forms a design, and then defeats it ; he gives with one hand, and he takes away with the other.

II. But it may be farther objected,—" That, as it was the intention of Moses to separate these people from all others, he therefore, gave them those cross and opposite institutions, as a barrier to all communication." To this I answer,

1. That were it indeed GOD, and not Moses, who projected this SEPARATION, the reason would be good. Because the immediate end of GOD's *separation* was twofold, to keep them unmixed ; and to secure them from idolatry : and such end could not be effected but by opposing those funda-

at the power of the king of Babylon, refused to stay any longer in Judea, *saying, No, but we will go into the land of Egypt, where we shall see no war, nor hear the sound of the trumpet, nor have hunger of bread, and there will we dwell.* chap. xlii. 14.

mental

mental principles of Egypt, with the doctrine of
ONE GOD, and the inftitution of a THEOCRACY.
But then this, which would be a good reafon, will
become a very bad objection.   Our Deift is to be
held to the queftion.   He regards Mofes as a mere
human Lawgiver.   But the fole end which fuch a
one could propofe by a *feparation*, was to preferve
his people pure and unmixed.   Now this could be
effected only by laws which kept them at home,
and difcouraged and prevented all foreign commerce : and thefe, by the fame means, bringing on
general poverty, there would be fmall danger of
their being much frequented, while they laboured
under that contagious malady.   This we know
was the cafe of Sparta.   It was their Lawgiver's
chief aim to keep them diftinct and unmixed.
But did he do this by inftitutions which croffed the
fundamental principles of the Religion and Policy
of Greece? By no means.   They were all of them
the fame.   The method he employed was only to
frame fuch Laws as difcouraged commerce and foreign intercourfe.   And thefe proved effectual.   I
the rather inftance in the Spartan, than in any
other Government, becaufe the end, which Mofes
and Lycurgus purfued in common, (tho' for different purpofes) of keeping their people *feparate*,
occafioned fuch a likenefs in feveral parts of the
two Inftitutions, as was, in my opinion, the real
origin of that tradition mentioned in the firft book
of Maccabees, That there was a Family-relation
between the two People.

2. But, fecondly, as it is very true, that the
mere intention of keeping a people feparate and
unmixed, (which is all, a human Lawgiver could
have in view) would occafion Laws in oppofition
to the cuftoms of thofe people with whom, from
their

their vicinity to, or fondneſs for, they were in moſt danger of being confounded; ſo, when I inſiſted on thoſe Anti-egyptian inſtitutions, which I gave as a certain proof of Moſes's *Divine Legation*, I did not reckon, in my account, any of that vaſt number of ritual and municipal laws, which, Manetho confeſſes, were *given principally in oppoſition to Egyptian cuſtoms* [d]. This a mere ſeparation would require: But this is a very different thing from the oppoſition to FUNDAMENTALS, here inſiſted on; which a mere ſeparation did not, in the leaſt, require.

III. But it may be ſtill further urged, " That reſentment for ill uſage might diſpoſe Moſes to obliterate the memory of the place they came from, by a Policy contrary to the *fundamental* Inſtitutions of Egypt." Here again our objecting Deiſt will forget himſelf. 1. He hath urged a CONFORMITY in the LAW to Egyptian Rites; and this, in order to diſcredit Moſes's *Divine Legation :* and we have allowed him his fact. Whatever it was therefore that engaged Moſes to his general OPPOSITION, it could not be reſentment: for that had certainly prevented all kind of conformity or ſimilitude.

2. But, ſecondly, ſuch effects of civil reſentment, the natural manners of men will never ſuffer us to ſuppoſe. We have in ancient hiſtory many accounts of the ſettlement of new Colonies, forced injuriouſly from home by their fellow-

---

[d] Ὁ δὲ πρῶτον μὲν αὐτοῖς νόμον ἔθετο, μήτε προσκυνεῖν θεὸς, μήτε τῶν μάλιϛα ἐν Αἰγύπτῳ θεμιϛευομένων ἱερῶν ζώ ων ἀπέχεϛαι μηδενὸς, πάντα τε θύειν κ᾽ ἀναλῶν· συνάπτεϛαι δὲ μηδινὶ πλὴν τῶν συνωμοϛμέ νων. Τοιαῦτα δὲ νομοθετήσας κ᾽ πλεῖϛα ἄλλα, μάλιϛα τοῖς Ἀιγυπτίοις ἐθιϛμοῖς ἐναντιεύμενα. Apud Joſeph. cont. Ap. l. i. p. 460, 461. Haverch. Ed.

citizens.

citizens. But we never find that this imbittered them againſt their Country-inſtitutions. On the contrary, their cloſe adherence to their native cuſtoms, notwithſtanding all perſonal wrongs, has in every age enabled learned men to find out their original, by ſtrong characteriſtic marks of relation to the mother city. And the reaſon is evident: INNATE LOVE OF ONE'S COUNTRY, whoſe attractive power, contrary to that of natural bodies, is ſtrongeſt at a diſtance; and INVETERATE MANNERS which ſtick cloſeſt in diſtreſs; (the uſual ſtate of all new Colonies) are qualities infinitely too ſtrong to give way to reſentment againſt particular men for perſonal injuries.

It is not indeed unlikely but that ſome certain ſpecific Law or cuſtom, which did, or was imagined to contribute to their diſgrace and expulſion, might, out of reſentment, be reprobated by the new Colony. And this is the utmoſt that the hiſtory of mankind will ſuffer us to ſuppoſe.

On the whole, therefore, I conclude that MOSES'S EGYPTIAN LEARNING IS A STRONG CONFIRMATION OF THE DIVINITY OF HIS MISSION.

The ſecond part of the propoſition is no leſs evident, *That the laws inſtituted in compliance to the people's prejudices, and in oppoſition to Egyptian ſuperſtitions, ſupport the ſame truth with equal ſtrength.* Had Moſes's Miſſion been only pretended, his conduct, as a wiſe Lawgiver, had doubtleſs been very different. His buſineſs had been then only to ſupport a falſe pretence to inſpiration. Let us ſee how he managed. He pretended to receive the whole frame of a national Inſtitution from GOD; and to have had the pattern of all its parts brought

him

him down from Heaven, to the Mount. But when this came to be promulged, it was seen that, the CEREMONIAL LAW being politically instituted partly in compliance to the people's prejudices, and partly in opposition to Egyptian superstitions, several of its Rites had a reference to the pagan superstitions in vogue. This, as we see, from the objection of the ignorant in these times, might have been an objection in those. And as an Impostor could not but have foreseen the objection, his fears of a discovery would have made him decline so hazardous a system, and cautiously avoid every thing that looked like an imitation. It is true, that, on enquiry, this unfolds a scene of admirable and superior wisdom : but it is such as an Impostor could never have projected ; or at least would never have ventured to leave to the mercy of popular judgment. We conclude, therefore, that this conduct is a clear proof that Moses actually received the Institution from GOD. Nor does this in anywise contradict what we have so much insisted on above, That a mere human Lawgiver, or even an inspired one, acting with free agents, is necessitated to comply with the passions of the People ; a compliance which would necessarily induce such a relation to Egypt as we find in the ritual Law : for we must remember too what hath been likewise shewn, that the *ends* of a divine and human lawgiver, both using the common means of a SEPARATION are vastly different ; the latter only aiming to keep the people unmixed ; the former, to keep them pure from idolatry. Now, in both cases, where the People are dealt with as free agents, some compliance to their prejudices will be necessary. But as, in the Institutions of a human Lawgiver pretending only to inspiration, such

com-

compliance in the RITUAL would be subject to the danger here spoken of; and as compliance in the FUNDAMENTALS, such as the object of Worship, a future State, and mode of civil Government, would not be so subject; and, at the same time, would win most forcibly on a prejudiced people, to the promoting the Legislator's *end*; we must needs conclude that these would be the things he would comply with and espouse. On the other hand, as a divine Lawgiver could not comply in these things; and as a RITUAL, like the mosaic, was the only means left of gaining his end, we must conclude that a divine Lawgiver would make his compliances on that side.

1. Let me only add one corollary to our BELIEVING ADVERSARIES, as a farther support of this part of the *proposition*; " That allowing the Ritual-law to be generally instituted in reference to Egyptian and other neighbouring Superstitions, the divine wisdom of the contrivance will be seen in redoubled lustre. One reason, as we have seen above, of the opposition to the notion of *such a reference* is, that the RITUAL LAW WAS TYPICAL, not only of things relating to that Dispensation, but to the Evangelical. This then they take for granted; and, as will be shewn hereafter, with good reason. Now an Institution of a body of Rites, particularly and minutely levelled against, and referring to, the idolatrous practices of those ages; and, at the same time, as minutely typical, not only of all the remarkable transactions under that Dispensation, but likewise of all the great and constituent parts of a future one, to arise in a distant age, and of a genius directly opposite, must needs give an attentive considerer the most amazing idea of divine wisdom.

wisdom [e]. And this I beg leave to offer to the consideration of the unprejudiced Reader, as another strong INTERNAL ARGUMENT THAT THE RITUAL LAW WAS NOT OF MERE HUMAN CONTRIVANCE.

2. Let me add another corollary to the UNBELIEVING Jews. We have seen at large how expedient it was for the Jews of the first ages, that the Ritual or ceremonial Law should be directed against the several idolatries of those ages. It was as expedient for the Jews of the later ages that this Law should be TYPICAL likewise. For had it not been *typical*, God would have given a Law whose reason would have ceased many ages before the *Theocracy* was abolished; and so have afforded a plausible occasion to the Jews for changing or abrogating them, on their own head.

3. Let me add a third corollary to the UNBELIEVING GENTILES. The Law's being *typical* obviates their foolish argument against Revelation, that the abolition of the *Mosaic* religion and the

---

[e] Hear what the learned Spencer says on this occasion : " Atque hac in re Deus sapientiæ suæ specimen egregium edidit, " et illi non absimile quod in mundo frequenter obfervemus : " in eo enim, notante *Verulamio*, dum *natura aliud agit, pro-* " *videntia aliud elicit* ; nam frondibus quas natura, confuetu- " dinem suam retinens, parit, utitur providentia ad cœli in- " jurias a fructu tenello propulfandas. Pari modo, cum Hebræ- " orum natio, confuetudinem fuam exuere nescia, ritus antiquos " impenfe defideraret, Deus eorum defiderio fe morigerum " præbebat ; fed eorum ruditate & impotentia puerili ad fines " egregios & fapientia fua dignos utebatur. Sic enim ritus anti- " quos populo indultos, circumftantiis quibufdam demptis aut " additis, immutavit, ut rerum cœleftium fchema repræfenta- " rent, oculis purgatio ibus facile percipiendum ; adeo ut Deus " puerilibus Ifraelitarum ftudiis obfequens, divina promoveret." *De Leg. Heb Rit.* p. 218.

eftablifhment of the *Chriftian* in its ftead, impeaches the wifdom of God, as implying change and incon- ftancy in his acting; for by his making the Law *typical*, the two religions are feen to be the two parts of one and the fame defign.

The great Maimonides, who firft [f] explained the CAUSES of the Jewifh Ritual in any reafonable manner

[f] In his *More Nevoch*. Par. III. This famous book (as is the fortune of all which bring new proofs for Revelation in a new way) hath undergone many heavy cenfures both from Jews and Chriftians. Thofe blame him for attempting to affign reafons for the Ceremonial ordinances; Thefe for explaining Scripture on the principles of Ariftotle. But both, as ufual, expofe their own ignorance and prevention. In this work, the excellent au- thor ftudied the real honour of GOD, together with the good of thofe to whom his difcourfe was addreffed. And becaufe its end and defign appears to be little underftood, and depends on a curious piece of hiftory, neglected by his editors and tranfla- tors, I fhall give the Reader a fhort account of it. In the firft flourifhing times of the Saracene Empire, (as we learn from William of Paris in his book *De Legibus*) a great number of Jews, devoting themfelves to the ftudy of the Ariftotelian phi- lofophy, (then cultivated by the Arabs with a kind of fcientific fanaticifm) and thereby contracting not only an inquifitive but a difputatious habit, fet themfelves to examine into the REASONS OF THE JEWISH LAWS; which, being unable to difcover, they too haftily concluded them to be ufelefs, abfurd, and of human invention; and fo apoftatized, in great numbers, from the Reli- gion of their fathers.—" Poftquam autem Chaldæis five Baby- " loniis & genti Arabum commixti funt, & mifcuerunt fe ftu- " diis eorum & philofophiæ; & fecuti funt opiniones philofo- " phorum; nefcientes legis fuæ credulitates & Abrahæ fidem " contra difputationes eorum & rationes defendere: hinc " eft quod facti funt in lege erronei, & in fide ipfius Abrahæ " hæretici; maxime poftquam regnum SARACENORUM dif- " fufum eft fuper' habitationem eorum. Exinde enim æterni- " tatem mundi & alios Ariftotelis errores fecuti funt multi " eorum. Hincque pauci veri Judæi (hoc eft, qui non in parte " aliquâ credulitatis fuæ Saraceni funt, aut Ariftotelicis con- " fentientes erroribus) in terrâ Saracenorum inveniuntur, de his " qui inter philofophos commorantur. Dedit enim cccafio- " nem

manner (and who, to obferve it by the way, faw
nothing in the LAW but *temporal fanEtions)* was fo
ftruck with the fplendor of divinity, which this
light reflected back upon the law, that in the entry on his fubject he breaks out into this triumphant boaft, EA TIBI EXPLICABO UT PLANE NON
AMPLIUS DUBITARE QUEAS ET DIFFERENTIAM
HABEAS QUA DISCERNERE POSSIS INTER ORDI-
NATIONES LEGUM CONDITARUM AB HOMINIBUS
ET INTER ORDINATIONES LEGIS DIVINÆ.

Thus the Reader fees what may be gained by
fairly and boldly fubmitting to the force of evidence.   Such a manifeftation of the divinity of the
Law, arifing out of the Deift's own principles, as
is fufficient to cover him with confufion!

" nem non levem apoftafiæ hujufmodi ea quæ videtur multo-
" rum mandatorum abfurditas vel inutilitas; dum enim appa-
" ret in eis abfurditas & inutilitas, nulla autem præceptionis
" aut inhibitionis earum ratio, nulla obfervantiarum utilitas,
" non eft mirum fi ab eis receditur: fed tanquam onera fuper-
" vacanea projiciuntur." *fol.* 18.   In thefe times, and under
this Empire, our Author wrote.   So that nothing could be
more ufeful than to fhew his apoftatizing brethren that the
SCRIPTURES might be defended, nay, even explained on the
principles of ARISTOTLE, and that the precepts of the CERE-
MONIAL LAW were founded in the higheft reafonablenefs and
convenience.——Maimonides, where, in his preface, he gives his
reafons for writing this difcourfe, plainly hints at that apoftafy—
Vertiginofos vero quod attinet, quorum cerebrum eft pollutum & vanis
futilibufque ac falfis opinionibus repletum, quique fibi imaginantur
fe magnos effe PHILOSOPHOS, *ac theologos, illos fcio fugituros a*
multis, contra multa etiam objectiones moturos.—Deus vero bene-
dictus novit, quantopere timuerim confcribere ea, quæ explicare &
confignare volui in hoc libro.   Nam quia talia funt de quibus nul-
lus ex gente noftra in hac captivitate quicquam fcripfit hactenus,
quâ ratione primus ego prodire in hac palæftra audeo: verum fuf-
fultus fum duobus principiis; primo, quod de iftius modi negotio dictum
fit, tempus eft faciendi Domino: IRRITAM FECERUNT LEGEM
TUAM, *&c. fecundo, eo quod fapientes noftri dicunt,* Omnia opera
tua fiant ad gloriam Dei.

And

And what is it, we lofe? Nothing fure very great or excellent. The imaginary honour of being original in certain Rites (confidered in themfelves) indifferent; and becoming good or bad by *compari-fon*, or by the *authority* which enjoins them, and by the object to which they are directed.

The Deift indeed pretends that, in the things borrowed from Egypt, the firft principles of Law and Morality, and the very triteft cuftoms of civil life, are to be included. The extravagance of this fancy hath been expofed elfewhere [s]. But as it s a fpecies of folly all parties are apt to give into, it may not be amifs to confider this matter of TRADUCTIVE CUSTOMS a little more particularly.

There is nothing obftructs our difcoveries in Antiquity (as far as concerns the nobleft end of this ftudy, the knowledge of mankind) fo much as that falfe, though undifputed Principle, that the general cuftoms of men, whether civil or religious, (in which a common likenefs connects, as in a chain, the Manners of its inhabitants, throughout the whole globe) are traductive from one another. When, in truth, the origin of this general fimi-litude, is from the famenefs of one common Na-ture, improved by reafon, or debafed by fuperfti-tion. But when a cuftom, whofe meaning lies not upon the furface, but requires a profounder fearch, is the fubject of inquiry, it is much eafier to tell us that the ufers borrowed it from fuch or fuch a people, than rightly to inform us, what common principle of REASON or SUPERSTITION gave birth to it in both.

[s] Vol. I. part 2d. p. 133.

How

How many able writers have employed their time and learning to prove that Chriſtian Rome borrowed their ſuperſtitions from the Pagan city? They have indeed ſhewn an exact and ſurpriſing likeneſs in a great variety of inſtances. But the concluſion from thence, that, therefore, the Catholic borrowed from the Heathen, as plauſible as it may ſeem, is, I think, a very great miſtake; which the followers of this hypotheſis might have underſtood without the aſſiſtance of the principle here laid down: ſince the riſe of the ſuperſtitious cuſtoms in queſtion were many ages later than the converſion of that imperial city to the Chriſtian Faith: conſequently, at the time of their introduction, there were no PAGAN prejudices which required ſuch a compliance from the ruling Clergy. For this, but principally for the general reaſon here advanced, I am rather induced to believe, that the very ſame *ſpirit of ſuperſtition,* operating in equal circumſtances, made both Papiſts and Pagans truly originals.

But does this take off from the juſt reproach which the Reformed have caſt upon the Church of Rome, for the practice of ſuch Rites, and encouragement of ſuch Superſtitions? Surely not; but rather ſtrongly fixes it. In the former caſe, the rulers of that Church had been guilty of a baſe compliance with the infirmities of their new converts: in the latter, the poiſon of ſuperſtition is ſeen to have infected the very vitals of its Hierarchy [h].

But

---

[h] The learned author of the elegant and uſeful *Letter from Rome* has here taken to himſelf what was meant in general of the numerous writers on the ſame ſubject; and ſo has done it the honour of a confutation, in a poſtſcript to the laſt edition
of

But then, truth will fare almoſt as ill when a right, as when a wrong principle, is puſhed to an extravagance.

of that *Letter*. But the ſame friendly conſiderations, which induced him to end the poſtſcript with declaring his unwillingneſs to enter further into controverſy with me, diſpoſed me not to enter into it at all. This, and neither any neglect of him, nor any force I apprehended in his arguments, kept me ſilent. However, I owe ſo much both to myſelf and the public, as to take notice of a miſrepreſentation of my argument ; and a change of the queſtion in diſpute between us : without which notice, the controverſy (as I agree to leave it where it is) can ſcarce be fairly eſtimated.——" A paragraph in Mr. " Warburton's *Divine Legation of Moſes* obliges me (ſays Dr. " Middleton) to detain the reader a little longer, in order to ob- " viate the prejudices which the authority of ſo celebrated a writer " may probably inject, to the diſadvantage of my argument.—— " I am a loſs to conceive what could move my learned friend to " paſs ſo ſevere a conſure upon an argument which is hitherto " been eſpouſed by all proteſtants ; admitted by many papiſts ; " and evaded rather than contradicted by any. But whatever " was his motive, which, I perſuade myſelf, was no unfriendly " one, he will certainly pardon me, if purſuing the full convic- " tion of my mind, I attempt to defend an eſtabliſhed principle, " confirmed by ſtrong and numerous facts, againſt an opinion " wholly new and ſtrange to me ; and which, if it can be ſup- " poſed to have any force, overthrows the whole credit and uſe " of my preſent work.——He allows that the writers, who have " undertaken to *deduce the rites of popery from paganiſm, have* " *ſhewn an exact and ſurpriſing likeneſs between them in a great* " *variety of inſtances.* This (ſays he) one would think, is " allowing every thing that the cauſe demands : it is " every thing, I dare ſay, that thoſe writers deſire *." That it is *every thing thoſe writers deſire,* I can eaſily believe, ſince I ſee, my learned friend himſelf hath conſidered theſe two aſſertions, 1. *The religion of the preſent Romans derived from that of their heathen anceſtors* ; and, 2. *An exact conformity, or uniformity rather of worſhip between popery and paganiſm,* he hath conſidered them, I ſay, as convertible propoſitions : for, undertaking, as his title page informs us, to prove *the religion of the preſent Romans derived from that of their heathen anceſtors*; and having gone through his argu- ments, he concludes them in theſe words, " But it is high

* Poſtſcript, p. 228.

" time

extravagance.   Thus, as it would be ridiculous to
deny, that the Roman laws of the Twelve Tables
were

" time for me to conclude, being persuaded, if I do not
" flatter myself too much, that I have sufficiently made good
" WHAT I FIRST UNDERTOOK TO PROVE, an exact con-
" formity, or uniformity rather, of worship between popery
" and paganism *." But what he *undertook to prove,* we see
was, *The religion of the present Romans derived from their hea-*
then ancestors: That I have therefore, as my learned friend
observes, *allowed every thing those writers desire,* is very likely.
But then, whether I have *allowed every thing that the cause demands,*
is another question : which I think can never be determined
in the affirmative, till it be shewn that no other probable cause
can be assigned of this *exact conformity between Papists and*
Pagans, but a borrowing or derivation from one to the other.
And I guess, that now this is never likely to be done, since
I myself have actually assigned another probable cause, namely
the same spirit of superstition operating in the like circumstances.

But this justly celebrated writer goes on—" This question
" according to his [the author of the D. L.] notion is not to
" be decided by facts, but by a principle of a different kind,
" a *superior knowledge of human nature* †." Here I am forced
to complain of a want of candour, a want not natural to my
learned friend.   For, whence is it, I would ask, that he col-
lects, *that, according to my notion, this question is not to be decided*
by facts, but a superior knowledge of human nature? From any
thing I have said? Or from any thing I have omitted to say?
Surely, not from any thing I have said, (tho' he seems to insinuate so much by putting the words, *a superior knowledge of*
human nature in Italic characters, as they are called) because I
leave him in possession of his *facts,* and give them all the vali-
dity he desires ; which he himself observes ; and, from thence,
as we see, endeavours to draw some advantage to his hypothesis :—Nor from any thing I have omitted to say ; for, in this
short paragraph where I deliver my opinion, and, by reason of
its evidence, offer but one single argument in its support, that
argument arises from a FACT, *viz.* that the *superstitious customs*
in question were many ages later than the conversion of the impe-
rial city to the Christian faith : whence I conclude, that the ruling Churchmen could have no motive in borrowing from Pa-

* Letter, p. 224.   † Postscript, p. 228.

were derived from the Greeks ; becaufe we have
a circumftantial hiftory of their traduction : fo it
would

gan cuftoms, either as thofe cuftoms were then fafhionable in
themfelves, or refpectable for the number or quality of their
followers. And what makes this the more extraordinary is,
that my learned friend himfelf immediately afterwards quotes
thefe words ; and then tells the reader, that *my argument con-
fifts of an* HISTORICAL FACT *and of a confequence deduced from
it*. It appears therefore, that, according to my notion, the
queftion *is* to be decided by *facts*, and not by a *fuperior knowledge of human nature*. Yet I muft confefs I then thought, and
do fo ftill, that a *fuperior knowledge of human nature* would do
no harm, as it might enable men to judge better of *facts* than
we find they are generally accuftomed to do. But will this
excufe a candid reprefenter for faying, that *the queftion, according to my notion, was not to be decided by facts, but a fuperior
knowledge of human nature?* However, to do my learned
friend all juftice, I muft needs fay, that, as if thefe were only
words of courfe, that is, words of controverfy, he goes on,
through the body of his poftfcript, to invalidate my argument
from *fact* ; and we hear no more of a *fuperior knowledge of
human nature* than in this place where it was brought in to be
laughed at.

As to the argument, it muft even fhift for itfelf. It has done
more mifchief already than I was aware of: and forced my
learned friend to extend his charge from the *modern* to the *ancient church of Rome*. For my argument, from the low birth
of the fuperftitions in queftion, coming againft his hypothefis,
after he had once and again declared the purpofe of his letter
to be the expofing of the heathenifh idolatry and fuperftition of
the PRESENT *church of Rome* ; he was obliged, in fupport of
that hypothefis, to fhew that even the early ages of the church
were not free from the infection. Which hath now quite
fhifted the fubject with the fcene, and will make the argument
of his piece from henceforth to run thus, *The religion of the
prefent Romans derived from their early Chriftian anceftors ; and
theirs, from the neighbouring Pagans*. To fpeak freely, my
reafoning (which was an argument *ad hominem*, and, as fuch, I
thought, would have been reverenced) reduced the learned
writer to this dilemma ; either to allow the fact, and give up
his hypothefis ; or to deny the fact, and change his queftion.
And he has chofen the latter as the leffer evil. As to the fact,
that the Churches of the firft ages might do that on their own
heads,

would be equally foolish not to own, that a great part of the Jewish ritual was composed in reference to the superstitions of Egypt; because their long abode in the country had made the Israelites extravagantly fond of *Egyptian* customs : but to think, (as some Deists seem to have done) that they borrowed from thence their common principles of morality, and the legal provisions for the support of such principles[1], is, whether we consider the Israelites under a divine or human direction, a thing equally absurd ; and such an absurdity as betrays the grossest ignorance of human nature, and the history of mankind.

And thus much concerning the ANTIQUITY of Egypt, and its EFFECTS on the divine legation of Moses.

heads, which Moses did upon authority, i. e. indulge their Pagan converts with such of their customs, as could not be easily abused to superstition, may be safely acknowledged. My learned friend has produced a few instances of such indulgence, which the censure of some of the more scrupulous of those times hath brought to our knowledge. But the great farraginous body of Popish rites and ceremonies, the subject of my learned friend's *Letter from Rome,* had surely a different original. They were brought into the Church when Paganism was in part abhorred and in part forgotten ; and when the same spirit of sordid superstition which had overspread the Gentile world, had now deeply infected the Christian.

[1] See Marsham.

THE
DIVINE LEGATION
OF
M O S E S
DEMONSTRATED.

BOOK V.

SECT. I.

HAVING now examined the CHARACTER
of the Jewish People, and the TALENTS of
their Lawgiver, I come next to confider the NA-
TURE of that Policy, which by his miniftry was
introduced amongft them. For in thefe two inquiries I hope to lay a ftrong and lafting foundation for the fupport of the third general propofition, *That the doctrine of a future ftate of rewards
and punifhments is not to be found in, nor did make
part of the Mofaic Difpenfation.*

We find amongft this people a Policy differing
from all the Inftitutions of mankind; in which the
two Societies, civil and religious, were perfectly
incorpo-

incorporated, with GOD ALMIGHTY, AS A TEM-
PORAL GOVERNOR, at the head of both.

The peculiar adminiſtration attending ſo ſingular a frame of Government hath always kept it
from the knowledge of ſuperficial obſervers. Chriſtian writers, by conſidering Judaiſm as a Religious
policy only, or a Church; and Deiſts, as a Civil
policy only, or a State; have run into infinite miſtakes concerning the reaſon, the nature, and the
end of its laws and inſtitutions. And, on ſo partial a view of it, no wonder that neither have done
juſtice to this amazing Œconomy. Let us ſuppoſe,
the famous picture of the female centaur by Zeuxis,
where two different Natures were ſo admirably incorporated, that the paſſage from one to the other,
as Lucian tells us [k], became inſenſible; let us, I
ſay, ſuppoſe this picture to have been placed before
two competent judges, yet in ſuch different points
of view, that the one could ſee only the *brutal*, the
other only the *human* part; would not the firſt have
thought it a beautiful horſe, and the ſecond, as
beautiful a woman; and would not each have given the creature ſuppoſed to be repreſented ſuch
functions as he judged proper to the ſpecies in
which he ranked it? But would not both of them
have been miſtaken; and would not a ſight of the
whole have taught them to rectify their wrong judgments? as well knowing that the functions of
ſuch a compounded animal, whenever it exiſted,
muſt be very different from thoſe of either of the

k Τὴν θήλειαν δὲ ἵππυ γε τῆς καλλίϛης, οἷαι μάλιϛα αἱ Θετ]αλαὶ
ιἱσιν, ἀδμῆτες, ἔτι κ) ἀϐαϊοι· τὸ δ' ἄνω ἡμίτομεν, γυναικὸς, πάγκαλον,
— κ) ἡ μίξις δὲ, κ) ἡ ἁρμογὴ τῶν σωμάτων, καθὸ συνάπ]εται κ) συν-
δεῖται τῷ γυναικείῳ τὸ ἱππικὸν, ἠρέμα, κ) ἐκ ἀθρόως μεταϐαίνουσα, κ)
ἐκ σωματαγωγῆς τερπομένη, λανθάνει τὴν ὄψιν ἐκ θατίρα, ἐις τὸ ἕτερον
ὑπατομένη. Ζεῦξις.

other,

other, singly and alone. From such partial judges of the LAW therefore, little assistance is to be expected towards the discovery of its true nature.

Much less are we to expect from the Jewish Doctors: who, though they still keep sheltered, as it were, in the ruins of this august and awful Fabric; yet patch it up with the same barbarity of taste, and impotence of science, that the present Greeks are wont to hide themselves amongst the mouldering monuments of Attic power and politeness. Who, as our travellers inform us, take a beggarly pride in keeping up their claim to these wonders of their Anceltors magnificence, by white-washing the parian marble with chalk, and incrusting the porphyry and granate with tiles and potsherds.

But least of all shall we receive light from the fantaftic visions of our english *Cocceians* [1]; who have sublimed the crude nonsense of the Cabalists, so long buried in the dull amusement of picking Mysteries out of letters, into a more spiritual kind of folly; a quintessence well defecated from all the impurities of sense and meaning.

Therefore, to understand the nature of the jewish Œconomy, we must begin with this truth, to which every page of the five books of Moses is ready to bear witness, *That the separation of the Israelites was in order to preserve the doctrine of the* UNITY, *amidst an idolatrous and polytheistic World.* The necessity of this provision shall be shewn at large hereafter [m]. At present we only desire the Deist would be so civil as to suppose there might possibly be a sufficient cause.

[1] The followers of *Hutchinson.*   [m] In the ninth book.

But

But now, becaufe it is equally true, that this *feparation* was fulfilling the promife made to ABRA-HAM their Father; thefe men have taken occafion to reprefent it as made for the fake of a FAVOURITE PEOPLE [n]. And then again, fuppofing fuch a partial diftinction to be inconfiftent with the divine attributes, have ventured to arraign the LAW itfelf of impofture.

But this reprefentation of the fact is both unjuft and abfurd. They cannot deny but it might be GOD's purpofe, at leaft, that it became his goodnefs, to preferve the doctrine of the UNITY amidft an idolatrous world. But this, (we know by the event) could never be effected but by a *feparation* of one part from the reft. Nor could fuch a feparation be made any otherwife than by bringing that part under God's peculiar protection: The confequence of which were GREAT TEMPORAL BLESSINGS. Now as fome one People muft needs be felected for this purpofe, it feems moft agreeable to our ideas of divine Wifdom, which commonly effects many ends by the fame means, to make the *bleffings* attendant on fuch a *felection*, the reward of fome high exalted virtue in the progenitors of the chofen People. But therefore to object that they were chofen as FAVOURITES, is both unjuft and abfurd. The *feparation* was made for the fake of Mankind in general; though one People became the honoured inftrument, in reward of their Forefathers' virtues. And this is the language of thofe very Scriptures which, as they pretend, furnifh the objection. Where God, by the Prophet Ezekiel, promifes to reftore the Ifraelites, after a fhort difperfion thro' the Countries, to their own land, he declares this

[n] See the firft vol. of the *Div. Leg.* p. 289. 2d edit.

to be the end of their separation: "Therefore "say unto the house of Israel, Thus saith the "LORD GOD, I DO NOT THIS FOR YOUR SAKES, "O HOUSE OF ISRAEL, BUT FOR MINE HOLY "NAME'S SAKE, which ye have profaned among "the heathen, whither ye went. And I will sanc-"tify my great name which was profaned amongst "the heathen, which ye have profaned in the midst "of them; and the heathen shall know that I am "the LORD, saith the LORD GOD, when I shall be "sanctified in you before their eyes [o]." What GOD himself says of the PEOPLE, St. Paul says of their LAW: "Wherefore then serveth the Law? "IT WAS ADDED BECAUSE OF TRANSGRESSIONS; "till the seed should come, to whom the promise "was made [p]." *It was added*, says the Apostle. To what? To the patriarchal Religion of the UNITY [q]. To what end? *Because of transgressions*, i. e. the transgressions of polytheism and idolatry; into which, the rest of mankind were already ab-

[o] EZEK. xxxvi. 22, 23. [p] GAL. iii. 19.

[q] Yet some writers against the Divine Legation will have it, that from the very context [ver. 16, 17. *To Abraham and his seed were the promises made*, &c. *The* COVENANT *that was confirmed before of God in Christ*, &c.] it appears that St. Paul means, the Law was ADDED not barely to the Patriarchal Religion, but to *the promise of the inheritance, the covenant that was confirmed before of God*; and from thence, conclude that the Jewish Religion had the doctrine of a future state. This it is to have a retrospective view, and with a *microscopic eye!* For had they, when they went *one* step backward, but gone *two*, they would have seen, St. Paul could not possibly have had their meaning in view, for at ver. 15. he expresly says,—though it be but a MAN'S COVENANT [much less if it be GOD'S] *yet if it be confirmed, no man disanulleth or* ADDETH *thereto.* The *Law* therefore mentioned as ADDED in the 19th verse, cannot be understood, in the Apostle's sense, as being added to the COVENANT *that was confirmed before of God in Christ*, or indeed to any thing, but to the Patriarchal Religion of the Unity.

forbed,

forbed, and the Jews at that time, haſtening apace; and from which, there was no other means of re-ſtraining them, than by this ADDITION; an addition that kept them ſeparate from all others, and preſerved the Doctrine of the UNITY till the *coming of the promiſed ſeed*.

But another thing offends the Deiſts: they cannot underſtand, let the end of this choice be what it would, why GOD ſhould prefer ſo perverſe and ſottiſh a People, to all others. One reaſon hath been given already; that it was for the ſake of their Forefathers, and to fulfill the promiſe made to the Patriarchs. But others are not wanting; and thoſe very agreeable to the ideas we have of infinite Wiſdom; ſuch, for inſtance, as this, That the EXTRAORDINARY PROVIDENCE, by which they were bleſſed and protected, might become the more viſible and illuſtrious. For had they been endowed with the ſhining qualities of the more poliſhed nations, the effects of that providence might have been aſcribed to their own power or wiſdom. Their impotence and inability, when left to themſelves, is finely repreſented in the Prophet Ezekiel, by the ſimilitude of the vine-tree: *Son of man, what is the vine-tree more than any tree, or than a branch which is amongſt the trees of the foreſt? Shall wood be taken thereof to do any work? or will men take a pin of it to hang any veſſel thereon? —Therefore thus ſaith the Lord God, As the vine-tree amongſt the trees of the foreſt* [¹], &c. For as the vine, which, with cultivation and ſupport is the moſt valuable of all trees, becomes the moſt worthleſs, when left neglected in its own natural ſtate: ſo the Jews, who made ſo ſuperior a figure under

[¹] Chap. xv. ver. 3.

the

the particular protection of GOD, when, for their fins, that protection was withdrawn, became the weakeft and moft contemptible of all tributary nations.

The Poet VOLTAIRE indeed has had a different revelation. "The pride of every individual a- "mongft the Jews (fays he) is interefted in be- "lieving, that it was not their DETESTABLE PO- "LICY, their ignorance in the arts, and their un- "politenefs, which deftroyed them; but that it is "GOD's anger which yet purfues them for their "idolatries[1]." This DETESTABLE POLICY (for fo, with the free infolence of impiety, characteriftic of thefe times, he calls the MOSAIC INSTITUTION) was a principle of independency: this *ignorance in the arts* prevented the entrance of luxury; and this *unpolitenefs* hindered the practice of it. And yet parfimony, frugality, and a fpirit of liberty, which naturally preferve other States, all tended, in the ideas of this wonderful Politician, to deftroy the Jewifh. Egypt was long loft for want of a fpirit of independency; Greece funk by its knowledge in the arts; and Rome was ruined by its politenefs: yet Judæa fuffered for the want of all thefe caufes of deftruction. Is not this more than a thoufand topical arguments, to prove, that they were ruined by nothing but by their idolatries, which brought down GOD's vengeance upon them? But any contrivance will ferve a Poet, any argument will fatisfy a Freethinker, to keep a GOD and his providence at a diftance. And that the PEOPLE were as DETESTABLE as their POLICY, the fame Poet, the virtu-

[1] L'orgueil de chaque Juif eft intéreffé à croire que ce n'eft point fa DETESTABLE POLITIQUE, fon ignorance des arts, fa groffiereté, qui l'a perdu; mais que c'eft la colere de Dieu qui le punit. *Rem. ix. fur les penfées de Pafcal.*

ous

ous Voltaire affures us—" We do not find, (fays
" he) throughout the whole annals of the HBEREW
" PEOPLE one generous action. They are utter
" ftrangers both to hofpitality, to beneficence,
" and to clemency. Their fovereign-good is the
" practice of Ufury, with all but their own na-
" tion. And this difpofition, the principle of all
" bafenefs, is fo inrooted in their hearts, that
" *Ufury is the conftant object of the figures they*
" employ in that fpecies of eloquence which is
" peculiar to them. *Their glory is to lay wafte*
" *with fire and fword, fuch paltry villages as they*
" *were juft able to ftorm : They cut the throats of the*
" *old men and children, and referve from flaughter only*
" *the marriageable virgins. They affaffinate their*
" *mafters when they are flaves. They are incapable*
" *of pardoning when they conquer.* THEY ARE THE
" FOES OF ALL MANKIND [t]."

Such is the ftrong colouring of our MORAL PAIN-
TER. He has dipt his pencil in fulphur to deli-
neate with horns and tails, thefe chofen inftruments
of God's vengeance on a devoted Nation, overrun
with UNNATURAL LUST and brutifh Idolatry ; for
to their deftruction, the murders, the rapine, and

---

[t] On ne voit dans toutes les Annales du peuple Hebreu aucune action généreufe. Ils ne connaiffent ni l' hofpitalité, ni la
liberalité, ni la clémence. Leur fovereign bonheur eft d' exer-
cer l' ufure avec les étrangers ; et cet efprit de ufure, principe
de toute lacheté, eft tellement enracine dans leurs coeurs, que
c'eft l' object continuel des figures qu' ils employent dans l' efpéce
d' eloquence qui leur eft propre. Leur gloire eft de mettre à
feu & a fang les petits villages, dont ils peuvent s'emparer.
Ils égorgent les vieillards & les enfans ; ils ne réfervent que les
filles nubiles ; ils affaffinent leurs Maitres quand ils font efclaves ;
ils ne favent jamais pardonner quand ils font Vainqueurs ; ILS
SONT LES ENNEMIS DU GENRE HUMAIN. *Addit. a l'Hift.*
Generale, p. 30.

2   the

the violations here charged upon the *Hebrew People*, allude. For the rest, it is so much below all criticism, that one is almost ashamed to touch upon it. Otherwise, we might observe, that, in his rage, he hath confounded the character of the ancient HEBREWS with that of the modern JEWS, two people as much unlike as the ancient Franks to modern Frenchmen.—We might be merry with the nonsense, of *Usury's being the object of their figures of eloquence*; which yet is not more ridiculous in the thought than absurd in the expression; his meaning, I suppose, being, that their figures of eloquence are formed from, and allude to, the circumstances attending their practice of *Usury*.

But the affair grows more serious, as we proceed with our *General Historian*; and we shall find that this unhappy People, however they may stand with their *God*, certainly, at present, for some reason or other, lye under the *Poet's curse*. And from his uncommon knowledge of their *Usury* and their *eloquence*, I should suspect, he had lately been transacting some money-matters with them, and had been not only out-witted but out-talked too into the bargain.

As to their HATRED OF ALL MANKIND, (the chopping-block of infidelity) we have it over again, and more at large, in another place. " You are " (says he to his reader) struck with that hatred " and contempt, which all people have always en- " tertained for the Jewish Nation. It is the una- " voidable consequence of THEIR LEGISLATION; " which reduced things to the necessity, that either " the Jews must enslave the whole world, or that " they, in their turn, must be crushed and destroy- " ed. IT WAS COMMANDED THEM to hold all other

" People

" People in abhorrence, and to think themselves
" polluted if they had eat in the same dish which
" belonged to a man of another Religion. BY THE
" VERY LAW ITSELF, they at length found them-
" selves the natural enemies of THE WHOLE RACE
" OF MANKIND ᵘ."

I believe it will not be easy to find, even in the
dirtiest sink of Freethinking, so much falshood,
absurdity, and malice heaped together in so few
words.   He says, *There was an inevitable necessity,
arising from the very genius of the Law itself, either
that this people should enslave the whole world, or that
they, in their turn, should be crushed and destroyed.*

It might be thought unreasonable to expect that
a Poet should read his Bible : but one might be
allowed to suppose that he had heard at least of its
general contents. If he ever had, could he, unmask-
ed, and in the face of the sun, have said, " That
the MOSAIC LAW directed or encouraged the Jewish people to attempt extensive conquests ?" That
very LAW, which not only assigned a peculiar and
narrow district for the abode of its followers ; but,
by a number of Institutions, actually confined
them within those limits : Such as the stated division of the land to each Tribe ; the prohibition of
the use of horse ; the distinction of *meats* into
clean and unclean ; the yearly visit of each individual to Jerusalem, with many others.   The Poet,

---

ᵘ — Vous etes frappés de cette haine & de ce mepris que
toutes les nations ont toujours eu pour la Nation Juive.   C'est la
suite inevitable de LEUR LEGISLATION ; il falait ou que ce
Peuple subjuguât tout, ou qu' il fut ecrasé.   Il lui fut ordonné
d' avoir, les nations en horreur, & de se croire souillés s'ils
avaient mangé dans un plat qui eût appartenu à un homme d'une
autre Loi — ils se trouvèrent PAR LEUR LOI MEME enfin Ennemis naturels du GENRE HUMAIN.   *Add. a l' Hist. Generale,*
p. 174.

who

who appears throughout his whole hiftory to be a much better Muffulman than a Chriftian, was furely, when he faid this, in fome pious meditation on the Alcoran; which indeed, by *the inevitable confequence of its Legiflation,* muft either fet the Saracens upon enflaving all mankind, or all mankind on extirpating fo pernicious a crew of mifcreants.

But *the Jews,* he tells us, *were* COMMANDED *to hold all other People in abhorrence.* If he had faid, *to hold their* IDOLATRIES *in abhorrence,* he had faid *true*; but that was faying nothing. To tell the world that *the Jews were commanded to hold the* PERSONS *of Idolaters in abhorrence,* was done like a Poet.

But when he goes on to fay, that *The Jews found,* BY THE VERY CONSTITUTION OF THE LAW ITSELF, *that they were the* NATURAL ENEMIES *of all mankind,* this was not like a Poet, being indeed a tranfgreffion of the PROBABLE : for by the *conftitution of the Law itfelf,* every Jew that could read, found all mankind to be his BRETHREN. For Mofes, to prevent any fuch eftrangement, which fome other parts of his Inftitution, if abufed, might occafion, was careful to acquaint the chofen Family with the origin of the human race, and of their defcent from one man and woman; and, in order to imprefs this falutary truth more ftrongly on their minds, he draws out an exact genealogy from Adam, not only of the direct line which was to inhabit the land of Judea, but of all the collateral branches by which the whole earth was peopled.

So that were our Poet to turn *Lawgiver,* (which he might as well do, as GENERAL HISTORIAN)
and

and fit down to contrive a method by which brotherly love and affection might be beft eftablifhed
amongft the fons of men, one might defy him,
with all his poetical or hiftorical invention, to hit
upon any more efficacious than that which Mofes
has here employed.   St. Paul, when he would enlarge the affections of the Athenians (to whom all
other nations, as well as the Jews, were become
BARBARIANS) to that extent which Chriftian benevolence requires, employed no other topic than
this, that GOD HAD MADE OF ONE BLOOD ALL
NATIONS OF MEN: and from thence inferred, that
they all ftand in the relation of BRETHREN to one
another.

But it may be afked, What are we then to think
of that ODIUM HUMANI GENERIS, with which the
ancient Pagans charged the Jews? I have fhewn,
in the firft volume of this work, that there was
not the leaft fhadow from *fact* to fupport this calumny; and that it was merely an imaginary
confequence, which they drew from the others declared hate and abhorrence of the Idols of Paganifm, and firm adherence to the fole worfhip of
the *one true God*.   But befides this original, the
Principles and Doctrine, there was another, the *Rites
and Ceremonies* of the Mofaic Religion; either of
them fufficient alone to perpetuate this wretched
calumny amongft ignorant and prejudiced men.
That the *Doctrine* was worthy of its original, the
enemies of Revelation confefs: That the eftablifhment of the *Ceremonies*, as they were neceffary to
fupport the *Doctrine*, were of no lefs importance,
I fhall now fhew our Poet.

To feparate one people from all others, in order
to preferve the doctrine of the *Unity*, was a juft
purpofe.

No

No feparation could be made but by a ceremonial Law.

No ceremonial Law could be eftablifhed for this
purpofe, but what muft make the Gentiles be
efteemed unclean by the feparated People.

The confequence of an eftimated *uncleannefs,*
muft be the avoiding it with horror: which, when
obferved by their enemies, would be malicioufly
reprefented to arife from this imaginary *odium humani generis.* What idea then muft we needs entertain, I will not fay of the Religion, but of the
common honefty of a modern Writer, who, without the leaft knowledge of the Jewifh Nation or
their Policy, can repeat an old exploded calumny
with the affurance of one who had difcovered a
newly acknowledged truth? But the Pagans were
decent when compared to this rude Libertine.
They never had the infolence to fay, that this pretended *hate of all mankind* was COMMANDED BY
THE LAW ITSELF. They had more fenfe as well
as modefty. They reverenced the great Jewifh
Lawgiver, whom they faw, by his account of the
origin of the human race, had laid the ftrongeft
foundation amongft his people of brotherly love
to all men. A foundation, which not one of the
moft celebrated Lawgivers of Antiquity had either
the wit to inforce, or the fagacity to difcover.

Well, but if the Jews were indeed that DE-
TESTABLE *People* which the Poet Voltaire reprefents them to be, they were properly fitted however with a *Law,* which, he affures us, was full
as DETESTABLE. What pity is it that he did not
know juft fo much of his Bible however, as might
ferve to give fome fmall countenance at leaft to his

impieties. We might then have had the *Prophet*
to fupport the *Poet*, where fpeaking, in the name
of God, he fays, — *I gave them Statutes that were
not good, and Judgments whereby they fhould not live*[x].
But to leave this to his maturer projects; and go
on with him, in his pious defign of *eradicating* this
devoted People; for he affures us, we fee, that
unlefs they be rooted out, their DETESTABLE PO-
LICY will fet them upon enflaving all mankind.

He hath fhewn the PEOPLE to be *deteftable*, and
their LAW *deteftable*; and well has he provided for
the reception of both, a moft *deteftable* COUNTRY.
You may, if you pleafe, fuppofe all this done in
vindication of the good providence of the God of
Ifrael; for a *People* fo bad, certainly deferved neither a better *Government* nor *Habitation*. No, he
had a nobler end than this, it was to give the lye
to the Legate of the God of Ifrael, who promifed
to them in his Mafter's name, *A land flowing with
milk and honey, the glory of all lands*. Having gotten Mofes at this advantage, by the affiftance of
Servetus and his followers, (for he always fpeaks
from good authority) he draws this delightful picture of the HOLY LAND. — " All of it which is
" fituated towards the fouth, confifts of DESERTS
" OF SALT SANDS on the fide of the Mediterra-
" nean and Egypt; and of HORRID MOUNTAINS
" all the way to Efiongaber, towards the Red-
" Sea. Thefe fands, and thefe rocks, at prefent
" poffeffed by a few ftraggling Arabian Robbers,
" were the ancient patrimony of the Jews[y]."

Now

---

[x] EZEKIEL. See p. 79. & *feq.*

[y] Tout ce qui eft fitué vers le midi confifte en deferts de
fables falés du côté, de la Mediterranée & de l' Egypte, et en
montagnes

Now admitting this account to be true: 1. In the first place, we may inform our Poet, that, from the face of a country lying desert, there is no safe judgment to be made of the degree of its fertility when well cultivated; especially of such a one as is here described, consisting of rugged mountains and sandy plains, which, without culture, indeed, produce nothing, but which, by human industry in a happy climate, may be made to vie with foils naturally the most prolific. 2. It appears from the vast numbers which this country actually sustained, in the most flourishing times of the Theocracy, that it well answered the character their Lawgiver had bestowed upon it, *of a land flowing with milk and honey.* 3. The Israelites, when they took possession of it, certainly found it to come up to the character which Moses had given them, of a place where they should find *great and goodly Cities which they had not builded, houses full of good things, which they had not filled, wells digged which they had not digged, and vineyards and olive trees which they had not planted*[z]. If, I say, they had not found it so, we should soon have heard of it, from the most turbulent and dissatisfied people upon earth. And it was no wonder they found it in this condition, since they had wrested it from the hands of a very numerous and luxurious People, who had carried arts and arms to some height, when they, in any sense, could be said to have *Cities fenced up to Heaven.* But the Poet has a solution of this difficulty; for to the Israelites, just

---

montagnes affreuses jusqu' a Esiongaber vers la Mer Rouge. Ces fables & ces rochers, habités aujourd hui par quelques Arables Volours, font l' ancienne patrie des Juifs. *Add. a l' Hist. Générale,* p. 83.

[z] DEUT. vi—viii.

got

got out of their forty years captivity in the wilderneſs, this miſerable country muſt needs appear a paradiſe, in compariſon of the Deſerts of Param and Cadiſh Barnea [a]. Now it is very certain, that no *Deſert* thereabout, could be more horrid or forbidding than that of Judea, as the Poet has here drawn the landſcape. But does he think they had quite forgot the fertile plains of Egypt all this time? And if they *compared* the promiſed Inheritance to the Wilderneſs on the one hand, would they not be as apt to *compare* it to Egypt on the other? And what Judea gained by the firſt it would loſe by the ſecond. But he will ſay, *that Generation* which came out of Egypt, *fell in the Wilderneſs.* What if they did? they left their fondneſs for its fleſh pots behind them, as we are ſufficiently informed from the exceſſive attachment of their poſterity for Egyptian luxury of every kind. 4. But let us admit his account of the ſterility of the promiſed Land, and then ſee how the pretenſions of the Moſaic Miſſion will ſtand. We will conſider this ſterility in either view, as *corrigible,* or as *incorrigible.*

If *corrigible,* we cannot conceive a properer region for anſwering the ENDS of Providence, as Moſes has delivered them unto us, with regard to this People. The firſt great bleſſing beſtowed on mankind, was to be particularly exemplified in the poſterity of Abraham, which was to be *like the ſand on the ſea-ſhore for multitude :* and yet they were to be confined within the narrow limits of a ſingle diſtrict : ſo that ſome proportionate proviſion was to be made for its numerous Inhabitants.

---

[a] —Ce pais fut pour eux une terre delicieuſe en comparaiſon des Déſerts de Param & de Cades-Barné. *ib.*

Affluence by commerce they could not have; for the purpose of their separation required, that Idolaters should no more be permitted to come and pollute them, than that they should go amongst Idolaters to be polluted by them: And accordingly, a sufficient care was taken, in the framing of their Laws, to hinder this communication at either end. Thus the advantages from commerce being quite cut off, they had only agriculture to have recourse to, for subsistance of their multitudes. And the natural sterility of the land would force them upon every invention to improve it. And artificial culture produces an abundance, which unassisted nature can never give to the most fruitful soil and most benignant climate. Add to this, that a People thus sequestered, would, without such constant attention to the art, and application to the labour, which the meliorating of a backward soil requires, soon degenerate into barbarous and savage manners; the first product of which has been always seen to be a total oblivion of a God.

But if we are to suppose what the Poet would seem to insinuate, in discredit of the Dispensation, that the soil of Judea was absolutely *incorrigible*; a more convincing proof cannot be given of that EXTRAORDINARY PROVIDENCE which Moses promised to them. So that if the *corrigibility* of a bad soil perfectly agreed with the END of the Dispensation, which was a separation, the *incorrigibility* of it was as well fitted to the MEAN, which was an *extraordinary Providence* For the fact, that Judea did support those vast multitudes being unquestionable, and the natural incapacity of the country so to do, being allowed, nothing remains but that we must recur to that *extraordinary Provi-*

dence

dence which not only was promifed, but was the natural confequence of a *Theocratic* form of government. But I am inclined to keep between the two contrary fuppofitions, and take up the premiffes of the one, and the conclufion of the other : to hold that the fterility of Judea was very corrigible; but that all poffible culture would be inadequate to the vaft numbers which it fuftained, and that therefore its natural produce was ftill further multiplied by an *extraordinary bleffing* upon the land.

To fupport this fyftem, we may obferve, that this extraordinary affiftance was beftowed more eminently, becaufe more wanted, while the Ifraelites remained in the *Wildernefs*. Moses, whofe word will yet go as far as our *General Hiftorian's*, fays, that when God took Jacob up, to give him his Law, he *found him indeed in a defert Land, and in the wafte howling Wildernefs* ; but it was no longer fuch, when now God had the leading of him. " *He led him about,*" [i. e. while he was preparing him for the conqueft of the promifed Land] " *He inftructed him,*" [i. e. by the Law, which he there gave him] " *He kept him as the apple of* " *his eye,*" [i. e. he preferved him there by his extraordinary Providence ;] the effects of which he defcribes in the next words,—" He made him ride " on the high places of the earth," [i. e. he made the Wildernefs to equal, in its produce, the beft cultivated places] " that he might eat the increafe " of the fields ; and he made him to fuck honey " out of the Rock, and oil out of the flinty Rock : " Butter of kine, and milk of fheep, with fat of " lambs, and rams of the breed of Bafhan" [i. e. as large as that breed] " and goats, with the fat " of kidneys of wheat," [i. e. the flour of wheat] " and

" and thou didst drink the pure blood of the
" Grape."

That this was no fairy-scene appears from the
effects.—" Jeshurun waxed fat, and kicked : thou
" art waxen fat, thou art grown thick, thou art
" covered with fatness; then he forsook God
" which made him, and lightly esteemed the Rock
" of his salvation [b], &c." This severe reproof
of Moses certainly did not put the Israelites in
an humour, to take the wonders in the foregoing
account on his word, had the facts he appeals to
been the least equivocal.

On the whole, we can form no conception how
God could have chosen a People and assigned them
a land to inhabit, more proper for the display of
his almighty Power, than the People of Israel
and the land of Judea. As to the People, the
PROPHET in his *Parable* of the Vine-tree, informs
us, that they were naturally, the weakest and most
contemptible of all nations : and as to the land, the
POET, in his *great Fable*, which he calls a General History, assures us, that Judea was the vilest
and most barren of all countries. Yet somehow
or other this *chosen People* became the Instructors
of mankind, in the noblest office of humanity,
the science of true Theology : and the *promised
Land*, while made subservient to the worship of one
God, was changed, from its native sterility, to a
region *flowing with milk and honey*; and, by reason
of the incredible numbers which it sustained, de-
servedly entitled the GLORY OF ALL LANDS.

This is the state of things which SCRIPTURE
lays before us. And I have never yet seen those

[b] DEUT. chap. xxxii. ver. 1c. *& seq.*

strong

strong reasons, from the schools of Infidelity, that should induce a man, bred up in any school at all, to prefer their logic to the plain facts of the Sacred Historians.

I have used their testimony to expose one, who, indeed, renounces their authority: but in this I am not conscious of having transgressed any rule of fair reasoning. The *Freethinker* laments that there is no contemporary Historian remaining, to confront with the Jewish Lawgiver, and detect his impostures. However, he takes heart, and boldly engages his credit to confute him from his own history. This is a fair attempt. But he prevaricates on the very first onset. The Sacred History, besides the many *civil* facts which it contains, has many of a *miraculous* nature. Of these, our Freethinker will allow the first only to be brought in evidence. And then bravely attacks his adversary, who has now one hand tied behind him: for the civil and the miraculous facts, in the Jewish Dispensation, have the same, nay, a nearer relation to each other, than the two hands of the same body; for these may be used singly and independently, tho' to disadvantage; whereas the civil and the miraculous facts can neither be understood or accounted for, but on the individual inspection of both. This is confessed by one who, as clear-sighted as he was, certainly did not see the [c] consequence of what he so liberally acknowledged. " The miracles in the Bible (says his philosophic lordship) " are not like those in Livy, detached " pieces, that do not disturb the civil History, " which goes on very well without them. But

---

[c] See the View of Lord Bolingbroke's Philosophy, p. 192. *& seq.* of the third edition.

" the

" the miracles of the Jewiſh Hiſtorian are inti-
" mately connected with all the civil affairs, and
" make a neceſſary and inſeparable part.   The
" whole hiſtory is founded in them; it conſiſts of
" little elſe, and if it were not an hiſtory of them,
" it would be a hiſtory of nothing [d]."

From all this, I aſſume that where an Unbeliever,
a Philoſopher if you will, (for the Poet Voltaire
makes them convertible terms) pretends to ſhew
the falſhood of Moſes's miſſion from Moſes's own
hiſtory of it; he who undertakes to confute his
reaſoning, argues fairly when he confutes it upon
facts recorded in that hiſtory, whether they be of
the miraculous or of the civil kind: ſince the two
ſorts are ſo inſeparably connected, that they muſt
always be taken together, to make the hiſtory underſtood, or the facts which it contains intelligible.

SECT. II.

ALLOWING it then, to have been GOD's purpoſe to perpetuate the knowledge of himſelf
amidſt an idolatrous World, by the means of a
ſeparated People; let us ſee how this deſign was
brought about, when the Family, he had choſen,
was now become numerous enough to ſupport itſelf under a *ſeparation*; and Idolatry, which was
grown to its moſt gigantic ſtature [e], was now to be
repreſſed.

·The

----

[d] Bolingb. poſth. works, vol. III. p. 279.

[e] —Il [Ninus fils de Belus] ne peut être inventeur de l'idolatrie qui etoit bien plus ancienne; je ne dis pas ſeulement en
Egypte, mais même au dela de l'Euphrate, puiſque Rachel de-
roba les Teraphims, &c. — Il faut aller en Egypte pour trouver
ſur

The Israelites, were, at this time, groaning under the yoke of Egypt; whither the all-wise providence

fur cela quelque chofe du mieux fondé. Grotius croit que, du temps de Joseph, l'idolatrie n'etoit point encore commune en Egypte. Cependant on voit des-lors dans ce pays un extrême attachement à la magie, à la divination, aux augures, à l'interpretation des fonges, &c. — Moyfe defend d'adorer aucune figure, ni de ce qui eft vifible dans les cieux, ni de ce qui eft fur la terre, ni de ce qui eft dans les eaux. Voila la defenfe generale d'adorer les aftres, les animaux, & les poiffons. Le veau d'or etoit une imitation du dieu Apis. La niche de Moloch, dont parle Amos, etoit apparemment portée avec une figure du foleil. Moyfe defend aux Hebreux d'immoler aux boucs, comme ils ont fait autrefois. La mort en l'honneur duquel il defend de faire le deuil, etoit le même qu'Ofiris. Beelphegor, aux myfteres duquel ils furent entrainez par les femmes de Madian, etoit Adonis. Moloch cruelle divinité, à laquelle on immoloit des victimes humaines, etoit commune du tems de Moyfe, auffi-bien que ces abominables facrificces. Les Chananeens adoroient des mouches & d'autres infectes, au rapport de l'auteur de la fageffe. Le même auteur nous parle des Egyptiens d'alors comme d'un peuple plongé dans toutes fortes d'abominations, & qui adoroit toutes fortes d'animaux, même les plus dangereux, & les plus nuifibles. Le pays de Chanaan etoit encore plus corrompu. Moyfe ordonne d'y abbattre les autels, les bois facrez, les idoles, les monumens fuperftitieux. Il parle des enclos, où l'on entretenoit un feu eternel en l'honneur du foleil. Voilà la plus indubitable epoque qui nous ayons de l'idolatrie. Mais ce n'eft point une epoque qui nous en montre fa fource & le commencement, ni même le progrés & l'avancement : elle nous préfente une idolatrie achevée, & portée à fon comble ; les aftres, les hommes, les animaux mêmes adorez comme autant divinitez ; la magie, la divination, l'impieté au plus haut point où elles puiffent aller ; enfin le crime, & les defordres honteux, fuites ordinaires du culte fuperftitieux & de regle. *Calmet Differt. fur l'Origine de l'Idolatrie*, tom. 1. p. 431, 432. Thus far this learned writer. And without doubt, his account of the early and over-bearing progrefs of idolatry is exact. Another writer who would pais for fuch, is in different fentiments. He thinks its rife and progrefs much lower. *If we look* (fays he) *as on ft the Canaanites, we fhall find no reafon to imagine that there was a religion different from that of Abraham. Abraham travelled up and down many years in this country, and was refpected by the inhabitants of it, as*

a perfon

dence of God had conducted them, while they where yet few in number, and in danger of mixing and confounding themselves with the rest of the Nations. In this distress, one of their own Brethren is sent to them with a message from GOD, by the name and character of the GOD OF THEIR FATHERS, whose virtues God had promised to reward with distinguished blessings on their Posterity. The message, accompained with *signs and wonders,* denounced their speedy deliverance from Egyptian bondage, and their certain possession of the land of Canaan, the scene of all the promised blessings. The People hearken, and are delivered. They depart from Egypt; and in the third month

---

a person in great favour with God, &c. And again, *Abraham was entertained by Pharaoh without the appearance of any indisposition towards him, or any the least sign of their having a different religion from that which Abraham himself professed and practised.* [*Connect. of Sac. and Prof. Hist.* vol. i. p. 309 and 312.] But here the learned author was deceived by mere modern ideas. He did not reflect on that general principle of *intercommunity,* so essential to paganism, which made all its followers disposed to receive the God of Abraham as a true, tho' tutelary, Deity. Josephus (the genius of whose times could not but give him a right notion of this matter) saw well the consistency between the veneration paid to Abraham's God, and the idolatry of the venerators; as appears from his making that Patriarch the first who propagated the belief of one God, after the whole race of mankind was sunk into idolatry; and at the same time making all those with whom he had to do, pay reverence to his God. Of Abraham he thus speaks, Διὰ τῦτο κỳ φρονεῖν ἐπ' ἀρετῇ μείζω τῶν ἄλλων ἡρμένω, κỳ τὴν περὶ τῦ Θιῦ δόξαν, ἣν ἅπασι συνέβαινεν εἶναι, καινίσαι κỳ μεῖαβαλεῖν ἔγνω. Πρῶτω ὖν τολμᾷ Θιὸν ἀποφήνασθαι δημιεργὸν τῶν ὅλων ἕνα. l. i. c. 7. He makes the idolatrous priests of Egypt tell Pharaoh at once, that the pestilence was sent from GOD in punishment for his intended violation of the stranger's wife: καὶα μῆνιν Θιῦ τὸ δεινὸν αὐτῷ παρεῖναι ἀπεσήμαινον οἱ ἱερεῖς, ἐφ' οἷς ἐθέλησεν ἐνυβρίσαι τῦ ξένε τὴν γυναῖκα. c. 8. And Abimelech, in the same circumstances, as ready to own the same author of his punishment. Φράζει πρὸς τὰς φίλας, ὡς ὁ Θεὸς αὐτῷ ταύτην ἐπαγάγοι τὴν νόσον ὑπὲρ ἐκδικίας τῦ ξένε φυλάσσων ἀνύβριστον αὐτῷ τὴν γυναῖκα. c. 12. *Antiq.*

from

from their departure, come to mount Sinai. Here
GOD first tells them by their Leader, MOSES, that,
*if they would obey his voice indeed, and keep his
Covenant, then they should be a* PECULIAR TREASURE
to him above all people, for that the WHOLE EARTH
was his [f]. Where we see an example of what hath
been observed above, that whenever an Institution
was given to this People, in compliance with the
notions they had inbibed in Egypt, a corrective
was always joined with it to prevent the abuse.
Thus God having here told them, that if they
would *obey his voice* they should be *his peculiar
treasure above all people*, (speaking in the character
of a *tutelary God*;) to prevent this compliance from
falling into abuse, as the division of the several
regions of the earth to several celestial rulers was
inseparably connected with the idea of a *tutelary
Deity*, he adds, as a reason for making this People
his Peculiar, a circumstance destructive of that
pagan notion of tutelary Gods——*for that the*
WHOLE EARTH *was his*. Well. The people consent [g];
and GOD delivers the Covenant to them, in the
words of the two Tables [h].

But this promise, of their being received for
GOD's *peculiar treasure*, could be visibly performed
no otherwise than by their separation from the rest
of mankind. As on the other hand, their separation could not have been effected without this visible protection. And this, Moses observes in his
intercession for the people : *For wherein shall it be
known here, that I and thy people have found grace in
thy sight? Is it not in that* THOU GOEST WITH US ?
So shall we be SEPARATED, *I and thy people, from
all the people that are upon the face of the earth* [i].

f EXOD. xix. 5.   g Ver. 8.   h Chap. xx.
i EXOD. xxxiii. 16.

The

The better, therefore to secure this separation, GOD proposes to them, to become their KING. And, for reasons that will be explained anon, condescends to receive. the Magistracy, on their free choice. —*And ye shall be unto me a kingdom of priests* [k], *and an holy nation.*—*And all the people answered together and said, All that the Lord hath spoken we will do* [l]. GOD then delivers them a Digest of their civil and religious Laws, and settles the whole Constitution both of Church and State. Thus the Almighty becoming their KING, in as real a sense as he was their GOD, the republic of the Israelites was properly a THEOCRACY; in which the two Societies, civil and religious, were of course intirely incorporated. A thing neither attended to nor understood. The name indeed is of familiar use: but how little men mean by it, is seen from hence, that those who, out of form, are accustomed to call it a *Theocracy,* yet, in their reasonings about it, consider it as a mere Aristocracy under the Judges; and as a mere Monarchy under the kings: whereas, in truth, it was neither one nor the other, but a real and proper THEOCRACY, under both.

Thus was this famous SEPARATION made. But it will be asked, Why in so extraordinary a way? A way, in which the sagacious Deist can discover nothing-but the marks of the Legislator's fraud, and the People's superstition.—As to what a mere human Lawgiver could gain by such a project, will be seen hereafter. At present, it will be sufficient,

---

[k] For where *God* is *King,* every *subject* is, in some sense or other, a *priest*; because in that case, civil obedience must have in it the nature of religious ministration.

[l] EXOD. xix. 6—8.

for the removal of thefe fufpicions, to fhew, that a THEOCRACY WAS NECESSARY, as the *feparation* could not be effected any other way.

It appears, from what hath been fhewn above, that the Ifraelites had ever a violent propenfity to mix with the neighbouring Nations, and to devote themfelves to the practices of idolatry : this would naturally, and did, in fact, abforb large portions of them. And the fole human means which preferved the remainder, was the feverity of their civil Laws againft idolatry[m]. Such Laws therefore were neceffary to fupport a *feparation*. But penal Laws, inforced by the ordinary Magiftrate, for matters of opinion, are manifeftly unjuft. Some way therefore was to be contrived to render thefe Laws equitable. For we are not to fuppofe GOD would ordain any thing that fhould violate the rule of natural juftice. Now thefe penal laws are equitable only in a Theocracy : therefore was a THEOCRACY NECESSARY.

That the punifhment of opinions, by civil Laws, under a THEOCRACY, is agreeable to the rules of natural juftice, I fhall now endeavour to prove.

[m] " If there be found amongft you, within any of thy gates " which the LORD thy GOD giveth thee, man or woman that " hath wrought wickednefs in the fight of the LORD thy GOD " in tranfgreffing his covenant, and hath gone and ferved other " Gods, and worfhiped them, either the fun, or the moon, " or any of the hoft of heaven, which I have not commanded ; " and it be told thee, and thou haft heard of it, and inquired " diligently, and behold, it be true, and the thing certain, that " fuch abomination is wrought in Ifrael ; then fhalt thou bring " forth that man or that woman (which have committed that " wicked thing) unto thy gates, even that man or that woman, " and fhalt ftone them with ftones till they die." DEUT. xvii. 2, 3, 4, 5.

Unbelievers

Unbelievers and intolerant Christians have both tried to make their advantage of this part of the Mosaic institution. The one using it as an argument against the divinity of the Jewish Religion, on presumption that such Laws are contrary to natural equity ; and the other bringing it to defend their intolerant principles by the example of Heaven itself. But they are both equally deceived by their ignorance of the nature of a *Theocracy :* which, rightly understood, clears the Jewish Law from an embarrassing objection, and leaves the rights of mankind inviolate.

Mr. Bayle, in an excellent treatise for Toleration, when he comes to examine the arguments of the Intolerants, takes notice of that which they bring from the example in question. " The fourth ob-
" jection (says he) may arise from hence, that the
" Law of Moses gives no toleration to idolaters,
" and false prophets, whom it punishes with
" death ; and from what the Prophet Elijah did
" to the Priests of Baal, whom he ordered to be
" destroyed without mercy. From whence it
" follows, that all the reasons I have employed,
" in the first part of this *commentary*, prove no-
" thing, because they prove too much ; namely,
" that the literal sense of the Law of Moses, as far
" as relates to the punishment of opinions, would
" be impious and abominable. Therefore, since
" GOD could, without violating the eternal order
" of things, command the Jews to put false pro-
" phets to death, it follows, evidently, that he
" could, under the Gospel also, command ortho-
" dox believers to inflict the same punishment upon
" heretics.

3   " I am

" I am not, if I rightly know myſelf, of that
" temper of mind; ſo thoroughly corrupted by the
" contagion of Controverſy, as to treat this objec-
" tion with an air of haughtineſs and contempt ;
" as is the way when men find themſelves inca-
" pable of anſwering to the purpoſe. I ingenu-
" ouſly own the objection to be ſtrong ; and that
" it ſeems to be a mark of God's ſovereign plea-
" ſure, that we ſhould not arrive at certainty in
" any thing, ſeeing he hath given exceptions in
" his holy word to almoſt all the common notices
" of reaſon. Nay I know ſome who have no
" greater difficulties to hinder their believing,
" that God was the author of the Laws of Moſes,
" and of all thoſe Revelations that occaſioned ſo
" much ſlaughter and devaſtation, than this very
" matter of intolerance, ſo contrary to our cleareſt
" ideas of natural equity ⁿ."

Whether Mr. Bayle himſelf, was one of theſe
backward believers, as by ſome of his expreſſions
he gives us reaſon to ſuſpect, is not material.
That he dwelt with pleaſure on this circumſtance,
as favouring his beloved ſcepticiſm, is too evident. But ſure he went a little too far when he
ſaid, God's *word contains exceptions to almoſt all the
common notices of reaſon*°. I hope to ſhew, before
I have done with Infidelity, that it contains exceptions to none. But the ſolution of this difficulty
was above his ſtrength, had he been ever ſo willing
to reconcile Scripture to Reaſon. Judea was a

ⁿ Voions preſentement cette iv. objection. On la peut tirer
de ce que la loi du Moïſe, &c. *Commentaire Philoſophique*, Part
ii. Chap. 4.

°—par les exceptions qu'il a miſes dans ſa parole à preſque
toutes les notions communes de la raiſon.

terra

terra incognita to this great Adventurer. : Our excellent countryman Mr. Locke, who wrote about
this time on the ſame ſubject, and with that force
and preciſion which is the character of all his writings, was much happier in his account of this
matter. *As to the caſe* (ſays he) *of the Iſraelites
in the Jewiſh Commonwealth, who being initiated into
the Moſaical rites, and made citizens of the commonwealth, did afterwards apoſtatize from the worſhip
of the* God *of Iſrael; theſe were proceeded againſt
as traitors and rebels, guilty of no leſs than high
treaſon: For the commonwealth of the Jews, different, in that, from all others, was an abſolute*
Theocracy; *nor was there, nor could there be,
any difference between the Commonwealth and the
Church. The Laws eſtabliſhed there concerning the
worſhip of the one inviſible Deity were the civil
Laws of that people, and a part of their political
Government, in which* God *himſelf was the Legiſlator*[p]. This he ſaid; and, for ought I can learn,
he was the firſt who ſaid it. : But this being all he
ſaid,

I ſhall endeavour to ſupport his ſolution by ſuch
other reaſoning as occurs to me.   It will be necef-
ſary then to obſerve, that God, in his infinite wiſdom, was pleaſed to ſtand in two *arbitrary* relations towards the jewiſh People, beſides that *natural* one, in which he ſtood towards them and
the reſt of mankind in common.   The firſt was
that of a *tutelary Deity, gentilitial* and *local*; the
God of Abraham, Iſaac, and Jacob, who was to
bring their poſterity into the land of Canaan, and
to protect them there, as his peculiar People.   The
ſecond was that of *ſupreme Magiſtrate and Lawgiver.*

[p] *Letter concerning Toleration,* p. 51, 52.

And in both thefe relations he was pleafed to refer it to the people's free choice, whether or no they would receive him for their God and King. For a tutelary Deity was fuppofed by the Ancients to be as much matter of election as a civil Magiftrate. The People, therefore, thus folemnly accepting him, thefe neceffary confequences followed from the Horeb contract.

I. Firft, that as the national God and civil Magiftrate of the Jews centered in one and the fame object, their civil Policy and Religion muft be intimately united and incorporated[9]; confequently, their religion had, and very reafonably, A public part, whofe fubject was the Society as fuch: tho' this part, in the national pagan Religions, which had it likewife, was extremely abfurd, as hath been fhewn more at large in the firft volume[r].

II. Secondly, as the two Societies were thoroughly incorporated, they could not be diftinguifhed; but muft ftand or fall together. Confequently the direction of all their civil Laws muft be for the equal prefervation of both. Therefore, as the renouncing him for King, was the throwing him off as God; and as the renouncing him for God, was the throwing him off as King; idolatry, which was the rejecting him as God, was properly the crimen læfæ majeftatis; and fo juftly punifhable by the civil Laws. But there was this manifeft

---

[9] Such a kind of union and incorporation was moft abfurdly affected by Mahomet in imitation of the *Jewifh* Œconomy; whence, as might be expected, it appears that neither he nor his affiftants underftood any thing of its true nature.

[r] P. 99. part 1. ed. 4.

difference

difference in these two cases, as to the effects. The renouncing GOD as civil Magistrate might be remedied without a total dissolution of the Constitution; not so, the renouncing him as tutelary GOD: because, though he might, and did ' appoint a deputy, in his office of KING, amongst the Jewish Tribes; yet he would have no substitute, as GOD, amongst the pagan Deities. Therefore, in necessity as well as of right, idolatry was punishable by the civil Laws of a THEOCRACY; it being the greatest crime that could be committed against the State, as tending, by unavoidable consequence, to dissolve the Constitution. For the one GOD being the supreme Magistrate, it subsisted in the worship of that GOD alone. Idolatry, therefore, as the renunciation of one GOD alone, was in a strict philosophic, as well as legal sense, the crime of lese-majesty. Let us observe farther, that as, by such INCORPORATION, religious matters came under civil consideration, so likewise civil matters came under the religious. This is what Josephus would say, where, in his second book against Apion, speaking of the Jewish Theocracy, he tells us that Moses did not make *Religion a part of Virtue, but Virtue a part of Religion*'. The meaning is, that, as in all human Societies, obedience to the Law is moral Virtue; under a THEOCRACY, it is Religion.

III. The punishment of Idolatry, by Law, had this farther circumstance of equity, that it was pu-

---

' The kings of *Israel* and *Judah* being, as we shall shew, indeed no other.

' Αἴτιον δ' ὅτι κỳ τῷ τρόπῳ τῆς νομοθεσίας πρὸς τὸ χρήσιμον πάντων ἀεὶ πολὺ διήνεγκεν· ἢ γὰρ μέρος τὴν ἀρετὴν ἐποίησε τὴν εὐσέβειαν, ἀλλὰ ταύτης τὰ μέρη τἄλλα συνῖδε κỳ κατέταξε· λέγω δὲ τὴν δικαιοσύνην, τὴν καρτερίαν, τὴν σωφροσύνην, τὴν τῶν πολιτῶν πρὸς ἀλλήλους ἐν ἅπασι συμφωνίαν. p. 483. *Hav. Ed.*

nishing

niſhing the rebellion of thoſe who had choſen the
Government under which they lived, when freely
propoſed to them. Hence, in the Law againſt
idolatry, the crime is, with great propriety, called
the TRANSGRESSION OF THE COVENANT ᵘ.

Thus we ſee, the Law in queſtion ſtands clear of
the cavils of Infidels, and the abuſe of Intolerants ˣ.
But

<hr/>

ᵘ DEUT. xvii. 2.

ˣ Theſe conſiderations will lead us to a right apprehenſion
of that part of the hiſtory of Jeſus, where James and John, on
the inhoſpitable behaviour of a village of Samaria, ſay to their
Maſter, in the Legal ſpirit of the Jewiſh Œconomy, *Lord, wilt
thou that we command fire to come down from heaven and con-
ſume them, even as Elias did? But he turned, and rebuked them,
and ſaid, Ye know not what manner of ſpirit ye are of. For the
Son of Man is not come to deſtroy mens lives, but to ſave them.*
[LUKE ix. 54, 55, 56.] *i. e.* You conſider not that you are no
longer under the Diſpenſation of Works (in which a ſeverity of
this kind was juſt and neceſſary) but, of Grace, in which all
reſtraint and puniſhment of opinions would be miſchievous and
unlawful. Here we ſee the very diſpoſition to intolerance in
James and John, is ſeverely cenſured. Yet the ſame temper in
Paul, even when proceeding into act, is paſſed over without reproof, when Jeſus, after his reſurrection, is pleaſed to reveal his
truth to him in a miraculous manner. Our Lord, inſtead of con-
demning the nature of the practice, only aſſures him of the vanity
of its effects, *It is hard for thee to kick againſt the pricks.* [ACTS
ix. 5.] The reaſon of this different treatment is evident. James
and John had given their names to the Religion of Jeſus, in which
all force was unjuſt. Paul was yet of the Religion of Moſes,
where reſtraint was lawful. On this account it is that this Apoſtle, when ſpeaking of his merits as a Jew, expreſſes himſelf in
this manner, *For ye have heard of my converſation in time paſt; how
that beyond meaſure I* PERSECUTED *the church of God, and
waſted it: and* PROFITED *in the Jew religion above many my
equals in mine own nation.* [GAL. i. 13.] Here he makes the
perſecution and the *profiting* to go hand in hand. And again,
*Though I might alſo have confidence in the fleſh. If any other
man thinketh that he hath whereof he might truſt in the fleſh, I
more: Circumciſed the eighth day, of the ſtock of Iſrael, of the
tribe of Benjamin, an Hebrew of the Hebrews; as touch-*
ing

But to this, the defender of *the common rights of subjects* may be apt to object, " that these penal laws were unjust, because no contract to give up the rights of conscience, can be binding."

To which I reply, with a plain and decisive fact, That none of all the idolatrous worship the Jews ever fell into, from the time of giving the Law to the total dissolution of the Republic, was MATTER OF CONSCIENCE; but always of convenience; such as procuring some temporal good, which they wantonly affected, or averting some temporal evil, which they servilely feared. The truth of which appears from hence, that, in the midst of all their idolatries, the GOD of their Fathers, as we shall see, was ever owned to be the Creator and first Cause of all things; and the Religion taught by Moses, to be a Revelation from heaven.

But it may be asked, What if their commission of idolatry had, at any time, proved matter of con-

---

ing the Law, a *Pharisee*; *concerning zeal,* PERSECUTING THE CHURCH; *touching the righteousness which is in the law, blameless. But what things were gain to me, those I counted loss for Christ* [PHIL. iii. 4.] Here he glories in the action, as plainly meritorious. And so indeed it was in a Jew, as appears from the commendations given to it in the case of Phineas, and others. Yet where he speaks of it, under his present character of a Christian, he condemns it as horrid and detestable; and this, in order to shew his followers how it ought to be regarded in the Religion of Jesus. To the Corinthians he says, *I am the least of the Apostles; that am not meet to be called an Apostle, because I* PERSECUTED *the church of God.* [1 EP. xv. 9.] And to *Timothy, I thank Christ Jesus our Lord, who hath enabled me, for that he counted me faithful, putting me into the ministry; who was before a blasphemer and a* PERSECUTOR, *and injurious. But I obtained mercy, because I did it in* IGNORANCE *and* UNBELIEF. [1 EP. i. 12.] *i. e.* being a Jew.

science;

ſcience ; i. e. ſuch an action as they thought they were obliged in duty to perform ?

I reply, the queſtion would have weight, had the Law in diſpute been of human inſtitution. But as it was given by God, who knows the future equally with the paſt and preſent, and ſaw the caſe would not happen, it is altogether impertinent. The Queſtion, indeed, points out to us the danger and abſurdity in any human legiſlature to make penal Laws for reſtraining the exerciſe of Religion, on any pretence whatſoever.

Thus it is ſeen, that a *ſeparation*, ſo neceſ-ſary to preſerve the Unity, could not have been ſupported without PENAL LAWS againſt idolatry ; and, at the ſame time, ſeen that ſuch penal laws can never be equitably inſtituted but under a Theocracy. The conſequence is, that A THEOCRACY WAS NE-CESSARY.

But this form of Government was highly convenient likewiſe. The Iſraelites, on their leaving Egypt, were ſunk into the loweſt practices of idolatry. To recover them, therefore, by the diſcipline of a *ſeparation*, it was neceſſary that the idea of God and his attributes ſhould be impreſſed upon them in the moſt *ſenſible* manner. But this could not be done, commodiouſly, under his character of God of the Univerſe : under his character of KING of Iſrael it well might. Hence it is, we find him in the Old Teſtament ſo frequently repreſented with affections analogous to human paſſions. The Civil relation, in which he ſtood to theſe people, made ſuch a repreſentation natural ; the groſſneſs of their conceptions made the repreſentation neceſſary ; and the guarded manner in which it was always
qualified,

qualified, prevented it from being mischievous. Hence, another instance of the wisdom of this Œconomy; and of the folly of Spinoza, and others, who would conclude from it, that Moses and the Prophets had themselves grofs conceptions of the Deity. Nor should the indiscretion of those Divines pass uncensured, who have taught that God, in the Old Testament, looks on man with a less gracious and benign aspect, than in the New. An error, which at one time gave birth to the most absurd and monstrous of the ancient herefies; and hath at all times furnished a handle to infidelity [y]. But God, whenever he represents himself under the idea of Lord of the Universe, makes one uniform revelation of his nature, throughout all his Dispensations, *as gracious and full of compassion; as good to* ALL, *and whose tender mercies are* OVER ALL HIS WORKS: yet condescending to become the tutelary God, and civil Magistrate of the Jews, it cannot but be, that he should be considered as having his peculiar inspection attached to this People, and as punishing their transgressions with severity.

These appear to me the true reasons of the *Theocratic* form of government. With such admirable wisdom was the Jewish Œconomy adapted, to effect the ends it had in view! Yet, notwithstanding the splendour of divinity which shines through every part of this Theocratic form, Mr. Foster, a dissenting preacher, tells us roundly, that it is all an idle dream; and that he will undertake

---

[y] *It must be owned* (fays Tyndal) *that the same spirit (I dare not call it a spirit of cruelty) does not alike prevail throughout the Old Testament: the nearer we come to the times of the Gospel, the milder it appeared.* Christianity as old as the Creation, p. 241. See too Lord Bolingbroke's posthumous works throughout.

to

to defend the Law, which punifhes idolatry with
death, " not on *dark and imaginary*, but on *clear*
" *and folid* principles; I therefore add, (fays he)
" fuppofing the Theocratic form of government
" amongft the Jews to be a point inconteftable, it
" *feems fcarce* capable of affording a *full and fa-*
" *tisfactory* anfwer to the objection raifed againft
" the hebrew Law for devoting idolaters to death,
" For when the people of Ifrael, fond of novelty,
" and of imitating the cuftoms of other nations,
" were ftubbornly and inflexibly refolved, not-
" withftanding all the remonftrances of the Pro-
" phet Samuel to the contrary, to have a vifible
" and mortal King; God upon this occafion de-
" clared, that they had *rejected him that he fhould*
" *not reign over them:* and as his former poli-
" tical reign is founded on a fuppofed compact
" between the Almighty Sovereign and his peo-
" ple, that *original compact* being now folemnly
" renounced on the part of the people, there muft
" of courfe be a diffolution or end of the Theo-
" cracy [z]."

He begins with calling the Theocracy *a dark
principle.* And yet, the account he gives of it
fhews, that he did not find it *dark*; and, what was
worfe, could not, with all his endeavours, make
it fo. He calls it *imaginary*; and yet the very Hiftory he quotes to prove its fhort duration, fhews,
even by his own proof, it was *not imaginary*, but
real.

Indeed, if that civil Government, which is founded on ORIGINAL COMPACT, were diffolvable at
pleafure, that is, as foon as one of the contracting

[z] Serm. vol. iii. p. 373—374.

parties

parties was grown weary of it, (which this Decider on Government and Laws exprefsly says it is) then Government, on its moft legitimate foundation, would be the moft *dark and imaginary* of all things. When the Parliament rofe up in arms againft Charles I. they wanted juft fuch a Preacher as this, (and yet they had many precious ones) to affure them, that *their renouncing* the King's Authority had fairly diffolved the Monarchy, and brought it to a lawful end. For the Leaders of that body, it is plain, knew nothing of this fecret, and were therefore at a great deal of pains to prove, and at laft could hardly get themfelves believed, that Charles himfelf had broken the *original Compact.* But unlefs this *Compact* ftands upon a different footing from all other compacts in the world, we may fafely pronounce, that a bargain or agreement, which has been made between two parties, can never be diffolved but by the confent of both of them ; or by a fundamental mifdemeanour in one ; if the other party chufes to exact the forfeiture. Now, in the cafe of the Jews under Samuel, there was a *renunciation,* it is true, on the part of the People, or, in plainer Englifh, a REBELLION. But GOD did not give way to it ; he would not (as on the pinciples of civil juftice he might) exact the forfeiture ; which was, the withdrawing his protection. All this will be proved at large in its place. The *Theocracy,* therefore, ftill continued under their Kings ; which were indeed no other than the *anointed,* or the Viceroys of GOD.—Such is our Preacher's fuccefs in attempting to fhew Mr. Locke's principle to be *dark and imaginary.* Let us fee next whether he has better fortune in proving his own to be *clear and folid.*

Now his way of juftifying the Law, which punifhed idolatry with death, without the aid of the
theocratic

theocratic principle is this.—" As the end for which
" the civil conſtitution of the Jews was formed,
" *viz.* to prevent their being over-run with ido-
" latry, (which as it prevailed amongſt the neigh-
" bouring nations, corrupted their internal ſenſe
" of the difference of good and evil, and baniſhed
" humanity and decency, and many of the moſt
" conſiderable and important of the ſocial virtues,
" by introducing ſhameful impurities and human
" ſacrifices, quite deteſtable to nature) as the end,
" I ſay, for which the civil conſtitution of the Jews
" was formed, appears, when thus explained, and
" abſtracted from all conſideration merely reli-
" gious, to be wiſe and gracious in itſelf; and as
" the judicial Laws in that ſcheme of Government
" were admirably adapted to ſubſerve and advance
" this wiſe and gracious end, it neceſſarily follows,
" that idolatry, which would have fruſtrated the
" whole deſign of the Conſtitution, and have en-
" tirely diſſolved and deſtroyed it, muſt, upon the
" ſame reaſons that are allowed to be juſt in all
" other Policies, have deſerved capital puniſh-
" ment[a]."

Here we ſee our Preacher approves himſelf juſt
as ſkilful in the *end* of Civil-government, as he
did before, in its *nature and eſſence.* He appears
not to know (what he might have ſeen proved in
the firſt volume of this work) that civil Society
muſt have one particular, diſtinct, and appropriated
end; and that this end can be no other than ſecurity to the temporal liberty and property of man; becauſe (as is there ſhewn) all other ends may be
attained without civil Society. This then is the
only proper end of Government. Yet our Preacher

[a] Page 375—376.

falls

falls into that exploded conceit, which makes any attainable end, so it be a good one, the legitimate business of civil Society, as such: which confounds this Society with all others, there being no way to keep the Civil distinct but by assigning it an end peculiar to itself. But his subject happening to be the *Jewish government,* it secured his reasoning from the glare of the absurdity. And his false and fallacious account of the *end* of its institution, with which he introduces his reasoning, gave a certain plausibility to the nonsense which followed. It is in these words, *The end for which the civil constitution was formed, was to prevent their being over-run with idolatry.* Now, by *civil constitution* a fair reasoner should mean (where the question is concerning the efficacy of a *mere* civil Government, in contradistinction to the Religious) the civil constitution of the Jews as it was so distinguished. But, in this sense, the *end* of the *civil constitution* of the Jews was the same with all other, namely, security to men's temporal liberty and property. It is true, if by their *civil constitution*, he meant both civil and religious, which here indeed was incorporated, and went under the common name of LAW; then indeed its *end was to prevent idolatry*; but then this is giving up the point, because that incorporation was the consequence of the *Theocratic* form of Government, or, to speak more properly, it was the THEOCRACY itself. Thus he comes round again to the place on which he had turned his back; and, before he knows where he is, establishes the very doctrine he would confute. In a word, our Preacher was got out of his depth; and here I shall leave him to sink or swim; only observing, that this great advocate of religious liberty has done his best (tho' certainly without design) to support a principle the most plausible of any
that

that Perfecutors for opinions can catch hold on, to juftify their iniquitous practice ; namely, *that civil government was ordained for the procuring all the good of all kinds, which it is even accidentally capable of advancing.* And to make fure work, he employs that adulterate glofs, which They fo artfully put upon their wicked practice ; *viz.* that it is *for the support of morality:* for who is fo purblind that he cannot fpy *immoralities* lurking in all heretical opinions? And thus it is that our Preacher defends civil Government, in punifhing opinions: *The idolatry of the neighbouring nations* (fays he) *corrupted their internal fenfe of the difference of good and evil, and banifhed humanity and decency, and many of the moft confiderable and important of the focial virtues.* A reafon conftantly in the mouths, whatever hath been in the hearts, of Perfecutors, from St. Auftin to St. Dominic [b].

II.

We come, in the next place, to fhew, that this Theocracy, as it was necessary, fo it would have an eafy reception ; being founded on the flattering notion, at that time univerfally entertained, of tutelary deities, *Gentilitial and Local.* Thus, to carry on his great purpofe, the Almighty very early reprefented himfelf to this chofen race, as a *Gentilitial* Deity, The God of Abraham, Ifaac, and Jacob [c]: Afterwards, when he preferred Judea

[b] Dr. Stebbing, tho' he differs from Mr. Fofter in moft other matters, yet agrees with him in this, " That the juftice and " equity of the Jewifh Law in punifhing Idolaters with death, " did not depend on the particular form of government." [*Hift. of Abraham*] In which he is much more confiftent than his diffenting neighbour. For the doctor approves of perfecutions for opinions ; whereas the minifter pretends to condemn it.

[c] See Jer. x, 16. and li. 19.

to all other countries for his perſonal reſidence, (on this account called His Land [d]) he came under their idea of a *Local* Deity : which notion was an eſtabliſhed principle in the Gentile world, as we have ſhewn above, from Plato. It was originally Egyptian ; and founded in an opinion that the earth was at firſt divided by its Creator, amongſt a number of inferior and ſubordinate Divinities. The Septuagint tranſlators appear to have underſtood the following paſſage, in the ſong of Moſes, as alluding to this opinion ;—*When the Moſt High divided to the nations their inheritance, when he ſeparated the ſons of Adam, he ſet the bounds of the people* ACCORDING TO THE NUMBER OF THE CHILDREN OF ISRAEL. *For the Lord's portion is his people :* Jacob *is the lot of his inheritance* [e] : For, inſtead of, *according to the number of the children of Iſrael* (which if they found in the text, they underſtood no more than later critics) they wrote καλὰ ἀριθμὸν Ἀγγέλων Θεῦ, ACCORDING TO THE NUMBER OF THE ANGELS OF God. Which at leaſt is intelligible, as referring to that old notion, original to the country where this tranſlation was made. And Juſtin Martyr tells us [f], that in the beginning, God had committed the government of the world to angels, who, abuſing their truſt, were degraded from their regency. But whether he learnt it from this tranſlation, or took it from a worſe place, I ſhall not pretend to determine.

The Land, thus ſelected by God for his perſonal reſidence, he beſtows upon his choſen People. *Be-*

[d] Levit. xxv. 23. Deut. xi. 12. Ps. x. 16. Is. xiv. 25. Jer. ii. 7. Chap. xvi. ver. 18. Ezek. xxxv. 10. Chap. xxxvi. ver. 5, 20. Chap. xxxviii. ver. 16. Wisd. of Sol. xii. 7.

[e] Deut. xxxii. 8, 9.   [f] *A*pologet. i.

hold (fays he) *the land of Canaan which I give unto
the children of Ifrael for a poffeffion* [g]. This too was
according to the common notions of thofe times.
Thus Jephthah, who appears to have been half
paganized by a bad education, fpeaks to the King
of the Ammonites, *Wilt not thou poffefs that which
Chemofh thy* GOD *giveth thee to poffefs? So, whomfoever
the Lord our* GOD *fhall drive out from before us, them
will we poffefs* [h].

It was no wonder, therefore, when GOD was
thus pleafed, for the wife ends of his providence, to
be confidered, by a prejudiced people, in this character, that all the pagan nations round about fhould
regard the GOD OF ISRAEL no otherwife than as a
local tutelary Deity; too apt, by their common
prejudices, to fee him only under that idea. Thus
he is called the GOD *of the Land* [i],—*the* GOD *of the
Hills* [k], &c. And it is exprefsly faid, that *they fpoke
againft the* GOD *of Jerufalem, as againft the Gods
of the people of the earth, which were the work of
the hands of man* [l]. By which is meant, that
they treated him as a local tutelary Deity, of a
confined and bounded power: for it was not the
old pagan way to fpeak againft one another's
Gods, in difcredit of their Divinity: and this circumfcribed dominion was efteemed, by them, no
difcredit to it: But, by the Jews, the worfhipers
of the true GOD, it was juftly held to be the greateft. Therefore, to call the GOD of Ifrael *the God
of the hills, and not of the plain*, was *fpeaking againft
him.*

---

[g] DEUT. xxxii. 49.   [h] JUDG. xi. 24.   [i] 2 KINGS,
xvii. 26. Chap. xviii. ver. 33, & *feq.*   [k] 1 KINGS,
xx. 23.   [l] 2 CHRON. xxxii. 19.

For, here again we must observe, that when God, agreeably to the whole method of this Dispensation, takes advantage of, or indulges his people in, any habituated notion or custom, he always interweaves some characteristic note of difference, to mark the institution for his own. Thus in this indulgence of their prejudices concerning a tutelary God.

1. He first institutes, upon it, a *Theocracy*; a practice just the reverse of paganism: for there Kings became Gods; whereas here God condescended to become King [m].

[m] It is strange to consider how much Dr. *Spencer* has mistaken this matter, where, in his reasons of a Theocracy *ex parte seculi*, as he calls them, he gives the following: " Seculi moribus " ita factum erat, ut Dii sui principatum quendam inter servos " suos obtinerent, & nomine rituque regio colerentur. Nam se- " culo illo Deos titulis illis *Molech, Elohim, Baalim* & hujusmodi " aliis, regibus & magnatibus tribui solitis, insignire solebant : " eos imperii arbitros plerumque ponebant, cum nec bella ge- " rere, nec civitatem condere, nec regem eligere, nec grandius " aliquid moliri solerent, priusquam Deos per oracula vel auf- " picia consuluissent." *Differ. de Theoc. Jud.* c. iii. p. 237. *Ed. Chap.* But these are no marks that the Pagans attributed any kind of civil regality to their Gods. As to their regal titles, those were what they had retained from the time of their real kingship in the state of humanity. And as to the consulting their oracles on all public affairs of moment, this was the consequence of pagan religion's having *a public as well as private part.* But, for an acknowledged God to be chosen and received by any people as their real Monarch or Civil Magistrate, was a thing altogether unknown to Paganism. The learned Marsham, with his usual bias, endeavours to insinuate, that the institution of a *Theocracy* was an imitation of Pagan Custom. — Moses pridem Θιοκρατιαν declaravit Ebraeorum Rempublicam ; ne sibi potestas regia deferretur : Athenienses autem Δικρατιαν suam ab Apolline retulerunt ; ut *regis* nomen *Jovi* cederet ; neque tam titulus quam potestas regia imminueretur. Sec. xiii. p. 340.—But the question here is not about the *name*, but the *thing*. The Pagans might call their national Gods by the name of Kings, and, by a bolder figure, might call their Government,

2. Secondly, he forbids all kind of community or intercourse between the God of Ifrael and the Gods of the Nations, either by joining their worſhip to his, or ſo much as owning their Divinity. Thus were the Ifraelites diſtinguiſhed from all other people in the moſt effeᶜtual manner : for, as we have often had occaſion to obſerve, there was a general intercommunity amongſt the Gods of paganiſm : They acknowledged one another's pretenſions; they borrowed one another's titles ; and, at length, entered into a kind of partnerſhip of Worſhip.   All the Pagan nations, we ſee, owned the God of Ifrael for a tutelary Deity [n]·   But His followers were not permitted to be ſo complaiſant. There was to be no fellowſhip between God and Belial ; though a good underſtanding always ſubſiſted between Belial and Dagon.

But, amidſt a vaſt number of charaᶜteriſtic circumſtances proving the origin of the Mosaic religion to have been different from that of every other nation, there is none more illuſtrious than this, *That the Moſaic religion was built upon a former,* namely the Patriarchal : whereas the various Religions of the Pagan world were all unrelated to, and independent of any other [o].

And yet the famous Author of *The grounds and reaſons of the Chriſtian Religion* hath been hardy enough to employ one whole chapter to prove, that

ment, put under the proteᶜtion of a tutelary Deity, by the name of a *Theocracy*; but a real Theocracy is that only where the Laws of the Inſtitution have all a reference to the aᶜtual rule of a tutelary God, whether the true God or falſe ones; and ſuch a Theocracy is no where to be found but in the land of Judea.

[n] 2 Kings xviii. 25.   Jer. iv. 2, 3.   [o] See vol. i. p. 279, *& ſeq.* ed. 2.

this

*this method of introducing Christianity into the world,
by building and grounding it on the Old Testament, is
agreeable to the common method of introducing new
Revelations, whether real or* PRETENDED, *or any
changes in religion; and also the nature of things* [p].

" For if (says he) we consider the various revolu-
" tions and changes in religion, whereof we have
" any tolerable history, in their beginning, we
" shall find them, for the most part, to be grafted
" on some old stock, or founded on some preceding
" revelations, which they were either to supply,
" or fulfil, or retrieve from corrupt glosses, inno-
" vations, and traditions, with which by time they
" were incumbered : and this, which MAY SEEM
" MATTER OF SURPRISE TO THOSE, WHO DO NOT
" REFLECT on the changeable nature of all things,
" hath happened ; though the old revelations far
" from intending any change, ingraftment, or new
" dispensation, *did for the most part declare they were
" to last for ever,* and did forbid all alterations and
" innovations, they being the last dispensation in-
" tended [q]."

Here are two things asserted : 1. That the build-
ing new Religions and new Revelations upon old
was agreeable to the common method of the ancient
world.   2. That it was agreeable to the nature of
things.   These are discoveries one would little
have expected.

I. Let us first examine his FACTS.—But to judge
truly of their force, we must remember, that the
observation is made to discredit what Believers call
true Revelation, by shewing that all false Religions
have taken the same method of propagation.

1. His firſt point is, *That this method was agree-able to the common practice of the ancient world.* Would not one expect now an inſtance of ſome confeſſedly falſe Religion, between the time of ABRAHAM and CHRIST, which pretended to be built on ſome preceding Revelation ? Without doubt: If it were only for this, that there is no other way of proving the propoſition. Beſides, to ſay the truth, ſuch an inſtance would be well worth attending to, for its extreme curioſity. But he could not give the reader what was not to be had: and therefore he endeavours to make up this de-ficiency of *fact*, by ſhewing, 1. That the JEWISH Religion, like the CHRISTIAN, pretended to be built on a preceding. " Thus the miſſion of Moſes " to the Iſraelites (ſays he) ſuppoſed a former re-" velation of God (who from the beginning ſeems " to have been conſtantly giving a ſucceſſion of dif-" penſations and revelations) to their anceſtors; " and many of the religious precepts of Moſes " were borrowed, or had an agreement with the re-" ligious rites of the heathens, with whom the " Iſraelites had correſpondence, and particularly " with the religious rites of the Egyptians, (who " upon that account ſeem confounded with the " Iſraelites by ſome pagans, as both their religious " rites were equally, and at the ſame time, pro-" hibited by others) to whoſe religious rites the " Iſraelites ſeem to have been *Conformiſts* during " their abode in Egypt[r]." Go thy way, for a good Reaſoner!——To prove that falſe revelations had the ſame pretenſions of dependency on a preceding, as the true have had, he ſhews that all the true had theſe pretenſions. But this is but half the atchieve-ment. The beſt part is ſtill behind. 'Tis a rarity;

[r] Page 22.

a blunder

a blunder ingrafted on a sophism. He was not content to say that Moses founded his Religion on the Patriarchal: he muſt needs go on,——*And many of the religious precepts of Moses were borrow-ed, or had an agreement with the religious rites of the Heathens, with whom the Israelites had correspondence, and particularly with the religious Rites of the Egyp-tians.*   Now, how it comes to paſs that Moses's borrowing from the religious Rites of the Egyp-tians, whoſe religion he formally condemned of falſhood, ſhould be metamorphoſed into an example of one Religion's being founded upon, or re-ceiving its authority from, another, I confeſs, I cannot comprehend.   If he were not at the head of the FREETHINKERS, I ſhould ſuſpect ſome ſmall confuſion in his ideas: and that this great Reaſoner was unable to diſtinguiſh between, *a Religion's ſup-porting itſelf on one preceding, which it acknowledged to be true:* and *a Religion's complying, for the ſake of inveterate prejudices, with ſome innocent practices of another religion, which it was erected to overthrow, as falſe.*   •

2. He ſhews next, that thoſe falſe religions which came AFTER the Jewiſh and the Chriſtian, and are confeſſed to mimick their peculiarities, pre-tended to be built on preceding revelations.——
" The miſſion of Zoroaſter to the Perſians ſuppoſed
" the religion of the Magians; which had been,
" for many ages paſt, the antient national religion
" of the Medes as well as Perſians.   The miſſion
" of Mahomet ſuppoſed Chriſtianity; as that did,
" Judaiſm [*]."   This is ſtill better.   The deſign of his general obſervation, *That it was the common method for new revelations to be built and grounded*

* Page 23.

on

on preceding revelations, was to fhew that the revelations, which we call true, imitated the falfe.
And he proves it,—by fhewing that the falfe imitated the true. That Mahomet's did fo, is agreed
on all hands. And thofe bewildered men who
would have us credit the ftory of a *late* Zoroafter,
do, and muft fuppofe that he borrowed from Judaifm. But the truth is, the whole is an idle tale,
invented by Perfian writers under the early Califs.
However, tho' the Zoroafter of Hyde and Prideaux be a mere phantom, yet the Religion called
by his name, was a real thing, and ftarted up in
the firft ages of Mahometifm, with a Bible to fupport its credit, in imitation of, and to oppofe to,
the Alcoran. But this neat device unluckily detects the whole impofture: For in the Age of
Mahomet, and in the time of the firft Commentators on the Alcoran, the Perfians were efteemed
by them, as Idolaters, and without a Bible; (and
they had good Opportunity, by their conftant
commerce thither, to be well informed:) Which is
agreeable to every thing that the earlier and the later
Greek Writers unanimoufly deliver of the Perfian Religion. But that, on the appearance of
Mahometanifm, the Perfians fhould do what the
Greeks did on the firft appearance of Chriftianity,
refine their old idolatrous worfhip, till they brought
it to what Hyde and Prideaux obferve it is at this
day, amongft the remainder of the Magian fect in
Perfia and India, is nothing ftrange. The wonder
is, that thefe learned men fhould have fwallowed fo
grofs a cheat, on the teftimony of later Mahometan Writers; who had fo many motives to fupport
it, and fo flender abilities to detect it; whofe propenfity to fabling is fo great as even to difcredit
any truth that refts on their authority; and whofe
talents in the art of lying are fo little proportioned

to

to their inclination to exercise it, that they never fail of defeating their own impositions.   This argument, therefore, was in all respects worthy the Author of *The Grounds and Reasons of the Christian Religion.*

3. Lastly, he tells us, that "'the Siamese and
" Brachmans both pretend that they have had a
" *succession of incarnate deities* amongst them, who
" at due distances of time, have brought new Re-
" velations from heaven; each succeeding one de-
" pending on the former; and that religion is to
" be conveyed on, in that way, for ever'."———
He promised to prove a succession of Religions in the ancient world, the later founded and depending on the preceding: And he proves—*a succession of incarnate deities*, talked of amongst the MODERN pagans of India and Siam; and, from this succession concludes for a succession of DEPENDING RELIGIONS, of which they have no kind of notion. Nor are these extravagancies, which their priests do indeed talk of, any other than late inventions of their priests, to oppose to Mahometan and Christian Missionaries.   But a *succession of incarnate deities* was so arch a ridicule on the mysteries of our holy faith, that it was to be brought in at any rate. But now the joke is over, let me tell him, he need not have gone so far for it.   Were not Cœlus, Saturn, Jupiter, Mars, *&c. a succession of incarnate deities?* yet were any of the Religions, which had those Gods for their author or object, FOUNDED or DEPENDENT on (tho' they succeeded to) one another? Here again, our sagacious Freethinker was at a fault; and, with all his logic, could not

---

† *Ibid.*

N 3   distinguish

diftinguifh between *one Religion's being built upon
another*, and *one Religion's fimply fucceeding another*.

II. He comes next to the NATURE OF THINGS.
The reader has feen how fhort he falls of his reckoning from *fact :* But let him fairly make up his
accounts, and we fhall not differ with him about
his way of payment ; but willingly receive his de-
ficiencies of Fact, in Reafon.——" If we confider
" (fays he) the *nature of things*, we fhall find that
" it muft be difficult, if not impoffible, to intro-
" duce amongft men (who in all civilized countries
" are bred up in the belief of fome revealed re-
" ligion) a revealed religion wholly new, or fuch
" as has no reference to a preceding one : for that
" would be to combat all men in too many refpects,
" and not to proceed on a fufficient number of
" principles neceffary to be affented to by thofe,
" on whom the firft impreffions of a new religion
" are propofed to be made [u]."

Here his head was full of the theologic ideas of
modern times ; where one Religion is maintained
and propagated on the deftruction of all the reft.
And that indeed would be *combating all men in too
many refpects*, without good evidence in the Religion
thus propofed. But had he had the leaft knowledge of Antiquity, he would have known that
the Gentile religions of thofe times were founded
on different principles, and propagated on different
practices. Not one of thofe numerous Religions
ever pretended to accufe another of falfhood ; and
therefore was never itfelf in danger of being fo
accufed. They very amicably owned one another's

[u] Page 23, 24.

pretenfions; and all that a new Religion claimed, was to be let into partnerfhip with the reft, whofe common practice was to trade in fhares [x].   Yet according to this great Philofopher, *it was difficult, if not impoffible—it was combating all men in too many refpects.—It was not proceeding on a sufficient number of principles neceffary to be affented to,* &c. But he can make Men, as well as Religions, change their natures when he wants them for fome glorious mifchief.   It is his more ufual way, and fo it is of all his fellows, to make the People, (the grofs body of mankind) run headlong into Religion, without the leaft inquiry after evidence.   But here we are told it *is very difficult, if not impoffible,* to induce them to think well of a Religion which hath not the moft plaufible evidence for its fupport: That the not giving them this, is *not proceeding on a sufficient number of principles,* but *combating all men in too many refpects,* &c.

And this is all we can get out of him, FROM THE NATURE OF THINGS.   But as he has raifed a curiofity which he knew not how to gratify, I fhall endeavour to fupply his ignorance ; and, from this *nature of things,* fhew the reader, 1. How the Religions of MOSES and JESUS muft NECESSARILY SUPPOSE a *dependency* on fome preceding.   2. How the ancient Religions of paganifm muft NECESSARILY NOT SUPPOSE any fuch *dependency ;* and 3. How it came to pafs, that more modern Impoftors, rifen fince the coming of Chriftianity, imitated the true, rather than the falfe Religions of ancient times, in this pretence to *dependency.*

I. The PATRIARCHAL, the JEWISH, and the CHRISTIAN Religions, all profeffed to come from

[x] See the firft vol. part II. p. 36. & *feq.* 4th Ed.

the

the only one GOD, the Creator of all things. Now as the whole race of mankind muft be the common object of its Creator's care, all his Revelations, even thofe given only to a part, muft needs be thought ultimately directed to the intereft of the whole : confequently, every later Revelation muft fuppofe the TRUTH of the preceding. Again, when feveral fucceffive Revelations are given by him, fome lefs, fome more extenfive, we muft conclude them to be the parts of ONE ENTIRE DISPENSATION ; which, for reafons beft known to infinite Wifdom, are gradually enlarged and opened : confequently every later muft not only fuppofe the TRUTH of every preceding Revelation, but likewife their mutual RELATION and DEPENDENCY. Hence we fee, there may be weighty reafons, why *God, from the beginning, fhould have been conftantly giving a fucceffion of Difpenfations and Revelations* [y]; as this Author, with a lewd fneer, feems to take a pleafure in obferving. If therefore, what we call the true Revelation came from GOD, thefe Religions muft needs be, and profefs to be, dependent on one another.

II. Let us fee next how the cafe ftood in the ancient Pagan world. Their pretended Revelations were not from the ONE GOD ; but all from local tutelary Deities ; each of which was fuppofed to be employed in the care of his own Country or People, and unconcerned in every Other's department. Confequently, between earlier and later Revelations of this kind, there could be no more dependency, than there was oppofition : But each ftood on its own foundation, fingle, unrelated, and original.

[y] Page 22.

III. But

III. But when, by the propagation of the Gospel, the knowledge of the ONLY ONE GOD was spread abroad over the whole earth, and the absurdities of Polytheism fully understood by the people, an Impostor, who would now obtrude a new Religion on the world, must of necessity pretend to have received it from that *only one God.* But the probability of his giving a Revelation now, being seen greatly to depend on his having given one before, our Impostor would be forced to own the truth of those preceding Religions, which professed to come from that GOD. And as the credit of the new Religion was best advanced by its being thought a finishing part of an incomplete Dispensation, he would, at the same time, bottom it on the preceding. Besides, as an Impostor must needs want that necessary mark of a divine Mission, the power of Miracles, he could cover the want no otherwise than by a pretended relation to a Religion which had well established itself by Miracles. And thus, in fact, MAHOMET framed the idea of his imposture. He pretended his new Religion was the completion of Christianity, as Christianity was the completion of Judaism ; for that the world not being to be won by the mild and gentle invitations of Jesus, was now to be *compelled to enter in* by Mahomet. And so again, to complete the imitation, this last and greatest Prophet, as his followers believe him to be, is pretended to be foretold in the New Testament, as the Messiah was in the Old.

Thus this notable observation, from whence the Author *of the Grounds and Reasons of the Christian Religion* endeavoured to deduce so discrediting a likeness between all *false* religion, and what we

believers

believers hold to be the *true*, comes, we fee, juft to nothing.

But he has yet another flagrant mark of *like-ness*, in referve : And thus he goes on, from dif-covery to difcovery.—*In building thus upon* PRO-PHECY (fays he) *as a principle, Jefus and his Apoftles had the concurrence of all fects of Religion amongft the Pagans.* Is it poffible ? Yes. *For the Pagans uni-verfally built their Religion on* DIVINATION[z]. As much as to fay, the people of Amfterdam, in build-ing their town-houfe upon piles, had (in the mode of laying a foundation) the concurrence of all the cities in England ; who build theirs upon ftone, or clay, or gravel. In the Jewifh writings there are Prophecies of a future and more perfect Difpenfa-tion; which, Jefus claiming to belong to HIS, his Religion was properly built upon PROPHECIES. The Heathens made Gods of their dead benefactors, and then confulted them at their fhrines, as Oracles ; they infpected the entrails of beafts ; they obferved the flight of birds ; they interpreted dreams and uncommon phænomena ; and all thefe things they called DIVINATION. But what likenefs is there be-tween thefe things and Prophecies, the Prophecies on which Jefus founded his Religion ? Juft as much as there is between TRUTH and what thefe men call, FREE-THINKING. But he has found a device to bring them related. 'Tis a mafter-piece ; and the Reader fhall not be robbed of it. *They* [the Pagans] fays he, *learnt that art* [Divination] *in fchools, or under difcipline, as the Jews did prophefy-ing in the fchools and colleges of the Prophets; where, the learned Dodwell fays, the candidates for Prophecy*

[z] *Grounds and Reafons, &c.* p. 27, 28.

were taught the rules of divination praƈtiſed by the Pagans, who were ſkilled therein, and in poſſeſſion of the art long before them [a]. This idle whimſy of the *learned Dodwell* concerning the ſchools of the Prophets has been expoſed, as it deſerves, already [b]. But for the ſake of ſo extraordinary an argument, (an *impiety*, grafted on its proper ſtock an *abſurdity*) it deſerves to be admitted, tho' it be but for a moment. The reaſoning then ſtands thus : Divination was an art learnt in the ſchools ; ſo was one kind of Prophecy, or the Jewiſh art of divination : thoſe who learnt this Jewiſh art of divination were taught the rules of pagan divination : THEREFORE pagan divination and ANOTHER kind of Prophecy, ſuch as foretold the coming of the Meſſiah, were things of the ſame kind. Incomparable reaſoner! and deſervedly placed at the head of modern Free-thinking ! But his learning is equal to his ſenſe, and his premiſes juſt as true as his concluſion : *The Pagans univerſally built their Religion on divination.* I believe there are few ſchool-boys, who would not laugh at his blunder, and tell him it was juſt otherwiſe, *that the Pagans univerſally built divination on their Religion.* All that was ever *built on divination* was now and then a Shrine or a Temple. To return,

III.

But theſe prejudices, concerning local tutelary Deities, which made the introduƈtion of a Theocracy ſo eaſy, occaſioned as eaſy a defeƈtion from the Laws of it.

1, For theſe tutelary Deities owning one another's pretenſions, there was always a friendly intercourſe

---

[a] See p. 42, *& ſeq.* of this Vol.   [b] P. 28.

of

of mutual honours, tho' not always, of mutual worſhip. For at firſt, each God was ſuppoſed to be ſo taken up with his own people, as to have little leiſure or inclination to attend to the concerns of others.—Now this prejudice was the *firſt* ſource of the Jewiſh idolatry.

2. But the pretenſions of theſe Gods being thus reciprocally acknowledged; and Some, by the fortunate circumſtances of their followers, being riſen into ſuperior fame, the Rites uſed in their Worſhip were eagerly affected. And this was the *ſecond* ſource of the Iſraelites' idolatry; exemplified in the erection of the GOLDEN CALF, and their fondneſs for all Egyptian ſuperſtitions in general.

3. But of theſe tutelary deities their being two ſorts, GENTILITIAL and LOCAL; the one ambulatory, and the other ſtationed; the latter were fixed to their poſts, as a kind of *heir-loom*, which they who conquered and poſſeſſed the country, were obliged to maintain in their accuſtomed honours. And whatever *gentilitial* Gods a People might bring with them, yet the *local* God was to have a neceſſary ſhare in the religious Worſhip of the new Comers. Nay it was thought impiety even in foreigners, while they ſojourned only in a ſtrange Country, not to ſacrifice to the Gods of the place. Thus Sophocles makes Antigone ſay to her father, that a ſtranger ſhould both venerate and abhor thoſe things which are venerated and abhorred in the city where he reſides [c]. Celſus gives the reaſon of ſo much complaiſance.—" Becauſe

---

[c] Τόλμα ξεῖν☉.
Ἐπὶ ξείνης, ὦ τλᾶμοι, ὅ, τι
Καὶ πόλις τέτροφεν ἄφιλον
Ἀποςυγεῖν κỳ τὸ φίλον ςέϐεσθαι.   *Act.* i. *Oedip. Colon.*

(says he) the several parts of the world were, from the beginning, diftributed to several powers, each of which has his peculiar allotment and refidence[d]." And thofe who were loth to leave their paternal Gods when they fought new fettlements, at leaft held themfelves obliged to worfhip them with the Rites, and according to the ufages of the Country they came to inhabit. Againft this more qualified principle of Paganifm, Mofes thought fit to caution his People, in the following words : *When the Lord thy* GOD *fhall cut off the nations from before thee, whither thou goeft to poffefs them, and thou fucceedeft them and dwelleft in their land; take heed to thyfelf that thou be not fnared by follow-ing them, after that they be deftroyed from before thee, and that thou* ENQUIRE NOT AFTER THEIR GODS, *faying,* HOW *did thefe nations ferve their Gods? even* SO WILL I DO *likewife*[e]. But the adoption of thefe new Gods, as well as of their Rites, was fo general, that David makes his being unjuftly driven into an idolatrous land, the fame thing as being forced to ferve idolatrous Gods. For thus he ex-poftulates with his perfecutor, " Now therefore I " pray thee let my lord the king hear the words of " his fervant : If the Lord have ftirred thee up " againft me, let him accept an offering : but if they " be the children of men, curfed be they before " the Lord ; for they have driven me out this day " from abiding *in the inheritance of the Lord, faying,*

---

[d] — ἀλλὰ κỳ ὅτι, ὡς εἰκὲς, τὰ μέρη τῆς γῆς ἐξ ἀρχῆς ἄλλα ἄλλοις ἐπισπίαις ἐπιμεμημένα, κỳ καΐα τινας ἐπικραΐείας δισειλημμένα, ταύτη κỳ διοικεῖται. κỳ δὴ τὰ παρ᾽ ἐκάσοις ὀρθῶς αν πραΐοιΐο ταύτη δρώμενα, ὅτη ἐκείνοις φίλον, παραλύειν δὲ ἀχ ὅσιον εἴναι τὰ ἐξ ἀρχῆς καΐα τόπυς ινομισμένα. *Orig. cont. Celf.* lib. v. p. 247. See the paffage, from *Plato*, p. 230, 231.

[e] DEUT. xii. 29, 30.

" GO SERVE OTHER GODS [f]." To the fame principle
Jeremiah likewife alludes, in the following words,
Therefore will I caft you out of this land, into a land
that ye know not, neither ye nor your fathers: and
THERE SHALL YE SERVE OTHER GODS *day and*
night, where I will not fhew you favour [g]. By
which is not meant that they fhould be *forced*, any
otherwife than by the fuperftitious dread of divine vengeance for a flighted worfhip: for at this
time civil reftraint in matters of religion was very
rare.

But the imaginary vengeance which the tutelary
GOD was fuppofed to take on thofe, who, inhabiting
his Land, yet flighted his Worfhip, was at length
really taken on the idolatrous Cutheans, when they
came to cultivate the land of Ifrael. For the Almighty having, in condefcenfion to the prejudices
of the Ifraelites, affumed the title of a TUTELARY
LOCAL GOD, and chofen Judea for his peculiar
regency; it appeared but fit that he fhould dif-
charge, in good earneft, the imaginary function
of thofe tutelary GODS, in order to diftinguifh
himfelf from *the lying Vanities* of that infatuated
age. Therefore when fo great a portion of his
Chofen people had been led captive, and a mixt
rabble of Eaftern idolaters were put into their
place, he fent plagues amongft them for their pro-
fanation of the holy Land. Which calamity their
own principles eafily enabled them to account for.
The ftory is told in thefe words: " And the king
" of Affyria brought men from Babylon, and from
" Cuthah, and from Ava, and from Hamath,
" and from Sepharvaim, and placed them in the
" cities of Samaria, inftead of the children of

[f] 1 SAM. xxvi. 19.   [g] Chap. xvi. ver. 13.

" Ifrael;

" Ifrael; and they poffeffed Samaria, and dwelt
" in the cities thereof.   And fo it was, at the be-
" ginning of their dwelling there, that they fear-
" ed not the Lord; therefore the Lord fent lions
" amongft them which flew fome of them.   Where-
" fore they fpake to the king of Affyria, fay-
" ing, The nations which thou haft removed, and
" placed in the cities of Samaria KNOW NOT THE
" MANNER OF THE GOD OF THE LAND : therefore
" he hath fent lions amongft them ; and behold
" they flay them, becaufe they know not the man-
" ner of the God of the land.   Then the king of
" Affyria commanded, faying, Carry thither one of
" the Priefts — and let him teach them *the manner*
" *of the God of the land.*——Then one of the Priefts
" came and dwelt in Bethel, and taught them
" how they fhould fear the Lord.   Howbeit every
" nation made Gods of their own—every nation
" in their cities wherein they dwelt.—So thefe
" nations feared the Lord and ferved their graven
" images, both their children and their childrens
" children, as did their fathers, fo do they unto
" this day [h]."

But leaft this account of the miraculous interpofition fhould be mifunderftood as an encouragement of the notion of local Gods, or of *in-*
tercommunity of worfhip, rather than a vindication of the fanctity of that Country, which was
confecrated to the God of Ifrael, the facred Hiftorian goes on to acquaint us with the perverfe influence this judgment had on the new inhabitants,
fo contrary to the divine intention.   " They
" feared the Lord, and ferved their own Gods
" after the manner of the nations, whom they

[h] 2 KINGS xvii. 24. *& feq.*

" carried

" carried away from thence.   Unto this day, they
" do after the former manners : they fear not the
" Lord, neither do they after their ftatutes, or after
" their ordinances, or after the Law and Com-
" mandment which the Lord commanded the
" children of Jacob whom he named Ifrael[1]."
They feared the Lord and ferved their own Gods;
that is, they feared the vengeance impending on
the exclufion of the Worfhip of the God of Ifrael.
But *they feared not the Lord, neither did after their*
Statutes.   That is, they tranfgreffed the Commandment which they found fo frequently repeated
in the Pentateuch, of joining no other Worfhip to
that of the God of Ifrael.

. .And this was the true reafon why the Kings of
Perfia and Syria, (when Judea afterwards became a
province to them) fo frequently appointed facrifices
to be offered to the *God of the land,* at Jerufalem,
in behalf of themfelves and families.   Nor was
the practice difufed when the Jews fell under the
Roman yoke ; both Julius Cæfar and Auguftus
making the fame provifion for the *felicity* of the
Empire.

Hence therefore the *third* fource of the Jewifh
idolatries.   It was this fuperftitious reverence to
local Deities within their own departments, which
made them fo devoted, while in Egypt, to the
Gods of that Country ; and when in poffeffion of
their own land, to the tutelary Gods of Canaan.

But this *intercommunity* of Worfhip, begun by
the migration of People and Colonies from one
country to another, grew more general, as thofe

migrations became more frequent. 'Till at length the frequency, aided by many other concurrent caufes (occafionally taken notice of in feveral places of this work) made the *intercommunity* univerfal: And this was the *laſt* fource of Jewifh idolatries. This drew them into the fervice of every God they heard of; or from whom they fancied any fpecial good might be obtained; efpecially the Gods of all great and powerful Nations. Thefe prejudices of opinion, joined to thofe of practice which they had learnt in Egypt, where the true caufes of their fo frequent lapfe into idolatry.

From all this it appears, that their defection from the GOD of Ifrael, wicked and abominable as it was, did not however confift in the rejecting him as a falfe God, or in renouncing the Law of Mofes as a falfe Religion; but only, in joining foreign Worfhip and idolatrous Ceremonies to the Ritual of the true GOD. Their bias to the ido- latries of Egypt was inveterate cuftom; their in- clination for the idolatries of Canaan was a prevail- ing principle that the tutelary God of the place fhould be worfhiped by its inhabitants; and their motive for all other idolatries, a vain expectation of good from the guardian Gods of famous and happy Nations.

Thefe were all inflamed by that common ftimu- lation of a debauched People, the luxurious and immoral rites of Paganifm; for it is to be obferv- ed that thefe defections generally happened amidft the abufes of profperity. There is a remarkable paffage in the Book of Jofhua which fets this matter in a very clear light. The Ifraelites having lapfed into idolatry, Jofhua drew together their Heads and Rulers at Shechem, in order to a reformation.

And the topic, he infifts upon for this purpofe, is not, that the God of Ifrael was the only true God, the Maker of all things; but that he was the family-God of the race of Abraham, for which he had done fo great things. And this he profecutes from the 2d verfe of the xxiv. chap. to the 13th. His conclufion from all is, " Now therefore fear the " Lord and *ferve him in fincerity, and in truth,* " and put away the Gods which your Fathers " ferved on the other fide of the flood and in " Egypt ᵏ." However (continues he) at leaft make your choice, and either ferve the Lord, or ferve the Gods of other People. ". *And the people* " *anfwered, God forbid we fhould forfake the Lord to* " *ferve other Gods* ˡ: for we acknowledge him to " be that God who has done fo great things for " us." To this Jofhua replies, " *Ye cannot ferve* " *the Lord; for he is an holy God: he is a jealous* " *God, he will not forgive your tranfgreffions, nor* " *your fins* ᵐ." From all this, it appears, that the point debated between Jofhua and his People, was not whether the Ifraelites fhould return to God, whom they had rejected and forfaken; but whether they fhould ferve him ONLY, or, as Jofhua expreffes it, *ferve him in fincerity and in truth.* For on their exclaiming againft the impiety of rejecting God, —" *God forbid, we fhould forfake the Lord*; we will " ftill ferve him ;" meaning along with the other Gods,—their Leader replies, *Ye cannot ferve the Lord, for he is an* HOLY *God: he is a* JEALOUS *God.* *i. e.* As a *holy God,* he will not be ferved with the lewd and polluted Rites of the Nations; and as a *jealous God,* he will not fuffer you to ferve Idols of wood and ftone with his Rites. The confequence is, You muft ferve him alone, and only with that worfhip which he himfelf hath appointed.

ᵏ Ver. 14.   ˡ Ver. 16, 17.   ᵐ Ver 19.

That

That this was the whole of their Idolatry, is farther seen from the accounts which the holy Prophets give us of it, in their reproofs and expostulations.

Isaiah says, *To what purpose is the multitude of your Sacrifices unto me, saith the Lord: I am full of the Burnt-offerings of Rams, and the Fat of fed Beasts, &c* [n]. To whom are these words addressed: To those who, besides their numerous Immoralities, there reckoned up at large, delighted in idolatrous worship in *Groves* and *high Places.* For the Denunciation is thus continued: *They shall be ashamed of the* Oaks *which ye have desired, and ye shall be confounded for the* Gardens *that ye have chosen* [o]. He describes them again in this manner: *A People that provoketh me to Anger continually* to my face, *that sacrificeth in Gardens; and burneth Incense upon Altars of Brick* [p]. Yet, at the same time, these men gloried so much in being the peculiar People of the Lord, that they said, *Stand by thyself, come not near to me, for I am holier than thou* [q].

Jeremiah draws them in the very same colours: *Though they say, The Lord liveth, surely they swear falsly* [r], i. e. vainly, idolatrously. Why? The Reason is given soon after; they swore likewise by their idols: *How shall I pardon thee for this? thy Children have forsaken me, and* sworn by them that are no Gods [s]. Again, *Will ye steal, murder, and commit adultery, and* swear falsly *and* burn incense unto Baal, *and walk after other Gods that ye know not;* [i. e. strange Gods]

[n] Chap. i. ver. 11.   [o] Ver. 29.   [p] Chap. lxv. ver. 3.   [q] Ver. 5.   [r] Chap. v. ver. 2.   [s] Ver. 7.

O 2   *and*

and come and STAND BEFORE ME IN THIS HOUSE,
*which is called by my Name, and say, We are delivered
to do all these Abominations* ᵗ *?* And in another place
we find them thus expostulating with the Prophet,
—*Wherefore hath the Lord pronounced all this Evil
against us? or what is our Iniquity, or what is our
Sin that we have committed against the Lord our* GOD ᵘ *?*
and the Prophet answering them in this manner,
—*because your Fathers have forsaken me, saith the
Lord, and walked after other Gods, and have served
them, and have worshiped them, and have foresaken
me, and have not kept my Law : And ye have done
worse than your Fathers* ˣ. But is it possible they
could be so exceeding stupid or impudent as to
talk at this rate, had they ever renounced the RE-
LIGION, or the GOD of their Forefathers?

EZEKIEL, likewise, shews plainly that their idolatries consisted in polluting the Religion of Moses
with foreign worship : " Son of man, these men
" have set up their idols in their heart, and put
" the stumbling-block of their iniquity before their
" Face : SHALL I BE INQUIRED OF *at all by them?*
" Therefore speak unto them, and say unto them,
" Thus saith the Lord GOD, Every man of the
" house of Israel that putteth up his idols in his
" heart, and putteth the stumbling-block of ini-
" quity before his face, and *cometh to the Prophet*, I
" the Lord will answer him that cometh according
" to the multitude of his idols ʸ, *&c.*" And
again : *As for you, O house of Israel, Thus saith the
Lord God, Go ye, serve ye every one his idols, and
hereafter also, if ye will not hearken unto me : but*
POLLUTE YE MY HOLY NAME NO MORE *with your*

ᵗ Chap. vii. ver. 9, 10.   ᵘ Chap. xvi. ver. 10.
ˣ Ver. 11, 12.   ʸ Chap. xiv. ver. 3, 4.

gifts and with your idols[z], i. e. with gifts offered
up to me with idolatrous Rites.   In another place
he giveth a terrible inſtance of this horrid mixture:
" They have committed adultery, and blood is in
" their hands, and with their idols have they com-
" mitted adultery, and have alſo cauſed their ſons,
" whom they bare unto me, to paſs for them
" through the fire to devour them.   Moreover
" this they have done unto me : THEY HAVE DE-
" FILED MY SANCTUARY IN THE SAME DAY,
" and have profaned my Sabbaths.   For when
" they had ſlain their Children to their idols, then
" THEY CAME THE SAME DAY INTO MY SANC-
" TUARY to profane it ; and lo, thus have they
" done in the midſt of mine houſe [a]."   Theſe, and
innumerable other paſſages in the Prophets to the
ſame purpoſe, evidently ſhew, that this defection
from the God of Iſrael conſiſted not in a rejection
of Him, or of his Law.

This appears ſtill more evident from the following conſiderations :

1. That, in the courſe of their idolatries, they
abuſed the memorials of their own Diſpenſation to
ſuperſtitious Worſhip.   Such·as the *Brazen Serpent*
of Moſes; to which, in the time of their kings,
they paid divine honours [b].   And I am much
miſtaken if the monument of *Twelve ſtones*, taken
out of Jordan, and pitched in Gilgal for a memorial of their miraculous paſſage [c], was not equally abuſed.   What induces me to think ſo, is the
following paſſage of ISAIAH : " Draw near hither,
" ye ſons of the ſorcereſs, the ſeed of the adulterer

---

[z] Chap. xx. ver. 39.   [a] Chap. xxiii. ver. 37,——39.
[b] 2 KINGS xviii. 4.   [c] JOSH. iv. 3, 20, 21, 22.

" and

" and the whore. Againſt whom do you ſport
" yourſelves ?—enflaming yourſelves with idols
" under every green tree, ſlaying the children in
" the valleys under the clifts of the rocks ?
" AMONG THE SMOOTH STONES OF THE STREAM
" IS THY PORTION; they, they are thy lot: EVEN
" TO THEM HÁST THOU POURED A DRINK-OFFER-
" ING, thou haſt offered a meat-offering. Should
" I receive comfort in theſe ᵈ ?"

2 The Iſraelites were moſt prone to idolatry in
PROSPEROUS TIMES; and generally returned to the
God of their fathers in ADVERSITY, as appears
from their whole hiſtory. Againſt this impotence
of mind they were more than once cautioned, before they entered into the Land of Bleſſings, that
they might afterwards be left without excuſe.
" And it ſhall be (ſays Moſes) when the Lord
" thy GOD ſhall have brought thee into the land
" which he ſware unto thy fathers, to Abraham,
" to Iſaac, and to Jacob, to give thee, great and
" goodly cities which thou buildeſt not, and houſes
" full of all good things which thou filledſt not,
" and wells digged which thou diggeſt not, vine-
" yards and olive-trees which thou plantedſt not,
" when thou ſhalt have eaten and be full; then
" beware left thou forget the Lord which brought
" thee forth out of the Land of Egypt from
" the houſe of bondage. Thou ſhalt fear the
" Lord thy GOD and ſerve him, and ſhalt ſwear
" by his name. Ye ſhall not go after other Gods,
" of the Gods of the people which are round about
" you ᶜ." However Moſes himſelf lived to ſee
an example of this perverſity, while they remained

ᵈ ISAIAH lvii. 3, & *ſeq.*
and chap. viii. ver. 11, & *ſeq.*

ᶜ DEUT. vi. 10, & *ſeq:*

in

in the Wildernefs : *But Jeshurun* (fays he) *waxed fat, and kicked : Thou art waxen fat, thou art grown thick, thou art covered with fatnefs; then he forfook God which made him, and lightly efteemed the Rock of his Salvation*[f]. And the Prophet HOSEA affures us, that the Day of profperity was the conſtant feafon of their idolatry : *Ifrael is an empty vine, he bringeth forth fruit unto himfelf:* ACCORDING TO THE MULTITUDE OF HIS FRUIT, HE HATH INCREASED THE ALTARS; ACCORDING TO THE GOODNESS OF HIS LAND THEY HAVE MADE GOODLY IMAGES[g]. And again: *According to their pafture fo were they filled;* THEY WERE FILLED, AND THEIR HEART WAS EXALTED : *therefore have they forgotten me*[h]. This, therefore, is a clear proof that their defection from the God of Ifrael was not any doubt of his goodnefs or his power, but a wanton abufe of his bleffings. Had they queftioned the truth of the Law, their behaviour had been naturally otherwife: they would have adhered to it in times of profperity; and would have left it in adverfity and trouble. This the Deifts would do well to confider.

3. The terms, in which God's warnings againft this defection are expreffed, plainly fhew that their lapfe into Idolatry was no rejection of him : he will have no FELLOWSHIP or COMMUNION with falfe Gods. The names employed to defign their idolatries are ADULTERY and WHOREDOM. And God's refentment of their defection, is perpetually expreffed by the fame metaphor : which fhews that his right over them was ftill acknowledged, juft as an adulterous wife owns the hufband's right,

[f] DEUT. xxxii. 15.   [g] Chap. x. ver. 1.   [h] Chap. xiii. ver. 6.

amidft

amidſt all her pollutions with ſtrangers. Where, we may obſerve, that though their idolatry is ſo conſtantly ſtyled ADULTERY, yet that of the Pagans never is; though it is very often called WHOREDOM. The reaſon of this diſtinction is plainly intimated in the following words of Ezekiel : " How weak " is thine heart, ſaith the Lord God, ſeeing " thou doſt all theſe things, the work of an " imperious whoriſh woman ? In that thou buildeſt " thine eminent place in the head of every way, " and makeſt thine high place in every ſtreet, and " has NOT BEEN AS AN HARLOT (in that thou " ſcorneſt hire) but AS A WIFE that committeth " ADULTERY, which taketh ſtrangers inſtead of " her huſband [i]." The Jews had entered into a covenant with God, which had made them his Peculiar : and when they had violated their plighted faith, they ſtood in that relation to him which an ADULTRESS does to her injured huſband. The Gentiles, on the contrary, had entered into no *excluſive* engagements with their Gods, but the practice of *intercommunity* had proſtituted them, as a common HARLOT, to all comers.

Thus much, however, muſt be confeſſed, that though the very worſt of their idolatry conſiſted only in mixing foreign Worſhip with their own; yet, in their mad attention to thoſe abominable things, God's Worſhip was often ſo extremely neglected, that He ſays, by the Prophet, *They have forſaken me, the fountain of living waters,* juſt as the Saint-worſhipers in the Church of Rome forſake God, when in their private devotions the Vulgar think only of their tutelary Saints.

---

[i] Chap. xvi. ver. 30, 31, 32.

The

The several principal parts, therefore, of the Israelitish idolatry were these,

1. Worshiping the true GOD under an image, such as the *golden Calves*, 1 KINGS xii. 28.

2. Worshiping him in Places forbidden, as in *Groves*, 2 KINGS xviii. 22.   Is. xxxvi. 7.

3. And by idolatrous Rites, such as *cutting themselves with knives*, JER. xli. 5.

4. By profaning the house of GOD with *idolatrous images*, JER. xxxii. 34.

5. By worshiping the *true* GOD *and Idols together*.

6. And lastly, by worshiping *idols alone*, JER. ii. 13. Yet by what follows, ver. 35. it appears, that even this was not a total apostacy from God.

If the Reader would know what use I intend to make of this account of the Jewish idolatry, to the main Question of my Work, I must crave his patience till we come to the last Volume.   If he would know what other use may be made of it, he may consider what hath been said above ; and be farther pleased to observe, that it obviates the objection of a sort of men equally unskilled in sacred and profane Antiquity ; (of whom more by and by) who, from this circumstance of the perpetual defection of the Jews into idolatry, would conclude that the Dispensation of GOD to them could never have been so illustrious as their history hath represented it. The strength of which objection rests on these two suppositions, that their idolatry
consisted

confifted in renouncing the Law of Mofes: And renouncing it as diffatisfied of its truth.   Both which
fuppofitions we have fhewn to be falfe: the neglect
of the law, during their moft idolatrous practice,
being no other than their preferring impure novel
Rites (which moft ftrongly engage the attention of
a fuperftitious people) to old ones, whofe fanctity
has no carnal allurements.   As to its original from
God, they never entertained the leaft doubt concerning it; or that the God of Ifrael was the Creator
of the Univerfe: They had been better inftructed.
—*Thus faith the Lord*, the HOLY ONE OF ISRAEL
and HIS MAKER [k]. — As much as to fay, the tutelary God of Ifrael is the Creator of the Univerfe:
Indeed, in the period juft preceding their Captivity, when the *extraordinary* providence was gradually withdrawing from them (a matter to be confidered hereafter more at large) they began to entertain
fufpicions of God's farther regard to them, *as his
chofen people*.   But that nothing of this ever contributed to their idolatry is plain from what we have
fhewn above, of its being a wanton defection in
the midft of peace, profperity, and abundance,
(the confeffed effects of the *extraordinary* providence
of the God of Ifrael) and of their conftantly returning to him in times of difficulty and diftrefs.

It is true, that this ftate of the cafe, which removes the infidel objection, at the fame time difcovers a moft enormous perverfity in that People;
who, although convinced of the truth of a Religion
forbidding all *intercommunity*, was forever running
aftray after foreign Worfhip.   However, would
we but tranfport ourfelves into thefe times, and remember what hath been faid of that great principle

k ISAIAH xlv. 11.

of

of INTERCOMMUNITY OF WORSHIP; and how early and deeply the Jews had imbibed all the essential superstitions of Paganism, we should not only abate of our wonder, but see good cause to make large allowances to this unhappy People.

But there is another circumstance in this affair too remarkable to be passed by in silence. As fond as the Jews were of borrowing their Neighbours' Gods, we do not find, by any hints in ancient history, either profane or sacred, that their Neighbours were disposed to borrow theirs. Nay, we are assured, by Holy Writ, that they did not. GOD, by the Prophet Ezekiel, addressing himself to the Jews, speaks on this wise :—*And the contrary is in thee from other women in thy* WHOREDOMS, WHEREAS NONE FOLLOWETH THEE TO, COMMIT WHOREDOMS : *and in that thou givest a reward, and no reward is given to thee ; therefore thou art contrary* [1]. I have shewn, elsewhere, that, by this, is meant, that no Gentile nation borrowed the Jewish Rites of Worship, to join them to their own. For as to Proselytes, or particular men converted to the service of the true God, we find a prodigious number in the Days of David and Solomon [m]. So again, in the Prophet Jeremiah, HATH A NATION CHANGED THEIR GODS, WHICH ARE YET NO GODS ? *But my people have changed their glory for that which doth not profit* [n]; *i. e.* Hath any of the Nations brought in the God of Israel into the number of their *false* Gods, as the Israelites have brought in theirs to stand in fellowship with the *true ?* For that the Nations frequently changed their tutelary Gods, or one idol for another, is too notorious to need any proof.

[1] Chap. xvi. ver. 34.   [m] 2 CHRON. ii. 17.
[n] Chap. ii. ver. 11.

This then is remarkable. The two principal reasons of the contrariety, I suppose, were these:

1. It was a thing well known to all the neighbouring Nations, that the God of Israel had an abhorrence of all *community* or alliance with the Gods of the Gentiles. This unsociable temper would deter those people (who all held him as a tutelary Deity of great power) from ever bringing him into the fellowship of their country Gods. For, after such declarations, they could not suppose his company would prove very propitious. And in truth, they had a single instance of his ill neighbourhood, much to their cost; which brings me to the second reason.

2. The devastation he brought upon the Philistines, while the ARK rested in their quarters. For they having taken it from the Israelites in battle, carried it, as another *Palladium* °, to Ashdod, and placed it in the temple of their God Dagon; who passed two so bad nights with his new Guest, that on the second morning he was found pared

---

° For this was the only use the Pagans ever thought of making of the Gods of their enemies when they had stolen them, or taken them away by force. Apion had mentioned one Zabidus an Idumean, who, when the Jews were warring against his countrymen, made a bargain with the enemy to deliver Apollo, one of their tutelary Gods, into their hands: and Josephus, when he comes to confute this idle tale, takes it for granted that the only supposed cause of such pretended traffic was to gain a new tutelary Deity; and on this, founds his argument against Apion: *How then,* says he, *can Apion persist in accusing us of not having Gods in common with others, when our forefathers were so easily persuaded to believe that Apollo was coming into their service?* Τί δ᾽ ἡμῶν ἔτι καλησορεῖ τὸ μὴ κοινὰς ἔχειν τοῖς ἄλλοις Θεὸς, εἰ ῥαδίως ὅτως ἐπείσθησαν οἱ πατέρες ἡμῶν, ἥξειν τὸν Ἀπόλλωνα πρὸς αὐτὸς. Vol. ii. p. 478.

away

away to his *fishy stump* [p]: And this difaster was followed with a defolating peftilence. The people of Afhdod, who hitherto had intended to keep the Ark as one of their Idol-protectors, now declare *it should not abide with them, for that the hand of the* God of Israel *was fore upon them, and upon Dagon their God* [q]. They fent it therefore to Gath, another of their cities; and thefe having carried it about in a religious proceffion, it made the fame havock amongft them [r]. It was then removed a third time, with an intent to fend it to Ekron; but the men of that city, terrified with the two preceding calamities, refufed to receive it, faying *they had brought the Ark of the God of Ifrael, to flay them and their people* [s]. At length the Philiftines by fad experience, were brought to underftand, that it was the beft courfe to fend it back to its owners: which they did with great honour; with gifts and trefpafs-offerings, to appeafe the offended Divinity [u]. And from this time we hear no more of any attempts amongft the gentile Nations to join the Jewifh Worfhip to their own. They confidered the God of Ifrael as a tutelary Deity, abfolutely UN-SOCIABLE; who would have nothing to do with any but his own People, or with fuch Particulars as would worfhip him alone; and therefore, in this refpect, different from all other tutelary Gods; each of which was willing to live in community with all the reft. This, the hiftorian Jofephus underftood to be their fentiment, when he makes the Midianitifh women addrefs the young men of Ifrael in the following manner : *Nor ought you to be blamed for honouring thofe Gods which belong to the*

---

[p] 1 Sam. v. 4, 5.   [q] Ver. 7.   [s] Ver. 9.
[r] Ver. 10.   [u] Chap. vi. ver. 3.

Country where you fojourn [x]. *Befides, our Gods are* COMMON TO ALL THE NATIONS, *yours to* NONE OF THEM [y].

And thus the matter refted, till occafion requiring that God fhould vindicate his property in that Country which he had chofen for his peculiar refidence, as a tutelary Deity. He then drove the Pagan inhabitants of Samaria into his worfhip, juft as he had driven the Philiftines from it : and, in both cafes, hath afforded to his fervants the moft illuftrious proofs of divine wifdom, in his manner of conducting this wonderful Œconomy to its completion.

But from this circumftance of the inability of the Law to prevent the Ifraelites from falling thus frequently into idolatry, a noble Writer [z] has thought fit to ground a charge of impofture againft the Lawgiver. It would therefore look like prevarication to let fo fair an opportunity, pafs by without vindicating the Truth from his mifreprefentations ; efpecially when the nature and caufes of that idolatry, as here explained, tend fo directly to expofe all his pompous fophiftry.

" One of the moft conceivable perfections of a
" law is, (fays his Lordfhip) that it be made with
" fuch a forefight of all poffible accidents, and

---

[x] See what hath been faid above concerning this imaginary obligation.

[y] Μέμψαιτο δ᾽ ἐδεὶς, εἰ γῆς εἰς ἣν ἀφίχθε τὲς ἰδίας αὐτῆς Θεὺς προτρέποισθε᾽ κỳ ταῦτα. τῶν μὲν ἡμεῖέρων κοινῶν ὄντων πρὸς ἄπαιλας, τῶ δ᾽ ὑμιῶέρα πρὸς μηδένα τοιῶτα τυγχάνοντ᾽. *Antiq. Jud.* l. iv. c. 6. Sect. 8.

[z] Lord Bolingbroke.

" with

" with such provisions for the due execution of it
" in all cases, that the law may be effectual to
" govern and direct these accidents, instead of
" lying at the mercy of them. Such a law would
" produce its effect, by a certain moral necessity
" resulting from itself, and not by the help of
" any particular conjuncture. We are able to
" form some general notions of laws thus per-
" fect; but to make them, is above humanity.
" ———To apply these reflections to the Law of
" Moses—We cannot read the Bible without be-
" ing convinced, that no law ever operated so
" weak and uncertain an effect as the Law of
" Moses did. Far from prevailing against acci-
" dents and conjunctures, the least was sufficient
" to interrupt the course and to defeat the designs
" of it; to make that people not only neglect
" the Law, but ceafe to acknowledge the Legif-
" lator. To prevent this, was the first of these
" designs; and if the second was, as it was, no
" doubt, and as it is the design or pretence of all
" laws, to secure the happiness of the people,
" THIS DESIGN WAS DEFEATED AS FULLY AS
" THE OTHER; for the whole history of this
" people is one continued series of infractions of
" the Law, and of national calamities. So that
" this law, considered as the particular law of this
" nation, has proved more ineffectual than any
" other law perhaps that can be quoted. If this
" be ascribed to the hardness of heart and obsti-
" nacy of the people, in order to save the honour
" of the Law, this honour will be little saved,
" and its divinity ill maintained. This excuse
" may be admitted in the cafe of any human law;
" but we speak here of a law supposed to be
" dictated by divine Wisdom, which ought, and
" which would have been able, if it had been
" such,

" fuch, to keep, in a ftate of fubmiffion to it,
" and of national profperity, even a people re-
" bellious and obftinate enough to break through
" any other. If it be faid the Law became inef-
" fectual by the fault of thofe who governed the
" people, their Judges and their Kings, let it be
" remembered that their Judges and their Kings
" were of GOD's appointment, for the moft part
" at leaft ; that he himfelf is faid to have been
" their King during feveral ages; that his pre-
" fence remained amongft them, even after they
" had depofed him; and that the High Prieft
" confulted him, on any emergency, by the Urim
" and Thummim. Occafional miracles were
" wrought to inforce the Law, but this was a
" ftanding miracle that might ferve both to explain
" and inforce it, by the wifdom and authority of
" the Legiflator, as often as immediate recourfe
" to him was neceffary. Can it be denied that
" the moft imperfect fyftem of human laws would
" have been rendered effectual by fuch means as
" thefe [a] ?"

I. The fum of his Lordfhip's reafoning amounts
to this, " That the Jewifh Law being ordained
for a certain end, it betrays its impofture by never
being able to attain that end. For, firft, if *infinite
Wifdom* framed the Law, it muft be moft perfect ;
and it is effential to the perfection of a mean, for
a Law is nothing but a mean, that it attain its
end. Secondly, if *infinite Power* adminiftered it,
that Power muft have rendered even the moft
imperfect fyftem effectual to its purpofe."

[a] Lord Bolingbroke's Works, vol. iii. p. 292, 293, 294.
Quarto Edition.

Thus,

Thus, we fee, his Argument, when reduced to order, divides itfelf into thefe two branches; Confiderations drawn, firft, from the *Wifdom,* and, then, from the *Power* of the Deity, to difcredit his workmanfhip.

1. We will take him at his beft, with the improvement of order; and firft examine his conclufions from the circumftance of *infinite Wifdom's framing the Law.*

Let us admit then for a moment, that his reprefentation of the *end* of the Law is exact; and that his affertion of its never gaining its end, is true: I anfwer, that this objection to the divine original of the JEWISH LAW holds equally againft the divine original of that Law of Nature, called the MORAL LAW. Now his Lordfhip pretends to believe that the *Moral Law* came from GOD: nay, that He was fo entirely the Author and Creator of it, that if he had fo pleafed, he might have made it effentially different from what it is. But yet the experience of all ages hath fhewn, that this Law *prevailed* ftill lefs *againft accidents and conjunctures* than the Mofaic. For if the Jews were always tranfgreffing their Law till the Captivity, yet after that difafter they as fcrupuloufly adhered to it; and in that attachment have continued ever fince: whereas, from the day the MORAL LAW was firft given to mankind, to this prefent hour, *the leaft accident was fufficient to interrupt the courfe,* and to *defeat the defigns of it.* How happened it therefore, that this acknowledged Law of GOD did not *govern and direct accidents, inftead of lying at the mercy of them?* Was it lefs *perfect* in its kind than the Mofaic? Who will pretend to fay That, who believes the Moral Law came directly from GOD, and was delivered intimately to Man, for the fervice of the whole Species ; while the Jewifh Law came lefs directly from him, as being conveyed thro' the miniftry of Mofes, for the fole ufe of the Jewifh People?

To thefe queftions his Lordfhip would be ready to anfwer, "That it is neceffary for the fubjects of a moral law to be endowed with free Will : That free Will may be abufed ; and that fuch abufes may render the moft *perfect* fyftem of Laws ineffectual." But this anfwer turns upon his Lordfhip, when applied to the defence of the Mofaic Law ; and turns with redoubled force.

We fee then how much he was miftaken in concluding, that, becaufe *perfection in its kind* is one of the effential qualities of a divine Law, therefore fuch a law muft of *neceffity* produce its effect. His beft reafon for this fancy is, that *he is able to form fome general notions of Laws thus perfect.* Which is no more than telling us, (notwithftanding his parade of infinuated ability) that he is able to conceive how the Will may be controlled, and how Man may be transformed into a Machine. It is true, he owns, that this fact, viz. *to make laws thus perfect, is above humanity.* It is fo ; and let me add, as much *below the Divinity*; whofe glory it is to draw his reafonable creatures with the *cords of a man.* A Law then, which produces its effects by a *certain neceffity*, muft do it by a neceffity which is *phyfical*, and not *moral*; it being the quality of *phyfical*, not of *moral neceffity*, that its effects cannot poffibly be *defeated.*

Thus, we fee, all there is of truth in his Lordfhip's affertion, of its being *effential to the perfection of a mean that it attain its end*, amounts only to
this,

this, A capacity in ſuch a *mean* to attain its end, naturally and of itſelf.   And this, we ſay, was the condition of the Moſaic Law ; whatever might be the actual ſucceſs.

The qualities of a Law capable of producing its effect, are to be ſought for à priori, as the Schools ſpeak, and not à poſteriori : And if here we find intrinſic marks of excellence in the particular Laws; of conſummate wiſdom in the general Frame and Conſtitution of them ; and can likewiſe diſcover thoſe *accidents*, which, at ſome periods of the Diſpenſation, hindred the *effect* ; we have done all that human reaſon can require, to vindicate this divine Law, from his Lordſhip's imputations of impoſture.

To treat this matter as it deſerves, would require a volume, tho' not ſo large as his Lordſhip's.   But a few words will ſuffice to give the reader a general idea of the truth.   And a general idea will be ſufficient to ſhew the futility of the objection.

The admirable proviſion made by the Jewiſh Law for preventing idolatry, may be ſeen in the following inſtances.

1. That each ſpecific Rite had a natural tendency to oppoſe, or to elude, the ſtrong propenſity to idolatrous Worſhip, by turning certain Pagan obſervances, with which the People were beſotted, upon a proper Object.—Hence that CONFORMITY between Jewiſh and Pagan Ceremonies, which ſo vainly alarms, and ſo vainly flatters, both the friends and enemies of Revelation.

2. That by their multiplicity, and the frequent returns of their celebration, they kept the People

conftantly bufied and employed; fo as to afford
fmall time or leifure for the running into the forbidden fuperftitions of Paganifm.

3. That the immediate benefits which followed
the punctual obfervance of the Law had a natural
tendency to keep them attached to it.

4. But laftly, and above all, that the admirable
coincidency between the *Inftitute of Law* and the
Adminiftration of Government, (whereby the Magiftrate was enabled to punifh idolatry with death,
without violating the rights of Mankind) went
as far towards the actual prevention of idolatrous
Worfhip, as, according to human conceptions,
Civil Law, whether of human or divine original,
could poffibly go. And refting the matter here, I
fuppofe, one might fafely defy his Lordfhip, with
all his legiflative talents, and his vain boaft of
them, *to form any general notions of a law more perfect*.

But this reafoning on the natural efficacy of the
Mofaic Law, by its innate virtue, to prevent and to
reftrain Idolatry, which it did not at all times, in
fact, prevent and reftrain, will be further fupported by this confideration: That the circumftance
which, from time to time, occafioned a defection
from the Law, was neither an indifpofition to its
eftablifhment; nor any incoherence in its general
Frame and Conftitution; nor averfion to any particular part, nor yet a debility or weaknefs in its
Sanctions. The fole caufe of the defection was an
inveterate prejudice, exterior and foreign to the
Law. The Ifraelites, in their houfe of bondage,
had been brought up in the principles of LOCAL
AND TUTELAR DEITIES and INTERCOMMUNITY OF
WORSHIP; principles often referred to, on various
occafions,

occasions, in the course of this work, for the illustration of the most important truths.   In these Principles, they saw the whole race of mankind agree :
and, from the Practice of them, in the worship of
tutelar Deities, they thought they saw a world of
good ready to arise.   But not only the hope of good,
but the fear of evil drew them still more strongly
into this road of folly.   Their Egyptian education
had early impressed that bugbear-notion of a set of
local Deities, who expected their dues of all who
came to inhabit the country which they had honoured with their protection [b]; and severely resented
the neglect of payment, on all new comers.   This
will easily account for the frequent defections of the
Israelities in the divided service of the Gods of Canaan.—But it is difficult for men fixed down to the
impressions of modern manners, to let themselves
into distant Times; or to feel the force of motives
whose operations they have never experienced :
Therefore, to convince such men that the early Jewish defections were not owing to any want of force
or virtue in the Law, but to the exterior violence
of an universal prejudice, it may be proper to observe, that, from the Babylonian Captivity to this
very time, the Jews have been as averse to Idolatry
under every form and fashion of it, as before they
were propense unto it.   If it be asked, what it was
that occasioned so mighty a change ?   I answer, It
was in part, the severity of that punishment which
they had felt; and in part, the abatement of that
foolish prejudice which they had favoured, of IN-
TERCOMMUNITY OF WORSHIP: This, tho' still as general as ever in the Pagan world, had yet lost greatly
of its force amongst the Jews, since they became

[b] See what has been said on this matter just above, in the
case of the *Cutheans*, inhabiting Samaria.

acquainted

acquainted with the principles of Gentile Philofophy; the founder parts of which being found conformable to the *reafonable* doctrines of their Religion, were applied by them to the ufe of explaining the Law. An ufe which this Philofophy was
never put to in the place of its birth, on account
of the *abfurdities* of Pagan Worfhip; for this kept
the principles of Philofophy and the practices of
Religion at too great a diftance to have any influence on one another. Such was the advantage
the followers of the Jewifh Law reaped from the
Greek Philofophy; an advantage peculiar to them;
and which made fome amends for the many fuperftitions of another kind, which the mixing Philofophy with Religion introduced into the practice
of the Law: fuperftitions which depraved, and at
length totally deftroyed the noble fimplicity of its
nature and genius. — But I anticipate a fubject for
which I fhall find a much fitter place.

At length then we fee, that the Law of Mofes
was, indeed, fuch a one as his Lordfhip would require in a LAW OF DIVINE ORIGINAL, namely,
that *it produced its effect*, if not by a *phyfical* neceffity which bears down all obftruction before it,
yet by a *moral*, which conftantly kept operating
when no foreign impediment ftood in the way!
So falfe is his Lordfhip's affertions, that *the* WHOLE
*hiftory of this people is one continued feries of infrac-
tions of the Law*. If, by the *whole*, he means (as
his argument requires he fhould mean) the whole
both of their facred and merely civil hiftory; and,
by *one continued feries of infractions of the Law*, their
lapfes into Idolatry; it is the groffeft mifreprefentation: the far greater part of their duration as a
diftinct People was free from idolatry; and an authentic account of this freedom is recorded in their
Annals.

Annals. But if by *their whole history,* he means (as his cause might necessitate him to mean) only the sacred books; and, by *their infraction of the Law,* only transgressions in lesser matters, it is illusory and impertinent.

2. We have seen the force of his Lordship's conclusion from the circumstance—*of infinite Wisdom's framing the Law:* We come next to the other circumstance, from which he deduceth the same conclusion, namely *infinite Power's administring the Law.*

" Let it be remembered (says his Lordship)
" that GOD himself is said to have been their King
" during several ages; that his presence remained
" amongst them, even after they had deposed
" him; and that the High Priest consulted him, on
" any emergency, by the Urim and Thummim.
" OCCASIONAL MIRACLES were wrought to inforce
" the Law, but this was a standing miracle that
" might serve both to explain and inforce it, by
" the wisdom and authority of the Legislator, as
" often as immediate recourse to him was necessary.
" *Can it be denied that the most imperfect system of hu-*
" *man Laws would have been rendered effectual by such*
" *means as these ?*"

This bad reasoning seems to be urged with much good faith, contrary to his Lordship's usual custom; and arises from his ignorance of a *Theocratic* administration, as the nature of the administration may be collected from the common principles of the Law of Nature and Nations.

Let us consider the affair dispassionately. God, in giving laws to his chosen people, was pleased,

more

more humano, to affume the title King, and to adminifter their civil affairs by a *Theocratic* mode of Government. Every ftep in this eftablifhment evinces,
that it was his purpofe to interfere no otherwife
than in conformity to that political affumption.
He proceeded on the moft equitable grounds of
civil Government: he became their *King* by free
choice. It muft needs therefore be his purpofe to
confine himfelf to fuch *powers of legiflation*, as human Governors are able to exert; tho' he extended the *powers of adminiftration* far beyond the
limits of humanity. His Lordfhip's ignorance of
fo reafonable a diftinction occafioned all this pompous Fallacy. He found in the Mofaic Difpenfation
OCCASIONAL MIRACLES pretended: and he imagined that, confiftently with this pretence, *Miracles* ought to operate throughout, rather than that
the *end* of the Law fhould be defeated. But, I
prefume, GOD could not, conformably to his purpofe of erecting a THEOCRACY, and adminiftering
it MORE HUMANO, exert miraculous powers in
legiflating, though he very well might, and actually
did exert them, in *governing:* becaufe, in legiflation, a *miracle*, that is, a fupernatural force added
to the Laws, to make them conftantly obeyed,
could not be employed without putting a force
upon the Will; by which God's Laws would indeed
produce their effect, but it would be by the deftruction of the fubject of them. The cafe was different in adminiftring the Laws made: here God
was to act *miraculoufly*; often out of wife choice,
to manifeft the nature of the Government, and the
reality of his *regal* character; fometimes out of
neceffity, for the carrying on of that Government
on the Sanctions by which it was to be difpenfed:
and all this he might do without the leaft force upon the Will.

This

This is sufficient to expose the futility of his Lordship's conclusion from the circumstance of *infinite Power's administring the Law*; it being essential to the Law, that *infinite Power administring it*, should restrain itself within such bounds as left the Will perfectly free. But *infinite Power*, restrained within such bounds, might sometimes meet with unsurmountable obstructions in the course of its direction, under a Theocracy administered *more humano.*

II. We have seen how weak his Lordship's reasoning is in itself: Let us now see how much weaker he makes it by ill management; till at length it comes out a good argument against his own objection.

" The Law of Moses (says his Lordship) was
" so far from prevailing over accidents and conjunc-
" tures, that the least was sufficient to interrupt the
" course and defeat the design of it, to make that
" people not only neglect the Law, BUT CEASE
" TO ACKNOWLEDGE THE LEGISLATOR. To pre-
" vent this was the *first of these designs:* and if the
" *second* was (as it was, no doubt) and as it is the
" design or pretence of all Laws, to secure the
" happiness of the people, THIS DESIGN WAS DE-
" FEATED AS FULLY AS THE OTHER: for the whole
" history of this people is one continued series of
" INFRACTIONS OF THE LAW, AND OF NATIONAL
" CALAMITIES."

To pass by that vulgar mistake (which has been sufficiently exposed above) that the Jews *ever ceased to acknowledge their Legislator*; let me observe it to his Lordship's credit, that he appears to have understood so much at least of the Mosaic Institution,

as

as to fee that the *firſt end* of it was peculiar to itſelf; and that that which is common to all civil Communities was but the *ſecond end* of This.

But is it not ſtrange, when he ſaw ſo far into the nature of the Jewiſh Conſtitution, that he ſhould not ſee that this *ſecond end* was entirely dependent on what he himſelf makes the principal; namely, to preſerve the Iſraelites from idolatry; but ſhould argue againſt the divinity of the Law, as if theſe ends were independant one of another; and that one might be obtained without the other. For, to aggravate the imbecillity of the Law, he informs us in the paſſage laſt quoted, " that it was not only unable to gain its firſt end, but its ſecond likewiſe: *that the one deſign was defeated as fully as the other*; that the people were not only idolaters in ſpiritual matters, but poor, miſerable, and calamitous in their civil intereſts." Strange! that he could not ſee, or would not acknowledge, that the LAW denounces their happineſs and miſery as citizens, in exact proportion to their adherence to, or their defection from, that Law; when he ſaw and confeſſed, (what their HISTORY records) that this was their invariable fortune. *The whole hiſtory of this people* (ſays his Lordſhip) *is one continued ſeries of infractions of the Law, and of national calamities.* Now if the whole frame of the Moſaic Law was ſo compoſed, as to do that by *poſitive* inſtitute which the Moral Law does by *natural*, viz. reward the obedient, and puniſh the diſobedient, (and it certainly was ſo compoſed, if a *continued ſeries of infractions* was followed by a *continued ſeries of calamities*) we muſt needs conclude that we have here the ſtrongeſt proof of that divine Wiſdom in the Conſtitution, which this great modern Lawgiver pretends to ſeek, but aſſures us he is not able

to

to find; and yet, at the fame time, brings this convincing circumftance of the *truth* of the LAW; but brings it indeed as an argument of its *falfhood.* — *This defign* (fays he) *was defeated as fully as the other.* Here his rhetoric, as ufual, got the better of his reafoning: Not content to fay,—*the whole hiftory of this People is one continued feries of infractions of the Law,*—he will needs add by way of exaggeration——AND OF NATIONAL CALAMITIES. Which has fo perverfe an influence on the argument as to undo all he had been labouring to bring about, by difcovering a connexion between *infractions* and *calamities,* which has all the marks of a divine contrivance.

Had it been the declared defign of their Lawgiver to *feparate* the two ends, and to form fuch an Œconomy as that the People under it might be flourifhing in Peace and affluence, while they were Idolaters in Religion; or, on the other hand, true Worfhippers and, at the fame time, calamitous Citizens; then to find them neither religious nor profperous, under a Law which pretended to procure truth without temporal felicity, or to eftablifh peace and profperity in the midft of error; this indeed (without taking in the perverfity of fuch a Syftem) would have fully difcredited the pretended original. But when, in this Law, truth and happinefs, error and mifery, are declared to have an infeparable connexion; the freethinking Politician, who fhews from hiftory that this connexion was conftant and invariable, is intrapped by the retorfion of nature and reafon, to prove againft himfelf the Divinity of that Inftitute he labours to difcredit.

Still further: When, on reading the hiftory of this extraordinary People, we find (as Jofephus

well

well expresses it) that, *in proportion to the neglect of the Law, easy things became unsurmountable, and all their undertakings, how just soever, ended in uncurable calamities*[c], we cannot but acknowledge the divine direction in every stage of such a Dispensation. For, to comprehend the whole of the Historian's meaning, we must remember, that there were some Laws given purposely to manifest the divinity of their original: such as that *against multiplying horses*; which, when it was transgressed, *easy things became unsurmountable*; and that which most facilitates a victory, a strong body of Cavalry intermixed with Foot, proved amongst the Israelites, a certain means of their defeat. So again, when they transgressed the Law which commanded *all the males to go annually to the temple*, the historian tells us, *their most just undertakings ended in incurable calamities*; and sure nothing could be more *just* than to defend their borders from invaders; yet they were sure to be most infested with them when they thought themselves best secured: that is, while there males were at home, when they should have been worshiping at the Temple.

III. But it is now time to come a little closer to his Lordship. He has been all along arguing on a FALSE FACT, which his ignorance of the nature of the Jewish Separation hindered him from seeing.

He understood, indeed, that this extraordinary Œconomy had, for its *primary end*, something very different from all other civil Policies; and that that

---

[c] — καθ' ὅσον δ' ἂν ἀποστῶσι τῆς τούτων ἀκριβοῦς; ἐπιμελείας, ἄπορα μὲν γίνεται τὰ πόριμα, τρέπεται δ' εἰς συμφορὰς ἀνηκέστους, ὅ, τι ποτ' ἂν ὡς ἀγαθὸν δρᾶν σπεύδωσιν. Antiq. v. 1. p. 4.

which

which was the first, (indeed the only end) in others, was but the secondary, end in this. Yet this primary end he saw so obscurely, as not to be able to make it out. He supposed it was *to keep the Israelites from idolatry*; whereas it was TO PRESERVE THE MEMORY OF THE ONE GOD IN AN IDOLATROUS WORLD, till the coming of Christ: To *keep the Israelites from idolatry*, was but the *mean* to this *end*. Thus has our political Architect " mistaken the " scaffold for the pile," as his harmonious friend expresses it. And the mistake is the more gross, as the notion of the ultimate end's being to *keep the Israelites from idolatry*, is founded in that vain fancy of Jewish pride, that their Fathers were selected as the favorites of God, out of his fondness for the race of Abraham.

Under this rectified idea therefore let us consider the truth of his Lordship's assertion, *That no Law ever operated so weak and uncertain an effect as the Law of Moses did: far from prevailing against accidents and conjunctures, the least was sufficient to interrupt the course, and to defeat the designs of it.*

Now if we keep the true end of the Law in view, we shall see, on the contrary, that it prevailed constantly and uniformly, without the least interruption, against the most violent *accidents*, and in the most unfavourable *conjunctures*; those I mean, which happened when their propensity to the practice of idolatry, and their prejudice for the *principle of intercommunity* were at the height: for amidst all the disorders consequent thereto, they still preserved the knowledge of the true God, and performed the Rites ordained by the Law. And the very calamities which followed the infraction of the

Law,

Law, of which the neighbouring Nations occafionally partook, were fufficient to alarm thefe latter,
when moft at eafe, amidft the imaginary protection
of their tutelary Gods, and to awaken them to the
awful fenfe of a BEING different, as well as fuperior
to their *National Protectors*. Which fhews, that
the Law ftill *operated its effect*, ftrongly and conftantly ; and ftill *prevailed againft accidents and conjunctures*, which it *governed and directed*, inftead of
lying at the mercy of them. But as it is very probable that the frequent tranfgreffions, which thofe
accidents and *conjunctures* occafioned, would in time
have defeated the end of the Law, the tranfgreffors
were punifhed by a feventy-years-captivity ; the
extraordinary circumftances of which, made fuch
an impreffion on their haughty mafters as brought
them to confefs that the *God of Ifrael* was the *true
God* ; and was fo feverely felt by them, that they
had an utter averfion and abhorrence of Idolatry or
the worfhip of falfe Gods, ever after. So that from
thence to the coming of Chrift, a courfe of many
ages, they adhered, tho' tributary and perfecuted,
and (what has ftill greater force than Perfecution,
if not thoroughly adminiftered) defpifed and ridi-
culed by the two greateft Empires of the world, the
Greek and Roman ; and tho' furrounded with the
pomp and fplendour of Pagan idolatries, recommended by the fafhion of Courts, and the plaufible
gloffes of Philofophers, they adhered, I fay ftrictly,
and even fuperftitioufly to the letter of that Law,
which allowed of no other Gods befides the God
of Ifrael. Now if this was not *gaining its end*, we
muft feek for other modes of fpeech, and other
conceptions of things, when we reafon upon Government and Laws.

Yet this was not all. For the LAW not only
gained its end, in delivering down the Religion of
the

the TRUE GOD into the hands of the REDEEMER OF MANKIND; who soon spread it throughout the whole Roman Empire; but even after it had done its deftined work, the vigour of the Mofaic Re-velation ftill working at the root, enabled a bold Impoftor to extend the principle of the UNITY, ftill wider, till it had embraced the remoteft re-gions of the habitable World: So that, at this day, almoft all the Natives of the vaft regions of higher Afia, whether Gentiles, Chriftians, or Mahome-tans, are the profeffed worfhipers of the ONE ONLY GOD.   How much the extenfion of the principle of the *Unity* has been owing to this Caufe, under the permiffion and direction of that Providence, which is ever producing *good out of evil*, is known to all who are acquainted with the prefent ftate of the Eaftern World.

The reafon why I afcribe fo much of this good, to the lafting efficacy of the Mofaic Law, is this; Mahumet was born and brought up an Idolater, and inhabited an idolatrous Country; fo that had he feen no more of true Religion than in the fuper-ftitious practice of the Greek Church, at that time over-run with faint and image-worfhip, it is odds but that, when he fet up for a Prophet, he might have made Idolatry the bafis of his new Religion: But getting acquainted with the Jews and their Scriptures, he came to underftand the folly of Gentilifm and the corruptions of Chriftia-nity; and by this means was enabled to preach up the doctrine of the ONE GOD, in its purity and in-tegrity.   It is again remarkable, that to guard and fecure this doctrine, which He made the funda-mental principle of Ifhmaelitifm, he brought into his Impofture many of thofe provifions which Mofes had put in practice to prevent the contagion of idolatry.

But

But the great Man with whom we have to do, is ſo ſecure of his fact, namely that *the Law was perpetually defeated, and never gained its end,* that he ſuppoſes his Adverſaries, the DIVINES, are ready to confeſs it; and will only endeavour to elude his inference by throwing the ill ſucceſs of its operations on the *hardneſs of the People's hearts and the impiety of their Governors* [d]. And this affords him freſh occaſion of triumph.

I will not be poſitive that this ſpecies of Divines is intirely of his own invention, and that this their apology for Moſes is altogether as imaginary as their famous CONFEDERACY [e] againſt God; becauſe I know by experience that there are of theſe Divines, who, in ſupport of their paſſions and prejudices, are always ready (as I have amply experienced) to admit what Scripture oppoſes, and to oppoſe what it admits, in almoſt every page. But the beſt Apologies of ſuch men are never worth a defence, and indeed are rarely capable of any.

To conclude: Such as theſe here expoſed, are all the reaſonings of his Lordſhip's bulky volumes: And no wonder; when a writer, however able in other matters, will needs dictate in a Science of which he did not poſſeſs ſo much as the firſt Principles.

S E C T. III.

HAVING thus ſhewn the nature of this THEOCRACY, and the attendant circumſtances of its erection; our next enquiry will be concerning its DURATION.

[d] Page 293—4.   [e] Vol. v. p. 305—307—393.

Most writers suppose it to have ended with the JUDGES; but scarce any bring it lower than the CAPTIVITY. On the contrary, I hold that, in strict truth and propriety, it ended not 'till the coming of CHRIST.

I. That it ended not with the Judges appears evident for these reasons:

1. Tho' indeed the People's purpose, in their clamours for a King, was to live under a gentile Monarchy like their idolatrous neighbours; (for so it is represented by God himself, in his reproof of their impiety [f]) yet in compassion to their blindness, he, in this instance, as in many others, indulged their prejudices, without exposing them to the fatal consequence of their project: which, if complied with, in the sense they formed it, had been the withdrawing of his *extraordinary protection* from them, at a time when they could not support themselves without it. He therefore gave them a *King*; but such an one as was only his VICEROY or Deputy; and who, on that account, was not left to the People's election, as he left his own Regality; but was chosen by himself: the only difference between God's appointment of the Judges and of Saul being this, that They were chosen by internal impulse; He, by Lots, or external designation.

2. This king had an unlimited *executive* power; as God's Viceroy must needs have.

3. He had no *legislative* power: which a Viceroy could not possibly have.

[f] 1 SAM. viii. 7.

4. He was placed and difplaced by God at pleafure: of which, as Viceroy, we fee the perfect fitnefs; but as Sovereign by the people's choice, one
cannot eafily account for; becaufe God did not
chufe to fuperfede the natural Rights of his People, as appears by his leaving it, at firft, to their
own option whether they would have God himfelf
for their King.

5. The very fame punifhment was ordained for
curfing the King as for blafpheming God, namely,
ftoning to death; and the reafon is intimated in
thefe words of Abifhai to David, *Shall not Shimei
be put to death for this, becaufe he curfed the* LORD's
ANOINTED [g]? This was the common title of the
Kings of Ifrael and Judah, and plainly denoted
their office of Viceroyalty: Improperly, and fuperftitioufly transferred, in thefe latter ages, to chriftian Kings and Princes.

From this further circumftance, a *Viceroyalty* is
neceffarily inferred: The throne and kingdom of
Judea is all along exprefly declared to be God's
throne and God's kingdom. Thus, in the firft
book of Chronicles, it is faid that *Solomon fat on
the* THRONE OF THE LORD, *as King, inftead of
David his father* [h]. And the queen of Sheba, who
vifited Solomon, to be inftructed in his wifdom,
and doubtlefs had been informed by him of the
true nature of his kingdom, compliments him in
thefe words: *Bleffed be the Lord thy God, which
delighted in thee to fet thee on* HIS THRONE, TO BE
KING FOR THE LORD THY GOD [i]. In like manner Abijah fpeaks to the houfe of Ifrael, on their

[g] 2 SAM. xix. 21.   [h] Chap. xxix. ver. 23.   [i] 2 CHRON.
ix. 8.

defection

defection from Rehoboam : *And now ye think to withſtand the* KINGDOM OF THE LORD *in the hands of the ſons of David* [k].   And to the ſame purpoſe, Nehemiah : *Neither have our kings, our princes, our prieſts, nor our fathers kept thy law, nor hearken-ed unto thy commandments, and thy teſtimonies where-with thou didſt teſtify againſt them.   For they have not ſerved thee in* THEIR KINGDOM [l].   The ſenſe, I think, requires that the Septuagint reading ſhould be here preferred, which ſays ΕΝ ΒΑΣΙΛΕΙΑ ΣΟΥ, IN THY KINGDOM.   And this the Syriac and Arabic verſions follow.   As Judea is always called *his kingdom,* ſo he is always called the *King of the Jews.*   Thus the Pſalmiſt : *Thine Altars, O Lord of Hoſts, my* KING *and my God* [m].   And again : *Let* Iſrael *rejoice in him that made him : let the child-ren of* Zion *be joyful in their* KING [n].   *And* thus the Prophet Jeremiah : *The* KING, *whoſe name is the Lord of Hoſts* [o].

7. The penal Laws againſt idolatry were ſtill in force during their Kings ; and put in execution by their beſt rulers, and even by men inſpired. Which, alone, is a demonſtration of the ſubſiſtence of the THEOCRACY ; becauſe ſuch laws are abſolutely un-juſt under every other form of Government.

As to the title of *King* given to theſe Rulers, this will have ſmall weight with thoſe who reflect that Moſes likewiſe, who was ſurely no more than God's deputy, is called King : *Moſes commanded us a Law; even the inheritance of the congregation of Jacob.   And he was* KING *in Jeſhurun, when*

---

[k] 2 CHRON. xiii. 8.   [l] Chap. ix. ver. 35.   [m] PSALM lxxxiv. 3.   [n] PSALM cxlix. 2.   [o] JER. li. 57.

the heads of the people, and the tribes of Israel were gathered together [p].

Let us now fee what the celebrated M. Le Clerc fays in defenfe of the contrary opinion, which fuppofeth the THEOCRACY to have ended with the Judges. Father Simon of the Oratory had faid, that *the republic of the Hebrews never acknowledged any other* CHIEF *than God alone, who continued to govern in that quality, even during the time in which it was fubject to Kings* [q]. This was enough to make his learned adverfary take the other fide of the queftion; who being piqued at Simon's contemptuous flight of his offered affiftance, in the project for a new Polyglott, revenged himfelf upon him in thofe licentious [r] Letters, intitled, *Sentimens de quelques Theologiens de Hollande*, where his only bufinefs is to pick a quarrel. He therefore maintains againft Simon, *That the Theocracy ceafed on eftablifhing the throne in the race of David* [s]. What

he

---

[p] DEUT. xxxiii. 4 and 5.

[q] La Republique des Hebreux differre en cela de tous les autres états du monde, qu'elle n'a jamais reconnu pour chef que Dieu feul, qui a continué de la gouverner en cette qualité dans les tems mêmes qu'elle a été foumife à des rois. *Hiftoire Crit. de l'ieux Tefl.* p. D5. *Ed. Rotterd.* 1685.

[r] I call them licentious, principally, for the extravagant Reafonings concerning the authority of the Pentateuch, and the divine infpiration of Scripture. The firft he retracted and confuted, when the fpirit of contradiction had given way to better principles; the other (which he had inferted into the *Letters* as the work of another man) he never, that I know of, attoned for, by any retractation whatfoever.

[s] Il paroît au contraire par l'Ecriture, que Dieu n'a gouverné la republique des Hebreux, en qualité de chef politique, que pendant qu'ils n'avoient point des rois, & peut-être au commencement

he hath of argument to support this opinion is but little; and may be summed up in the following observation, *That God did not* PERSONALLY *interfere with his directions, nor discharge the functions of a Magistrate after the establishment of the Kings as he had done before* [t]. But this, instead of proving the abolition of the *Theocracy*, only shews that it was administered by a *Viceroy*. For in what consists the office of a Viceroy but to discharge the functions of his Principal? He had been a cipher, had God still governed *immediately* as before. Mr. Le Clerc could see that God acted *by the ministry of the Judges* [u]. If then the Theocratic function could be discharged by deputation, why might it not be done by Kings as well as Judges? The difference, if any, is only from less to more, and from occasional to constant. No, says our Critic, the cession was in consequence of his own declaration to Samuel: *For they have not rejected thee, but they have* REJECTED ME, *that I should not reign over them* [x]. This only declares the sense God had of their mutinous request; but does not at all imply

ment que les rois furent etablis, avant que la famille de David fut affermie sur le trône d'Israel. *Sentimens, &c.* p. 78.

[t] — Pendant tout ce temps-la, Dieu fit les fonctions de roi, Il jugeoit des affaires — il repondoit par l'oracle — il regloit la marche de l'armée — il envoyoit même quelquefois un ange — On n'étoit obligé d'obeïr aveuglement, qu'aux seuls ordres de Dieu. Mais lors qu'il y eut des rois en Israël, & que le royaume fut attaché à la famille de David, les rois furent maitres absolus, & Dieu cessa de faire leurs fonctions. p. 78, 79.

[u] — au lieu qu'auparavant Dieu lui-même la faisoit, *par le ministere des Juges,* qu'il suscitoit de temps en temps au milieu d'Israël. *Def. des Sent.* p. 121.

[x] — C'est pour cela que Dieu dit à Samuel, lors qu' Israël voulut avoir *un roi pour le juger à la maniére de toutes les nations: ce n'est pas toi qu'ils ont rejetté, mais moi, afin que je ne regne point sur eux,* 1 SAM. viii. 7.

that

that he gave way to it. For who, from the like words (which exprefs fo natural a refentment of an open defection) would infer in the cafe of any other monarch, that he thereupon ftepped down from his throne, and fuffered an ufurper to feize his place? This, we fee, was poor reafoning. But, luckily for his reputation, he had an Adverfary who reafoned worfe. — However Simon faw thus much into Le Clerc's cavil, as to reply, *That all he had faid was quite befide the purpofe, for that the thing to be proved was, that, after the eftablifhment of the Kings, God was no longer the civil Chief* [y]. On which Le Clerc thus infults him: *As much as to fay, that in order to prove God was no longer Chief of the Hebrews after the election of a King, it is befide the purpofe to fhew, he never afterwards difcharged the functions of a Chief of the republic. It is thus this great Genius happily unravels matters, and difcovers, in an inftant, what is, and what is not to the purpofe* [z]. Whether Simon indeed knew *why* Le Clerc's objection was nothing to the purpofe, is to be left to God and his own confcience, for he gives us no reafons for the cenfure he paffes on it: but that it was indeed nothing to the purpofe, is moft evident, if this propofition be true,

[y] Je paffe fous filence le long difcours de Mr. le Clerc touchant le pouvoir de Dieu fur les Ifraëlites avant l'etabliffement des rois, d'où il pretend prouver que Dieu pendant tout ce temps-la fit la fonction de roi. Tout cela eft hors de propos, puis qu'il s'agit de prouver qu'apres ces temps-la Dieu n'a plus été leur chef: & c'eft ce qu'on ne prouvera jamais. *Reponfe aux Sentimens de quelques Theol. de Hol.* p. 55.

[z] — C'eft à dire que pour prouver que Dieu n'a pas été chef des Hebreux, aprés l'election des rois, il eft hors de propos de prover qu'il n'a plus fait les fonctions de chef de la republique. C'eft ainfi que ce grand genie debrouille heureufement les matieres, & découvre d'abord ce qui eft hors de propos, de ce qui ne l'eft pas. *Defenf. des Sentimens*, p. 120.

" That

" That a King does not ceafe to be King, when he puts in a Viceroy, who executes the regal office by deputation."

Le Clerc returns to the charge in his *Defenfe of the Sentiments:* — " The Ifraelites did not reject " God as Protector, but as civil Chief, as I ob- " ferved before. They would have a King who " fhould determine fovereignly, and command " their armies. Which, before this, God himfelf " did by the miniftry of the Judges, whom he " raifed up, from time to time, from the midft of " Ifrael. In this fenfe we muft underftand abfo- " lutely the words of God, in Samuel, *that I* " *fhould not reign over them*[a]." It is indeed ftrange, that, after writing two books, he fhould ftill infift on fo foolifh a paralogifm[b], That God's *giving up* his office of civil Chief, was a neceffary confe- quence of the People's *demanding* it. For, that they did demand it, I acknowledge. Let us confi- der then this whole matter a little more attentively.

Samuel (and I defire the Deifts would take no- tice of it) had now, by a wife and painful direction of affairs, reftored the purity of Religion, and ref- cued his Nation from the power of the Philiftines, and their other hoftile neighbours ; againft whom

---

[a] Les Ifraëlites ne rejetterent pas Dieu comme protecteur, mais comme chef politique, ainfi que je l'ai marqué. Ils vou- lurent un roi qui les jugeât fouverainement, & qui commandât leurs armées, au lieu qu'auparavant Dieu lui-même le faifoit, par le miniftere des juges, qu'il fufcitoit de temps en temps au milieu d'Ifrael.—En ce fens il faut entendre abfolument les paroles de Dieu dans Samuël, *afin que je ne regne point fur eux,* p. 121.

[b] However, foolifh as it is, the Reader hath feen, how a late Sermonizer has borrowed it, and how little force he has added to it.

they were utterly unable to make head when he entered upon the public Adminiſtration. At this very time, the People, debauched, as uſual, by power and proſperity, took the pretence of the corrupt conduct of the Prophet's two ſons [c], to go in a tumultuary manner, and demand a King. But the ſecret ſpring of their rebellion was the ambition of their leaders; who could live no longer without the ſplendour of a regal Court and Houſhold; Give me (ſay they, as the Prophet Hoſea interprets their inſolent *demand*) a king and princes [d]; where every one of them might ſhine a diſtinguiſhed Officer of State. They could get nothing when their affairs led them to their Judges' poor reſidence, in the *Schools of the Prophets*, but the Gift *of the Holy Spirit* [e]; which a Courtier, I preſume, would not prize even at the rate Simon Magus held it, of a paultry piece of money.——This it was, and this only, that made their demand criminal. For, the chuſing Regal rather than Ariſtocratic Viceroys was a thing plainly indulged to them by the Law of Moſes, in the following admonition: *When thou art come into the land which the Lord thy God giveth thee, and ſhalt poſſeſs it, and ſhalt dwell therein, and ſhalt ſay, I will ſet a* King *over me, like as the nations that are about me: Thou ſhalt in any wiſe ſet him King over thee, whom the* Lord thy God shall chuse: *one from amongſt thy Brethren ſhalt thou ſet King over thee: Thou mayeſt not ſet a Stranger over thee which is not thy brother* [f]. The plain meaning of which caution is, that they ſhould take care, when they demanded a King, that they thought of none other than ſuch a King who was to be God's Deputy. As therefore Court-ambition

---

[c] 1 Sam. viii. 5. and xii. 12.
[e] 1 Sam. x. 10. and Chap. xix.
[d] Chap. xiii. ver. 10.
[f] Deut. xvii, 14, 15.

only

only was in the wicked view of the Ringleaders
of theſe malecontents, and no fooliſh fears for the
State, or hopes of bettering the public Adminiſtration, it is evident to all acquainted with the
genius of this Time and People, that compliance
with their demand, muſt have ended in the utter
deſtruction of the Moſaic Religion as well as Law.
But it was God's purpoſe to keep them SEPARATE,
in order to preſerve the memory of himſelf amidſt
an idolatrous World.   And this not being to be
done but by the preſervation of their Religion and
Law, we muſt needs conclude that he would not
give way to their rebellious demand.

And what we are brought to conclude from the
reaſon of the thing, the *hiſtory* of this tranſaction
clearly enough confirms.   For it having now informed us how God conſented to give this People
a King; To ſhew us, that he had not caſt off the
Government, but only transferred the immediate
Adminiſtration to a Deputy, and conſequently, that
their King was *his* Viceroy, it tells us next, how He
was pleaſed to bring them to repentance in an extraordinary way; the gracious method he commonly
employed when he intended to pardon.   Samuel aſ-
ſembled the People[g]; and to convince them of their
crime in demanding a King, called down the preſent vengeance of their offended God in a ſtorm of
thunder and rain at the time of wheat harveſt [h].
This ſudden deſolation brings them to a ſenſe of
their guilt, and they implore mercy and forgive-
neſs: " And all the People ſaid unto Samuel,
" Pray for thy ſervants unto the Lord thy God,
" that we die not; for we have added unto all our
" ſins this evil, to aſk us a King.   And Samuel

---

[g] 1 Sam. xii.   [h] 1 Sam. xii. 17, 18.

" ſaid

6

" faid unto the People, fear not: (ye have done all
" this wickednefs : yet turn not afide from follow-
" ing the Lord, but ferve the Lord with all your
" heart; and turn ye not afide : for then fhould
" you go after vain things, which cannot profit
" nor deliver, for they are vain) For the Lord
" will *not.forfake his People*, for his great Name's
" fake : becaufe it hath pleafed the Lord to *make*
" *you his People* [i]." Here, we fee, they repent,
are pardoned, and received again into Grace, as
appears by the concluding promife, that the *Theo-*
cratic form fhould be continued. They are ready
to give up their King, and yet a regal chara&er
is inftituted. The plain conclufion from all this
is, that their King was given, and, now at leaft,
received, as God's DEPUTY.

But Father Simon is at length provoked into a
Reafon, and that, to fay the truth, no weak one.
God, he obferves, kept the election of their King
in his own hands [k]. But *this*, Le Clerc fays, *proves*
nothing. How fo ? *Becaufe, according to this reafon-*
ing, we fhould be obliged to fay that God oftener dif-
charged the functions of civil Chief in the idolatrous
realm of the ten Tribes than in that of Judah: for
that was elective, this, hereditary [l]. And what if we
do ?

---

[i] Ver. 19. *& feq.*

[k] Et une preuve même qu'il ne ceffoit pas d'être leur chef
par cette election, c'eft qu'il s'en rend le maître. *Reponfe aux*
Sentimens, p. 55.

[l] Pour ce que dit M. Simon que Dieu *fe rend maitre de l'elec-*
tion des Rois, il ne s'enfuit nullement qu'il continuât d'être pour
cela chef politique de la republique d'Ifraël; puifque fi cela
étoit, il faudroit dire que Dieu faifoit beaucoup plus fouvent
les fonctions de chef de l'etat dans le royaume Idolatre des dix
tribus, que dans celuy de Juda. Car ce derniere royaume étoit
hereditaire,

do? Where will be the harm of it? The two king-
doms made up but one Commonwealth; of which
God, as Head, governed by two Viceroys.   And
if he oftener acted immediately in the kingdom of
Israel, there was a plain reason for it; Its inhabitants were more given to idolatrous worship; and
needed more the frequency of an extraordinary re-
straint.   And in effect, we find he did interfere
greatly in other instances, as well as in the election of their Kings.

In truth, F. Simon seemed to see as little into the
force of the obfervation *(that God referved the choice
of their King to himfelf)* when he urged it, as M.
Le Clerc did, when he defpifed it: yet it is ftrongly
conclufive for the continuation of the Theocracy.
For had the vifible King which the Ifraelites demanded been granted to them, that is, a King in
his own right, fovereign, and at the head of a new
Conftitution, or indeed, any other than a Viceroy
to the KING of the Theocracy, the choice of him
would have been referved to the People.   It was a
natural right; and more than that, a right which
God did not think fit to take from them, when he
firft accepted the regal office for himfelf.   But if
the People have, by natural Law, a right to chufe
their own King, that King hath, by civil Law, a
prerogative to chufe his own Deputy.   When we
fee him therefore exercife this prerogative, we may
be affured that the King chofen was no other than
his Deputy, as SOVEREIGN of the Theocracy.
But to return to the two Combatants.——Here
the Difpute ended; and for farther fatisfaction,

hereditaire, & étoit poffedé par la maifon de David, fans qu'il
fût befoin d'aucune élection, au lieu qu'il le fit plufieurs elec-
tions dans celui des dix tribus. *Defenfe des Sentimens,* p. 121,
122.

Le

Le Clerc refers us to a book of Spencer's, written profeſſedly upon this very ſubjeĉt[m]. It is his tract *De Theocratia Judaica*. What is to be found there, beſides the arguments which Le Clerc has borrowed from it, and which have been conſidered already, I ſhall now with ſome reluĉtance inform the Reader.

This treatiſe is by no means in the number of thoſe on which Spencer raiſed his reputation. He goes on a wrong hypotheſis; he uſes weak arguments; and he is confuſed and inconſiſtent in his aſſertions.

1. He thinks the Theocracy was eſtabliſhed by degrees[n], and abrogated by degrees[o]. A conceit highly abſurd, as GOD was the Lawgiver, and Supreme Magiſtrate of the Jews.—He thinks the firſt ſtep to its introduĉtion was their proteĉtion at the Red Sea[p]; and the firſt ſtep to its aboli-

---

[m] Il n'eſt pas neceſſaire que je m'arrête d'avantage à cela, après ce qu'en a dit le ſavant *Spencer* dans un traité qu'il a fait exprès ſur cette matiere. *Lib. i. de Legg. Heb. Ritual. Defenſe des Sent.* p. 122.

[n] — Neminem in ſacris literis vel mediocriter verſatum latere poteſt *Theocratiam* in ipſo rerum Iſraeliticarum exordio aliquatenus obtinuiſſe, ad ἀκμὴν autem non niſi gradatim & poſt legem in Sinai datam perveniſſe. *Vol. i. p.* 239.

[o] Cum autem regiminis hujus, non ſimul & ſemel, ſed per gradus quoſdam, jaĉturam ſecerint, placet hic veritatis fugientis veſtigia gradatim premere. *Id. ib.*

[p] Gradum primum ad poteſtatem regiam obtinendam feciſſe videtur Deus, cum gentem Iſraeliticam inſigni illo potentiæ & bonitatis ſuæ documento (Ægyptiorum in Mari Rubro ſubmerſione) ſibi devinxiſſet. *Id. ib.*

tion,

tion, their demand of a King [q]: That it was still more impaired when Saul and David got possession of the throne [r]: That it approached much nearer to its end when it became hereditary, under Salomon [s]: and yet, for all this, he confesses that some obscure footsteps of it remained even to the time of Christ [t].

. 2. In his reasoning for the abolition of the Theocracy, instead of employing the general principles of civil Policy, which were the only means of coming to the truth, he insists much on the disuse of Urim and Thummim, &c. which Le Clerc borrowed from him; and which hath been already considered. He brings the despotic power of the Kings [u], as another argument; which, I think, proves just the contrary. For if so be, that these Kings were the Viceroys of God, whose power was despotic, their power must be despotic too, i. e. independent on all but the Sovereign. Not so, if they were Monarchs in their own right.

[q] Primo itaque ad certum affirmo, quod Israelitæ, regem sibi dari postulantes, gradum primum ad imperii hujus desideratissimi ruinam fecisse videantur. *Id. ib.*

[r] Dei regimen multo magis imminutum est, cum Deus *Saulem* & *Davidem* ad rerum arbitrium evocasset. p. 240.

[s] Salomone rerum potito, Theocratia multo vicinior ἀφανισμῷ non immerito censeatur.

[t] Judæi Theocratiæ veteris indicia & vestigia quædam obscuriora, ad extrema usque politiæ suæ tempora retinuere — ipso Domini nostri seculo, Hierosolyma *civitas magni regis* audiit. *Ib.*

[u] — adeo ut hinc constet eos se pro regibus gessisse, & potestatem arbitrariam exercuisse. *Ib.*

3. Though,

3. Though, as we observed, Spencer, in the second section of his fourth chapter, supposes a gradual decay of the Theocracy; and that even some obscure footsteps of it remained to the time of CHRIST; yet, in the following section, he, all the way, argues upon the supposition of an absolute and entire abrogation by the establishment of the Kings [x] [y]. To proceed.

II. That

[x] — Regiminis hujus mutati vel abrogati causa principalis — De regiminis hujus abrogati effectu vel eventu breviter disserendum est — &c. p. 241,—243.

[y] Dr. Sykes has undertaken to confute the censure here passed upon Dr. Spencer. *Here it is* (says this Answerer) *that Mr. W. attacks Dr. Spencer's dissertation on the Jewish Theocracy. Are we not now from hence to* IMAGINE *that Dr. Spencer was one of those writers that supposed the Theocracy to have ended with the Judges?* [An examination of Mr. W's account, &c. p. 168.] What demands of *imagination* his trade of Answering may have upon him, I do not know. But from my words, a fair reasoner would *imagine* nothing but that I meant to prove what I said; namely, that Dr. Spencer's discourse of the Theocracy is *weak and inconsistent.*

His first charge (says he) *against Spencer is, that he thought the Theocracy was established by degrees, and abrogated by degrees.* " A conceit highly absurd," *says* Mr. W. *But wherein lies the absurdity of this gradual progress and gradual declension?* [p. 170.] The *Absurdity* lies here. When God is pleased to assume the character of civil Magistrate, he must, like all other Magistrates, enter upon his office at once, and (as common sense requires) abdicate it at once. Now the Government under such a Magistrate is what we properly call a Theocracy. Therefore to talk of *the gradual progress* and *gradual declension* of this mode of civil relation, is the same as to talk of the gradual progress and gradual declension of Paternity, or any other mode of natural relation; of which, I suppose, till now, no body ever heard.

He goes on — *if there be any absurdity or inconsistency, in this manner of speaking, it may be* JUSTIFIED *by Mr. W's own authority.* That is, my absurdity will justify another Man's. But this

II. That this Theocracy, the administration of which lay, as it were, in abeyance during the Captivity,

this is doing me an honour which I do not pretend to. Well, but how do I *justify* Dr. Spencer? Why, I say, it seems, " That in " the period immediately preceeding the Jewish Captivity, on " the gradual withdrawing the extraordinary Providence from " them, they began to entertain doubts concerning God's " further peculiar regard to them as his chosen People." *So that here* (says Dr. Sykes) *he expresly owns a* GRADUAL WITH-DRAWING OF THE EXTRAORDINARY PROVIDENCE from the Jews. *And where is the absurdity of Dr. Spencer's* GRADUAL DECLENSION OR IMMINUTION OF THE THEOCRACY, *which Mr. W's gradual withdrawing of the extraordinary Providence is not liable unto. Or was not the gradual withdrawing of the extraordinary Providence a proper imminution of the Theocracy?* [p. 171.] He is so pleased with this argument that he repeats it at p. 218. Yet who would have suspected him of what he here discovers, a total ignorance of any difference between the FORM of Government and the ADMINISTRATION of it. Now Dr. Spencer talked of the gradual decline of the *form of Government*, which I thought absurd: I spoke of the gradual decline of the *administration* of it; which, whether it be equally absurd let those determine who have seen (unless perhaps the rarity of the fact has made it escape observation) an *administration* of Government grow worse and worse, while the *form* of it still continued the same.

. So much as to Spencer's *absurdity.* We come next to his *inconsistency,* in supposing some foot-steps of the Theocracy till the time of Christ, and yet that it was entirely abrogated by the establishment of the Kings. Of this inconsistency, Dr. Spencer is absolved by the dexterity of our Answerer, in the following manner: *Here again is Dr. Spencer much misrepresented, from not considering* WHAT HE MEANT *by the* ABROGA-TION *of God's Government. Not that the Theocracy entirely ceased; but the Government received an* ALTERATION *and* ABATE-MENT. *And therefore he uses more than once the phrase of* RE-GIMINIS MUTATI, *in this very section; Where is the absurdity and inconsistency of this way of reasoning, unless abrogation is made to signify a total abolition, and duration is to be construed cessation?*

He asks, *where is the absurdity of this way of reasoning?* I did not accuse Spencer of *absurdity in his way of reasoning,* but of

tivity, was again exercifed after the return from it,
is evident from the exprefs declaration of the Almighty,

of *contradiction in his way of expreffion*. I fee no *reafoning*
there is, or can be. in a man's delivering what he thinks a fact;
fuch as his opinion of the duration of a form of Government.
But he who cannot diftinguifh *reafoning* from *expreffion*, may be
well excufed for confounding the *form of Government*, and the
adminiftration of Government with one another.

However, *Spencer* (he fays) *is much mifreprefented; he did not
mean by* ABROGATION *a* CEASING; *but an* ALTERATION *and*
ABATEMENT. It feems then, a writer is *much mifreprefented* if,
when he is charged with an inconfiftent *expreffion*, his *meaning*
may be proved confiftent. A good commodious principle for
the whole clafs of Anfwerers! But he tells us that *abrogation*
[regimen abrogatum] does not fignify *ceafing*. Where did he
get his latin? for the Roman writers ufe it only in the fenfe of
diffolution, abolition, or the *entire ceafing* of an office or command. What then does it fignify? ALTERATION (he fays) *and*
ABATEMENT. But now where did he get his Englifh? Our
Country writers, I think, ufe the word *alteration* to fignify a
change; and *abatement*, to fignify no change; no alteration
in the qualities of things, but a diminution only in the vigour
of their operations. What the *alteration* of a Theocracy, or
any other form of Government is, we well underftand; but
what the *abatement* of it is, one is much at a lofs to conceive.
However, this I know, that Dr. Sykes here confirms what I
charge upon him, the confounding the mode of Government
with the adminiftration of it: *Alteration* being applicable to the
former, and *abatement*, only to the latter.

But his inference from this fpecial reafoning, is worth all
the reft — *and* THEREFORE *Spencer ufes, more than once, the
phrafe of* regiminis MUTATI, *in this very fection*. *Therefore!*
Wherefore? Why, becaufe by *abrogati* he meant only *abated*,
therefore he *ufes* mutati, *more than once* to explain himfelf.
That is to fay, " becaufe, by *totum*, I mean *pars*, THERE-
FORE I ufe *omne* more than once, to explain my meaning."
Well, if he did not clear it up before, he has done it now.

—— *And where* (fays he) *is the abfurdity or inconfiftency of
this way of reafoning?* Nay, for that matter, the *reafoning* is
full as good as the Criticifm. But here he fhould have ftopped;
for fo fatal is his expreffion, when the fit of Anfwering is upon
him,

mighty, by the Prophet Haggai: *Yet now be strong, O Zerubbabel, saith the Lord, and be strong,*

him, that he cannot aſk quarter for one blunder without committing another. — *Unleſs* ABROGATION *is made to ſignify a* TOTAL ABOLITION, *and* duration *is conſtrued to be* ceſſation. — " I can find (ſays he) no abſurdity nor inconſiſtency in Dr. Spencer, without perverting the common ſignification of words :" — *without calling duration ceſſation.* —— This is his Argument; and ſo far was well. But he goes on — *and abrogation, a total abolition.* Here he ſinks again; for *abrogation* was *abolition*, amongſt all nations and languages, till Dr. Sykes firſt pleaded in *abatement.* Well, but our Anſwerer will go farther: and having ſo ably vindicated Dr. Spencer, he will now ſhew, tho' the Dr. be *conſiſtent*, yet ſo am not I: for that I hold, the extraordinary Providence entirely ceaſed on the return from the Captivity: From whence, (ſays this ſubtile logician) I argue thus, " If the EXTRAORDINARY PROVIDENCE " entirely ceaſed *on the full Settlement of the Jews after their* " *Return*, it ceaſed ſome centuries at leaſt before the days of " Chriſt; and CONSEQUENTLY the THEOCRACY muſt have " ceaſed ſome centuries before the days of Chriſt. How then " is Mr. W. conſiſtent about the duration of the Theo- " cracy, ſince he pleads for its continuance till Chriſt's time, " and yet maintains that IT entirely ceaſed ſo long before his " time * ?"

The argument, we ſee, gathers even as it rolls from his mouth. In the beginning of the ſentence, The *ceaſing of an extraordinary Providence* only implied in conſequence, the *ceaſing of the Theocracy*; but, before we get to the end, an *extraordinary Providence* and a *Theocracy* are one and the ſame thing. " *Mr. W. pleads for its* [a Theocracy's] *continuance* " *till Chriſt's time, and yet maintains that* IT *entirely ceaſed* " *ſo long before his Time.*" Thus again to the ſame purpoſe at p. 178. " Or by what rule does he form a judgment that " WHAT was gradually decaying to the Captivity, was entirely " to ceaſe after their Return and full Settlement ; and yet WAS " to continue till Chriſt's Time ?" — Nay, if he begins to talk of *Rules*, let me aſk him *by what Rule* he found out, " that " a *Monarchy* and an exact *Adminiſtration of Juſtice* are one " and the ſame thing ?" The truth is, our Examiner was thus grievouſly miſled by the ambiguity of the *Engliſh* word THE

* Exam. of Mr. *W*'s Account, *&c.* p. 173—4.

*ftrong, O Joßhua, Son of Joßedech .the High Prieft,
and be ftrong, all ye People of the Land, faith the
Lord, and work : for I am with you, faith the Lord
of Hoßts*; ACCORDING TO THE WORD THAT I CO-
VENANTED WITH YOU WHEN YOU CAME OUT OF
EGYPT, SO MY SPIRIT REMAINETH AMONGST
YOU : *fear ye not* ª. What was that *Covenant?*
That Ifrael fhould be his People, and He, their
God and *King*. Therefore it cannot barely mean,
that he would be their God, and they fhould be
his People ; for this was but *part* of the *Covenant*.
Nor can it mean that they fhould be conducted
by an extraordinary providence, as at their coming
out of Egypt, and during the firft periods of the
Theocracy ; for this was but the *effects* of the *Covenant :* and befides, we know that that difpenfation of Providence foon ceafed after the Re-eftablifhment. The meaning therefore muft be, that
he would ftill continue their KING as well as God.
Yet at the fame Time, when this Theocracy was
reftored, it was both fit, on account of its own
dignity, and neceffary for the People's affurance,

GOVERNMENT ; which fignifies either the MODE of Civil Policy, or the ADMINISTRATION of it. But was this to be expected of a man who had been all his life-time writing ABOUT
GOVERNMENT ?

To conclude this long note, The charge againft SPENCER
was of *abfurdity* and *contradiction* in one fingle inftance amidft
a thoufand excellencies. Dr. Sykes affumes the honour of his
Defence. But with what judgment, he foon gives us to underftand, when he could find no other part of that immortal Book
to do himfelf the credit of fupporting, but the *difcourfe concerning the Theocracy*; much in the fpirit of that ancient Advocate of
Cicero, who while the Patriot's character was torn in pieces by
his Enemies, would needs vindicate him from the imputation of
a Wart upon his Nofe, againft his Friends.

ª Chap. ii. ver. 4, 5.

that

that it should be attended with some unusual difplay of divine favour.   Accordingly,   Prophets
were raised up; and an extraordinary Providence,
for some short time, adminiftered, as appears from
many places in thofe Prophets [b].

III. That the Theocracy continued even to the
coming of Christ, may be feen from hence.—

1. Whenever it was abrogated, it muft needs be
done in the fame folemn manner in which it was
eftablifhed ; fo that the one might be as well known
as the other : becaufe it was of the higheft importance to a people fo ftrictly bound to obedience,
not to be miftaken concerning the power under
which they lived.   Natural equity requires this
formality as a neceffary concomitant in the im-
pofing and abrogating of all civil laws and inftitutions whatfoever.   Now the Theocracy having
never been thus abolifhed till the coming of Chrift,
we conclude that it continued to fubfift till that
time.

2. Nor indeed, could it have been abolifhed
without diffolving the whole frame of the Republic;
fince all the Laws of it, whether as to their equity,
force, or fitnefs, as well as the whole Ritual of Worfhip, refpected, and referred to God as civil Gover-
nour. But neither by the declaration of any Prophet,
nor by the act of any good King, did the Inftitution
fuffer the leaft change in any of its parts, from the
time of its eftablifhment by Mofes to its diffolution by Jesus Christ, either by addition, correction, or abrogation.   Confequently, the *Theocracy*

[b] Hag. i. 6—11.   Chap. ii. ver. 16—19.   Zech. viii. 12.
Mal. iii. 10, 11.

was exifting throughout that whole period. Nothing being more abfurd than to fuppofe that national Laws, all made in reference to the form of
Government, fhould remain unvariable, while the
Government itfelf was changed. For what the
Author of the epiftle to the Hebrews fays of the
Priest (in a Conftitution where the two Societies
were incorporated) muft be equally true of the
King. — The Priesthood being changed,
there is made also, of necessity, a change of
the Law [c]. And now it was that Jesus, the Messiah, who is here fpoken of as making this change,
in quality of Priest, made it likewife in quality
of King. For, as we learn from the hiftory of
his Miniftry, he came as Heir of God, to fucceed
immediately without any interregnum, in his Father's kingdom : God having delivered up to
his Son the kingdom, of which the Father was, till
then, in poffeffion. And this change in the Government, from the *temporal Theocracy* of God the
Father, to the *fpiritual Kingdom* of God the Son,
was made in the fame folemn and authentic manner
in which that Theocracy was introduced. God
raifed up from amongft his chofen People, a *Prophet like unto Mofes*, who exercifed the *Legiflative* power, like Mofes ; and affumed the *Regal*
power, like God. He gave a new Law to be
adminiftered in a new Kingdom, and confirmed
the divinity of the Difpenfation by the moft ftu-
pendous miracles. Thus, we find, the Theocracy
did indeed fubfift till the coming of Chrift.

And this Abolition of it by the Son of God,
I take to be the true completion of that famous
prophecy of Jacob, of which fo much hath been
written and difputed. The Sceptre shall not

c Chap. vii. ver. 12.

DEPART

DEPART FROM JUDAH, NOR A LAWGIVER FROM
BETWEEN HIS FEET, UNTIL SHILOH COME [d], i. e.
the THEOCRACY shall continue over the Jews [e] until Christ come to take possession of his Father's
Kingdom: For there was never any *Lawgiver* [f],
in *Judah*, but GOD by the ministry of Moses, until
the coming of his SON.

JESUS the MESSIAH, the best interpreter of the
Oracles of GOD, of which he himself is the capital subject, and for whose sake the *chain of Pro-
phesies* was so early drawn out, and extended to
such a length, seems to have paraphrased and explained the words of Jacob concerning the *departure of the Sceptre from Judah*, by his declaration recorded in St. Matthew, THE PROPHETS
AND THE LAW PROPHESIED TILL JOHN [g], i. e.
" the Mosaic Law, and the Theocratic Government by which it was dispensed, continued in
Being till the approach of this harbinger of
Christ, John the Baptist; but was then superseded
by the promulgation of a *new Law* and the establishment of a *new Kingdom.*"

[d] Gen. xlix. 10.

[e] Who took their Name from the Tribe of *Judah*; the rest
being incorporated in that Tribe, or extinguished in Captivity.

[f] *Mhhokek, Legislator*, aut *Legis interpres.* But the first is
its original and proper Signification. And thus Isaiah [chap.
xxxiii. ver. 22.] " The Lord is our *Judge*, the Lord is our LAW-
GIVER, [*Mhhokekenou*] the Lord is our *King*, he will save us."
Where the word *Mhhokek* is used in its proper Signification of
Lawgiver; the other Sense of Dispenser or Interpreter of the
Law being contained in the titles of *Judge* and *King*.

[g] Matth. xi. 13.

R 3   But

But as this interpretation is so different from the common, and underftands the Prophefy as fortelling. that the Jewifh nation fhould not be bereft of Sovereign Power, by falling under a foreign Yoke, till the Advent of the Messiah, the Reader will excufe me, if I detain him a little longer on fo important a fubject.

The common notion of the *Sceptre of Judah*, is explained three different ways, each of which has it's particular Followers.

1. Some fuppofe the *Sceptre of Judah* to fignify the SOVEREIGNTY OF THE JEWISH NATION at large.

2. Others again fuppofe it to fignify the SOVEREIGNTY OF THE TRIBE OF JUDAH.

3. And a third fort contend that it fignifies not a fovereign or regal, but a TRIBAL SCEPTRE only.

In the Senfe of a *Sovereignty in the Jewifh people at large*, which is the moft general interpretation, and, in my Opinion, the moft natural of the three, (as the whole People were long denominated from that tribe) the pretended Prophefy was not only never fulfilled, but has been directly falfified: becaufe long before the *coming of Shilo*, or of Chrift, the Sceptre or Sovereignty in the Jewifh people was *departed*. During the Babylonian and Perfian Captivity, and while afterwards they continued in a tributary dependence on the Greeks, they could, in no reafonable fenfe, be faid to have retained their *Sceptre*, their Sovereignty, or independent

pendent Rule.   But it may be replied, " that the
Prophecy by *departure*, meant a final departure ;
and in thefe inftances it was but temporary : for
CYRUS reftored the *Sceptre* to them ; and when it
was again loft in the grecian Empire, the MACCA-
BEI recovered it for them." Though this be allowed, yet we muft ftill confefs, that the Romans, who,
under Pompey reduced Judea to a dependant Province, effectually overthrew the Prophecy. POMPEY
took Jerufalem ; and left to Hyrcanus, the laft of
the Afmonean family, only the office of High-Prieft.
From this time, to the birth of Chrift, it was
ever in dependence on the Romans, who difpofed
of all things at their pleafure.   The Senate gave
the Government of Judæa to Antipater;   and
then to Herod his Son, under the title of King.
And Archelaus, on the Death of his Father, did
not dare to take poffeffion of this fubject-king-
dom, till he had obtained leave of Auguftus : who
afterwards, on complaint of the Jews againft him,
banifhed him into the Weft, where he died.   Now
the precarious Rule of a dependent Monarch
could no more be called a *Sceptre* (which in the
figurative mode of all languages, fignifies *Sovereignty*) than the condition of the Jews could be
faid to be fovereign, when this Archelaus was depofed, and Coponius a Roman Knight made procurator of Judæa, at that time which the fupporters
of this interpretation fix for the *Departure of the
Sceptre.*

I reckon for nothing another objection which
has been made to the common interpretation,
" That after the return from the Captivity, the
Jews were, from time to time, under a form of
Government refembling rather the Ariftocratic
than the Monarchic ;" becaufe the *Sceptre* or Sove-

reignty, belongs equally to all thofe Forms. This then makes no more againft the common interpretation, than the other, I am now going to mention, makes for it, namely, that the Senate of Rome gave the Government of Judæa to Herod under the title of KING; fince the dependent rule of this Roitelet was as certainly the *departure of a Sceptre*, as a Sovereignty under an ariftocratic Government was the *continuance* of it.

The learned Father Tournemine was fo embarraffed with thefe difficulties, that in a differtation on *the Sceptre of Judah*, he endeavours to fhew, that the proof of the predicted birth of Chrift from this Prophefy, arifes not from the *departure of the Sceptre*, but from its re-eftablifhment under the Meffiah[h]. Which thefis, (as the intelligent reader may obferve) fairly put him in the road; and, had it been purfued, would have led him, to the fenfe I am here endeavouring to eftablifh.

The fecond branch of the common interpretation is, That, by the *Sceptre* is fignified a *civil fovereignty in the tribe of Judah*. This, in my opinion, has ftill lefs of ftability than the other. It fuppofes that the *Sceptre*, or the fupreme rule of the Jewifh People, remained in natives of that Tribe, from the time of David to the coming of Chrift. But Petavius hath fhewn, that from the giving of the Prophecy to the time of David, (a Space of above fix hundred Years) there was but one or two Rulers defcended from the Tribe of Judah: And that from the death of Sedecias to the birth of Chrift (a fpace of near the fame number of years) all the Rulers of the Jewifh People were of other

[h] Journal de Trevoux. Mars 1705. & Feb. 1721.

Tribes;

Tribes; the Afmonean princes particularly being all of the tribe of Levi[1]? The Abbé de Houteville, who, at a very eafy rate, hath obtained the reputation of an able defender of Revelation[k], hath indeed invented a curious expedient to evade this difficulty. His fyftem is, that the rulers of the tribe of Levi (and fo I fuppofe of the reft) exercifed this Sovereignty by leave, or deputation from the Tribe of Judah. To fuch wretched fhifts are learned men reduced, when they have reverfed the order of things, and made Truth to wait upon their Syftems; inftead of making their Syftems fubfervient to Truth.

Thefe two fenfes, (by one or other of which the common interpretation hath been long fupported) being found on a ftricter fcrutiny, to be intenable, men caft about for a third: and a happy one it was thought to be, which contrived, that, *Sceptre* fhould fignify a *domeſtic*, not a *civil* rule; a TRIBAL, not a SOVEREIGN *Sceptre*; and of which, they fay, JUDAH, at the giving of the Prophecy, was already poffeffed. This expedient, the learned Dr. Sher-

[1] — At complures antiquorum recentiorumque qui in illa Jacobi fententia *Judam* peculiari de tribu intellexerunt, id fibi Patriarcham voluiffe credunt, ex ftirpe ac progenie *Judæ* filii ipfius perpetuo Judæis præfuturum aliquem eorumque fore principem, donec Chriftus adveniat. Sed in hujus reddenda dicti ratione multum æftuant, fiquidem vetuftatis omni tefte memoriâ refelluntur, quæ non folum ante Davidem unum alterumve duntaxat ex illa tribu rexiiſe populum oftendit, annis circiter 675 ab edita prohetia; fed etiam poft Sedecias necem, occafumque Urbis & Templi ad Chriftum ufque de alia quam *Judæ* ftirpe duces extitiffe annis 588; et enim Machabæos conftat ex Levitica et Sacerdotali progenie defcendere. *Ration. Temporum,* Par. II. L. III. C. 16.

[k] See his book intitled, *Religion préuvée par les Faits.*

lock,

lock, Bifhop of London, has honoured with his fupport and protection[1].

It would be want of refpect to fo eminent a Perfon, to pafs over this refinement with the fame flight notice that has been given to the other two. I fhall therefore do myfelf the honour to confider his Lordfhip's reafoning more at large.

His Lordfhip's firft argument in fupport of a *tribal Sceptre* is—That the *Sceptre's not* DEPART-ING *from Judah* fhews plainly that Judah had a Sceptre when the prophecy was given.—" Is there " any fenfe (fays his Lordfhip) in faying that a " thing fhall not *depart*, which never was yet in " *poffeffion?* The prophecy is not a *grant* of the " Sceptre, but a *confirmation* of it. Now a con- " firmation of nothing, is nothing: And, to " make it fomething, the *poffeffion* of the thing " *confirmed* muft be fuppofed. I know not by " what rules of language or grammar, thefe words " can be conftrued into a *grant* of the Scep- " tre. And tho' fo many writers and interpre- " ters have followed this fenfe, yet I do not re- " member to have feen one paffage or parallel " expreffion from the Scripture, or any other " author, produced to juftify the interpreta- " tion [m]."

Is there any Senfe (his Lordfhip afks) *in faying a thing fhall* not DEPART which *never was yet in pof-feffion?* Yes certainly, a very good one, in a PRO-

---

[1] *Ufe and Intent of Prophefy.* Differt. III. 5th Edit. 1749.

[m] Page 326—7.

phesy, where the ſubject is not of a preſent but
of a future poſſeſſion ; and where the Holy Spirit
is wont to *call the things that are not, as though
they were.* The Subject is a *Sceptre,* which could
in no ſenſe, not even in the ſenſe of a *tribal ſceptre,* be in poſſeſſion of Judah before he became a
Tribe. His Lordſhip indeed ſuppoſes he became
a Tribe immediately after the death of Jacob.—
*This power in the hands of the Tribes took place im-
mediately upon the death of Jacob* [a]. But if it did ?
Was not that acceſſion as properly *future,* as if it
had been a thouſand years after ? Judah then, at
the time of this Prophecy, not being in poſſeſſion
of his Sceptre, *a confirmation of nothing is nothing,*
&c. ſo that all the abſurdities here imagined,
ſtick to his Lordſhip's Æra of the *Sceptre,* as well
as to the common one. But let us ſuppoſe that
Jacob's Prophecy and death were individual; and
then ſee how he proves his aſſertion, that Judah
and the Reſt became Tribes immediately on the
death of Jacob. His proof is a little extraordinary—*When Moſes and Aaron led them into
the Wilderneſs* (ſays his Lordſhip) *we hear of the*
Elders *of the people, and the* Rulers *of the congregation* [b], His aſſertion, is that the *tribal ſceptre* ſprung up from the aſhes of Jacob ; and his
proof, that it aroſe and flouriſhed in the Wilderneſs. This is indeed the truth ; it was a Native
of that place; as may be fairly *preſumed* from
the occaſion which the Iſraelites had of a tribal
rule, (namely, to fit them for the warfare they
were now about to undertake) and as may be fairly *proved* from the firſt chapter of the book of
Numbers—" And the Lord ſpake unto Moſes in
" the wilderneſs of Sinai: Take ye the ſum of

---

[a] Page 323.　　　[b] Page 323.

"all the congregation of the Children of Israel, "after their families, by the house of their Fa-"thers——*all that are able to go forth to war in* "*Israel*; Thou and Aaron shall number them with "their armies. And with you, there SHALL BE "A MAN of every tribe; every one HEAD OF "THE HOUSE of his Fathers——and they as-"sembled all the congregation; and they declared "their pedigrees, after their families, by the "house of their Fathers—These were those which "were numbered: and the PRINCES OF ISRAEL "BEING TWELVE MEN, EACH ONE WAS FOR THE "HOUSE OF HIS FATHERS. And the Children of "Israel shall pitch their tents, every man by his "own camp, and every man by his own standard, "throughout their Hosts——And the Children of "Israel did according to all the Lord commanded "them [p]." Then follows the order of the Tribes in their tents [q]. Now surely, this detailed account of these *tribal Sceptres* hath all the marks of a new Institution.

The Bishop's hypothesis therefore is without foundation: the *Sceptre* was something in *reversion*. Indeed the particular words, as well as the general nature of Prophesy, declare the subject to be of things future.—"And Jacob called to his "sons, and said, *Gather yourselves together that I* "*may tell you what shall befall you* IN THE LAST "DAYS [r]." The Bishop owns, that *most of the Interpreters*, from these words, *take it for granted, and it is the common notion, that the Sceptre was not to be settled in Judah's family till some ages after the death of Jacob* [s]. I think thay had reason

[p] Numb. i. 4—5—18—44—52—54. [q] Chap. ii.
[r] Gen. Chap. xlix. ver. 1. [s] Page 326.

so

ſo to do.   How does his Lordſhip prove they had not? In this manner. " The obſervation, when " rightly applied, is right.   And if the *continu-* " *ance* of the Sceptre of Judah be, as I ſuppoſe, " the thing foretold, it extends to the very laſt " days of the Jewiſh State ; and in this reſpect the " interpretation is juſtified '." *i. e.* if you will agree that *futurity* refers to the *continuance,* and not to the *eſtabliſhment* of the Sceptre, his Lordſhip will ſhew you, how well he can evade this objec- tion.   But tho' we were inclined to be thus com- plaiſant, the book of Numbers would not ſuffer us ; which informs us (we ſee) that even the *tribal Sceptre* was eſtabliſhed long after the death of Jacob. But to go no farther than the Prophefy.   If each Tribe had a Scepter then exiſting, how happened it that Judah's is only named, *by way of* CONFIR- MATION, as his Lordſhip will have it.   For, *by way of* GRANT, we find Dan too had a Sceptre — *Dan* SHALL *judge his People as one of the Tribes* [or SCEP- TRES] *of Iſrael.*   But then Dan's is a *reverſionary* Sceptre ; and ſuch a one deſtroys all his Lordſhip has been erecting.

To proceed — *The Prophefy* (ſays the Biſhop) *is not a* GRANT *of a ſceptre, but a* CONFIRMATION. The Prophefy itſelf plainly intimates the contrary. Jacob having told his ſons that he would inform them *of what ſhould befall them in the laſt days,* when he comes to Judah, he ſays, *Thy Father's Children ſhall bow down before thee* ".   This, if it was any thing, was the promiſe of a future Sceptre ; and conſequently it was the *grant.*

The Biſhop goes on—*Now a confirmation of nothing is nothing.*   Without doubt.   But he ſup-

' Page 327.   " Ver. 8.

pofes, (what I have fhewn to be a miftake) that
there was no *grant*. If there were a *grant*, then
the confirmation of it was the confirmation of
fomething. He feems to be apprehenfive of fo
obvious an anfwer, for he immediately adds—*I
know not by what rules of language or grammar thefe
words can be conftrued into a* GRANT *of the Sceptre*.
By the plaineft *rule* in the world; that of *common
fenfe*, the firft and capital *rule* in every Art as well
as *grammar*. For if Jacob made a declaration
concerning fome future prerogative, as the words
—*Thy father's Children fhall bow down before thee*
—prove he did; and that this was the firft time
that Judah heard of it, as the words—*I will tell you
what fhall befall you in the laft days*—prove it was;
What can this Prophecy be but *the* GRANT *of a
Sceptre?*

    " Though fo many writers and interpreters (fays
" the Bifhop) have followed this fenfe, yet I do
" not remember to have feen one paffage or pa-
" rallel expreffion from the Scripture or any other
" writer produced to juftify the interpretation."
As for *any other Writers* than thofe of Scripture, I
know of none who have prophefied: and the language of prophefy hath peculiarities unknown to
other Compofitions. But a *Scripture-writer* I am
able to produce; and the fame who has recorded
this Prophecy of Jacob.—On Abraham's departure out of Haran, he being then feventy-five years
of age, *the Lord*, as Mofes tells us, *appeared unto
him and faid*—*Unto thy* SEED *will I give this Land* [x].
Was this now a *grant*, or a *confirmation* only of SEED?
" A confirmation only, fays his Lordfhip: All
the *grant* contained in thefe words is the grant of

[x] Gen. chap. xii. ver. 7.

                      the

the LAND : and this shews, (will he say) that the
Seed was now exiling : for a nonentity is incapable
of receiving any grant or donation : besides, *a
confirmation of nothing is nothing,* and so on."—
Notwithstanding all this, it so happens that Abraham had then *no Seed.*

Here now is a *parallel expression,* which holds
a fortiori. For if it be a little anomalous
to talk of a *thing's departing which was never yet in
possession,* it seems to be much more absurd to talk
of *giving* to persons who were never yet in Being.
Besides, the promise of Rule actually accompanies the promise of its duration : but the express
promise of Seed does not accompany the promise
of a provision for it: I suppose the reason of this
difference of expression in the two places is, because to get a Son is a much commoner case than
to get a Sceptre.

His Lordship having thus shewn, that Judah's
Sceptre was a *Sceptre in possession,* he will prove next,
that it was not a *civil,* but a *tribal Sceptre* ; which
did not stretch its sovereignty over a whole nation,
but was confined to the œconomic rule of the single
tribe of Judah.—" Another thing supposed (says
" he) by most interpreters is, that the *Sceptre,*
" here mentioned, is an emblem of Dominion
" over all the tribes of Jacob. But how can that
" be? Had not Jacob settled a *sceptre* in every
" tribe ? as is evident, ver. 16. *Dan shall judge his
" people as one of the Sceptre's of Israel.* Suppose
" a Father has divided his estate amongst twelve
" Sons, and should say of one of them, *The
" Estate shall not depart from John, for many ages* ;
" could you possibly suppose him to mean more
" than the *share* of the Estate given to John ?
I " Could

" Could you underſtand him to mean that all the
" eſtate, the twelve ſhares, ſhould come to John
" and continue in his family? The caſe is the
" ſame here. Twelve Princes are created; Of one
" of Them Jacob ſays, *the Sceptre ſhall not de-*
" *part from him until Shiloh come.* Is it not plain
" then, that the Sceptres are diſtinguiſhed here;
" and that it is foretold of one, that it ſhall long
" outlaſt the reſt?—conſequently the Sceptre here
" is an emblem of Authority IN AND OVER ONE
" TRIBE ONLY [y]."

His Lordſhip's reaſoning, on which he grounds
his parallel, ſtands thus—Judah's ſceptre was the
ſame with Dan's: now Dan's was a *tribal* Sceptre;
therefore Judah's. But the very words of the Prophecy ſhew that the Sceptres were *ſpecifically* different. Of Dan it is ſaid, he ſhall judge his People AS ONE OF THE TRIBES OR SCEPTRES OF IS-
RAEL. Here is a *tribal* Sceptre marked out in expreſs and proper terms. But of Judah's Sceptre
it is ſaid, THY FATHER'S CHILDREN SHALL BOW
DOWN BEFORE THEE. Who were theſe *Children*
but the eleven tribes? So that here a *civil* and a
ſovereign Sceptre, is as properly and expreſly marked out for Judah, as before, a *tribal* one for Dan.
This ſhall judge his own tribe; but the other ſhall,
with his own tribe, judge the reſt alſo. And yet
if you will rely on his Lordſhip's Authority, he
has *a caſe in point*; and he aſſures us " that Judah's
grant is the ſame as that of a Father's to his Son
John, who when he had divided his eſtate amongſt
his twelve Sons ſhould ſay of John's part, that it
ſhould not depart for many ages."

[y] Page 328——9.

He

He tells us next, " that the sense of the word Lawgiver will follow the fate of the word *Sceptre*[z]." In this, I perfectly agree with him. And therefore as his sense of the word *Sceptre* is found to be erroneous, his sense of the word *Lawgiver* must fall with it.

All that follows has nothing to do with the question of a *tribal Sceptre*, till we come to page 344. From thence to 350, he endeavours to take advantage of the hypothesis, to shew that this *tribal Sceptre* never departed from Judah till the coming of Christ: And here he had an easy task. But unluckily confounding *oeconomic* with *civil* Rule, he embarasses himself as much, to make out the completion of the Prophecy, as the supporters of the other two branches of the common interpretation are wont to do.—As where he talks of the Jews in Babylon *ordering all matters relating to their own* CIVIL *and* ECCLESIASTICAL *Affairs*[a].—Their *coming back to their own Country as a people and a nation* GOVERNED BY THEIR OWN LAWS —*though never* SO FREE A PEOPLE *as they had been formerly. They lived under subjection to the Persian Monarch, and under the empire of the Greeks and Romans*[b].—*The Evangelists shew that they lived under their* OWN LAWS, *and* EXECUTED JUDGMENT *amongst themselves*[c].—*Had the exercise of* JUDICIAL AUTHORITY *amongst themselves*[d]. Thus, like the Successors of Peter, who enlarged his *Rock* into a *Citadel*, his Lordship at last lengthens his *tribal* Sceptre into a *sovereign*. But if here he extends it over a People and Nation, he contracts it as much by and by; and we see it shrink up into a mere

[z] Page 329.   [a] Page 345.   [b] Page 347.   [c] Page 349.   [d] Page 350.

philofophical or Stoical Regality. His Lordfhip undertakes to prove that the Jews were a FREE PEOPLE, from their own confcioufnefs of their free condition. —*When our Saviour* (fays the Bifhop) *tells the Jews* " The truth fhall make you free." *they reply,* " We are Abraham's Children, and were never " in bondage to any man ͤ." This his Lordfhip urges as a proof of their *Civil freedom.* But if the Jews, who expected a carnal Meffiah to lead real armies againft their enemies, could fuppofe that Jefus made them an offer of fending *Truth* in perfon, to execute this commiffion for them, their ftupidity muft have exceeded every thing we have been told of it, by their Enemies. To be plain with his Lordfhip, the fubject here debated, between Jefus and his Adverfaries, is moft foreign from his Lordfhip's purpofe. Our bleffed Saviour is here addreffing himfelf to the PHARISEES, a rank of men not ignorant of the Greek philofophy, (tho' greatly miftaking its ufe when they brought fo much of it into the Law) and therefore, with a Stoical dignity, he tells them—*the truth fhall fet you free.* They anfwer him in the fame tone, *We are Abraham's Children, and were never in bondage to any man.* That is, " Our principles are of divine extraction, and we never fuffered ourfelves to be inflaved to human decifions." *Surely* (fays his Lordfhip) *they had not forgot their captivity in Babylon.* Forgot! Why, Jefus had faid nothing to put them in mind of it. The queftion is not about their freedom from Babylon, but from Error.— *Much lefs* (fays he) *could they be ignorant of the power of the Romans over them at that time, and yet we fee they account themfelves free.* And why fhould they not, when the Queftion between Jefus

ͤ Page 349.

and them was only who should make them so, HE
or ABRAHAM.   Strange! that his Lordship's own
account of their *civil condition* under the *power of
the Romans*, should not have brought him to see,
that the subject in hand was only of their *moral
Condition.*   Stranger still! that his solution of this
difficulty should not have led him to discover that it
was but imaginary—*they were free* (says his Lordship) *for they lived by their own Laws and executed
judgment amongst themselves.*—Had he added—*but,
at the precarious nod of an arbitary Tyrant*—it would
doubtless have given great force to his observation :
For, about this time, Coponius, a Roman Knight,
was named Procurator of Judea.   Nay, even the
precarious privilege of punishing capitally was
now taken from them : They had a pagan Governor ; and Justice was administered, not by
their own Forms of Law, but by the Roman.   An
admirable character of *civil freedom !*

His Lordship seems to be no happier in answering other's objections, than in urging his own
proofs.   " You will say (continues he) why did
" not Jacob foretell also the continuance of the
" Sceptre of Benjamin ? For the tribe of Ben-
" jamin run the same fortune with that of Judah :
" they went together into captivity : they returned
" home together ; and were both in Being when
" *Shiloh* came [f]."

Upon my word, a shrewd objection.   Let us
see how his Lordship quits his hands of it.   His
first answer is,—*That from the division of the Kingdom after the death of Solomon, the tribe of Benjamin and the remnant of Israel, that is, part of all*

---

[f] Page 355.

the

the other tribes, ADHERED TO JUDAH AS THEIR
HEAD [g].

Here his Lordſhip ſeems fairly to have given up
the Cauſe; his anſwer proving, in ſo many words,
that *Judah's Sceptre* was not *tribal,* but *civil.*
Let us examine it ſtep by ſtep. *Benjamin and the
remnants of all the other tribes adhered to Judah as
their head.* Now ſuch an adherence can be no
other than an acknowledgement of a *Civil Sceptre*
in Judah. Yet his Lordſhip gives this as a reaſon
why the continuance of Judah's Sceptre is foretold,
and not Benjamin's. Therefore the Sceptre, whoſe
continuance is foretold, was a *civil,* not a *tribal,*
Sceptre, even on his own principles. If this needed a ſupport, the words of the Prophecy afford it
amply : his Lordſhip ſays, that *Benjamin and
the remnants of all the other tribes adhered to Judah
as their* HEAD ; *and this adherence,* Jacob foretells
—*Thy Father's children ſhall* FALL DOWN *before
thee.*

Suppoſing therefore that this Sceptre of Judah
were of the *civil* kind, his Lordſhip, it muſt be
owned, has given a very ſatisfactory reaſon why
Benjamin's *tribal* ſceptre was not mentioned. But
if both were *tribal* Sceptres, the *continuance* of
Benjamin's had as good a claim to the Prophet's
notice (for any thing the Biſhop has ſhewn to
the contrary) as Judah's. Since, as *Tribes,*
they both continued to exiſt, and to exiſt diftinct.

His ſecond anſwer to the Objection ſeems as little ſatisfactory as the firſt—*Though the continuance of*

[g] Page 355—6.

the

the SCEPTRE *of Benjamin is not foretold, yet the continuance of the tribe or* PEOPLE *of Benjamin is distinctly foretold*[h]. Would you desire a more conclusive argument against his own notion of a *tribal Sceptre?* If this prophetic Sceptre of Judah was a *civil* one, there is a very good reason why the *continuance of the people,* and not of the *Sceptre* of Benjamin should be foretold; because what Judah and Benjamin had in common was their continuing to exist as distinct tribes; the *Sceptre* being peculiar to the first: But if a *tribal* Sceptre be the subject of the Prophecy concerning Judah, then no possible reason can be assigned why the *continuance* of Benjamin's Sceptre should not be honoured with the divine notice as well as Judah's; since his Lordship assures us—*they both run the same fortune ; they went together into captivity; they returned together to Judea; and were both in being when Shiloh came.* And while a *Tribe* continues distinct, a *tribal Sceptre* continues with it; just as the head of a family exists so long as there is a family to govern.

All this considered, his Lordship, in my humble opinion, had done well not to load himself with more than he had occasion to carry: especially as he had so little to answer for, in the success of this hypothesis; for he tells us at the end of his DISSERTATION, *that he has nothing more to add, but to acquaint the reader that the interpretation of Jacob's Prophesy now advanced, was not a mere invention of his own; that it was, as to the main point, the same with that which is the fourth in* HUETIUS, *and by him rejected, but for such reasons as had been fully obviated in this dissertation.*—That *it was the same which* JUNIUS *and* TREMELLIUS, *and our own learn-ed Countryman,* AINSWORTH, *had espoused; and which not many years ago was revived and improved by Mr.* JONCOURT [i].

Now, from what hath been said it appears, that of all the three branches, into which the common interpretation spreads, though they be equally weak, the laft betrays its weaknefs moft. But, what is of principal confideration, it is, of all the three, leaft fuitable to the DIGNITY OF PROPHECY; the whole body of which has a perpetual reference to one or other of the great parts of the Difpenfa-tion of Grace. Now the firft branch refers with fuitable dignity to a whole People at large: the fecond to the fame People under the Government of one certain line: while the third concerns only the fortunes of a fingle Tribe, and under a Family-idea.

The common interpretation therefore being fhewn fo very exceptionable in all its branches, what remains for us to conclude but that the true and real meaning of the *Sceptre of Judah* is that THEO-CRATIC GOVERNMENT which God, by the vicege-rency of Judges, Kings, and Rulers exercifed over the Jewifh nation? We have fhewn from various confiderations of weight, that this THEOCRACY, which was inftituted by the miniftry of Mofes, continued over that People till the coming of Shiloh or Chrift; THAT PROPHET *like unto Mofes* whom God had promifed to *raife up.* And to fup-port what hath been urged from reafon, to illuft-rate this important truth, we have here a Pro-phetic declaration enouncing the fame thing,———

[i] Page 358.

the

the sceptre shall not depart from Judah till Shiloh come:
Shiloh is Christ. Now Christ is not the Successor
of those VICEGERENTS of the Jewish State, but
of God himself, the KING of the Jews. The
Sceptre therefore which descends to him, thro' the
hands of those vicegerents, is not merely a CIVIL,
but a THEOCRATIC *Sceptre.* This, at the same
time, explains the Evangelic doctrine of CHRIST's
KINGDOM, arising out of the *Theocracy* or *Kingdom
of God.* Hence the distinction in that famous
declaration of Christ, so much abused to factious
and party purposes, that HIS KINGDOM WAS NOT
OF THIS WORLD : The Theocracy which was administred over the Jews only, and in a carnal
manner, was a *Kingdom of this world:* but when
transferred to Shiloh, and extended over all mankind, and administred in a spiritual manner, it became a *Kingdom not of this world.* And the making
the *Sceptre of Judah* neither *Tribal,* nor MERELY
Civil, but properly *Theocratic,* clears the Prophesy
from those insuperable difficulties which render all
the other interpretations hurtful or dishonourable
to the Prophetic system in general.

Thefe are the superior advantages of the fense I
have here endeavoured to establish. Nor are these all
the advantages. The Prophesy is seen to embrace a
much nobler object than was imagined. It was
suppofed to relate only to the fortunes of the
Jewish Oeconomy, and we find it extends itself to
the *whole Dispensation of Grace.* It was considered
but as a simple PROPHECY, while it had the dignity
of a REVELATION. It was mistaken for the *species,*
when it is indeed, of the *genus.*

But to all this an *Answerer* may reply. 1.
" That, as we admit the THEOCRACY to be *a King-*

dom of this World, the same objection will lie as well against the CONTINUANCE or duration of a *Theocratic* Sceptre as of a mere *Civil* one." But here we must diftinguifh. The Theocracy was indeed carnal in its *adminiftration*, but in its *original* it was Divine. Therefore, as where the fubject is of the *continuance* of a *mere civil* Sceptre, we cannot but underftand the *continuance of its adminiftration*, becaufe the adminiftration is infeparable from the exiftence; fo where the fubject is of the continuance of a *Theocratic* Sceptre, we muft underftand that continuance to confift in its remaining unrevoked, fince what is of divine original exifts, independently of its being actually adminiftered; it exifts till it be formally abrogated. This difference is evident from the nature of things. Forms of Government ordained by Men ceafe when Men no longer adminifter them: becaufe, in the non-adminiftration of them, they are naturally fuppofed to revoke what they had ordained: But men's ceafing to adminifter (whether by choice or force) a Form of Government given by God, does not, (on any rules of logic or ideas of nature) imply God's revocation of that form of Government.

Again, we muft remember what has been faid of the effect and confequence of a THEOCRACY. It not only *united*, but *incorporated* the two Societies, civil and religious, into One. And this incorporated body of the Jewifh State went by the name of THE LAW. Now under that part of the Law which more intimately regarded Religion, the Jews always lived FREE till the publication of the Gofpel; though the other part of it, regarding the fovereign adminiftration of civil policy and juftice, they had loft from the time of Pompey. For a
power

power precariously enjoyed, and ready to be abolished at the nod of a Conqueror, can never be called *Sovereign* (which implies the being free and independant) without the worst abuse of words, which is, the quibbling upon them. So that a Sovereignty in this Theocracy was still administered to the last, tho' in part. However this partial exercise was consentaneous to the System on which this Theocracy was dispensed; its Administration being ordained to have a gradual decline. The Jews, for their transgressions, being first of all deprived of that natural effect of Theocratic rule, the *extraordinary providence :* and then, for their incorrigible manners, further punished by an infringement of their civil sovereignty : but still the Theocracy, as to that more essential, the Religious part, remained unhurt till the coming of Christ : And let it be observed, that it was this part in particular which was to be assigned over to him, from the Father. Thus, as I said before, this is not so properly a *prediction* of human events, as a *revelation* concerning the course of God's Dispensation.

2. Secondly it hath been objected " that according to the sense here put upon the *Sceptre*, it should have been said—*the Sceptre shall not depart from* JEHOVAH *instead of* JUDAH.". But such Objectors do not advert, that the Theocracy was administered by Vicegerents of JUDAH. And this likewise will account for the expression of a *Lawgiver between his feet.*

3. Lastly it may be said, " That by this interpretation of the *Sceptre of Judah* we deprive the Prophesy of one principal part of the information it was supposed to give, namely, the TIME of Christ's

Chrift's advent, which the common interpretation is fuppofed to fix exactly." To this I anfwer, that Religion lofes nothing by this change, fince there are fo many other Prophefies which point out the *time* with infinitely more precifion. On the other hand, Religion gains much by it, in evading a number of objections, which had ftigmatized the fuppofed Prediction with apparent marks of falf-hood.

Thus we fee this noble Prophecy, concerning the transfer of the Kingdom of GOD, to CHRIST, con-tains a matter of much greater dignity in itfelf, and of much greater moment for the fupport of CHRISTI-ANITY than could arife from the perplexed quef-tion about the reign of the Afmonean Princes, or the Continuance of the power of life and death amongft a tributary People. For, in predicting the *Abolition of the Law*, it fupplies us with a new and excellent Argument for the Converfion of the Jewifh People, fatally perfuaded of its *eternal obli-gation*.

The Reafons of my being fo particular concern-ing the duration of the THEOCRACY are various, and will be feen as occafion offers. Only the rea-der may here take notice, that it was neceffary for the prefent purpofe, to fhew its continuance throughout the whole duration of the Republic, in order to vindicate the juftice of thofe Laws all along in force, for the punifhment of idolatrous Worfhip.

SECT. IV.

THUS far as to the nature and duration of the Mofaic Republic. Let us now fee what PECULIAR CONSEQUENCES neceffarily attended the admini-

administration of a THEOCRATIC form of Government.

One necessary consequence was an EXTRAORDINARY PROVIDENCE. For the affairs of a People under a Theocracy, being administered by God as King; and his peculiar and immediate administration of human affairs being what we call *an extraordinary Providence*, it follows that an extraordinary Providence must needs be exercised over such a People. My meaning is, that if the Jews were indeed under a Theocracy, they were indeed under an extraordinary Providence : And if a Theocracy was only pretended, yet an extraordinary Providence must necessarily be pretended likewise. In a word, they must be either both true or both false, but still inseparable, in reality or idea. Nor does this at all contradict (as was suggested by Doctor SYKES even after he had seen his suggestion confuted) what I observe concerning the gradual decay and total extinction of the extraordinary Providence, while the Theocracy yet existed. For when I say *an extraordinary Providence was one necessary consequence of a Theocracy*, I can only mean that it was so in its original constitution, and in the order and nature of things : not that in this, which was matter of compact, the contravening acts of one Party might not make a separation. For, as this extraordinary Providence was (besides it being a mode of administration arising out of a Theocracy) a reward for obedience, it became liable to forfeiture by disobedience, tho' subjection to the Government still continued. I beg leave to illustrate this position both by a foreign and a domestic instance. The Ærarii in the Roman State were such who, for their crimes, were deprived of the right of Citizens : Yet these delinquents were obliged to

pay

pay the public taxes.   At home, a voice in the fupreme Council of the kingdom is the neceffary
confequence of an Englifh Barony; yet they may
be feparated by a judicial Sentence; and actually
have been fo feparated; as we may fee in the two
famous cafes of Lord Verulam, and the Earl of
Middlefex, in the reign of James the Ift; who were
both deprived of their feats in the Houfe of Lords,
and yet held their Baronies, with all the other
rights pertaining to them.   Thus a Punifhment of
this kind was inflicted on the rebellious Ifraelites:
they were deprived of the *extraordinary Providence*:
and were yet held fubject to the *Theocracy*, as appears from the Sentence pronounced upon them,
by the mouth of the Prophet Ezekiel:—" Ye
" polluted yourfelves with your idols even unto
" this day: and fhall I be enquired of by you,
" O houfe of *Ifrael?* As I live, faith the Lord
" God, *I will not be enquired of by you.   And*
" *that which cometh into your Mind fhall not be at*
" *all, that ye fay, We will be as the Heathen, as*
" *the Families of the Countries to ferve Wood and*
" *Stone.*   As I live, faith the Lord, *with a mighty*
" *Hand, and with a ftretched out Arm, and with*
" *Fury poured out will I rule over you,   And I will*
" *bring you out from the People, and will gather*
" *you out of the Countries wherein ye are fcattered,*
" with a mighty Hand, and with a ftretched out
" Arm, and with Fury poured out.   And I will
" bring you into the Wildernefs of the People,
" and there will I plead with you Face to Face.
" *Like as I pleaded with your Fathers in the Wilder-*
" *nefs of the Land of* Egypt, fo will I plead with
" you faith the Lord.   And *I will caufe you to*
" *pafs under the Rod.*   And *I will bring you into*
" *the* Bond of the Covenant."   Chap. xx. ver.
31—37.   It is here we fee denounced, that the
extra-

extraordinary Providence ſhould be withdrawn; or, in Scripture phraſe, *that God would not be enquired of by them*; That they ſhould remain in this con- dition, which their *Fathers* had occaſionally felt *in the wilderneſs*, when the extraordinary Providence, for their ſignal diſobedience was, from time to time, ſuſpended: And yet, that, tho' they ſtrove to diſperſe themſelves amongſt the People round about, and projected *in their minds to be as the heathen, and the families of the Countries to ſerve wood and ſtone*, they ſhould ſtill be under the govern- ment of a THEOCRACY; Which, when adminiſter- ed without an extraordinary Providence, the bleſſ- ing naturally attendant on it, was, and was juſtly called, THE ROD AND BOND OF THE COVE- NANT.

But now if you will believe a Profeſſor of Divi- nity and a no leſs eminent dealer in Laws, the caſe grows worſe and worſe, and, from a contradiction in my ſyſtem, it becomes a contradiction in God's. For thus Dr. RUTTHERFORTH deſcants upon the matter. " As the Law was gradually deprived of " its Sanction, the *Obligation* of it grew continual- " ly weaker, till at laſt, after the people were re- " turned from the Captivity, it muſt have ceaſed " to oblige them at all. For whatever may be " the caſe of God's MORAL LAW, yet moſt cer- " tainly, as he withdraws the Sanctions of his " POSITIVE ones, he takes off ſomething from " their obligation; and when he has wholly with- " drawn the promiſe of reward and the threaten- " ing of puniſhment, THOSE LAWS OBLIGE NO " LONGER[k]." To this *Determination* of the learn- ed Profeſſor, concerning OBLIGATION, I have

[k] Page 329.

nothing to oppofe but the *Determination* of God himfelf: who, by the mouth of one of his Prophets, declares, That the *Laws fhall ftill oblige, tho' the Sanction be withdrawn.* " Ye pollute your felves " with your Idols, &c."—as the reader may find it tranfcribed juft above.   Here God declares he would withdraw that extraordinary Providence which naturally attended a Theocracy—*I will not be enquired of by you.* " Yet do not (fays he) deceive your felves in an expectation that, becaufe for your crimes I withdraw this fanction of my Law, the Law will oblige no longer,——*and that which cometh into your mind fhall not be at all, that ye fay we will be as the heathen:* For, in order to the bringing about my own great purpofes, I will ftill continue you a felect and fequeftered people —*I will bring you out from the people, and will gather you out from the Countries wherein you are fcattered.* And will ftill rule over you by my Law; now, in my wrath, as before in my mercy. *With fury poured out I will rule over you, and bring you into the bond of the Covenant.*"

I fuppofe the thing that led our Doctor into this rafh judgment, That *when the fanctions of a pofitive law are withdrawn, the obligation to the law ceafes,* was his totally mifunderftanding the principles of the beft writers on the Law of Nature: Not by their fault, I dare affure the Reader.— *The Law of Nature* is written in the heart; but by Whom, is the queftion.   And a queftion of much importance; for if not written by a competent Obliger it is no Law, to bind us.   The enquirers therefore into this matter had no other way of coming to the Author of the Law but by confidering the effects which the obfervance or inobfervance of it would have on mankind.   And they

they found that the obfervance tended to the benefit of all, the inobfervance to their deftruction. They concluded therefore that it muft needs have been given by God, as a Law to mankind; and thefe effects of its obfervance or inobfervance they called the *fanction*. Hence it appears that the knowledge of our *obligation to the Law of nature* arifes from the knowledge of the *fanction*. And, this fanction away, we had not been obliged, becaufe we could never have difcovered any real ground of obligation.

But the *pofitive Law of the Jews* was written in ftone by the finger of God, in a vifible manner; in which the fenfes of the People were appealed to, for the truth of the tranfaction. Here the knowledge of their obligation did not arife from their knowledge of the fanction, but from quite another thing, namely, the immediate knowledge they had by their fenfes, that God, their fovereign Lord and Mafter, gave them the Law. To inforce which, a *fanction* indeed, was added; but a fanction that added nothing to the obligation, nor confequently that took from it, when it was withdrawn.

This is a plain and clear ftate of the cafe. Yet fo miferably has our Profeffor miftaken it, that for want of feeing on what principle it was which the writers on the Law of Nature proceeded, when they fuppofed *obligation to depend on the fanction*, he hath, of a particular cafe, made a general maxim: and in applying that maxim, he hath turned every thing topfy turvy, and given us juft the reverfe of the medal. He fuppofes the taking the fanction from the moral Law might not deftroy the obligation, (which it certainly would) — *whatfoever,* fays he, *might be the caufe of God's moral Laws;*

I   and

and that taking away the fanction from his pofitive Law would deftroy the obligation; (which it certainly would not.)

What might further miflead our Profeffor (for the more fuch men read the lefs they underftand) is the attribute the Roman Lawyers give to fuch civil Laws as are made without a penal fanction. Thefe they are wont to call, *Leges imperfectæ :* And our great Civilian might believe that this affigned *imperfection* had a reference to the *obligation* they impofed, whereas it refers to the *efficacy* they were able to work.   He fhould have known at leaft this firft principle of Law, That it is the Authority of the Lawgiver, not the Sanction he annexes to his Law, which makes it, I will not fay, operate *properly* (for this is nothing to the purpofe) but makes it oblige *really,* which is only to the purpofe.   In a word I know of nobody but Hobbes, befides this Doctor, who pretended to teach that the *obligation* to Laws depended upon their *fanction :* and this he did, becaufe he derived all *right* and *wrong* from the Civil Magiftrate : which, for ought I know, our learned Profeffor may do likewife, as only miftaking *right* and *wrong* (by a blunder like to the foregoing) for *good* and *evil.*   Yet hath this grave man written moft enormoufly both on Laws and Morals : And is indeed a great Writer, juft as the mighty Gaint, Leon Gawer, was a great Builder ; cf whom the Monk of Chefter fo fweetly fings.

    " The Founder of this City, as faith Polychronicon,
    " Was Leon Gawer, a mighty ftrong Giant,
    " Which builded Caves and Dunceons manya one :
    " No goodly Building, ne proper, ne pleafant."

But our bufinefs at prefent is not with the actual adminiftration of an extraordinary Providence, but with the Scripture reprefentation of fuch an adminiftration.   And this the facred hiftory of the Jews attefts in one uniform unvaried manner; as well by recording many inftances of it in particular, as by conftantly referring to it in general.

I. The firft is in the Hiftory of MIRACLES. For an equal Providence being, by the nature of man's fituation and affairs, neceffarily adminiftered partly by ordinary and partly by extraordinary means, thefe latter produce what we call *Miracles*, the fubject of the facred Writers their more peculiar regard.   But I apprehend it would be thought perfuming too much on the reader's patience, to expect his attention, while I fet myfelf formally to prove that many *miracles* are related in the facred hiftory of the Ifraelites.

The fimpler fort of Deifts fairly confefs that the Bible records the working of many Miracles, as appears even from the free names they give to thofe accounts.   But there are refiners in Infidelity, fuch as SPINOZA and his mimic TOLAND; who acknowledge many of the facts recorded, but deny them to have been miraculous.   Thefe are to our purpofe, and an Appeal to the common fenfe of Mankind is a fufficient anfwer to them all.   And furely I fhould have done no more, had they not attempted to draw in to their Party much honefter Men than themfelves.   For fuch, therefore, even charity requires us to attempt fome kind of defenfe.

The infamous *Spinoza* would perfuade us that JOSEPHUS himfelf was as backward in the belief of Miracles as any modern Pagan whatfoever. The handle, for his calumny, is [1] that Writer's relation of the *paſſage* of the *Red-ſea*; which he compares to Alexander's thro' the *Pamphylian*, and which concludes with ſaying that *every Man may believe of it as he pleaſes*. No unuſual way with this Hiſtorian of introducing or ending a miraculous Adventure. This hath indeed ſo libertine an air, that it hath betrayed ſome Believers into the ſame falſe judgment concerning Joſephus; as if he afforded only a political or philoſophical belief to theſe things; and gave a latitude to *thoſe of his own Religion*, to think as they ſhould ſee cauſe.

But here lies the difficulty; the Hiſtorian is every now and then putting on a very different aſpect, and talking like a moſt determined Believer. Many are the places where he expreſſes the fulleſt and firmeſt aſſent to the *Divinity* of the *Moſaic* Religion, and to the *Truth* of the ſacred

---

[1] — Scriptura de natura in genere quibuſdam in locis affirmat eam fixum atque immutabilem ordinem ſervare. — Philoſophus praeterea in ſuo *Eccl.* clariſſime docet nihil novi in natura contingere. — Haec igitur in Scriptura expreſſe docentur, at nullibi, quod in natura aliquid contingat, quod ipſius legibus repugnet, aut quod ex iis nequeat ſequi, adeoque neque etiam Scripturae affingendum. — Ex quibus evidentiſſime ſequitur miracula res naturales fuiſſe. — Attamen — de his unicuique, prout ſibi melius eſſe ſentiet, ad Dei cultum & religionem integro animo ſuſcipiendum, liberum eſt exiſtimare. Quod etiam JOSEPHUS SENTIT; ſic enim in concluſione *l. 2. Antiq.* ſcribit, *Nullus vero diſcredat verbo miraculi, ſi antiquis hominibus, & malitia privatis via ſalutis liquet per mare facta, ſive voluntate Dei, ſive ſponte revelata:* dum & eis, qui cum Alexandro rege Macedoniae fuerunt olim, & antiquitus a reſiſtentibus Pamphylicum mare diviſum ſit, & cum aliud iter non eſſet, tranſitum *praebuit iis, volente Deo, per eum Perſarum deſtruere principatum; & hoc confitentur omnes, qui actus Alexandri ſcripſerunt,* DE HIS ITAQUE, SICUT PLACUERIT CUILIBET, EXISTIMET. Haec ſunt verba Joſephi, ejuſque DE FIDE MIRACULORUM JUDICIUM. *Tract. Theologico-Pol. C.* vi. *de Miraculis,* p. 81, 82.

Volumes.

Volumes. To mention only one or two, from a
Book so known, and in a point so notorious. The
following words of his Introduction (where he
cannot possibly be considered as a translator, or
relator only of what he found in the *sacred books*,
from which he composed his history) these, I
say, shew in how different a light he regarded *Moses* from all other Lawgivers: " And now I earnestly
" intreat all who take these Volumes in hand, to
" apply themselves with their whole faculties to the
" contemplation of the Divine Nature, and then
" turn to our LAWGIVER, and see whether he has
" not made a representation of that Nature entirely
" worthy of it; always assigning such Actions to
" GOD, as become his excellence, and preserving
" the high subject clear from any impure mixture
" of FABLE. Though if we consider the distance
" and antiquity of the Time he wrote in, we can-
" not but understand he was at full liberty to invent
" and falsify at pleasure. For he lived full two
" thousand years ago—A distance of Time to
" which even the Poets dared not to carry up
" the birth of their Gods, the actions of their
" Heroes, or the establishment of their Laws[m]."
Here, we see, the Historian expresly declares that
MOSES in his writings employed *no degree of fiction*,
so common in the practice of other ancient Lawgivers.

[m] Ἤδη τοίνυν τὰς ἐπεξομένας τοῖς βιβλίοις παρακαλῶ τῶν γνώμην
Θεῷ προσανέχειν, ᾗ δοκιμάζειν τὸν ἡμέτερον Νομοθέτην, εἰ τήν τε
φύσιν αὐτῷ ἀξίως κατιδὼν, ᾗ τῇ δυνάμει πρεπούσας ἀεὶ τὰς πράξεις ἀπέθηκε, πάσης καθαρὸν τὸν περὶ αὐτῷ φυλάξας λόγον τῆς παρ'
ἄλλοις αἰσχίνης μεθοδολογίας· καίτοιγε, ὅσον ἐπὶ μήκει χρόνῳ ᾗ πα-
λαιότητι, πολλὴν ἴχων ἄδειαν ψευδῶν πλασμάτων. γέγονε γὰρ πρὸ ἐτῶν
δισχιλίων, —— ἐφ' ὅσον πλῆθ⊙ αἰῶνος ἐδ' αὐτῶν οἱ ποιηταὶ τὰς γενέσεις
τῶν Θεῶν, μήτιγε τὰς τῶν ἀνθρώπων πράξεις, ἢ τὰς νόμους ἀνενεῖκειν
ἐτόλμησαν. Vol. i. p. 3, 4.

And how *truly* divine he fuppofed the Law, appears from his obferving, in the fame place, that, while the *Jews* religioufly obferved its Precepts, all things went well and profperoufly; but that, whenever they tranfgreffed, then nothing but difafters followed. And left any one fhould pretend, he meant no more than that national happinefs was the natural confequence of adhering to the Laws of their Country; or that thofe Laws, being founded on Juft and Right, God (whofe general Providence it is agreed he acknowledged) would reward the virtuous obfervers, whatever were the original of fuch Laws; left, I fay, this fhould be pretended, he adds, that thefe difafters followed whenever they tranfgreffed the Law, though in purfuit of things juft and good. His words are thefe : " Upon the whole, what the Reader of " this Hiftory may chiefly learn from it is this : " That thofe, who obfequioufly ftudy the Will of " God, and reverence his well eftablifhed Laws, " pafs their lives in incredible profperity; Hap- " pinefs, the reward from God, ever attending " their obedience. But in proportion to their " neglect of thefe Laws, eafy things become un- " furmountable, and all their undertakings, *how* " *juftly foever directed*, end in incurable calamities ᵃ." In which words, I take it for granted, he had the cafe of *Saul* particularly in his view. Again, fo full was his perfuafion of the Divinity of the Law, that he extols the *Jews* for fuffering *Ptolemy*; the

ᵃ Τὸ ζύμπλον δὲ μάλιςά τις ἂν ἐκ ταύτης μάθοι τῆς ἱτορίας, ἐθελή- ϲας αὐτὴν διελθεῖν, ὅτι μὲν τοῖς Θεῦ γνώμη καλακολυθῦσι, κ̀ τὰ κα- λως νομοθετηθέντα μὴ τολμῶσι παραβαίνειν, πάντα καλορθῦται πέρα πίςεως, κ̀ γέρας εὐδαιμονίας πρόκειται παρὰ Θεῦ· καθ᾿ ὅσον δ᾿ ἂν ἀπόςῶσι τῆς τέτων ἀκριβῦς ἐπιμελείας, ἄπορα μὲν γίνεται τὰ πόριμα, τρέπεται δ᾿ εἰς ζυμφορὰς ἀνηκέςυς, ὅ, τι ποτ᾿ ἂν, ὡς ἀγαθὲν δρᾷν ϲπυδάζωσιν. Vol. i. p. 3, 4.

fon

son of *Lagus*, to take their City by storm on the seventh day, rather than violate the *Sabbatic* rest. *Agatharchides* (says he) *thinks this scruple worthy of contempt and laughter. But those who weigh it without prejudice, will see something truly great, and deserving of the highest commendations, in thus always preferring their Piety towards God, and adherence to his Law, before their own safety, or even the freedom of their Country* °.

These passages, we see, have all the marks of a very zealous Believer.   And what makes the greatest difficulty of all, is, that the very places in which the Historian uses such offensive latitude of expression are those where he employs his utmost endeavours to shew the real Divinity of his Religion ; of which these *Miracles* are produced as evidence ; an evidence he studiously seeks, and seems to dwell upon with pleasure.

This varying aspect, therefore, so indifferently assumed, creates all the embarass.   But would men only do in this case what they ought to do in all, when they pass their judgment on an ancient writing, that is, consider the *End,* and *Time,* and *Genius* of the Writer, together with the Character of those to whom the work is addressed ; they would find *Josephus* to be indeed a steady Follower of the Law, and a firm Believer of its *miraculous* establishment ; and, at the same time, discover the easy solution of all those untoward appearances which have brought his Religion into question.

° Τῦτο μὲν 'Αγαθαρχίδη καταγίλωἶ᾿ ἄξιον δοκεῖ· τοῖς δὲ μὴ μετὰ δυσμενείας ἐξεῖάζεσι φαινέῖαι μέγα κ᾽ πολλῦν ἄξιον ἐξωμίων, εἰ κ᾽ ζωῆνρίας κ᾽ παῖριδὅ᾽ ἀνθρωποί τινες νόμων φυλακὴν κ᾽ τὴν πρὸς Θεὸν εἰσέβιιαν᾿αεὶ πρϋῦμῶσιν.   Vol. ii. p. 458.

The

The cafe, with our Hiftorian, ftood thus: His Country was now in great diftrefs; its Conftitution overturned, and his Brethren in apparent danger of utter Extirpation. Calamities arifing as much from the ill-will which the Heathens had entertained of their Religion ᵖ for its *unfociable* nature, as for their own turbulent and rebellious Carriage. This ill-will had been much increafed by their fuperior Averfion to *Chriftianity*, confidered by them as a Sect of *Judaifm*; which had carried its infociability as far, and its pretenfions much farther: fo far as to infift on the neceffity of all Mens fubmitting to its dominion, and renouncing their own Country Religions as the Impoftures of Politicians; or the Inventions of evil Demons. This put the Heathen World into a flame, and produced thofe mad and wicked Perfecutions that attended the firft Propagation of the *Chriftian* Faith ᑫ. Such was the unfriendly ftate of things, when *Jofephus* undertook an Apology for his Nation, in the HISTORY OF ITS ANTIQUITIES. Now as their conquerors' averfion to them, arofe from the fuppofition that their Religion required the belief and obedience of all

---

ᵖ It was one of the principal Accufations which *Apion*, at that time, brought againft the *Jews*, that they would not have Gods in common with other Nations; as we learn from *Jofephus*'s tract againft him, τί δ' ἡμῶν ἔτι κατηγορεῖ το μὴ κοινὲς ἔχειν τοῖς ἄλλοις θεὸς, Vol. ii. p. 477, 478. And *Celfus* calls that famous Maxim, *A man cannot ferve two Mafters* (on which he fuppofed *Chriftians* founded the fame principle) THE VOICE OF SEDITION when men are for breaking off all fociety and commerce with the reft of mankind. Εἶθ' ἑξῆς ἐκείνοις ἡμᾶς εἰσάγει λέγοντας πρὸς τὴν ἐπαπόρησιν αὐτῶ, Σέλλοιθ' ἡμᾶς ᾗ τὰς Δαίμονας θεραπεύειν, ὅτι οὐκ οἶόντε δυλεύειν τὸν αὐτὸν πλείοσι κυρίοις. Τᾶτο δ', ὡς οἴεται ΣΤΑΣΕΩΣ εἶναι ΦΩΝΗΝ, τῶν (ὡς αὐτὸς ὠνόμασεν) ἀποτειχιζόντων ἑαυτὰς ᾗ ἀπορϟηγνύντων ἀπὸ τῶν λοιπῶν ἀνθρώπων. Orig. cont. Celf. p. 380.

ᑫ See the firft volume, p. 291. Ed. 2.

Mankind

Mankind (for they had, as we obferved, confounded *Judaifm* with *Chriftianity*) to wipe off this invidious imputation, we muft conclude, would be ever in the Author's thoughts.   So that when the courfe of his Hiftory leads him to fpeak of the effects of God's extraordinary Providence in his conduct of this People, he fometimes adds to his relation of a miraculous adventure, *but in this every Man may believe as he pleafes.*   A declaration merely to this effect :   " The *Jewifh* Religion was given by " God for the ufe of his chofen People, therefore " the Gentiles might believe as they pleafed.   The " *Jews* did not pretend they fhould leave their " own Country Religion to embrace theirs ' : " That in this they were different from the *Chrif-* " *tian* Sect, which required all Mankind to follow " the Faith of a crucified Saviour under pain of " total deftruction'.   But that yet they were not " fo

---

' In his Tract againft *Apion* he has thefe remarkable words : *It is becoming Men of prudence and moderation carefully to obferve their own Country Laws concerning Religious matters, and to a- void calumniating the cuftoms of others.   But this Man* [Apion] *abandoned his own Religion, and has fince employed himfelf in inventing lies of ours.* Δεῖ γὰρ τὰς εὐθρενϖϯΙας τοῖς μὲν οἰκείοις νόμοις περὶ τὴν εὐσέβειαν ἀκριβῶς ἐμμένειν, τὰς δὲ τῶν ἄλλων μὴ λοιδορεῖν· ὁ δὲ τὰτας μὲν ἔφυγε, τῶν ἡμιτέρων δὲ κατεψεύσατο.   Vol. ii. p. 480. This was carrying his complaifance to the Gentiles extremely far.   But the neceffity was preffing ; and he miffes no opportunity of conciliating their good-will.   Thus in his *Antiquities,* a work, as we obferved, entirely apologetical, he tells the Reader, l. iii. c. 6. that the feven branches of the golden Candleftick fignified the *feven Planets.*   But in his *Wars of the Jews,* l. vii. c. 5. § 5. he affures us they fignify the Reverence in which the *Jews* held the *Number Seven.*   But, Allegory for Allegory, he thought, I fuppofe, one as good as the other, and therefore might be allowed to ufe what beft ferved his occafions.

' The Jews fucceeded in their endeavours to diftinguifh Their cafe from the Chriftians, So that while the ftorm fell upon the

" fo *unhofpitable*, but that they received with open
" arms all who were willing to worfhip one God
" the Creator of the Univerfe[1]." Thus we fee
how it came to pafs, (which was the main difficulty) that the places where he gives fuch a latitude
of Belief, are thofe very places where he moft
labours to prove the Divinity of his Religion.

But this folution clears up all difficulties, and
fhews the Hiftorian's great confiftency, as well as
artful addrefs, throughout the whole work. *Jofephus* profeffes the moft awful regard to the facred
Volumes ; and yet, at the fame time, takes fuch
liberties of going from their authority, that it pro-
voked the honeft refentment of a late excellent
Writer[u] to the following afperities: " Nec levis fit
" fufpicio illum Hebraice non fciviffe, cum multis
" indiciis linguæ ejus imperitiam prodat. Quivis
" certe, cui vel mica falis eft, fentiat illum Hiftorias
" Sacras pro arbitrio interpolaffe, demendo, ad-
" dendo, immutando, ut Antiquitates fuas ad Lec-
" torum Græcorum & Romanorum palatum ac-
" commodaret." But this licenfe, though furely

latter, the other enjoyed a calm. As we may fully underftand
by that paffage in St. Paul to the Galatians. *As many as d fire
to make a fair fhew in the flefh, they conftrain you to be circum-
cifed, only left they fhould fuffer perfecution for the crofs of Chrift.*
c. vi. 12. On which Limborch obferves very juftly,—Qui non
zelo pietatis, aut pro lege Mofis, moti id urgebant ; fed tantum
ut placerent Judæis ; quia nempe videbant perfecutiones quotidie
magis magifque Chriftianis a Gentibus inferri, *Judæos autem ab
illis effe immunes,* hac ratione eas, tanquam ipfi effent Judæi,
ftuduerunt declinare. *Amic. Collatio,* p. 164.

[t] —— κỳ τẽτο μỏνον ἔιναι κοινỏν, εἰ βỏλονται, πρὸς αὐτὺς κỳ πᾶσιν ἀνθρώποις, ἀφικνυμένοις εἰς τὸ ἱερὸν σέϐειν τὸν Θεὸν. Vol. i.
p. 556.

[u] Bifhop Hare.

to be condemned, was however fomething more legitimate and fober than is generally fuppofed. His deviations from Scripture being in thofe places *only,* where an exact adherence to it would have increafed that general averfion to his Nation, whofe effects were at that time fo much to be dreaded, either as expofing the *perverfe nature* of the People, or the *unfociable genius* of their Religion.   To give an inftance or two of each:

1. The *murmuring* of the *Ifraelites,* for *bread* and *flefh* in the Wildernefs, is reprefented in Scripture, and juftly [x], as an act of horrid ingratitude towards God.   Yet *Jofephus* makes *Mofes* own they had reafon for their complaints [y].   And in the execrable behaviour of the Men of *Gibeah* to the *Levite* and his wife, though Scripture exprefly fays they attempted a more unnatural crime than adultery, yet the Hiftorian paffes this over in filence, and makes all the perfonal outrage attempted, as well as committed, to be offered to the woman [z]. The Reader will now eafily account for what Mr. *Whifton* could not, his Author's omiffion of the ftory of the *golden Calf* [a].   For this was fo amazing
a per-

___

[x] EXOD. xvi.

[y] παθεῖν δ' ουκ αλόγως αυτὰς διὰ την ἀπάτην τᾶτο νομίσας.   *Antiq. Jud.* l. iii. c. 1. § 5.

[z] *Antiq. Jud.* l. v. c. 2. § 8.

[a] " There is, amongft many other things that *Jfephus's* " copy appears to want, one omiffion of fo important a nature " — the hainous Sin of the golden Calf. — What makes it " ftranger is this, that *Jofephus's* account is not only negative, " by a bare omiffion, but pofitive, by affording an exact cohe- " rence without it, *nay fuch a coherence as is plainly inconfiftent* " *with it.* And what ftill makes it more furprifing is, that *Jo-*
" *fephus*

a perverfity, at that juncture, that it muft have made the very *Pagans* themfelves afhamed of their *Jewifh* brethren in idolatry.

2. Again, we are told in Scripture, that when the *Cutheans*, or *Samaritans*, heard that the *Jews*, who were returned from the Captivity, were re-building the Temple, they came and defired to be partners in the work, and joint Worfhipers of the God for whom it was erected; to which the *Jews* gave this round reply: *You have nothing to do with us, to build an Houfe unto our God, but we ourfelves together will build unto the Lord God of* Ifrael, *as King* Cyrus *the King of* Perfia *hath com-manded us* [b]. And *Nehemiah*, on the fame occa-fion, gave them a ftill rougher anfwer: *The God of Heaven he will profper us, therefore we his Ser-vants will arife and build : but you have no Portion, nor Right, nor Memorial in* Jerufalem [c]. This was a tender place: it was touching upon the very fore, in an exprefs declaration of the *Unfociablenefs* com-plained of. The ftory therefore, we may be fure, was to be foftened before the Gentiles were to be

---

" *fephus* frequently profeffes, neither to add to nor to take away " from the facred Books." *Differt.* II. p. xlv. Some other Li-berties, which *Jofephus* took with Scripture for the end above explained, made this learned Writer conclude that the Hiftorian had an *earlier and more uncorrupt copy of the Old Teftament than any we now have : for that his accounts are more exact, confiftent, and agreeable with Chronology, with natural Religion, and with one another.* p. xxxv. Yet, after all, the fatal omiffion of the golden Calf brings him to confefs, *that* Jofephus's *copy appears to* WANT *many things* which are in ours. p. xlv. Thus forely diftreffed is this good man in the fupport of a wild extravagant hypothefis; while every one elfe fees that all the omiffions and alterations (which fometimes make his copy *good*, fometimes *bad)* were defigned deviations from the facred Volumes to con-ciliate the good-will of his mafters.

[b] Ezra, iv. 3.   [c] Neh. ii. 20.

intrufted

intrusted with it. Accordingly, *Josephus* makes them speak in these obliging terms: *That they could not possibly admit them as partners in the work; for that the command to build the Temple was directed to them first by* Cyrus, *and now by* Darius : *That indeed they were at liberty to worship along with them : and that this was the only Community, in religious matters, that they could enter into with them, and which they would do with as many of the rest of Mankind, as were willing to come up to the Temple to adore the God of Heaven*[d]. The reason the *Scripture Jews* give for the refusal of the offer to be joint partners with them in their work and worship is, that it was a Temple built in the *Land of Israel*, and to the honour of the *God of Israel*. The reason *Josephus's Jews* give for their refusal is obedience to the King of Persia : else, as for *community* of worship, they were very ready to receive them.

And now was not that a wise [e] project which proposed reforming the *sacred Text* by the Writings of *Josephus?*

But this Explanation will enable us to conclude with certainty against that *spurious* passage concerning CHRIST. I think I have already offered one demonstrative argument against it[f]. And I suppose, the many marks of forgery are so glaring, that most men would be willing to give

---

[d] — Ἔφασαν, '' τῆς μὲν οἰκοδομίας αὐτὸς ἀδύνατοι εἶναι κοινωνεῖν, αὐτῶν προσταχθένταν κατασκευάσαι τὸν ναὸν, πρότερον μὲν ὑπὸ Κύρου, νῦν δὲ ὑπὸ Δαρείου· προσκυνεῖν δὲ αὐτοῖς ἐφιέναι· καὶ τοῦτο μόνον εἶναι κοινὸν, εἰ βούλοιται, πρὸς αὐτὲς κỳ πᾶσιν ἀνθρώποις, ἀφικνουμένοις εἰς τὸ ἱερὸν σέβειν τὸν Θεόν. Vol. i. p. 556.

[e] Mr. Whiston's.   [f] See vol. i.

it up, were *Josephus*'s silence on so extraordinary an occasion but easy to be accounted for. Now we have so far laid open his conduct as to see, that the preaching up of CHRIST was an affair he would studiously decline. His great point, as we observed, was to reconcile the Gentiles to his Countrymen. But the *Pagan* aversion was greatly increased by the new Sect of *Christians*, sprung, as was well known,. from the Country of *Judea*. It was therefore utterly destructive of his purpose to shew, as he must have done, in giving them an account of CHRIST, the close connexion between the two Religions. Of all dangerous subjects, therefore, *Josephus* would be careful to avoid this [g]. So that (certain as I am of the Writer's purpose, and not ignorant of the liberty he took even with the sacred Records, when ·it served his ends, of adding and omitting at pleasure) I should have been as much surprised to have found the *History* of JESUS in his Works as others are to be told that it is not there. This too will equally well ·account for his omission of Herod's slaughter of the Children at Bethlehem, which Scaliger so much wondered at [h]; which Collins so much triumphed in [i]; and for the sake of which, our

---

[g] " La plus forte preuve qu' on ait, pour soutenir que le passage en question, ou' il est parlé de JESUS CHRIST, est de *Joseph*, c'est qu'il n'est pas croyable, qu'il n'ait rien dit de JESUS CHRIST. Photius fournit une réponse a ce raisonnement, en parlant de *Juste de Tiberide*, qui a ecrit l' Histoire des Juifs en Grec, et qui vivoit du tems de Joseph, avec qui il a eü de grands demelez. Juste de Tiberide, dit Photius n'a point parlé de JESUS CHRIST parce qu'il etoit Juif de Nation et de Religion." *P. Simon Bibl. Crit.* v. 2. p. 41.

[h] *Animad. in Chron. Eusebii.*   [i] *Scheme of literal Prophecy considered.*

Whitby

Whitby seemed ready to give up the truth of the story [k].

Thus did this excellent Writer out of extreme love to his Country (the most pardonable however of all human frailties) make too free with Truth and Scripture ; though most zealously attached to the Religion of his Forefathers : as those Men generally are who love their Country best. And a *Jew* he strictly was, of a very different Stamp too, from that poor paltry Mimic of the *Greek* Sophists, *Philo* [l]. Of whom his Master *Plato would have said*, what *Josephus* tells us *Aristotle did say*, of one of his *Jewish* Acquaintance, A GREEK HE WAS, AND NOT IN SPEECH ONLY, BUT IN SOUL LIKEWISE [m].

I judged it of importance to set this matter in a true light: Because many, I supposed, would think it a fair prejudice against the Divinity of the *Mosaic* Religion, had a person, so eminent amongst his Countrymen while the Republic was yet existing, and of so learned an age ; so conversant in the *Jewish* Records, and so skilled in the best *Grecian* Literature; had such a one afforded only a political or philosophic Faith to the sacred Volumes. But then it will follow on the other hand, that the sincere *Belief* of one, so circumstanced, will be as fair a prejudice in its favour.

[k] *Comment. on the New Testament.*

[l] *Philo*, in his life of *Moses*, brings in the *Egyptian* Priests reasoning on the *Platonic* principles, concerning the soul that informed *Moses's* body ; which is altogether as well judged, as if a modern Writer of the life of *Ptolemy* the Astronomer should bring him in explaining Sir *Isaac Newton's Principia.*

[m] Ἑλληνικὸς ἦν, ἃ τῇ διαλέκτῳ μόνον, ἀλλὰ κỳ τῇ ΨΥΧΗ.

Not

NOT that I am over fond of this kind of evidence, in matters where every one is obliged to judge for himfelf; and confequently, where every one, on a due application to the fubject, is capable of judging. Much lefs would I lay great weight on the opinions of Men out of their own Profeffion, however eminent in any other. What is it to Truth, for inftance, what a Courtier judges of a Church; a Politician of Confcience; or a Geometer, grown gray in *Demonftration*, of *moral Evidence?*   To go on:

MIRACLES, therefore, as they are recorded to be continued through fo large a period of this Republic, I give for one proof that the Scriptures have reprefented the Ifraelites as living under an extraordinary Providence. I fay, as they are recorded to be fo *continued:* For when miracles are only given at the firft propagation of a Religion, (as of the Chriftian) they are to be no otherwife efteemed of, than as the Credentials of a new Revelation: Thefe being like the Cloud which conducted the Ifraelites in their journeyings in the wildernefs; the other like the fame Cloud which abode upon the Mercy-feat: Thefe like the Manna rained down from heaven only for a prefent fubfiftence; the other like the fame Manna preferved uncorrupted in the Ark, to be a teftimony to future ages.

II. This extraordinary Providence is reprefented as adminiftered. 1. Over the State in general. 2. Over private Men in particular. And fuch a reprefentation we fhould expect to find from the nature of the Republic; becaufe, as an extraordinary Providence over the STATE neceffarily follows GOD's being their TUTELARY DEITY; fo an

extra-

extraordinary Providence to PARTICULARS follows
as necessarily from his being their SUPREME MA-
GISTRATE[n].

As

[n] Here Dr. Sykes appears again upon the stage. " The
" Scripture representation of the Theocracy, as Mr. Warbur-
" ton (says he) assures us, was, 1. *Over the State in general:* and
" 2. *Over private Men in particular.* I have no doubts about
" the former of these cases: For where a law was given by
" God, and he condescended to become King of a Nation,
" and a solemn Covenant was entered into by the People and
" by God, as their King, and where blessings were solemnly
" promised upon obedience to the Law, or curses were de-
" nounced upon disobedience: and this by one who was able
" to execute whatever he engaged; no doubt can be about
" the reciprocal obligations, or about God's performing his
" part of the obligation, since it is his property not to lie
" nor deceive. Temporal Rewards and Punishments being
" then the sanction of the Jewish Law, these must be dispensed
" by God so as to make the State happy and flourishing if they
" keep the Law, or else miserable if they disobeyed it. The
" Blessings and Curses were general and national, agreeable
" to the character of a King, and a legal Administration:
" such as related to them as a People; and not to particular
" persons." [Exam. of Mr. W's. account, &c. p. 186—7.]

Here, he assures us, *he has no doubts about the extraordinary
Providence over the State in general.* And he tells us his reason,
———Because *the Law was given by God, and he condescended
to become the* KING *of the Nation, by a solemn Covenant made
with the People.* Now if this very reason be found to hold
equally strong for an extraordinary Providence over PARTICU-
LARS, the point will be soon decided between us. Let me ask
him then, what those reasons are whereby he infers that, from
God's becoming King of a Nation, he must administer an extraordinary Providence over the *State in general,* which do not equally conclude for God's administring it over *Particulars?* Is not
his inference founded upon this, That where God condescends
to assume a *civil* character, he condescends to administer it in a
civil manner? which is done by extending his care over the
whole. If our Doctor should say, his inference is not thus founded; I must then beg leave to tell him, that he has no foundation at all to conclude from God's being *King,* that there was an
extraordinary Providence exerted over the *State in general.* If

he

As to this Providence over the State, it would
be abſurd to quote particular texts, when the

he confeſſes that it is thus founded ; then I infer, upon the ſame
grounds, an extraordinary Providence over *Particulars.* For the
juſtice of the Regal office is equally pledged to extend its care to
Particulars as well as to the *general.* It may be aſked then, what
hindered our Doctor from ſeeing ſo ſelf-evident a truth ? I reply,
the miſtake with which he firſt ſet out; and which yet ſticks to
him. I have obſerved before, what confuſion he ran into by not
being able to diſtinguiſh between the *Form of Government* and the
Adminiſtration of it. Here again he makes the ſame blind
work, from not ſeeing the difference between a Legislator
and a King. — *For where a* Law (ſays he) *was given by God,
and he condeſcended to become the* King *of a Nation,* &c. implying that in his opinion, the *giving a Law,* and the *becoming a
King,* was one and the ſame thing. Hence it was, that as the
Legiſlative power, in the inſtitution of good Laws, extends its
providence only over the State in general, he concluded, that
the executive power, in the adminiſtration of thoſe Laws, does
no more. Which brings him to a concluſion altogether worthy
both of himſelf and his premiſes. — *The Bleſſings and Curſes*
(ſays he) *were general and national, agreeable to the character of
a King and a legal Adminiſtration.* — What ! Is it only agreeable to the character of a King and a legal Adminiſtration to
take care of the *State in general,* and not of *Particulars?* So, according to this new ſyſtem of Policy, it is agreeable to the Conſtitution of *England* to fit out fleets, to protect the public from
inſults, and to enact Laws to encourage commerce ; but not to
erect Courts of Equity, or to ſend about itinerant Judges. What
makes his ignorance in this matter the more inexcuſable is that
I had pointed out to him this diſtinction, in the following
paſſage; the former part of which he has quoted, but dropt
the latter, as if determined that neither himſelf nor his reader
ſhould be the better for it. My words are theſe : *It* [the extraordinary Providence] *is repreſented as adminiſtred,* 1. *Over
the State in general.* 2. *Over private men in particular. And
ſuch a repreſentation we ſhould expect to find from the nature of
the Republic;* because as an extraordinary Providence over the State necessarily follows God's
being their tutelary Deity [in which capacity he gave
them Laws] so an extraordinary Providence to Particulars follows as necessarily from his being
their supreme Magistrate [in which capacity he adminiſtered them.]

8

whole

whole BIBLE is one continued history of it.
Only it may not be amiss to observe, that from
a passage in Ezekiel, where GOD says, *Because
that* Moab *and* Seir *do say,* BEHOLD THE HOUSE
OF JUDAH IS LIKE UNTO ALL THE HEATHEN °, it
appears the Jews had boasted, and the Gentiles,
till then, had acknowledged, that they were under
an extraordinary Providence. As this therefore
is so plain, I shall not hazard the obscuring it by
many words; but go on to shew, that Scripture
represents this Providence as administered likewise
to Particulars.

In the Dedication of the first Temple, SOLOMON
addresses his Prayer to GOD, that the Covenant
between him and the People might remain for ever
firm and inviolate, and the old Oeconomy be still
continued. And after having enumerated divers
parts of it, he proceeds in this manner : " When
" the heaven is shut up, and there is no rain,
" because they have sinned against thee; yet if
" they pray towards this Place, and confess thy
" name, and turn from their sin when thou dost
" afflict them : Then hear thou from heaven, and
" forgive the sin of thy SERVANTS, and of thy
" PEOPLE ISRAEL, when thou hast taught them
" the good way, wherein they should walk ; and
" send rain upon the Land, which thou hast
" given unto thy People for an inheritance. If
" there be dearth in the Land, if there be pesti-
" lence, if there be blasting or mildew, locust or
" caterpillers; if their enemies besiege them in
" the cities of their Land; whatsoever sore, or
" whatsoever sickness there be: Then what prayer
" or what supplication shall be made *of* ANY

" MAN, or of all thy PEOPLE ISRAEL, *when*
" EVERY ONE *shall know his own sore, and his own*
" *grief,* and shall spread forth his hands in this
" house; then hear thou from heaven and for-
" give, and RENDER UNTO EVERY MAN accord-
" ing unto all his ways, whose heart thou know-
" est[P]." Solomon in this petition, which, with
respect to the given *Covenant,* we might properly
call a PETITION OF RIGHTS, speaks the language
of one who extended the temporal sanctions of the
Law to PARTICULARS and INDIVIDUALS. For he
desires God, according to the terms of the Covenant, to render unto *every man according to all his*
ways. But when is it that he prays for the exertion
of this extraordinary providence to particulars? At
the very time when it is administring to the state
in general.—*If there be dearth in the land,. if there*
be pestilence, if there be blasting or mildew, locust or
caterpillers, if their enemies besiege them, &c. The
necessary consequence is, that as sure as Solomon
believed an extraordinary Providence exercised to
the State in general, so surely did he believe it

[P] 2 CHRON. vi. 28. *& seq.* To this it has been objected,
" That Solomon here prays for scarce so much in behalf of
" his own People, as he doth ver. 32. for every *stranger* that
" shall come and worship in the Temple." But the Objector
should have observed that there is this difference, — the prayer
for the Israelites was founded on a Covenant; the prayer for the
Stranger, on no Covenant. That for the Israelites begins thus,
O Lord God of Israel there is no God like thee, which KEEPETH
COVENANT—and as he proceeds, the reason of his petition all
along goes upon their being possessors of the *promised Land,* the
great object of the Covenant, ver. 25-27-31. But the prayer for
the *Stranger,* ver. 32. is founded altogether on another principle,
namely, for the sake of God's glory amongst the heathen.
Moreover concerning the Stranger [words implying a new consi-
deration] *if they come and pray in this house, then hear from the*
heavens — THAT ALL PEOPLE OF THE EARTH MAY KNOW
THY NAME AND FEAR THEE.—

exercised

exercised to individuals in particular. The Psalmist
bears his testimony to the same Oeconomy : *I have
been young* (says he) *and now am old: yet have I not
seen the Righteous forsaken, nor his seed begging their
bread*[q]. God himself declares it, by the Prophet
Isaiah *: Say ye to the Righteous that it shall be well
with him : for they shall eat the fruit of their doings.
Wo unto the Wicked, it shall be ill with him : for the
reward of his hands shall be given him*[r]. And a-
gain : *He that walketh righteously and speaketh up-
rightly,* &c, *he shall dwell on high : his place of defence shall be the munitions of rocks, bread shall be
given him, his waters shall be sure*[s]. And we learn,
from a parabolical command in Ezekiel, how exactly these promises were fulfilled : " And the Lord
" said unto him, Go through the midst of the
" city, through the midst of Jerusalem, and set a
" mark upon the foreheads of the men that sigh,
" and that cry for all the abominations that be
" done in the midst thereof. And to others he
" said in mine hearing, Go ye after him through
" the city, and smite : let not your eye spare,
" neither have ye pity. Slay utterly old and
" young, both maids and little children, and wo-
" men ; *but come not near any man upon whom is
" the mark* ; and begin at my Sanctuary[t]," &c.
The

----

[q] Psal. xxxvii. 25. But the whole book of Psalms is one
continued declaration of the administration of an extraordinary
Providence to particulars, in the exact distribution of rewards
and punishments. See the *Argument of the D. L. fairly stated,*
p. 57 to 75, where the learned Writer has evinced the truth in
question beyond the possibility of a reply.

[r] Chap. iii. ver. 10, 11.   [s] Chap. xxxiii. ver. 15, 16.

[t] Chap. ix. ver. 4—6. To this Testimony from Ezekiel, Dr.
Sykes objects, that " It is but a parabolical command : and no

" argu-

The fame Prophet in another place, alluding to Abraham's interceffion for Sodom, declares from God,

" argument can be drawn from parables for an equal providence
" over particulars, but at moft for a particular and peculiar Dif-
" penfation." *Defence*, p. 61. This is the pleafanteft of Anfwerers.—If this *parabolical command* does not mean what itfelf
fays it does mean, namely, " that virtuous individuals fhould
" be diftinguifhed from the wicked, in a general calamity ;"
what then does it mean? Why, *at moft, but a particular and peculiar Difpenfation.* And in what, I pray you, does a *particular
and peculiar Difpenfation* confift, if not in a diftinction between
the virtuous and the wicked, in a general calamity? But he had
fome confufed notion that there was a difference between a parabolical and a real reprefentation : and therefore he makes it to
confift in this, that *no argument can be drawn from* the former.—
Now, if from Jefus's parable of the rebellious Hufbandmen (who
wounded their Lord's Servants and killed the Heir, and for their
pains were ejected from their poffeffions, and the vineyard let to
other Hufbandmen) I fhould conclude, " that he meant the Jews,
who had murdered the Prophets which were fent unto them,
and were ready to murder the Meffiah likewife, and that for
this crime they fhould be deprived of the bleffing of the Gofpel,
and the Gentiles received into the Kingdom of Chrift, in their
ftead, I make no doubt but, if it ferved our Doctor's purpofe of
anfwering, he would reply, *It is but a parabolical tale, and no
argument can be drawn from parables, of Chrift's fufferings and
the rejection of the Jews, &c. but, at moft, that the Jews were
rebels and murderers, and would be treated as fuch.*"

Another Anfwerer is yet more fhamelefs. " As to the para-
" bolical command in Ezekiel (fays Dr. Rutterforth) the very
" fame promifes were exactly fulfilled to the Chriftians. *Rev.*
" vii. 1--2--3."—If you afk *when, where,* and *how,* you would
embarrafs, but not difconcert him. Yet, as he affures us, thefe
promifes were exactly fulfilled to Chriftians, he muft give us
leave to affure him, that it could be only in a *fpiritual* fenfe :
for St. Paul tells us, that the Jews had the *promife of the life
that now is,* and the Chriftians of *that which is to come.* I
doubt then the learned Profeffor was a little diforiented when
he called the *promifes* in Ezekiel and in the Revelations, *the fame.*
There is a ftrange perverfity in thefe men. The promifes
under the *Law* they tell us are to be underftood SPIRITU-
ALLY, and this, in order that they may bring Judaifm to Chriftianity : But then, to bring Chriftianity back to Judaifm, they
tell

God, that when his judgments come out against
the land of Judea, the Righteous, found in it, should
save only themselves; which plainly shews a providence extending to particulars.—" Son of man,
" when the land sinneth against me by trespassing
" grievously, then will I stretch out mine hand
" upon it, and will break the staff of the bread
" thereof, and will send famine upon it, and will
" cut off man and beast from it. Though these
" three men Noah, Daniel, and Job, were in it
" they should deliever but their own souls by their
" righteousness, faith the Lord God." Ch. xiv.
13—14. But God, by the Prophet *Amos*, describes this administration of Providence in the
fullest manner : " Also I have witholden the rain
" from you, when there were yet three months to
" the harvest ; *and I caused it to rain upon one city,*
" *and caused it not to rain upon another city : one*
" *piece was rained upon, and the piece whereupon*
" *it rained not, withered.* So two or three cities
" wandered unto one city to drink water; but
" they were not satisfied: yet have ye not return-
" ed unto me, faith the Lord. I have smitten
" you with blasting and mildew, &c[u]." And
again : *Lo, I will command, and I will sift the house*
of Israel *amongst all Nations, like as corn is sifted*
in a sieve, yet shall not the least grain fall upon the
earth[x].

tell us on the other hand, that the promises under the *Gospel*
are to be understood CARNALLY. But what is to be expected,
or rather what is not to be expected, from a man who dares to
assert, that there was no more an extraordinary Providence under the Jewish than under the Christian Dispensation ; in open
defiance of the Prophets and the Apostles, of Moses and of
Jesus Christ.

[u] Chap. iv. ver. 7—11.   [x] Chap. ix. ver. 9.

These

Thefe declarations of God's providence are fo exactly correfpondent to Solomon's petition; that they feem as it were the FIAT to it [y].

Thus we fee the Law, as well by its exprefs declarations as by its effential nature and genius, extended its fanctions of temporal rewards and punifhments as well to Particulars as to the General. And as in civil Government, univerfal practice fhews the neceffity of a more exact difpenfation of punifhment than of reward, fo we may obferve from the paffages laft quoted that the Mofaic Law had the fame attention; which occafioned the Wife Man to fay, *Behold the Righteous fhall be recompenfed in the Earth:* MUCH MORE *the Wicked and the Sinner* [z].

The infpired writers of the NEW TESTAMENT give evidence to this difpenfation of Providence under the OLD. The Author of the epiftle to the Hebrews argues from it as a thing well known and generally allowed: *For if the Word fpoken by Angels was ftedfaft, and* EVERY TRANSGRESSION AND DISOBEDIENCE RECEIVED A JUST RECOMPENCE OF REWARD, *how fhall we efcape if we neglect fo great falvation* [a] *?*

[y] Yet Dr. Sykes fcruples not to fay, " The paffage from " Amos does not prove an *equal* or *unequal* Providence, but a " peculiar interpofition OCCASIONALLY adminiftered." Def. p. 61. As I would be willing that every thing of this learned Anfwerer's fhould be put to ufe, I would recommend this obfervation to the reader as a paraphrafe on the words of the Apoftle, where he fays that, under the Mofaic Difpenfation " the " word fpoken by Angels was STEDFAST, and EVERY tranfgref- " fion and difobedience received a juft recompence of reward." *Heb.* ii. 2.

[z] PROV, xi, 31.   [a] Chap, ii. ver. 2, 3.

St,

St. Paul, in his epistle to the Romans, speaking of the advantages which Christianity had over Judaism, says: *Therefore being justified by faith, we have peace with God through our Lord Jesus Christ. By whom also we have access by Faith into his Grace, wherein we stand, and rejoice in hope of the glory of God. And not only so, but* WE GLORY IN TRI-BULATION ALSO, *knowing that Tribulation worketh patience*[b], *&c.* Here St. Paul opposing the advantages which the Gentile Converts had by FAITH, to those which the Jews, in contempt to the Gentiles, gloried to have by the LAW, adds, in order to shew those advantages in their highest superiority, that the Christian Gentiles could glory even in that which was the very opprobrium of the Jews, namely *tribulation.* For the sanction of the Jewish Law being temporal rewards and punishments, administered by an equal providence; *Tribulation* was a punishment for crimes, and, consequently, an high opprobrium[c]. But the followers of Christ, who were taught, *that we must through much* TRIBULATION *enter into the kingdom of God*[d], had the same reason to *glory* in the roughness of the road, as the ancient Agonistæ had in

[b] ROM. v. 1, *& seq.*

[c] To this Dr. Sykes replies, "The equal providence over "the Jews by his own confession had ceased some hundred of "years, and therefore at the writing of this epistle, *Tribulation* "was deemed by no body more an opprobrium of the Jews, or "a punishment of their crimes, than it was of other people." *Defence, p.* 62. This great Divine did not perceive that St. Paul is here speaking of the different *genius* of the two Religions, Judaism and Christianity, not of the *condition* of the two People at the time he wrote: and consequently, as what was once true would be always true, the Apostle considers the *nature* of the two Dispensations as invariable.

[d] ACTS xiv. 22.

the

the toils which procured them the victory. This is urged with great address. But the Critics, not taking the Apostle's meaning, have supposed in their usual way, that he here broke in upon his argument, with an idea foreign to the point in hand.

This will help us to explain an odd remark of the excellent Maimonides: *That their wise men talked of a thing which was* NOT TO BE FOUND *in the* LAW, *namely, that which some of them call the* CHASTISEMENTS OF LOVE, *by which they meant that* TRIBULATIONS *might befall a man without any precedent sin*[e], *and only in order to multiply his reward. And that this was the very opinion of the Sect called* Muatzal, *of which, or in favour of which opinion, there is not one single word to be found in the Law*[f]. This seems to have perplexed our Rabbi; and with cause. He lived when his countrymen were under a common providence, and had the doctrine of a future state of rewards and punishments, which, he took for granted, was always in the Jewish Œconomy. These things disabled him from seeing that — NO CHASTISEMENTS OF LOVE was a necessary consequence of temporal re-

---

[e] This explanation was necessary; For, another kind of *chastisements of Love* there was in the *Law*, namely, *paternal chastisements*. Thus *Moses: Thou shalt also consider in thine heart, that as a man chasteneth his son, so the Lord thy God chasteneth thee.* DEUT. viii. 5.

[f] Unum tamen occurrit in verbis sapientum nostrorum, quod NON INVENITUR IN LEGE; id nempe, quod quidam eorum dicunt CASTIGATIONES AMORIS. Juxta hanc enim sententiam possunt TRIBULATIONES alicui evenire sine præcedente peccato, sed ut multiplicetur ejus Remuneratio. Atque hæc ipsissima est sententia Sectæ Muatzali, de qua, aut pro qua ne verbulum quidem in Lege reperitur. *More Nevoch. Buxtorfii*, p. 381.

wards and punishments administered by an equal providence: And likewise that when this sanction ceased, and a future state was known, then CHAS- TISEMENTS OF LOVE became a necessary conse- quence.

But if by the LAW, Maimonides did (as the Jews frequently do) include the writings of the Pro- phets, then he was very much mistaken in saying there is not one word in it concerning the *chastise- ments of love.* For Zechariah, prophesying of a NEW Dispensation, describes this sort of *chastise- ments* in very express terms: " And I will bring " the third part thro' the fire, and *will refine them* " *as silver is refined,* and *will try them as gold is* " *tried:* and they shall call on my name, and I " will hear them." So admirably do all the parts of God's grand Œconomy support one an- other.

We have seen what testimonies their coeval writers afford of an extraordinary Providence. But we must not suppose the Jews always held the same language. The difference is great between the early and later Jews, even during the existence of the Republic. Take an instance from the Pfalmist, and the writer of Ecclesiasticus. The former says, *I have been young and now am old, yet have I not seen the Righteous forsaken, nor his Seed begging their bread*[g]. The latter, — *Look at the* GENERATIONS OF OLD, *and see: Did ever any trust in the Lord and was confounded? Or did any abide in his Fear and was forsaken? Or whom did he ever despise that called upon him*[h] ? The Pfalmist living under an *extraordinary* Providence appeals to his

[g] PSAL. xxxvii. 25.   [h] Chap. ii. ver. 10.

own times; the Author of Ecclesiasticus living when it was long ceased, appeals to former times. But as we have been told, that this talk of a particular Providence is only an Eastern Hyperbole, in which every thing is ascribed to God, I think it not improper to take notice here of one singular circumstance in favour of the Reporters.

We may observe then, that the spirit of *Gentilism* was always uniform; and, throughout its whole duration, had ever the same unvaried pretensions to divine Intercourse, supported by the same sort of Oracles and Divinations. But amongst the *Jews* matters were on another footing. After their perfect settlement, on their return from Captivity, (when we know from the course and progress of God's Oeconomy, that the extraordinary Providence was to cease) we hear no more of their pretences to it, though they now adhered more strictly than ever to the Religion of their forefathers. They made no claim, as we see by the excellent Writer of the first Book of *Maccabees*, either to *Prophets*, *Oracles*, or *extraordinary Dispensations*. When they write unto the *Lacedemonians*, for the renewal of their Alliance, they tell them, at the same time, that they need it not, FOR THAT THEY HAVE THE HOLY BOOKS OF SCRIPTURE IN THEIR HANDS TO COMFORT THEM [1]. Language very different from their forefathers', when God was wont to send immediate help from the Sanctuary. How ingenuously does the same Historian relate the misfortune of *Bethsura*, caused by the observance of the Sabbatic Year [m]? A misfortune of which we have no instance before the Captivity; and therefore a plain evidence that the extraordinary Providence

---

[1] Chap. xii. ver. 9.   [m] 1 Macc. vi. 49.

was indeed withdrawn.   Besides if we consider the nature of the *Religion*, the genius of the *People*, and the circumstances of the *Time*, we shall find, they all concurred to favour the continuance of a pretension to an extraordinary Providence, had it been *only a pretension*.

1. The *Mosaic Religion*, like the *Pagan*, had a *public part*, and therefore the *Jews* might, with the greatest ease, have still carried on the Superstition of *Oracles*, had their Oracles been indeed a superstition; especially as they were now become so closely attached to their Religion.   For when did ever *Greece* or *Italy* confess that their *Oracles* were become *dumb*, 'till the Consulters had generally forsaken them, and the whole frame of their Religion was falling to pieces? Besides, the practice of this Superstition had been as easy as it was commodious; for the Oracular Voice was wont to come from the *Mercy-Seat* behind the *Veil*.

2. The *genius of the People* too would have contributed to the continuance of this claim.   For some how or other, it was become their character *to require a Sign*[n]; and tho', now, really superstitious, yet the humour spent itself rather in telling lyes of former times[o], than in inventing any of their own.

This

---

[n] 1 Cor. i. 22.

[o] The Writer of the *first Book of Maccabees* appears to have lived in the times he wrote of; and we find no wonders nor prodigies in his History.   But a long time after comes the Author of the *second Book*, an Epitomizer of one *Jason* of *Syrene*; and he largely supplies what he thought the other wanted.   This Man is such a lover of prodigies, that, when he has made a monstrous lye, and so frighted himself at the size of it that he dare not tell it out, he insinuates it [as chap. xii. ver. 22. —

is

This, on a fuppofition of the human invention of their Law, is altogether unaccountable. But take the matter as we find it in their facred Books, and nothing is more eafy. For if they had indeed been long accuftomed to a *miraculous* Difpenfation, they would, ever after, be ftrongly difpofed *to require a Sign*; but it would be only fuch a *Sign* as bore the evident marks of a Divinity; which not being to be had in human inventions, they would be kept fafe from delufions, and made fenfible of the difference of times : And fuch was, in fact, their cafe.

3. Add to all this, that the *time of the Maccabees* was the feafon of Enthufiafm, when that airy Spirit is at its height; after the national Genius, long funk by oppreffion, begins to rife and recover itfelf to a vindication of public Liberty. And of this we have a fignal inftance in the perfon of *Judas Maccabæus* himfelf; who, in imitation of *Gideon*, would fet upon an army of twenty thoufand foot and two thoufand horfe, with only eight hundred ftraggling defperado's; which rafh and fanatic attempt was followed with the fortune that might, at this time, have been expected [p].—In fuch a feafon too, artful Leaders are moft difpofed to fupport themfelves by infpirations; have moft need of them ; and are thought, by the People, moft worthy to receive them.

There is the fame difference between the Writers of the New Teftament and of the Old, as between

ἐκ τῆς τοῦ παῦλα ἐφοςῶν᳉ ἐπιφανίας. Chap. xv. ver. 27. τῇ τοῦ Θιῦ ἐπιφανεία.] Nay he even ventures at an apology for *lying Wonders*, [Chap. xv. ver. 11.] and under this encouragement falls a lying to fome purpofe, [Chap. xii. ver. 16.]

P 1 Mac. ix. 6.

the

the Writers of the several ages of the Old. The Apostles (who worked *Miracles* as well as Moses and the Prophets) represent the followers of CHRIST as under the same *common* Providence with the rest of mankind : Unlike in this, to the first propagators of the LAW, who always declared the Israelites to be under an *extraordinary* Providence.

From all this I conclude, that as amidst the concurrence of so many favourable circumstances, no such claim was made ; but that, contrary to the universal practice of all false Religions, the *Jews*, saw and owned a great change in the Divine Oeconomy, that therefore their former pretensions to the peculiar protection of Heaven were TRUE.

But it hath been objected that the early sacred Writers themselves frequently speak of the *inequality of* Providence to *Particulars*[q] : and in such a manner as Men living under a common Providence are accustomed to speak. It is very true that these Writers do now and then give intimations of this *inequality*. And therefore, though we shall hereafter prove an extraordinary *Providence* to have been actually administered, in which, not only this objection will be seen to drop of itself, but the particular passages, on which it is founded, will be distinctly considered ; yet, for the Reader's satisfaction, it may not be amiss to shew here, that these representations of *ine-*

---

[q] — Asaph de Dei providentia dubitavit, & fere a vera via deflexisset—Salomon etiam, cujus tempore res Judæorum in summo vigore erant, suspicatur omnia casu contingere—Denique omnibus fere prophetis hoc ipsum valde obscurum fuit, nempe quomodo ordo naturæ & hominum eventus cum conceptu quem de providentia Dei formaverant, possent convenire. — *Spinozæ Theologico-Pol.* p. 73, 74.

quality

quality are very confiftent with that before given of the extraordinary Providence. We fay therefore,

I. That when the Sacred Writers fpeak of the *inequalities* of Providence, and the unfit diftribution of things, they often mean that ftate of it amongft their *Pagan* neighbours, and not in *Judea*: As particularly in the Book of *Pfalms* and *Ecclefiaftes*[r].

II. We fometimes find Men complaining of *inequalities* in events, which were indeed the effects of a moft *equal* Providence. Such as the punifhment of *Pofterity* for the crimes of their *Forefathers*; and of *Subjects* for their *Kings*. Of the firft, the Prophet *Ezekiel* gives us an inftance in the People's cafe: *What mean ye, that you ufe this Proverb concerning the Land of* Ifrael, *faying, The Fathers have eaten four grapes, and the Childrens teeth are fet on edge*[s]?—Of the fecond, *David* gives it in his own; not duly attending to the juftice of this proceeding, where he fays, *But thefe Sheep, what have they done*[t]? And that he was fometimes too hafty in judging of thefe matters appears from his own confeffion: *Behold, thefe are the ungodly, who profper in the world, they increafe in riches.— When I thought to know this, it was too painful for me: until I went into the Sanctuary of God; then underftood I their end. Surely thou didft fet them in flippery places: thou caftedft them down into deftruction.—So foolifh was I, and ignorant: I was as a beaft before thee*[u]. That is, I underftood not the courfe of thy juftice, till I had confidered the *way* in which an equal Providence muft neceffarily be ad-

---

[r] See Appendix. [s] Chap. xviii. ver. 2. [t] 2 SAM. xxiv. 17. [u] PSALM lxxiii. 12———22.

ministered

ministered under a *Theocracy,* and the *consequences* of such an Administration. For,

III. Even admitting the reality of an *equal* Providence to Particulars in the *Hebrew* State, the administration of it must needs be attended with such circumstances as sometimes to occasion those observations of *inequality.* For 1. it appears, from the reason of the thing, that this administration did not begin to be exerted in particular cases till the civil Laws of the Republic had failed of their efficacy. Thus where any crime, as for instance disobedience to Parents, was *public,* it became the object of the civil Tribunal, and is accordingly ordered to be punished by the Judge[x]. But when *private* and secret, than it became the object of Divine vengeance [y]. Now the consequence of this was, that when the Laws were remissly or corruptly administered, *good* and *ill* would sometimes happen unequally to men. For we are not to suppose that Providence, in this case, generally, interfered till the corrupt administration itself, when ripe for vengeance, had been first punished. 2. In this extraordinary administration, one part of the wicked was sometimes suffered as a scourge to the other. 3. The extraordinary Providence to the State might sometimes clash with that to Particulars, as in the plague for numbering the people. 4. Sometimes the extraordinary Providence was suspended for a season to bring on a national repentance: But at the same time this suspension was publicly denounced[z]. And a very severe punishment it was, as leaving a State which had not the sanction of a

---

[x] EXOD. xxi. 15, and 17.   [y] DEUT. xxvii. 16. and PROV. xxx. 17.   [z] ISAIAH iii. 5. Chap. lix. ver. 2. Chap. lxiv. ver. 7.

future

future ftate of rewards and punifhments in a very
difconfolate condition. And this was what occafioned the complaints of the impatient *Jews*, after they had been fo long accuftomed to an extraordinary adminiftration [a].

IV. But the general and full folution of the difficulty is this, The common caufe of thefe complaints arofe from the GRADUAL WITHDRAWING
the extraordinary Providence. Under the *Judges*
it was perfectly equal. And during that period of
the *Theocracy*, it is remarkable that we hear of no
complaints. When the people had rebellioufly
demanded a king, and their folly was fo far complied with, that God fuffered the *Theocracy* to be
adminiftered by a *Viceroy*, there was then, as was
fitting, a great abatement in the vigour of this *extraordinary* Providence; partly in natural confequence, God being now farther removed from the
immediate adminiftration; and partly in punifhment of their rebellion. And foon after this it is
that we firft find them beginning to make their
obfervations and complaints of *inequality*. From
hence to the time of the *Captivity*, the *extraordinary* Providence kept gradually decaying, till on
their full reeftablifhment, it intirely ceafed [b]. For
what

---

[a] Is. v. 19. JEREM. xvii. 15. AMOS, v. 18. ZEPH. i. 12.
MALAC. ii. 17.

[b] I will only obferve at prefent, what the leaft reflection on
this matter fo naturally fuggefts, that this *complaint of inequality*
never could have come from *good men*, as it did even from *Jeremiah* himfelf, who thus expoftulates with the Almighty: *Righteous art thou, O Lord, when I plead with thee: yet let me talk
with thee of thy judgments: Wherefore doth the way of the Wicked
profper? Wherefore are all they happy that deal very treacheroufly?*
[Chap. xii. ver. 1.] It never, I fay, could have come from
fuch

what great reasons, besides punishment for their crimes; and what consequences it had on the religious sentiments of the People, will be occasionally explained as we go along.

But now, let it be observed, that tho' I have here accounted for the *appearances* of an unequal Providence, yet this is ex abundanti; the very nature of my general argument evincing, that there must needs have been an equal Providence actually administered : for a People in society, without both a future State and an equal Providence, could have no belief in the moral government of God : And under such circumstances, it hath been shewn, that they could not long subsist, but must fall back again into all the confusion of a savage state. We must conclude therefore, that what *appearances* soever there may be of inequality in the administration of Providence, in the early times of the Jewish Theocracy, they are *but appearances:* that is, nothing which can really affect such a mode of administration [a]. The Adversaries therefore of the

such men, had they been *at all acquainted* with the Doctrine *of a future state of rewards and punishments*; or had they not been *long accustomed* to an *extraordinary Providence*.

[a] Mr. Chubb, in some or other of his Tracts, has, as I remember, made an unusual effort; an effort to be witty. He observes, that the Author of the *Divine Legation* has done the Unbeliever's business for him; " by proving that an equal Providence was *promised*; while the Bible shews that it was not *performed.*" But he might have known, that the Author did not furnish Infidelity with this foolish objection; it lay open to them. And he might have seen, that the folly of it was here effectually exposed. However, Mr. Chubb was a very extraordinary personage; and might have said with the reasoning Rustic in Moliere — Oui, si j' avois étudié j' aurois eté songer a des choses ou l' on n' a jamais songé. As it was, he did wonders.

the *Divine Legation*, fuch of them, I mean, who profefs themfelves Believers, fhould confider that,
while they oppofe the reality of an *extraordinary*
Providence over the Jewifh people, they are
weakening the evidence for the miracles recorded
in the Old Teftament. But this is the leaft of
their care. One of them with an affurance, that
hath fomething in it of a prodigy, affirms, " that
the Providence adminiftered under the *Law* was
exactly the fame kind with that adminiftered under the *Gofpel*ᵈ." How this could be the cafe
without impeaching the veracity of God himfelf,
as not making good his repeated engagements,
this man would do well to confider before he becomes the fcorn and contempt of Unbelievers.
But as fuch fort of men bear worfe the difgrace of
folly than impiety, I fhall confider this Portent on
its ridiculous fide only.

Temporal rewards and punifhments adminiftered by the hand of God, followed, as a confequence, from the Jewifh Government's being *Theo-
cratical*; and an *extraordinary* Providence followed,
as a confequence, from the difpenfation of temporal
rewards and punifhments. Yet here we have a
Regius Profeffor of Divinity affirming, That both
temporal Sanctions and *an extraordinary Providence*
are adminiftered under the *Gofpel* in the very
fame manner they formerly were under the *Law*.
In which it is difficult to determine what' moft
to admire; his modefty or his wit. For if it does

He began with defending the reafonablenefs of Chriftianity, and
carryed on his work fo fuccefsfully, that, before he gave over,
he had reafoned himfelf out of Religion.

ᵇ Dr. Rutherforth.

honour

honour to his wit to maintain conclusions destitute
of their premisses, it as strongly recommends his
modesty to contradict the whole tenour of the
New Testament. But there is neither end nor
measure to party-bigottry. Faustus, the Mani-
chean, contended that the Jews and Christians got
the doctrine of the one only God from the Gentiles.
Is this a wilder fancy than what many modern
Divines have asserted, that the Gentiles got the
doctrine of future rewards and punishment from
the Law of Moses? Or are either of these more extravagant than the folly I am going to expose,
namely, That *the temporal sanctions of the* LAW
are transferred into the GOSPEL? Now, if you
should ask whether the Gospel claimed to be a
Theocracy; I suppose at first, they would say *no*;
till they found the advantage you get over them
by this answer. And then I make no doubt,
they would as readily say, *yes*. For what should
hinder them? Does the Gospel disclaim, in stronger terms, its being a TEMPORAL KINGDOM, when
Christ says, *his Kingdom was not of this world,*
than it disclaims TEMPORAL SANCTIONS, when it
says *Yea, and all that will live godly in Jesus Christ
shall suffer persecution*[c], or than it disclaims an *extraordinary providence* where it declares that the
Jews had *the promise of the life that now is,* and
the Christians *of that which is to come* [d] ?

But not to stretch our conjectures to the lengths
these men are disposed to go; let us consider how
far they have already gone. They say *the temporal
sanctions of the Law are transferred into the Gospel:*
and they prove it by these two notable texts.

[c] 2 TIM. iii. 12.   [d] 1 TIM. iv. 8.

The firſt is of St. PAUL, " Children, obey
" your parents in all things: for this is right.
" *Honour thy Father and thy Mother* (which is
" the firſt commandment with promiſe) that it
" may be well with thee, and thou mayeſt live
" long on the earth ᶠ." All that I here find
transferred, from the Law to the Goſpel, are the
words of the fifth Commandment. For the Apoſtle
having ſaid, *Children, obey your parents in the Lord:
for this is right*; he ſupports his exhortation by a
quotation from the Decalogue; juſt as any modern
preacher, but This, would do, without ever dream-
ing of *temporal ſanctions* in the Goſpel; the obſervation, the Apoſtle makes upon it being in theſe
words—*which is the firſt commandment with promiſe*;
as much as to ſay, " You may ſee, from this circumſtance, how very acceptable the performance
of this duty is, to God :" The only inference
which common ſenſe authoriſes us to draw from it
being what, in another place, he thus expreſſes,—
Godlineſs [or the obſervance of God's commands]
*is profitable unto all things, having the promiſe of the
life that now is* [under the LAW] *and of that which
is to come* [under the GOSPEL.]

The other colour for this clandeſtine *transfer* of
temporal ſanctions, is from St. PETER : " Who is
" he that will harm you, if you be followers of
" that which is good ᵍ." So ſays the Apoſtle; and
ſo too ſaid his Maſter; to whoſe words Peter alludes, *Fear not them which kill the body: but rather
fear him which is able to deſtroy body and ſoul in Hell* ʰ.
But as if the Apoſtle had it in his thoughts to guard
againſt this abſurd viſion of *temporal ſanctions*, he

ᶠ Ερη. vi. 2, 3.　　ᵍ 1 Pet. iii. 13.　　ʰ Matt. x. 28.

immediately

immediately ſubjoins,—" But, and if ye ſuffer for righteouſneſs ſake, happy are ye."

Our Doctor having ſo well made out this point, we need not wonder at his confidence, when he aſſures us, *that there is full as good evidence of an extraordinary providence under the chriſtian Diſpenſation as under the Jewiſh.* This though the language of Toland, Tindal, Collins, and the whole tribe of Free-thinkers, yet comes ſo unexpected from a Regius Profeſſor of Divinity, that we ſhould be very careful not to miſtake his meaning.

If, by *full as good*, he would inſinuate that an *extraordinary providence* was adminiſtered under both Diſpenſations, I ſhall be in pain for his intellects : if he would inſinuate, that an *extraordinary providence* was adminiſtered in neither, I ſhall be in pain for his Profeſſorſhip. But he is in pain for nothing ; as the reader may perceive by his manner of ſupporting this impertinent paradox. His proofs follow with equal eaſe and force.———*I ſay unto you, that if two of you ſhall agree on earth, as touching any thing that they ſhall aſk it ſhall be done for them of my Father which is in Heaven* [i].—*And every one that hath forſaken houſes, or brethren, or ſiſters, or father, or mother, or wife, or children, or lands, for my name's ſake, ſhall receive an hundredfold, and ſhall inherit everlaſting life* [k].—*Take therefore no thought ſaying, What ſhall we eat ? or what ſhall we drink ? or wherewithal ſhall we be cloathed ? for your heavenly father knoweth that you have need of all theſe things. But ſeek ye firſt the Kingdom of God and his righteouſneſs, and all theſe things ſhall*

[i] M a t t h. xviii. 19.   [k] M a t t h. xix. 29.

be

be added unto you [1]. And again, *If ye aſk any thing
in my name, I will give it* [m].—" No more, my moſt
wiſe Friend! Thou haſt my wonder; that's enough.
My underſtanding ſhall come after;" ſaid, once
on a time, a plain good man to a profound Philoſopher like this.

Now not to repeat again the illogical bravado of
taking and ſupporting a *concluſion* divorced from
its *premiſſes*; ſuch as is the contending for temporal ſanctions and an extraordinary providence
where there was no Theocracy, from whence they
could be derived; we have here a Profeſſor of
Divinity who has his elements of Scripture-inter-
pretation yet to learn. The firſt rule of which
is, 1. " That *all*, does not ſignify *all ſimply*, but
all of one kind; and, of what kind, the context
muſt direct us to determine." When therefore,
the members of Chriſt's *ſpiritual Kingdom* are
promiſed they ſhall obtain *all* they aſk, this *all*
muſt needs be confined to *things ſpiritual.* Now
when here we find thoſe, who are bid to leave their
temporal poſſeſſions and propagate the Goſpel,
have the promiſe of a hundred fold, are we to
ſeek for the performance, in Paleſtine, or in a
better Country [n]? Again, Where under the *Law*,
we read of *temporal Promiſes*, we read likewiſe that
they were fulfilled. Where, under the Gospel,
we read that *thoſe who, for the ſake of Chriſt, forſake houſes, or brethren or ſiſters, or father or mother,
or wife or children, or lands, ſhall receive an hundredfold*, What are we there to look for? For the good
things of this world, which this ſharp-ſighted
Doctor is ſo eager and intent to find?—Now admit

[1] Matth. vi. 31. *& ſeq.*   [m] John xiv. 14.
[n] Heb. xi. 16.

there

there might be no great inconvenience in receiving a hundred *houses* for one; would not a hundred *wives* a little embarras his Professorship? And as to the *house and land*—Where did he learn that this was literally fulfilled, even to those who had the best title to them if they were literally promised, I mean the Apostles, yet these we always meet on foot; strangers upon earth; and without either house or home. He, who then passed for a learned Apostle, once at Rome, indeed, got a warm *house* over his head; yet let us not forget that it was but a *hired* one. Here, in this Capital of the World, he received all who came to him. But tho' a good Divine, as times then went, he never rose to a Regius Professorship.

The second elementary rule of interpretation is, " That all the promises of *extraordinary* blessings, made to the first propagators of the Gospel, are not to be understood as extending to their successors of all Ages, or to the Church in general." To apply this likewise to the thing in question. If it should be admitted that great *temporal blessings* were promised to the first disciples of Christ, it will not follow that their successors had a claim to them, any more than they had to their *spiritual gifts and graces*, such as the power of working miracles, prophesying, speaking with tongues, *&c.* Because, as divine Wisdom saw these latter to be necessary for the discharge of their peculiar function; so divine Goodness might be graciously pleased to bestow the Other on them, as the reward of their abundant Faith, and superior Courage in the day of trial, when the Powers of this world were bent on their destruction. But this (blessed be God) is neither the learned Professor's case, nor mine. The worst that has be-

fallen

fallen me in the defence of Religion is only the railings of the Vile and Impotent: and the worſt that is likely to befal him is only the ridicule of all the reſt. Happy had it been for himſelf and much happier for his hearers, had our Profeſſor's modeſty diſpoſed him rather to ſeek inſtruction from thoſe who have gone before, than to impart it to thoſe who are to come after. HOOKER has ſo admirably expoſed this very ſpecific folly which our Doctor has run into, of arguing againſt his ſenſes, in making the Diſpenſation of Providence under the *Moſaic* and *Chriſtian* Oeconomies to be the ſame, that I cannot do him better ſervice than to tranſcribe the words of that divine ornament of the Engliſh Prieſthood.——" Shall we then here-
" upon ARGUE EVEN AGAINST OUR OWN EXPE-
" RIENCE AND KNOWLEGE? Shall we ſeek to
" perſuade men that, of neceſſity, it is with us as
" it was with them, that becauſe God is ours, in
" all reſp cts, as much as theirs, therefore, either
" no ſuch way of direction hath been at any time,
" or if it have been, it doth *ſtill continue* in the
" Church? or if the ſame do not continue, that
" yet it muſt be, at the leaſt, ſupplied by ſome
" ſuch means as pleaſeth us to account of equal
" force? A more dutiful and religious way for us,
" were to admire the Wiſdom of God which
" ſhineth in the beautiful variety of things, but
" moſt in the manifold and yet harmonious diſ-
" ſimilitude of thoſe ways, whereby his Church
" upon earth is guided from age to age through-
" out all the generations of men °."

But this was one of the charitable expedients employed to ſet me right, and to prevent the diſ-

---

° Eccl. Pol. b. iii. ſec. 10.

grace of scribling much to no purpose. However, as in a Work of this nature, which partakes so much of the History of the human mind, I may be allowed occasionally, and as it falls in my way, to give as well, examples of its more uncommon degrees of depravity and folly, as of its improvements and excellencies, I shall go on. My constant friend Dr. Stebbing proceeds another way to work, but all for the same good end. He desires me and my reader to consider, " what it was that " Moses undertook; and what was the true end of " his Mission. It was to carry the children of Israel " out of Egypt, and put them in possession of the " Land of Canaan, in execution of the Covenant " made with Abraham. The work in the very " NATURE of it *required* the administration of an " *extraordinary* Providence; of which it OUGHT " THEREFORE TO BE PRESUMED that Moses had " both the *assurance* and *experience:* otherwise he " would have engaged in a very MAD undertak-" ing, and the people would have been AS MAD " in following him. THIS SHORT HINT POINTS " OUT THE TRUE INTERNAL EVIDENCE of *Moses's* " *Divine Legation,* and this evidence *has no sort of* " *dependence* upon the belief or disbelief of the " doctrine of a future state. For supposing (what " is the truth) that the Israelites did believe it; " what could this belief effect? It might carry " them to Heaven, and would do so if they made " a proper use of it, but it could not put them " in possession of the Land of Canaan. Mr. " Warburton therefore has plainly mistaken his " point."

This intimation of my mistake is kind: and I should have taken his *hint,* as *short* as it is, but for the following reasons.

1. This

1. This *hint* would serve the Mufti full as well, to prove the *Divine Legation of Mahomet* : for thus we may suppose they would argue.—" Mahomet's work was not like Moses's, the subdual of a small tract of Country, possessed by seven Tribes or Nations, with a force of some hundred thousand followers; but the conquest of almost all Asia, with a handful of Banditti. Now *this work*, says the learned Mahometan, *in the very nature of it, required the administration of an extraordinary providence, of which* IT OUGHT THEREFORE TO BE PRESUMED, *that Mahomet had both the assurance and experience; otherwise he would have engaged in a very mad undertaking, and the people would have been as mad in following him.*"

Thus hath the learned Doctor taught the Mufti how to reason. The worst of it is, that I, for whom the kindness was principally intended, cannot profit by it, the argument lying exposed to so terrible a retortion. To this the Doctor replies, that the cases are widely different: and that I myself allow them to be different, for that I hold, the Legation of Moses to be a true one; and the Legation of Mahomet, an imposture.—Risum teneatis Amici.

But there is another reason why I can make nothing of this gracious *hint*. It is because I proposed to PROVE (and not, as he says, I ought to have done, TO PRESUME upon) the Divinity of Moses's mission, by an *internal argument*. Indeed he tells me, that if I be for *proving*, he has *pointed out* such a one to me. He says so, 'tis true : but in so saying, he only shews his ignorance of what is meant by an INTERNAL ARGUMENT. An internal argument is such a one as takes for its medium some

notorious

notorious Fact, or circumstance, in the frame and constitution of a Religion, *not in contest* ; and from thence, by necessary consequence, deduces the truth of a fact supported by testimony which *is in contest.* Thus, from the notorious Fact of the omission of a future State in Moses's institution of Law and Religion, I deduce his *Divine Legation.*

But the learned Artist himself seems conscious that the ware he would put into my hands, is indeed no better than a counterfeit piece of trumpery; and so far from being an *internal argument,* that it is no argument at all: For he tells us, It ought therefore to be presumed, *that Moses had both the assurance and experience* that God governed the Israelites by an extraordinary Providence.

But what follows is such unaccountable jargon! —*For supposing the Israelites did believe a future State, what would this belief effect ? It might carry them to Heaven, but it could not put them in possession of the land of Canaan.* This looks as if the learned Doctor had supposed that, from the truth of this assertion, *That no civil Society under a common Providence could subsist without a future state,* I had inferred, that, *with a future state,* Society would be able to work wonders.—What efficacy a future state hath, whether little or much, affects not my argument any otherwise than by the oblique tendency it hath to support the reasoning: and I urged it thus;—" Had not the Jews been under an *extraordinary providence,* at that period when Moses led them out to take possession of the land of Canaan, they were most unfit to bear the want of the doctrine of a *future state:*"—Which ob-

servation

fervation I fupported by the cafe of Odin's followers, and Mahomet's; who, in the fame circumftances of making conquefts, and feeking new
habitations, had this Doctrine feduloufly inculcated
to them, by their refpective Leaders. And the
Hiftories of both thefe Nations inform us, that
nothing fo much contributed to the rapidity of
their fucceffes as the enthufiafm which that Doctrine infpired.

And yet, to be fure, the Doctor never faid a
livelier thing, who is celebrated for faying many,
than when he afked,—*What could this belief effect?*
It might carry them to Heaven; but it could not put
them in poffeffion of the Land of Canaan. Now unluckily, like moft of thefe witty things, when
too nearly infpected, we find it to be juft the reverfe of the truth. The *belief* could never *carry*
them to Heaven, and yet was abundantly fufficient,
under fuch a leader as Mofes, *to put them in pof-*
feffion of the land of Canaan. The Arabians' *belief*
of a future ftate could never, in the opinion at
leaft of our orthodox Doctor, carry them to Heaven; yet he muft allow it enabled them to take
and keep poffeffion of a great part of Europe and
Afia. But the Doctor's head was running on the
efficacy of the *Chriftian Faith,* when he talked of
belief carrying men to heaven.—Yet who knows, but
when he gave the early Jews the knowledge of a
future ftate, he gave them the *Chriftian faith* into
the bargain?

SECT. V.

THUS we fee that an EXTRAORDINARY
PROVIDENCE WAS THE NECESSARY CONSE-
QUENCE OF A THEOCRACY; and that this Provi-
dence

dence is represented in Scripture to have been really administered. TEMPORAL REWARDS AND PUNISHMENTS, therefore, (the effects of this providence) and *not future*, MUST NEEDS BE THE SANCTION of their Law and Religion.

Having thus prepared the ground, and laid the foundation, I go on to shew that future Rewards and Punishments, which COULD NOT BE THE SANCTION of the Mosaic Dispensation, WERE NOT TAUGHT in it at all : and that, in consequence of this Omission, the PEOPLE had not the doctrine of a future state for many ages. And here my arguments will be chiefly directed against the believing part of my Opponents; no Deist[p], that I know of, ever pretending that the doctrine of a future state was to be found in the Law.

MOSES delivered to the Israelites a complete Digest of Law and Religion : but, to fit it to the nature of a Theocratic Government, he gave it perfectly incorporated. And, for the observance of the intire Institution, he added the sanction of rewards and punishments : both of which we have shewn to be necessary for the support of a Repub-

---

[p] The Atheist *Vanini*, indeed, seems to rank Moses in the number of those Politicians, who, he says, promised a *future state* that the cheat might never be found out. — In unica naturæ lege, quam *natura*, quæ Deus est *(est enim principium motus)* in omnium gentium animis inscripsit. Cæteras vero leges non nisi figmenta & illusiones esse asserebant, non a cacodæmone aliquo inductas *fabulosum namque illorum genus dicitur a philosophis*, sed a *principibus ad subditorum pædagogiam excogitatas*, & a sacrificulis ob honoris & auri aucupium confirmatas, non miraculis, *sed scriptura, cujus nec originale ullibi adinvenitur, quæ miracula facta recitet*, & bonarum ac malarum actionum repromissiones polliceatur, *in futura tamen vita*, ne fraus detegi possit. — *De admirandis naturæ arcanis.*

Q

lic :

lic: and yet, that civil Society, as such, can administer only one [q].

Now in the Jewish Republic, both the rewards and punishments promised by heaven, were TEMPORAL only. Such as health, long life, peace, plenty, and dominion, &c. Diseases, immature death, war, famine, want, subjection, and captivity, &c. And in no one place of the Mosaic Institutes is there the least mention, or any intelligible hint, of the rewards and punishments of another life.

When SOLOMON had restored the integrity of Religion; and, to the regulated purity of Worship, had added the utmost magnificence; in his DEDICATION of the new-built Temple, he addresses a long prayer to the God of Israel, consisting of one solemn petition* for the continuance of the OLD COVENANT made by the ministry of Moses. He gives an exact account of all its parts, and explains at large the SANCTION of the Jewish Law and Religion. And here, as in the writings of Moses, we find nothing but TEMPORAL rewards and punishments; without the least hint or intimation of a future state.

The holy PROPHETS speak of no other. Thus Isaiah: " Then shall he give the rain of thy
" seed that thou shalt sow the ground withal,
" and bread of the increase of the earth, and it
" shall be fat and plenteous; and in that day shall
" thy cattle feed in large pastures.—And there
" shall be upon every high mountain, and upon

----

[q] *i. e.* Punishments. See the first vol. p. 16. 4th ed.

" every

" every high hill, rivers and ftreams of water'."
And Jeremiah: " I will furely confume them,
" faith the Lord; there fhall be no grapes on the
" vine, nor figs on the fig-tree, and the leaf fhall
" fade, and the things that I have given them
" fhall pafs away from them.—I will fend fer-
" pents and cockatrices amongft you, which will
" not be charmed, and they fhall bite you, faith
" the Lord '." Nay fo little known, in thefe
times, was any other kind of rewards and punifhments to the Jewifh People, that, when the Prophets foretell that NEW Difpenfation, by which, *life
and immortality were brought to light*, they exprefs
even thofe future rewards and punifhments under
the image of the prefent. Thus Zechariah, prophefying of the times of CHRIST, defcribes the
punifhment attendant on a refufal of the terms of
Grace, under the ideas of the Jewifh Œconomy:
" And it fhall be that whofo will not *come up* of
" *all the families of the earth* unto *Jerufalem*, to
" worfhip the *King* the Lord of Hofts, even upon
" them SHALL BE NO RAIN '." I would have
thofe men well confider this, who perfift in thinking " that the early Jews had the doctrine of a
future ftate of rewards and punifhments, though
Mofes taught it not exprefly to them;" and then
tell me why Zechariah, when prophefying of the
Gofpel-times, fhould chufe to exprefs thefe *future*
rewards and punifhments under the image of the
prefent?

Indeed, were it not for the amazing prejudices
which have obtained on this fubject, a writer's
pains to fhew that a future ftate of rewards and

' Chap. xxx. ver 23, 25.   ' Chap. viii. ver. 13, 17.
' Chap. xiv. ver. 17.

'punifhments made no part of the Mofaic Difpenfation, would appear as abfurd to every intelligent·
reader, as his would be who fhould employ many
formal arguments to prove that Sir Ifaac Newton's
Theory of Light and Colours is not to be found in
Ariftotle's books *de Cælo, & de Coloribus*. I will
therefore for once prefume fo much on the privilege
of Common Senfe, as to fuppofe, the impartial
reader may be now willing to confefs, that the
doctrine of Life and Immortality was not yet
known to a people while they were *fitting in darknefs, and in the region and fhadow of death* [u] ; and
go on to other matters that have more need to be
explained.

II.

I fhall fhew then, in the next place, that this
OMISSION was not accidental; or of a thing which
Mofes did not well underftand : but that, on the
contrary, it was a defigned omiffion ; and of a thing
well known by him to be of high importance to
Society.

I. That the doctrine of a future ftate of Rewards and Punifhments was ftudioufly omitted,
may appear from feveral circumftances in the book
of Genefis. For the hiftory of Mofes may be divided into two periods; from the Creation to his
Miffion; and from his Miffion to the delivering
up his Command to Jofhua : The firft was written
by him in quality of HISTORIAN ; the fecond, of
LEGISLATOR ; in both of which he preferves an
equal filence concerning the doctrine of a future
ftate.

[u] MATTH. iv. 16.

1. In the history of the *Fall of Man* it is to be observed, that he mentions only the instrument of the agent, the SERPENT; not the agent himself, the DEVIL: and the reason is plain; there was a close connection between that agency,—The spiritual effects of the Fall,—the work of Redemption,—and the doctrine of a future State. If you say, the connection was not so close but that the Agent might have been mentioned without any more of his history than the temptation to the *Fall*; I reply it is true it might; but not without danger of giving countenance to the impious doctrine of *Two Principles*, which at this time prevailed throughout the Pagan world. What but these important considerations could be the cause of the omission [x]? when it is so evident that the knowledge of this grand enemy of our welfare would have been the likeliest cure of Pagan superstitions, as teaching men to esteem of Idolatry

---

[x] The miserable efforts of these men to evade the force of a little plain sense is deplorable. " Moses (says one of them) " could not omit the mention of the *Devil* for the reason given " by the author of the D. L. because he mentions him ex- " pressly and represents him as the patron, if not as the author, " of idolatry." Deut. xxxii. ver. 17. *Rutherforth's Essay*, p. 294. — The words of Moses are these, — *They sacrificed to* DEVILS; *not to God*; *to Gods whom they knew not, to new Gods that came newly up, whom your fathers feared not.* The Hebrew word here translated *Devils*, is *Schedim*, which the best interpreters tell us, has another signification. The true God being *Schaddei*, the *omnipotent and all sufficient*; the gentile Gods by a beautiful opposition, are called *Schedim, counterfeit Gods.* And the context, where they are called *new Gods*, shews this interpretation to be true. But admit that, by Schedim is to be understood *evil spirits:* by these spirits are not meant fallen Angels, but the souls of wicked men. These were the *Demons* of Paganism; but the *Devils* discovered by Revelation have a different nature and original: Accordingly, the Septuagint, which took *Schedim* in the sense of the souls of wicked men, translates it by δαιμόνια.

no otherwife than as a mere diabolical illufion. And in fact we find, that when the Ifraelites were taught, by the later Prophets, to confider it in this light, we hear no more of their Idolatries. Hence we fee, that the folly of thofe who, with *Collins*, would have a mere ferpent only to be underftood, is juft equal to theirs who, with the *Cabbalifts*, would have that ferpent a mere Allegory.

2. In the hiftory of Enoch's *tranflation* [y] to Heaven [z], there is fo ftudied an obfcurity that feveral of the Rabbins, as Aben Ezra and Jarchi, fond as they are of finding a future ftate in the Pentateuch, interpret this tranflation as only figni-fying an immature death. *And Enoch walked with God, and he was not, for God took him.* How diffe-rent from the other hiftory of the tranflation of Elijah? " And it came to pafs when the Lord would " take up Elijah into Heaven by a whirlwind, that " Elijah went with Elifha from Gilgal, *&c.*—And " it came to pafs as they ftill went on and talked, " that behold there appeared a chariot of fire, and " horfes of fire, and parted them both afunder, " and Elijah went up with a whirlwind into Hea-" ven [a]." But the reafon of this difference is evi-dent: When the latter hiftory was written, it was thought expedient to make a preparation for the dawning of a *future ftate* of reward and punifhment, which in the time of Mofes had been highly impro-per. The reflections of an eminent Critic on this oc-cafion, will fhew how little he penetrated into the true defign of this Œconomy. " Mirum eft " Mofem rem tantam, fi modo immortalem He-" nochum factum CREDIDIT, tam obiter, tamque

[y] GEN. v. 24.   [z] HEB. xi. 5.   [a] 2 KINGS ii. 1, 11.

" obfcure,

" obſcure, quaſi EAM LATERE VELLET, perſtrinx-
" iſſe. Fortè cum hæc ex antiquiſſimis monumentis
" exſcriberet, nihil præter ea quæ nobis tradidit
" invenit, quibus aliquid adjicere religio fuit [b]."
For Moſes both knew and *believed* the Immortality
of Enoch, and purpoſely obſcured the fact, from
whence it might have been collected.   But what is
moſt ſingular in this reflection is, that the learned
Commentator, to aggravate the obſcurity, ſays it
is as obſcure, as if he purpoſely deſigned to hide it,
ſuppoſing ſuch a deſign to be the higheſt improbability ; which was indeed the fact, and is the
true ſolution of the difficulty.

3. In his hiſtory of the Patriarchs, he entirely
omits, or throws into ſhade, the accounts of thoſe
Revelations, with which, as we learn from the
writers of the New Teſtament, ſome of them
were actually favoured, concerning the Redemption of mankind.   Of theſe favours we ſhall give
ere long a great and noble inſtance, in the caſe of
ABRAHAM, who, as we are aſſured by JESUS himſelf, *rejoiced to ſee* CHRIST'S *day, and ſaw it, and
was glad.*

From whence therefore could all this ſtudied
caution ariſe, but to keep out of ſight that doctrine,
which, for ends truly worthy of the divine Wiſdom, he had omitted in his Inſtitutes of Law and
Religion.   This ſhews the weakneſs of that eva-
ſion, which would reconcile the OMISSION, to the
People's KNOWLEDGE of the doctrine, by ſuppoſing they had been ſo well inſtructed by the Patriarchs, that Moſes had no occaſion to ſay any
thing farther on that ſubject.

[b] Vid. *Clericum* in GEN. v. 24.

Let

Let me obferve by the way, that thefe confiderations are more than a thoufand topical arguments to prove, that Mofes was the real author of the book of Genefis. But the proof deduced therefrom will be drawn out and explained at large hereafter.

II. That the importance of this Doctrine to Society was well underftood by Mofes, may appear from a particular provifion in his Inftitutes, (befides that general one of an extraordinary providence) evidently made to oppofe to the inconvenient confequences of the OMISSION.

We have fhewn at large, in the firft volume, that under a common or unequal providence, civil Government could not be fupported without a Religion teaching a future ftate of reward and punifhment. And it is the great purpofe of this work to prove, that the Mofaic Religion wanting that doctrine, the Jews muft REALLY have enjoyed that equal providence, under which holy Scripture reprefents them to have lived: and then, no tranfgreffor efcaping punifhment, nor any obferver of the law miffing his reward [e], human affairs might be

---

[e] Dr. Sykes in difputing with me, as we have feen above, on this queftion, *Whether the extraordinary Providence was only over the State in general, or whether it extended to Particulars,* having fufficiently puzzled himfelf and his reader; To recover the ground he had loft, on a fudden changes the queftion, and now tells us, that it is, " *Whether an extraordinary Providence* " *was adminiftered to Particulars* IN SUCH A MANNER *that* " *no tranfgreffor of the Law efcaped punifhment, nor any ob-* " *ferver of the Law miffed his reward,*" " which Mr. Warbur-" ton reprefents (fays he) to be the ftate of the Jews under an " equal Providence." [Exam. p. 187-8] Now what his drift was in this piece of management, is eafily underftood. It was to introduce a commodious Fallacy under an ambiguous expreffion;

be kept in good order, without the doctrine of a future State.

Yet

pression; which should be always at hand to answer his occasions. And indeed, the cautious reader, (and I would advise no other to have to do with him) will suspect no less, when he observes that the words, [*no Transgressor escaped Punishment, nor any Observer of the Law missed his Reward*] quoted from me, are not to be found in that place where I state the nature of the extraordinary Providence; but here, where I speak of the consequences of it, in the words above — *We have shewn at large*, &c. What now has this ANSWERER done? He has taken the words [*no Transgressor escaping Punishment, nor any Observer of the Law missing his Reward*] from their natural place; misrepresented their purpose; and given them to the reader as my DEFINITION of an extraordinary Providence to Particulars. And not content with all this, he has put a false and sophistical sense upon them, *viz.* THAT NO ONE SINGLE PERSON, WITHOUT EXCEPTION, ever escaped Punishment, or missed his Reward. And in this sense, by the vilest prevarication, he repeats and applies them, on every following occasion, as the sole answer to all my reasonings on the subject of an extraordinary Providence. It will be proper then to shew, that the words could not mean, by any rules of just construction, that every *single person, without exception*, was thus punished and rewarded; but only that this extraordinary Providence over Particulars was so exactly administered, that no one could hope to escape it, or fear to be forgotten by it.

. First then, let it be observed, that the words are no absolute assertion; but a consequence of something asserted. — AND THEN *no Transgressor escaping*, etc. which illative words the honest Examiner omitted. — What I had asserted was simply this, that the extraordinary Providence over the Jews was in Scripture represented as administered over Particulars; but that this very administration would of necessity be attended with some inequalities. Must not then the consequence I draw from these premises be as restrained as the premises themselves? Secondly, I said, that God had promised an equal Providence to Particulars, but that he had declared, at the same time, how it should be administered, *viz.* in such a manner as would occasion some few exceptions. If therefore Dr. Sykes would not allow me, he ought to have allowed God Almighty at least, to explain his own meaning. Thirdly, had the words been abso-

lute

Yet ſtill the violence of irregular paſſions would make ſome men of ſtronger complexions ſuperior to all the fear of *perſonal temporal evil*. To lay hold therefore on Theſe, and to gain a due aſcendant over the moſt determined, the puniſhments, in this Inſtitution, are extended to the POSTERITY

lute, as they then might have admitted of two ſenſes, did not common ingenuity require, that I ſhould be underſtood in that which was eaſieſt to prove, when either was alike to my purpoſe? But there was ſtill more than this to lead an ingenuous man into my meaning; which was, that he might obſerve, that I uſed, throughout my whole diſcourſe of the Jewiſh Œconomy, the words *extraordinary Providence* and *equal Providence*, as equivalent terms. By which he might underſtand that I all along admitted of exceptions. Fourthly, If ſuch rare caſes of exception deſtroyed an equal Providence to *Particulars*, (which Providence I hold) it would deſtroy, with it, the equal Providence to the *State*, (which Dr. Sykes pretends to hold.) But if not for the ſake of truth in opinion, yet for fair dealing in practice, Dr. Sykes ſhould have interpreted my words not abſolutely, but with exceptions. For thus ſtood the caſe. He quoted two poſitions from the *Divine Legation*. 1. That there was an extraordinary Providence over the State in general. 2. Over private men in particular. He grants the firſt; and denies the ſecond. But is not the extent of that providence underſtood to be in both caſes the ſame? Now in that over the *State*, he underſtands it to have been with exceptions, as appears from his own mention of the caſe of Achan, p. 190. and of David, p. 197. Ought he not then, by all the rules of honeſt reaſoning, to have underſtood the propoſition-denied, in the ſame ſenſe he underſtands the Propoſition-granted? If in the adminiſtration over the State in general, there were ſome few exceptions, why not in That over private men in particular?

But if now the candid reader ſhall aſk me, Why I employed expreſſions, which, when divorced from the context, might be abuſed by a Caviller to a perverſe meaning, I will tell him. I uſed them in imitation of the language of the Apoſtle, who ſays that, under the Jewiſh Œconomy, EVERY *tranſgreſſion and diſobedience received a juſt recompence of reward**. And if He be to be underſtood with latitude, why may not I?

* HEB. ii. 2.

of

of wicked men; which the inſtinctive fondneſs of Parents to their offspring would make terrible even to thoſe who had hardened themſelves into an inſenſibility of perſonal puniſhment: *I the Lord thy God am a jealous God, viſiting the iniquity of the Fathers upon the Children unto the third and fourth generation of them that hate me* [d].

Now that this puniſhment was only to ſupply the want of a *Future ſtate* is evident frem hence [e], Towards the concluſion of this extraordinary Œconomy, when GOD, by the later Prophets, re-

[d] EXOD. xx. 5. Chap. xxxiv. 7. But as GOD acted with them in the capacity of the Creator and Father of all Men, as well as of tutelary God and King, he was pleaſed, at the ſame time, to provide that they ſhould never loſe the memory of the attributes of the Almighty: and therefore adds, — *And ſhewing mercy unto thouſands in them that love me and keep my commandments.* NUMB. xiv. 18. DEUT. v. 9.

[e] " The Author of the D. L. (ſays Dr. Sykes) goes on, and " obſerves that this puniſhment [of viſiting the iniquities of " Fathers upon their Children] *was only to ſupply the want of a* " *future ſtate.* But how will this *extraordinary œconomy* SUP-" PLY this want? The Children at preſent ſuffer for their " Parents' crimes; and are ſuppoſed to be puniſhed when they " have no guilt. Is not this a plain act of HARDSHIP? And " if there be no future ſtate or compenſation made, the hard-" ſhip done muſt continue for ever a hardſhip on the unhappy " ſufferer." [Exam. of Mr. W's. account, &c. p. 202—3.] For a Reaſoner, it would be hard to find his fellow. 1. The queſtion is, whether this Law of puniſhing, was a SUPPLY to the want of a future ſtate? If it laid hold of the paſſions, as he owns it did, it certainly was a SUPPLY. However, he will prove it was none. And how? Becauſe it was a HARD-SHIP. 2. He ſuppoſes, I hold, that when Children were *puniſhed*, in the proper ſenſe of the word, they were innocent, whereas I hold, that then they were always guilty. When the innocent were affected by their Parents' crimes, it was by the deprivation of benefits, in their nature forfeitable. 3. He ſuppoſes, that if Moſes taught no future ſtate, IT WOULD FOL-LOW, that there was none.

veals

veals his purpose of giving them a NEW *Dispensation*ᶠ, in which a Future state of reward and punishment was to be *brought to light*, it is then declared
in the most express manner, that he will abrogate
the Law of punishing Children for the crimes of
their Parents. JEREMIAH, speaking of this *new*
Dispensation, says: " In *those days* they shall say
" no more, The Fathers have eaten a sour grape,
" and the Children's teeth are set on edge : but
" *every one shall die for his own iniquity*, every man
" that eateth the sour grape, his teeth shall be set
" on edge. Behold the days come, saith the
" Lord, that I will make a NEW COVENANT with
" the House of Israel,——NOT according to the
" Covenant that I made with their Fathers in the
" day that I took them by the hand to bring them

ᶠ To this it hath been objected — " As to the proof, that
" visiting the iniquities of Parents on their Children was designed
" to supply the want of a future state, because in a *new Dis-
" pensation*, it is foretold, that this mode of punishing will be
" changed, this argument will not be admitted by the Deists,
" who do not allow that a *new Dispensation* is revealed under
" the phrase of a *new Covenant*." Here the Objector should
have distinguished — The Deists make two different attacks on
Revelation. In the one, They dispute that order, connexion,
and dependency between the two Dispensations, as they are delivered in Scripture, and maintained by Believers : In the other,
they admit (for arguments' sake) this representation of revealed
Religion ; and pretend to shew its falshood, even upon that footing. Amongst their various arguments in this last method of attack, one is, that the Jewish Religion had no sanction *of a future
state*, and so could not come from God. [See Lord Bolingbroke's Posthumous Writings.] The purpose of this work is to
turn that circumstance against them : and from the omission of
the Doctrine, demonstrate the Divine original of the Law. So
that the Reader sees, I am in order, when, to evince a *designed*
omission, I explain the Law of punishing the crimes of Fathers
on the Children, from the different natures of the two Dispensations ; as going upon principles acceded to, tho' it be only
disputandi gratia, by the Deists themselves.

" out

" out of the land of Egypt [s], &c.   And EZE-
KIEL fpeaking of the fame times, fays: " I will
" give them one heart, and will put a NEW fpirit
" within you, &c.——But as for them, whofe
" heart walketh after the heart of their abominable
" things —— *I will recompenfe their way* UPON
" THEIR OWN HEADS, faith the Lord God [h]."
And again : " What mean ye, that you ufe this
" Proverb concerning the land of Ifrael, faying,
" The Fathers have eaten four grapes, and the
" Childrens' teeth are fet on edge [i]? As I live,
" faith the Lord God, Ye fhall *not have occafion*
" *any more to ufe this Proverb in Ifrael.*   Behold all
" fouls are mine, as the foul of the Father, fo
" alfo the foul of the Son is mine : *the foul that*
" *finneth, it fhall die* [k]."

And yet (to fhew more plainly that the *abrogation* of the Law was folely owing to this *new* Difpenfation) the fame Prophets, when their fubjeƈt
is the *prefent* Jewifh Œconomy, fpeak of this very
Law as ftill in force.   Thus JEREMIAH : " Thou
" fheweft loving kindnefs unto thoufands, and
" *recompenfeft the iniquity of the Fathers into the*
" *bofom of their Children* after them [l]."   And
HOSEA : " *Seeing thou haft forgotten the Law of thy*
" *God, I will alfo forget thy Children* [m]."

---

[s] Chap. xxxi. 30—33.   [h] Chap. xi. ver. 19—21.

[i] It hath been objeƈted, " That the Prophet here upbraids
" the Jews as blameable in the ufe of this proverb."   Without
doubt.   And their fault evidently confifted in this, That they
would infinuate that an *innocent* pofterity were punifhed for
the crimes of their forefathers ; whereas we have fhewn, that
when *the childrens' teeth were fet on edge,* they likewife had been
tafting.

[k] Chap. xviii. ver. 2—4.   [l] Chap. xxxii. ver. 18.
[m] Chap. iv. ver. 6.

From

From all this I conclude, That, whoever was the real Author of what goes under the name of the *Law of Moſes*, was at leaſt well acquainted with the *importance* of the doctrine of a future ſtate of reward and puniſhment ; and provided well for the *want* of it.

But the blindneſs of Infidelity is here moſt de-plorable. The Deiſts are not content with con-demning this Law of injuſtice, but will accuſe the Diſpenſation itſelf of inconſiſtence ; pretending that the Prophets have directly contradicted Moſes in their manner of denouncing puniſhment.

It is indeed the ſtanding triumph of infidelity. *But let us return* (ſays Spinoza) *to the Prophets, whoſe diſcordant opinions we have undertaken to lay open.* —— *The* xviiith *chap. of* Ezekiel *does not ſeem to agree with the* 7th ver. *of the* xxxivth *chap. of* Exodus, *nor with the* 18th ver. *of the* xxxiid chap. of Jeremiah, &c*[n].* — " There are ſeveral
" miſtakes (ſays Tyndal) crept into the Old
" Teſtament, where there's ſcarce a chapter which
" gives any hiſtorical account of matters, but
" there are ſome things in it which could not be
" there originally. — It muſt be owned, that the
" ſame ſpirit (I dare not call it a ſpirit of cruelty)
" does not alike prevail throughout the Old Teſta-
" ment ; the nearer we come to the times of the
" Goſpel, the milder it appears : for though God
" declares in the Decalogue, that he is *a jealous*
" *God, viſiting the iniquity of the parents upon the*
" *children to the third and fourth Generation,* and

<hr>

[n] — Sed ad Prophetas revertamur, quorum diſcrepantes opi-niones etiam notare ſuſcepimus — Cap. ſaltem xviii. Ezech. non videtur convenire cum verſu 7. cap. xxxiv. Exod. nec cum ver. 18. Cap. xxxii. Jer. &c. *Tract. Theologico-Pol.* p. 27, 28.

" accordingly

" accordingly Achan, with all his family, was
" deftroyed for his fingle crime; yet the Lord af-
" terwards fays, *The foul that finneth it fhall die*;
" *the fon fhall not bear the iniquity of the father*[o],
" &c[p]."

I. Let us fee then what thefe men have to fay
on the firft point, the *injuftice of the Law.* They
fet out on a falfe fuppofition, that this method of
punifhment was part of an univerfal Religion given
by God as the Creator and Governor of mankind:
whereas it is only part of a civil Inftitute, given
by him to *one People,* as their *tutelary God* and
civil Governor. Now we know it to be the practice
of all States to punifh the crime of lefe Majefty
in this manner. And to render it juft, no more

---

[o] *Chrift. as old as the Creation,* p. 240, 241.

[p] Dr. Stebbing has thought fit to fupport this charge of contradiction urged by Spinoza and Tyndal, very effectually. He
infults the author of the D. L. for pretending to clear up a
difficulty, where there was none. " He [the author of the
" D. L.] has alfo juftified the equity of *another Law,* that of
" *punifhing pofterity for the crimes of their forefathers.* — Tho'
" it is one of the plaineft cafes in the world, that God doth
" this EVERY DAY in the *ordinary* exercife of his Providence."
Hift. of Abr. p. 89. — MOSES fays, *God will vifit the iniquity of
the Fathers upon the Children.* JEREMIAH and EZEKIEL fay as
exprefsly, that *God will not do fo.* See, exclaim *Spinoza* and *Tyndal,* the difcordancies and contradictions amongft thefe Prophets.
Softly, replies the Author of the *Divine Legation,* You miftake
the matter; the contradiction is all a fiction of your own brains:
Mofes fpeaks of the *Jewifh* Difpenfation; and Jeremiah and
Ezekiel, of the Chriftian. I deny that, cries Dr. Stebbing,
*punifhing pofterity for the crimes of their Fathers is done every day
under the Chriftian Difpenfation.* And thus the objection of
Spinoza and Tyndal, by the kind pains of Dr. Stebbing, remains not only unanfwered, but unanfwerable. And yet this is
the man, whofe zeal would not let him reft till he had refcued
Revelation from the difhonours brought upon it by the Author
of the *Divine Legation.*

is

is required than that it was in the Compact (as it certainly was here) on men's free entrance into Society.

When a *guilty* Posterity suffered for the crimes of their Parents, they were deprived of their natural unconditional rights; when an *innocent*, they only forfeited their conditional and civil: But as this method of punishment was administered with more lenity in the Jewish Republic, so it was with infinite more rectitude, than in any other. For although God allowed capital punishment to be inflicted for the crime of *lese majesty*, on the *Person of the offender*, by the delegated administration of the Law; yet concerning his *Family* or *Posterity* he reserved the inquisition of the crime to himself, and expresly forbid the Magistrate to meddle with it, in the common course of justice. *The Fathers shall not be put to death for the Children, neither shall the Children be put to death for the Fathers: every man shall be put to death for his own sin* [q]. And we find the Magistrate careful not to intrench on this part of God's jurisdiction. We are told, that as soon as Amaziah the son of Joash king of Judah became firmly established in the throne, *He slew his servants which had slain the King his Father. But the* CHILDREN *of the murderers he slew not: according unto that which is written in the book of the law of Moses,* [Deut xxiv. 16.] *wherein the Lord commanded saying, The Fathers shall not be put to death for the Children, &c* [r]. Yet such hath been the perversity or stupidity of Freethinking, that this very text itself hath been charged with contradicting the xxth chapter of Exodus. Now God's appropriating to himself the

[q] Deut. xxiv. 16.   [r] 2 Kings xiv. 5, 6.

execution

execution of the Law in question would abundantly justify the equity of it, even supposing it had been given by him as part of an *universal religion.* For why was the Magistrate forbidden to imitate God's method of punishing, but because no power less than omniscient could, in all cases, keep clear of injustice in such an inquisition ?

But God not only reserved this method of punishment to himself, but has graciously condescended to inform us, by his Prophets, *after what manner* he was pleased to administer it. YOUR INIQUI-TIES (says he) AND THE INIQUITIES OF YOUR FATHERS TOGETHER, *which have burnt incense upon the mountains, and blasphemed me upon the hills : therefore will I measure their former work into their bosom* [s]. And again : " But ye say, Why ? doth not the Son " bear the iniquity of the Father ? When the Son " hath done that which is lawful and right, and " hath kept all my statutes, and hath done them, " he shall surely live — But when the Righteous " turneth away from his righteousness and com-" mitteth iniquity—shall he live [u] ?"

[s] Is. lxv. 7.   [t] EZEK. xviii. 19 and 24.

[u] Yet Doctor Sykes modestly tells his reader, that " there is not " any ground or foundation for this distinction ; for that the in-" nocent posterity were sometimes deprived of life for the crimes " of their Parents in virtue of this Law."—But here, as the Doctor has not to do with me, but with the Prophet, I leave it to be adjusted between them, as the Public shall think fit to arbitrate. — Another has even ventured to ask, " How the Posterity, if " it suffer for its own guilt, can be said to suffer for the trans-" gressions of its Parents ?" As this doubt arises from the Prophets words, *Your iniquity and the iniquities of your fathers together,* &c. I think myself not concerned to satisfy it, till these Writers have more openly rejected the authority of the Prophets.

So much for that cafe in which the Pofterity were *iniquitous*, and fuffered punifhment, in the ftrict and proper fenfe of the word. But doubtlefs, an innocent Pofterity were fometimes punifhed, according to the denunciation of this Law, for the crimes of their wicked Fathers[x]; as is done by modern States, in attaint of blood and confifcation: and this, with the higheft equity in both cafes.

In our Gothic Conftitutions, the throne being the fountain of honour and fource of property, *Lands* and *Titles* defcend *from it*, and were held as FIEFS *of it*, under perpetual obligation of military and civil fervices. Hence the LAWS OF FORFEITURE for high treafon[y], the moft violent breach

of

---

[x] This appears from the rife of that proverb in Ifrael, *The Fathers have eaten four grapes, and the Childrens teeth are fet on edge.*

[y] It is obfervable that by our own Conftitution, no forfeitures attend capital condemnations in the Lord High Admiral's and Conftable's Courts. And why? the reafon is plain; thofe Judicatures proceed on the Roman, and not on the municipal laws of a feudal Government. Not but that the neceffities of ftate frequently obliged other Governments which never had been feudal, to have recourfe to an extemporaneous confifcation. Even Rome itfelf fometimes exercifed the feverity of this punifhment, even before it fell under the feet of its Tyrants. Cicero, to excufe the confifcations decreed againft Lepidus, which affected his children, the nephews of Brutus, fays to this latter: Nec vero me fugit quàm fit acerbum, parentium fcelera filiorum pœnis lui. Sed hoc PRÆCLARE LEGIBUS COMPARATUM eft, ut caritas liberorum amiciores parentes reipublicæ redderet. *Ep. ad Brutum liber,* Ep. 12. And again : In qua videtur illud effe crudele, quod ad liberos, qui nihil meruerunt, pœna pervenit. SED ID ET ANTIQUUM EST, ET OMNIUM CIVITATUM. Ep. 15. Again, the fame neceffities of State have obliged Governments which had been

originally

of the condition on which thoſe *fiefs* were granted. Nor was there any injuſtice in the forfeiture of what was acquired by no natural right, but by civil compact, how much ſoever the confiſcation might affect an innocent poſterity.

The ſame principles operated under a Theocracy. God ſupported the Iſraelites in Judea, by an extraordinary adminiſtration of his providence. The conſequence of which were great temporal bleſſings to which they had no natural claim ; given them on condition of obedience. Nothing therefore could be more equitable than, on the violation of that condition, to withdraw thoſe extraordinary bleſſings from the Children of a Father thus offending. How then can the Deiſt charge this Law with injuſtice ? ſince a Poſterity when *innocent* was affected only in their civil conditional rights ; and, when deprived of thoſe which were natural and unconditional, were always guilty.

From all this it appears, that the excellent Grotius himſelf had a very crude and imperfect notion of the whole matter, when he reſolved the juſtice of it intirely into God's ſovereign right over his creatures. " Deus quidem in lege Hebræis " data paternam impietatem in poſteros ſe vindi- " caturum minatur : ſed ipſe Jus Dominii plenif- " ſimum habet, ut in res noſtras, ita in vitam " noſtram, ut munus ſuum, quod ſine ulla cauſa

---

originally feudal, but were ſo no longer to retain this *Law of forfeiture,* eſſential to feudal Government even after all the feudal tenures had been aboliſhed. But he, who would ſee the Law of Forfeiture defended on the more general principles of natural juſtice and civil policy, may have full ſatisfaction, in the very elegant and maſterly Diſcourſe ſo intitled.

" & quovis

" & quovis tempore auferre cuivis, quando vult,
" poteft [z]."

II. As to the fecond point, the charge of *Con-tradiction in the Difpenfation*, we now fee, that, on the contrary, thefe different declarations of God's manner of punifhing in two fo diftant Periods, are the MOST DIVINE INSTANCE of conftancy and uni-formity in the manifeftations of eternal Juftice: So far are they from any indication of a *milder or feverer Spirit*, as Tyndal with equal infolence and folly hath objected to Revelation. For while a *future ftate* was kept hid from the Jews, there was abfo-lute need of fuch a Law to reftrain the more daring Spirits, by working on their inftincts; or, as Cicero expreffes it —— ut caritas libero-rum amiciores Parentes Reipublicæ redderet. But when a doctrine was *brought to light* which held them up, and continued them after death, the objects of divine juftice [a], it had then no farther ufe;

---

[z] *De Jure Bel. & Pac.* vol. ii. p. 593. *Ed. Barbeyrac, Amft.* 1720.

[a] Here Dr. Sykes, who fo charitably takes the *Deifts'* part, all the way, againft the Author of the D. L. fays, " It would " have been well TO HAVE TOLD US what this *doctrine* was " which was *brought to light*, and which *held up* thefe daring " tranfgreffors, and which *continued* them after death the objects " of divine juftice." *Defence*, p. 83. Can the Reader, when he cafts his eye upon the text, and fees that *I had told him*, in fo many words and letters, that it was a FUTURE STATE, think the grave Doctor in his fenfes? But this quotation from him will have its ufe. It will ferve for a fpecimen and example of the miferable difpofitions with which an *Anfwerer by profeffion* ad-dreffes himfelf to confute Writers who have taken fome pains to confider their fubject, and to exprefs their meaning.

He goes on objecting to this *unknown* doctrine. He afks " *how this doctrine did thefe things?*" That is, how the doctrine of use; and was therefore reasonably to be abolished with the rest of the judicial Laws, peculiar to the Mosaic Dispensation.   But these men have taken it into their heads (and what comes slowly in, will go slowly out) that it was repealed for its *injustice*; tho' another reason be as plainly intimated by the Prophets, as the circumstances of those times would permit; and so plainly by JEREMIAH, that none but such heads could either not see or not acknowledge it.   In his thirty first chapter, foretelling the advent of the NEW Dispensation, he expresly says, this Law shall be revoked : IN THOSE DAYS *they shall say no more, The Fathers have eaten a sour grape, and the Childrens' teeth are set on edge. But every one shall die for his own iniquity* [b].   Yet, in the very next chapter, speaking of the OLD Dispensation, under which they then lived, he as expresly declares the Law to be still in force. *When*

of a *future state* could extend beyond the present life ? This shews at least, he was in earnest in his ignorance, and perfectly well assured that *I had not told him what the doctrine was.*

He proceeds with his interrogations, and asks, *Why the punishing Children for their Fathers' faults had no further use after the bringing in a future state ?* I had told him long ago. it was because the punishment was employed only to supply the want of a future state. But to this, he replies, — *nothing hindered its being added to the doctrine of a future state.* It is very true : nor did any thing hinder *temporal rewards* from being added to the doctrine of a future state under the Gospel, yet when a future state was brought to light, by that Dispensation, both one and the other were abolished.   But is it not a little strange that the Doctor, in thus insisting on its *further use*, on account of its being able to restrain more daring Spirits, by laying hold of their instincts, at all times, as well under an *unequal* as under an *equal* providence, should not see he was arguing against the DIVINE WISDOM, who by the mouth of the Prophet declared it of no further use under the Gospel-dispensation ?

[b] Ver. 29, 30.

*I had delivered the evidence of the purchase unto
Baruch, I prayed unto the Lord, saying,——Thou
shewest loving kindness unto thousands, and recompensest
the iniquity of the fathers into the bosom of their Children after them*[c]. Is this like a man who had forgot himself? or who suspected the Law of cruelty
or injustice?

But the ignorance of Free-thinking was here unaffected; and indeed the more excusable, as the
matter had of old perplexed both Jews and Christians. The Synagogue was so scandalized at Ezekiel's Declarations against this mode of punishment, that they deliberated a long time whether
he should not be thrown out of the Canon, for
contradicting Moses in so open a manner[d]. And
Sentence had at last past upon him, but that one
Chananias promised to reconcile the two Prophets.
How he kept his word, is not known, for there is
nothing of his extant upon the subject; only we
are told that he approved himself a man of honour,
and, with great labour and study, at length did the
business[e].

ORIGEN

[c] Ver. 16 and 18.

[d] Les Juifs disent qu'Ezechiel etoit serviteur de Jérémie, &
que le Sanhedrin delibera long-tems, si l'on rejetteroit son
Livre du Canon des Ecritures. Le sujet de leur chagrin contre ce Prophete vient de son extreme obscurité, & de ce qu'il
enseigne diverses choses contraires à Moise — Ezechiel, disent
ils, a declaré, *Que le fils ne porteroit plus l'iniquité de son pere,*
contre ce que Moise did expressément, *Que le Seigneur venge
l'iniquité des Peres sur les Enfans, jusqu' à la troisieme & quatrieme
generation.* Calmet, Dissert. vol. ii. p. 361.

[e] Ezechielis sententias adeo sententiis Mosis repugnantes in-
venerunt Rabini, qui nobis illos (qui jam tantum extant) libros
Prophetarum reliquerunt, ut fere deliberaverint, ejus librum
inter

ORIGEN was so perplexed with the different assertions [f] of these two Prophets, that he could find no better way of reconciling them than by having recourse to his *allegorical* fanaticism, and supposing the words of the first to be a Parable or Mystic speech; which, however, he would not pretend to decipher.   This learned Father, having quoted some pagan Oracles intimating that Children were punished for the crimes of their Forefathers, goes on in this manner: "How much " more equitable is what our Scriptures say on this " point? *The Fathers shall not be put to death for* " *the Children, neither shall the Children be put to* " *death for the Fathers : every man shall be put to* " *death for his own sin.* DEUT. xxiv. 16, *&c.—* " But if any one should object that this verse of " the oracle,

" *On the Childrens Children and their Posterity* ;

" is very like what Scripture says, that GOD *visits* " *the iniquity of the Fathers upon the Children unto*

inter canonicos non admittere, atque eundem plane abscondidissent, nisi quidam Chananias in se suscepisset ipsum explicare, quod tandem magno cum labore & studio (ut ibi narratur) aiunt ipsum fecisse, qua ratione autem non satis constat. — *Spinozæ Tract. Theologico-Pol.* p. 27, 28.   In the mean time it may be worth observing, that the explanation which I have here offered, cuts off the only means the modern Jews have of accounting for their long Captivity upon the Principle of the LAW's being still in force.   Limborch urges Orobio with the difficulty of accounting for their present dispersion any other way than for the national crime of rejecting Jesus as the Messiah ; seeing they are so far from falling into Pagan idolatries, the crime which brought on their other Captivities, that they are remarkably tenacious of the Mosaic Rites.   To which Orobio replies, " that they are not their own sins for which they now suffer, but the sins of their forefathers."   Now Ezekiel has declared (and I have reconciled that declaration to the *Law and the Prophets)* that this mode of punishment hath been long abolished.

[f] EXOD. xx.   EZEK. xviii.

" *the*

" *the third and fourth Generation of them that hate*
" *him,* EXOD. xx. 5. he may learn from *Ezekiel*
" that those words are a PARABLE; for the Pro-
" phet reproves such as say, *The Fathers have*
" *eaten four Grapes, and the Childrens teeth are set*
" *on edge;* and then it follows: *As I live, faith*
" *the Lord, every one shall die for his own sins only.*
" But this is not the place to explain what is
" meant by the PARABLE of *visiting iniquity unto*
" *the third and fourth generation* ⁵." There could
hardly be more miftakes in fo few words. The
two texts in Deuteronomy and Exodus, which
Origen reprefents as treating of the fame fubject,
treat of fubjects very different: the firft, as we
have fhewn above, concerns the Magiftrate's execution of the Law; the other, that which God
referves to himfelf. Again, becaufe the text of
Exodus apparently occafioned the Proverb mentioned by Ezekiel and Jeremiah, therefore by a
ftrange blunder or prevarication, the Father brings
the Proverb in proof that the Law which gave
birth to it, was but a Proverb or *parable* itfelf ʰ.

II.

⁵ Ὅρα δὲ ὅσῳ τᵘτᵘ βέλλιον τὸ, Οὐκ ἀποθανᵘᵘ̃lαι, &c. ἰὰν δὲ τις
ὅμοιον εἶναι λέγη τῷ

Ἐς παίδων παῖδας οἳ κ̃ ὄπισθεν γίνωῃlαι,

τὸ, Ἀπℴδιδὰς ἁμαρℓίας παℓέρων ἐπὶ τέκνα, ἐπὶ τρίτην κ̃ τℓάρℑην
γενεὰν τοῖς μισᵘσῖ [με] μαθέτω, ὅτι ἐν τῷ Ἰεζεκιὴλ παραℓολὴ τὸ
τοιᵘτον εἶναι λέλεκℑαι, αἰτιωμένῳ τὰς λέγοℓας, Οἱ παℓέρες ἔφαℑον ὄμφα-
κα, κ̃ οἱ ὀδόℓ̃les τῶν τέκνων ἡμωδίασαν· ᾧ ἐπιφέρℓαι, Ζῶ ἐγὼ, λέγℰι
Κύρι℥, ἀλλ᾽ ἢ ἕκας℥ τῇ ἑαυτᵘ ἁμαρℓίᾳ ἀποθανεῖlαι. Οὐ καλὰ τὸν
παρℴℓα δὲ καιρόν ἐςι, διηγήσασθαι. τί σημαίνℰι ἡ περὶ τᵘ τρίτην κ̃
τℓαρℑην γενεὰν ἀποδιδόασθαι τὰς ἁμαρℓίας παραℓολή. *Cont. Celf.*
p. 403.

ʰ Having thus reconciled the two Prophets, Mofes and
Ezekiel, on this point, one may be allowed to wonder a little
at the want of good faith even in M. Voltaire, when it comes
to a certain extreme.

This

II.

We have now fhewn that Moses did not teach a future ftate of reward and punifhment; and that he

This celebrated Poet has, like an honeft man, written in defence of RELIGIOUS TOLERATION : and to inforce his argument has endeavoured, (not indeed like a wife one, who fhould weigh his fubject before he undertakes it) to prove, that all Religions in the world, but the Chriftian, have tolerated diverfities of opinion. This common weaknefs of rounding one's Syftem, for the fupport of a plain Right which requires no fuch finifhing, hath led him into two of the ftrangeft paradoxes that ever difgraced common fenfe.

The one, that the *Pagan Emperors* did not perfecute the Chriftian Faith : The other, that the *Jewiſh Magiſtrate* did not punifh for Idolatry.

In fupport of the firft, his *bad faith* is moft confpicuous ; in fupport of the latter, his *bad logic.*

If there be one truth in Antiquity better eftablifhed than another, it is this, That the Pagan Emperors did perfecute the Chriftians *for their faith only*; eftablifhed, I fay, both by the complaints of the Perfecuted, and the acknowlegment of their Perfecutors. But this being proved at large in the preface to this very Volume, it is enough to refer the Reader thither.

The other Paradox is much more pleafantly fupported. He proves that the Mofaic Law did not denounce punifhment on religious errors, (tho' in direct words, it does fo) nor did the Jewifh Magiftrate execute it, (tho' we have feveral inftances of the infliction recorded in their hiftory.) — And what is the convincing argument he employs? It is this, *The frequent defections of the Jewiſh People into Idolatry, in the early times of their apoſtacies?* An argument hardly fo good as this,—*The Church of Rome did not perſecute, as appears from that general defection from it, in the ſixteenth Century.* I fay, Mr. Voltaire's argument is hardly fo good as my illuftration of it, fince the defection from the Church of Rome ftill continues, and the Jewifh defections into Idolatries were foon at an end.

But we are not to think, this Paradox was advanced for nothing, that is, for the fake of its own fingular boldnefs, (a

motive

he omitted it with defign; that he underftood its
great importance to fociety; and that he provided
for

motive generally fufficient to fet reafon at defiance) nor even
for the fupport of his general queftion. It was apparently advanced to get the eafier at his darling fubject, THE ABUSE OF
THE MOSAIC RELIGION, that *Marotte* of our party-coloured
Philofopher.

Take this inftance, which is all that a curfory note will be
able to afford.

Mr. Voltaire, fpeaking of the *rewards* and *punifhments* of
the Jewifh Difpenfation, expreffes himfelf in this manner,
" Tout etait temporel ; et c' eft la preuve que le favant Evêque
Warburton apporte pour démontrer que la Loi des Juifs, était
divine ; parce que Dieu même étant leur Roi, rendant juftice
immédiatement apris la tranfgreffion ou l' obeiffance, n' avoit
pas befoin de leur révéler une Doctrine qu' il réfervait au tems
ou' il ne governerait plus fon peuple. Ceux qui par ignorance
prétendent que Moyfe enfeignait l' immortalité de l' ame, ôtent
au nouveau Teftament un de fes plus grands avantages fur
l' ancien *." Would not any one now believe (who did not
know Mr. Voltaire) that he quoted this argument, as what he
thought a good one, for the divinity of the Mofaic Religion?
Nothing like it. It was only to find occafion to accufe the Old
Teftament of contradiction. For thus he goes on, — " Cependant malgré l' énoncé précis de cette Loi, malgré cette décla-
ration expreffe de Dieu, qu' il punirait jufqu' à la quatriéme
génération ; *Ezechiel* annonce TOUT LE CONTRAIRE aux Juifs,
et leur dit, que le Fils ne portera point l' iniquité de fon pere :
il va même jufqu' à faire dire a Dieu, qu' il leur avait *donné des
preceptes qui n' etaient pas bons* †."

As for the *precepts which were not good*, the Reader will fee
that matter explained at large, as we go along. What I have
to do with Mr. Voltaire at prefent, is to expoftulate with him
for his ill faith ; that when he had borrowed my argument for
the divinity of the Mofaic Miffion from that mode of punifhment, he would venture to invalidate it from an apparent contradiction between MOSES and EZEKIEL ; when, in that very
place of the *Divine Legation* which he refers to, he faw the
two Prophets reconciled by an argument drawn from the true

* Page 132.   † Page. 133.

for the want of it.   And if we may believe a great
Statesman and Philosopher, " Moses had need of
" every SANCTION that his knowledge or his ima-
" gination could suggest to govern the unruly
" people, to whom he gave a Law, in the name
" of God [i]."

But as the proof of this point is only for the sake
of its Consequence, that *therefore the people had not
the knowledge of that doctrine,* our next step will be
to establish this Consequence : Which (if we take
in those circumstances attending the *Omission,* just
explained above) will, at the same time, shew my
argument in support of this *Omission* to be more
than *negative.*

Now though one might fairly conclude, that the
Peoples' not having this Doctrine, was a necessary
consequence of Moses's not teaching it, in a Law

natures of two approximating Dispensations ; an argument
which not only removes the pretended contradiction, (first insisted on by *Spinosa,* and, through many a dirty channel, derived,
at length, to Mr. Voltaire) but likewise supports that very
mark of divinity which I contend for.

But it is too late in the day to call in question the Religion or
the good faith of this truly ingenious man.   What I want, in this
Discourse *sur la Tolérance,* is his CIVIL PRUDENCE.   As an AN-
NALIST, he might, in his *General History,* calumniate the Jewish
People just as his passions or his caprice inclined him : But when
he had assumed the character of a DIVINE, to recommend *Toleration* to a Christian State, could he think to succeed by abusing
Revelation? He seems indeed, to have set out under a sense of
the necessity of a different conduct : But coming to his darling
subject an abuse of the Jews, he could not, for his life, sus-
tain the personage he had assumed, but breaks out again into all
the virulence and injustice with which he persecuted this unhappy
People in his *General History* ; and of which the Reader will see
a fair account, in this volume, b. v. sect. 1.

[i] *Bolingbroke's Works,* vol. v. p. 513.

which forbids the leaſt addition [k] to the written In-ſtitute; yet I ſhall ſhew, from a circumſtance, the cleareſt and moſt inconteſtable, that the Iſraelites, from the time of Moſes to the time of their Cap-tivity, had not the doctrine of a future ſtate of reward and puniſhment.

The Bible contains a very circumſtantial Hiſtory of this People throughout the aforeſaid period. It contains not only the hiſtory of public occur-rences, but the lives of private perſons of both ſexes, and of all ages, conditions, characters and complexions; in the adventures of Virgins, Ma-trons, Kings, Soldiers, Scholars, Merchants and Huſbandmen. All theſe, in their turns, make their appearance before us. They are given too in every circumſtance of life; captive, victorious; in ſickneſs, and in health; in full ſecurity, and amidſt impending dangers; plunged in Civil buſi-neſs, or retired and ſequeſtered in the ſervice of Re-ligion. Together with their Story, we have their Compoſitions likewiſe. Here they ſing their tri-umphs; there, their palinodia. Here, they offer up to the Deity their hymns of praiſe; and there, pe-titions for their wants: here, they urge their moral precepts to their Contemporaries; and there, they treaſure up their Prophecies and Predictions for poſterity; and to both, denounce the promiſes and threatenings of Heaven. Yet in none of theſe dif-ferent circumſtances of life, in none of theſe various caſts of compoſition, do we ever find them acting on the motives, or influenced by the proſpect of future rewards and puniſhments; or indeed expreſſ-ing the leaſt hope or fear, or even common curioſity concerning them. But every thing they do or ſay

[k] Deut. iv. 2. Chap. xii. ver. 32.

reſpects

respects the present life only ; the good and ill of which are the sole objects of all their pursuits and aversions [1].

Hear then the sum of all. The sacred Writings are extremely various both in their subject, style, and composition. They contain an account of the Creation, and Origine of the human race ; the history of a private Family, of a chosen People, and of exemplary men and women. They consist of hymns and petitions to the Deity, precepts of civil life, and religious Prophecies and Predictions. Hence I infer that as, amidst all this variety of writing, the Doctrine of a future state never once appears to have had any share in this People's thoughts ; it never did indeed make part of their

[1] This is the precise character of the writings of the Old Testament. And this state of them (to observe it only by the way) is more than a thousand answers to the wild suspicions of those writers, who fancy that the Jews, since Christ, have corrupted their sacred Scriptures, to support their superstitions against the Gospel ; and amongst other erasements have struck out the Doctrine of life and immortality; which, say these Visionaries, was, till then, as plainly taught in the Old as in the New Testament : For had these supposed Impostors ever ventured on so bold a fraud as the adulterating their sacred Writings, we may be well assured their first attempt would have been to add the doctrine of a future state, had they not found it there, rather than to take it away if they had : since the *omission* of the doctrine is the strongest and most glaring evidence of the *imperfection of the Law* ; and the insertion of it would have best supported what they now hold to be one of the most *fundamental* points of their Religion.— But this is not a folly of yesterday. Irenæus tells us that certain ancient Heretics supported their wild fancies against Scripture, which was against them, by the same extravagant suspicion, that it had been interpolated and corrupted. Notwithstanding, I am far from thinking these Moderns borrowed it from them. They found it in our common Nature, which always goes the nearest way to work, to relieve itself.

Religious

Religious opinions ᵐ.   And when, to all this, we
find, their *occasional* reasoning only conclusive on
the

ᵐ We shall now understand the importance of a remark,
which the late Translator of Josephus employs to prove the
genuineness of a fragment or homily, given by him to that Historian : " There is one particular observation (says he) belong-
" ing to the contents of this fragment or homily, that seems
" to me to be DECRETORY, and to determine the question
" that some of this Jewish church, that used the Hebrew copy
" of the Old Testament, nay rather, that Josephus himself in
" particular was the author of it.   The observation is this,
" that in the present address to the Greeks or Gentiles there
" are near forty references or allusions to texts of the New
" Testament; AND NOT ONE, TO ANY OF THE OLD TESTA-
" MENT either in Hebrew or Greek; and this in a discourse
" concerning HADES ; which yet is almost five times as often
" mentioned in the Old Testament as in the New.   What can
" be the reason of this ? But that the Jewish Church at Jerusa-
" lem used the Hebrew Bible alone, which those Greeks or
" Gentiles, to whom the address is here made, could not un-
" derstand ; and that our Josephus always and only used the
" same Hebrew Bible ?" *Mr. Whiston's Differt.* prefixed to his
Transl. of Josephus, p. 105. — *What can be the reason* (says he)
of this mystery ? He unfolds it thus : *The Jewish Church of Jerusalem used the Hebrew Bible alone, which those Greeks or Gentiles, to whom the address is here made, could not understand.* So
that because the Audience did not understand Hebrew, the
Preacher could not quote the texts, he had occasion for, in
Greek.   But he supposes the Author could not quote the Greek,
because it must needs have been that of the *Septuagint* ; which
the Jewish Church at Jerusalem would not use.   Now admit
there were no other Greek to be had, or allowed of, Can any
man believe that if this Jewish Preacher would turn himself to
the Gentiles, he could be such a bigot as to be afraid of quoting
the Old Testament in a language they understood, because his
Church used only the Original which they understood not ? Or
if he had been such a bigot, Would he have dared to preach to
the Gentiles at all ? What then but the fondness for an hypothesis could make men ramble after such reasons, when so obvious an one lies just before them ? Why did he this, do you
ask ? For this plain reason : His subject was a *future state of reward and punishment,* and he had more sense than to seek for
it where it was not to be found.   *Oh but* HADES *is almost five
times as often mentioned in the Old Testament as in the New.*   Indeed ! But the fragment is not about the *word,* but the *thing.*
In

the suppofition that a future state was not amongst
the Religious doctrines of the People, the above
confiderations, if they needed any, would receive
the strongest support and confirmation. To give
one example out of many. The Psalmist says,
For the rod of the Wicked shall not rest upon the
lot of the Righteous: lest the Righteous put forth
their hands unto iniquity [n]. That is, " God will
vigoroufly administer that *extraordinary Providence*
which the nature of the Difpenfation required to be
administered, lest the Righteous, not seeing themfelves exempt from the evils due to wickednefs,
should conclude that there was no moral Governor
of the world; and fo, by making their own private
interest the rule of their actions, fall into the practice of all kind of iniquity." But this could never
be the confequence where an unequal difpenfation
of Providence was attended with the knowledge
and belief of a future state. And here I will appeal
to thofe who are most prejudiced against this reafoning. Let them fpeak, and tell me, if they were now
first shewn fome hiftory of an old Greek Republic,
delivered in the form and manner of the Jewifh,
and no more notice in it of a future state, Whether
they could poffibly believe that that Doctrine was
National, or generally known in it. If they have
the least ingenuity, they will anfwer, They could

In the Old Teftament it fignified the receptacle of *dead bodies*;
in the New, the receptacle of *living fouls.* But though this
learned writer can, without doubt, laugh at thofe who feek the
Trinity in the Old Teftament, yet he can in good earneft go
thither in fearch of a *Future state.* Yet this latter is not in any
comparifon fo clearly hinted at as the other: and no wonder;
a Future state is circumfcribed to the New Teftament, as *brought*
to light by the Gofpel; but the doctrine of the Trinity is no
where faid to be fo circumfcribed.

[n] Ps. cxxv. 3.

not

not. On what then do they support their opinion here, but on religious Prejudices ? Prejudices of no higher an original than some Dutch or German System : for, as to the BIBLE, one half of it is silent concerning *life and immortality* ; and the other half declares that the doctrine was *brought to light through the Gospel.*

But to set this argument in its fullest light. Let us consider the History of the rest of mankind, whether recorded by Bards, or Statesmen ; by Philosophers, or Priests : in which we shall find the *doctrine of a future state* still bearing, throughout all the various circumstances of human life, a constant and principal share in the determinations of the Will. And no wonder. We see how strong the Grecian world thought the sanction of it to be, by a passage in Pindar, quoted by Plutarch in his tract of *Superstition*, where he makes it one circumstance of the superior happiness of the Gods, over men, that they stood not in fear of Acheron.

But not to be distracted by too large a view, let us select from the rest of the Nations, one or two most resembling the Jewish. Those which came nearest to them, (and, if the Jews were only under human guidance, indeed extremely near) were the SUEVI of the north, and the ARABS of the south. Both these People were led out in search of new Possessions, which they were to win by the sword. And both, it is confessed, had the doctrine of *a Future state* inculcated unto them by their leaders, ODIN and MAHOMET. Of the Arabs we have a large and circumstantial history : Of the Suevi we have only some few fragments of the songs and ballads of their Bards; yet they
equally

equally serve to support our Conclusion. In the large history of the Saracen Empire we can scarce find a page, and in the Runic rhymes of the Suevi scarce a line, where the doctrine of a future state was not pushing on its influence. It was their constant Viaticum through life; it stimulated them to war and slaughter, and spirited their songs of triumph; it made them insensible of pain, immoveable in danger, and superior to the approach of death[o].

For,

[o] To all this, Dr. Stebbing has an *Answer* ready, "The "History of the persecution under Antiochus (says he) is writ- "ten by two Historians, namely, the Author of the first book "of Maccabees, and the Author of the second. This last "writer has recorded the profession of the Martyrs concerning "their belief of the doctrine of the Resurrection; but the "first has entirely omitted it: nor is there one word about a "resurrection or future state to be found throughout his whole "History, though it is certain it was now the national be- "lief. *So* UNSAFE *a thing is it to rely upon the* MERE *silence* "*of historians,* when they undertake to write a history *not of* "*doctrines* but of the transactions of men." *Exam.* p. 116.

I will tell him of an unsafer thing: which is, venturing to draw *parallel cases*; as he has done here; for they may happen, (as hath happened here) to be *cases most unlike.*

In a large and miscellaneous Volume, composed by various Writers of different times and states, and containing the Law, the Religion, and the History of the Jews, from Moses to the Captivity, neither the Doctrines of the resurrection nor a future state are ever once mentioned.

This is the Fact. And to obviate my inference from it, — "That the Jews, during that period, were unacquainted with "the Doctrines," this able Divine opposes the two books of *Maccabees,* containing the story of one short period, when, it is confessed, these Doctrines were of national belief; in the first of which Books, there is no mention of the Doctrine, and in the second, a great deal: the reason both of the mention and of the silence being self evident. It is recorded in the *second* book, where there is a detailed account of the Martyrs for the

Jewish

For, what Cicero fays of Poetry in Rome, may be more truly applied to the Doctrine of a Future ftate

Jewifh Faith: it is omitted in the *firft*, where there is no account of any fuch thing.

Yet thefe are brought as *parallel cafes :* Let us therefore do them all honour.

1. Several Volumes of the facred Canon contain a *hiftory of doctrines*.

The two books of Maccabees contain only a *hiftory of civil transactions*.

2. None of the infpired Writers of the Canon before the Captivity ever once mention the Doctrines of a refurrection or a future ftate.

Of the two books of Maccabees, one of them mentions the Doctrines fully and at large.

3. The facred Canon comprifes a vaft period of time, and treats of an infinite variety of matters.

The two books of Maccabees are fmall tracts of an uniform fubject, and contain only the ftory of one revolution in the Jewifh State.

Unconfcious, as fhould feem, of all this difference, the learned Doctor concludes — *So unfafe a thing it is to rely on the* MERE SILENCE *of Hiftorians, when they undertake to write a hiftory* NOT OF DOCTRINES, *but of the transactions of Men.* In which, thefe THREE FALSEHOODS are very gravely and magifterially infinuated : That the Writers of the two books of Maccabees are equally *filent* with the Writers of the Canon : 2. That all the Writers of the Canon are writers of a Hiftory, *not of the Doctrines,* but merely of the civil transactions of men, equally with the writers of the two Books of Maccabees : And 3. That the thing relied on by me, is the MERE SILENCE of Hiftorians. Which falfehood if the Reader does not fee from what has been faid above, he may be pleafed to confider, that *mere filence* is when a Writer omits to fay a thing which it was indifferent to his purpofe whether he faid or not. But when he omits to

fay

state amongst these Barbarians: " Ceteræ neque
" temporum sunt, neque ætatum omnium, neque
                              " locorum.

say a thing, which it was much to his purpose to say, this is
not a *mere silence*. It is a *silence* attended with a *circumstance*,
which makes the evidence drawn from that *silence* something
more than negative, and, consequently, something more than
mere silence. So much for Dr. Stebbing.

A Cornish Writer * pursues the same argument against the
Divine Legation ; but takes his *parallel* much higher. " There
" is no one (says he) who reads HOMER that can doubt whether
" a Future state were the popular belief amongst the Greeks in
" the times he writes of. And yet, by what I remember of
" him, I believe it would be difficult to produce SIX instances
" in all his poems of any actions either entered upon or avoided
" from the EXPRESS motive of the rewards or punishments to
" be expected in the other world."

I inferred from a Future state's NEVER being mentioned in the
Jewish History, amongst the motives of men's actions, (after it
had been omitted in the Jewish Law and Religion) that it was
not of popular belief amongst that people. Now here comes an
Answerer, and says, that it is not mentioned above SIX TIMES
EXPRESSLY in Homer, and yet that no body *can doubt whether
it were not the popular belief amongst the Greeks*. The good
cautious man! Had it been but ONCE EXPRESSLY mentioned in
the Old Testament, I should no more have doubted of its being
of popular belief amongst the Jews, than he does. Why then
do we doubt so little, in the case of the Greeks, but for the
same reason why we ought to doubt so much in the case of the
Jews! HOMER, (who gives a detailed account of a future state)
this writer allows, has mentioned it about *six times* as a motive.
The SCRIPTURES (which, together with the history, deliver
the Law and Religion of the Jews, in which a future state is
omitted) mention it *not once*, as a motive. But this Answerer
would make the reader believe, I made my inference from the
paucity, and not from the *want*, of the mention. The same
may be observed of another expression of this candid Gentle-
man's — *express motive*. Now much less would have satisfied
me; and I should readily have allowed that the Jews had the
popular belief amongst them had the *motive been but once fairly
implied*.

* Mr. Peters.

                                                        But

" locorum. Hæc ftudia adolefcentiam alunt, fe-
" nectutem oblectant, fecundas res ornant, AD-
" VERSIS PERFUGIUM AC SOLATIUM PRÆBENT ᴾ."
But

But let us take him at the beft, and fuppofe Homer did not
afford one fingle inftance. What, I pray you, has HOMER in
common with MOSES? Suppofe, I fhould affirm from the Greek
Hiftory, That the ancient WORTHIES always proportioned
their work to their ftrength and bulk; and that my Anfwerer
was not in an humour to let this pafs; but, to confute me,
would prefs me with the high atchievements of TOM THUMB, as
they are recorded in his authentic ftory; who was as famed for
his turbulence in king Arthur's Court, as Achilles was in Aga-
memnon's: Would not this be juft as much to the purpofe, as
to put the *Iliad* and the *Odyffey* in parallel with the *Law and the
Prophets?*

But Homer's poems have been fo long called the *Bible of the
Pagans,* that this Anfwerer appears, in good earneft, to have
taken them for *religious Hiftory*; otherwife how could it have
ever entered into his head to make fo ridiculous a comparifon?
My reafoning with regard to SCRIPTURE ftood thus. — As all
good Hiftory deals with the motives of men's actions, fo the
peculiar bufinefs (as it feems to me) of *religious Hiftory* is to
fcrutinize their *religious Motives*: Of thefe, the principal is the
confideration of a Future ftate. And this not being fo much as
once mentioned in the ancient Jewifh Hiftory, it is natural to
conclude that the Jews of thofe times had it not. But now,
what has Homer's poems to do in this matter? I apprehend
they are no *religious Hiftory*; but compofitions as far removed
from it as poffible, namely a *military* and *civil* Romance, brim-
full of fabulous trumpery. Now in fuch a work, the writer
furely would be principally folicitous about the *civil* motives of
his Actors. And Homer, who is confeffed to underftand what
belonged to every kind of Compofition, would take care to keep
within his fubject; and, to preferve decorum, would content
himfelf with fupplying his Warriors and Politicians with fuch
motives as might beft fet off their Wifdom and their Heroifm:
fuch as the *love of power,* in which I comprife, revenge on their
Enemies; the *love of plunder,* in which is included their paffion
for fair Captives; and the *love of glory,* in which, if you pleafe,
you may reckon their regard for their Friends and their Country.
—But in Homer's military and political Romances *there are hardly*

ᴾ *Pro Archia Poeta,* Sect. 7.

fix

But this is not all.   For we find, that when a future state became a popular doctrine amongst the Jewish People (the time and occasion of which will be explained hereafter) that then it made as considerable a figure in their Annals, by influencing their determinations [q], as it did in the history of any other people.

Nor is it only on the silence of the sacred Writers, or of the speakers they introduce, that I support this conclusion ; but from their positive declarations ; in which they plainly discover that there was no popular expectation of a future state, or Resurrection.   Thus the woman of Tekoah to David : *For we must needs die, and are as water spilt on the ground, which cannot be gathered up again* [r]. Thus Job : *As the cloud is consumed, and vanisheth away : so he that goeth down to the grave shall come up no more* [s].   And again : " There is hope of a " tree,

---

six instances in which a future state is mentioned as the express motive ; therefore the perpetual silence on this point, in the *religious History* of the JEWS, and the perpetual mention of it in the *religious Histories* of the SUEVI and the SARACENS, conclude nothing in favour of the argument of the *Divine Legation.*

[q] See the second book of Maccabees.   [r] 2 SAM. xiv. 14.

[s] Chap. vii. ver. 9.   To this Dr. Stebbing objects, that " it " means no more than that man was not to be restored to his " earthly human state." *Exam.* p. 60. and to confirm this, he appeals to the tenth verse of this chapter, which runs thus, *He shall return no more to his house; neither shall his place know him any more.* ·But the learned Doctor should have reflected, that if Job says the dead man *returns no more to his house,* he gives a reason for his so saying, very inconsistent with the Doctor's interpretation of the 9th verse of the viith chapter.   It was, because the dead man was got into *the land of darkness and the shadow of death* [chap. x. 21.] it was because he was *not awake*

" tree, if it be cut down, that it will fprout again
" —though the root thereof wax old in the earth,
" and the ftock thereof die in the ground, yet
" through the fcent of water, it will bud and
" bring forth boughs like a plant. But man
" dieth and wafteth away : yea, man giveth up the
" ghoft, and where is he? As the waters fall from
" the fea, and the flood decayeth and drieth up :
" fo man lieth down and rifeth not till the Hea-
" vens be no more, they fhall not awake nor be
" raifed out of their fleep ^t." Here the Jewifh
Writer, for fuch he was, as fhall be fhewn hereafter (and might, indeed, be underftood to be fuch
from this declaration alone) oppofes the revival of
a *vegetable* to the irrecoverable death of a rational *animal*. Had he known as much as St. Paul,
he had doubtlefs ufed that circumftance in the
vegetable world (as St. Paul did) to prove analogi-
cally, the revival of the rational *animal*.

The Pfalmift fays, *In death there is no remembrance of thee: in the grave who fhall give thee
thanks* ^u ? And again: *What profit is there in my
blood, when I go down to the pit? Shall the duft
praife thee, fhall it declare thy truth* ^x ? And again,
" Wilt thou fhew wonders to the dead? Shall
" the dead ARISE and praife thee? Shall thy lov-

---

ncr could be raifed out of his fleep [Chap. xiv. 12.] But the very
fubject which Job is here treating confutes the Doctor's interpretation : He is complaining that life is fhort, and that after death
he fhall no more fee good, for that he *who gocth down to the grave
fhall come up no more; he fhall return no more to his houfe* [ver. 7,
8, 9, 10.] which at leaft *implies* that there was no good to be
expected any where, but in this world : And this expectation is
cut off in *exprefs terms.*

^t Chap. xiv. ver. 7—12.　　^u Pf. vi. 5.　　^x Pf.
xxx. 9.

" ing

" ing kindnefs be declared in the grave, or thy
" faithfulnefs in deftruction ? Shall thy wonders
" be known in the dark ? and thy righteoufnefs in
" the land of forgetfulnefs *[y]* ?

The writer of the book of Ecclefiaftes is ftill
more exprefs : *For the living know that they fhall
die : but the dead know not any thing, neither have
they any more a* REWARD, *for the memory of them is
forgotten*[z].

Hezekiah, in his fong of Thankfgiving for his
miraculous recovery, fpeaks in the fame ftrain :
" For the grave cannot praife thee, death cannot
" celebrate thee : they that go down into the pit
" cannot hope for thy truth. The living, the
" living, he fhall praife thee, as I do this day :
" The father to the children fhall make known
" thy truth [a]."

---

[y] PSALM lxxxviii. 10—12.

[z] Chap. ix. ver. 5. To this fenfe of the text, Dr. Stebbing
objects, and fays, that *by no reward is meant none in this world.*
Exam. p. 63—4. and in fupport of his interpretation, quotes
the words of the verfe immediately following—*neither have they
any more a portion for ever in any thing that is done under the fun.*
Now I agree with the learned Doctor that thefe words are an
explanation of the foregoing, of the *dead's not having any more
a reward:* and from thence draw juft the contrary inference,
That the facred writer, from the confideration of the dead's not
returning to life to enjoy their reward, concluded that, when
once death had feized them, they could have no reward at all ;
not even that imaginary one, the living in the memory of men,
for the memory of them (fays he) *is forgotten.* So again from
the confideration in ver. 6. that the dead *had neither love, hatred
nor envy,* he had concluded ver. 5. that THEY KNEW NOT ANY
THING. — But the *premiffes* and the *conclufion* not being in
their ufual order, our learned *Doctor's* Logic did not reach to
take the force of the *Preacher's.*

[a] Is. xxxviii. 18, 19.

Laftly

Laftly Jeremiah, in his *Lamentations* and complaints of the people, fays: OUR FATHERS HAVE SINNED AND ARE NOT, AND WE HAVE BORN THEIR INIQUITIES [b]. Which implies, that the fathers being dead bore no part of the punifhment of their fins, but that all was thrown upon the children. But could this have been fuppofed, had the People been inftructed in the doctrine of future rewards and punifhments:

Yet a learned *Anfwerer*, in contradiction to all this, thinks it fufficient to fay, That " thefe paf-" fages may imply no more than that the dead can-" not fet forth God's glory *before men*, or make his " praife to be known *upon earth* [c]." Now I think it muft needs *imply* fomething more, fince the *dead* are faid to be unable to do this under the earth as well as upon it. For it is the *Grave* which is called the *land of forgetfulnefs*, or that where all things are forgotten. And in another place it is faid, *The dead praife not the Lord, neither any that go down into filence* [d]. Surely, a plain intimation that all intercourfe of praife between man and his Maker ceafed on death, as well below ground as above; otherwife why did the facred writer tell us it was the *Grave* which was the place of *filence* to the dead? If the Anfwerer's interpretation be right, *this world*, and not the other, was the place. Had the Pfalmift fuppofed, as the Doctor does, that the *dead* continued in a capacity of *remembring the goodnefs of God*, this remembrance could be no where more quickly or forceably excited than in that World where the divine goodnefs is clearly unveiled to *the fpirits of juft men made perfect* [e]? On the con-

[b] Chap. v. ver. 7.   [c] Dr. Stebbing's Exam. &c. p. 64.
[d] Pf. cxv. 17.   [e] HEB. xii. 23.

trary, the *Grave* is uniformly reprefented by all of them, as the *land of darkrefs, filence, and forgetfulnefs.*

But fince, of all the facred writers, the Pfalmift is he who is fuppofed by the adverfaries of the D. L. to have moft effectually confuted the Author's fyftem, I fhall quote a paffage from his hymns which, I think, fairly enough decides the controverfy.—Hitherto we have only heard him fay, that the *dead forget God*; we fhall now find him go further, and fay that *God forgets them.*— " I am counted with them that go down into the pit—Free amongft the dead, like the flain that lie in the grave, *whom thou rememberest no more:* and THEY ARE CUT OFF FROM THY HAND [f]. Let the ferious reader take notice of the laft words,— *they* [the dead] *are cut from thy hand,* i. e. they are no longer the object of thy Providence or moral Government. On this account it is, that in the begining of the fentence he calls thefe *dead* Free ; that is, manumifed, fet at liberty; in the fame fenfe that Uzziah the leper's *freedom* is fpoken of by the facred hiftorian.—*And Uzziah the King was a Leper, and dwelt in a feveral houfe* [or, as the margin of our tranflation tells us, it fignifies in the hebrew, a FREE HOUSE, or *houfe of freedom*] *being a Leper, for he was* CUT OFF *from the houfe of the Lord.* The phrafe of *cutting off,* &c. fignifying the fame in both places, the taking away all intercourfe and relation between two: And if that intercourfe confifted in *fervice* on the one fide, and protection on the other, as between Lord and Subject, Mafter and Servant, he who owed *fervice is* with great propriety of figure faid to be FREE or MANUMISED. Hezekiah, as quoted above, delivers the very fame fentiment, tho' in a different expreffion—*they that go down into the pit cannot hope for* THY TRUTH. What this *truth* is, the following words declare,—*the living, the living, they fhall praife thee.* THE FATHER TO THE CHILDREN SHALL MAKE KNOWN THY TRUTH. As much as to fay, " the *truth* not to be hoped for by them who go down into the pit, is *The nature and the hiftory of God's Difpenfation to his chofen people*;" in which, by a particular precept of the LAW, the Fathers were commanded to inftruct their Children. Thus the Pfalmift and this other Jewifh Ruler agree in this principle, that the Dead are no longer the objects of God's *general* Providence, or of his *particular :* which evinces what I was to prove, " THAT THE BODY OF THE EARLY JEWS HAD NO EXPECTATIONS OF A FUTURE STATE OF REWARDS AND PUNISHMENTS." And here let me take notice of a paffage which the contenders for the contrary Doctrine much confide in. It is where David, fpeaking of his dead child, fays, *I fhall go to him, but he will not return to me.* But whither was he to follow his departed child ? He himfelf tells you,—into a land of *darknefs, filence* and *forgetfulnefs,* where he was to be no longer in a capacity of *remembring the goodnefs and mercy of God,* or even of *being remembered* by him ; but was to be *cut off from his hand,* that is, was to be no longer the object of his Providence or moral Government.

To proceed. If now we fet all thefe paffages together, we find it to be the fame language throughout, and in every circumftance of life ; as well in the cool philofophy of the author of

Eccle-

2

Ecclefiaftes, as amidft the diftreffes of the Pfalmift, and the exultations of good Hezekiah.

But could this language have been ufed by a People inftructed in the doctrine of life and immortality? or do we find one word of it, on any occafion whatever, in the Writers of the New Teftament, but where it is brought in to be confuted and condemned [g]?

All this, to thoughtful men, will, I fuppofe, be deemed convincing. Whence it follows that their fubterfuge is quite cut off, who pretend, that Mofes did not indeed propagate the Doctrine of a future ftate of rewards and punifhments in *writing*, but that he delivered it to TRADITION, which conveyed it fafely down through all the ages of the Jewifh Difpenfation, from one end of it to the other. For we fee, he was fo far from teaching it, that he ftudioufly contrived to keep it out of fight; nay provided for the want of it: and the people were fo far from being influenced by it, that they had not even the idea of it. Yet the writers of the Church of Rome have taken advantage of this filence in the Law of Mofes concerning a future ftate, to advance the honour of TRADITION : For, not feeing the doctrine in the WRITTEN LAW, and fancying they faw a neceffity that the Jews fhould have it, they concluded (to fave the credit of the Jewifh Church and to advance the credit of their own) that Mofes had carefully inculcated it, in the TRADITIONAL. This weighty point, Father Simon proves by the *fecond book of Maccabees*; and triumphs over the

---

[g] " *Let us eat and drink, for to-morrow we die.* Be not deceived: evil communications corrupt good manners, &c." 1 Cor. xv. 32.

Proteftants

Proteſtants and Socinians (as he call them) for their folly in throwing that book out of the Canon, and thereby diſabling themſelves from proving a future ſtate, from the old Teſtament [h].

A very worthy proteſtant Biſhop does as much honour to *Tradition,* in his way. In ſome *Miſcellanies* of the Biſhop of Cloyne, publiſhed in 1752, we find theſe words—" Moſes, indeed, " doth *not inſiſt on a future ſtate,* THE COMMON " BASIS OF ALL POLITICAL INSTITUTIONS.—The " belief of a future ſtate (which it is manifeſt " the Jews were poſſeſſed of *long before the coming* " *of Chriſt)* ſeems to have obtained amongſt the " Hebrews from primæval TRADITION, which " might render it unneceſſary for Moſes to *inſiſt* on " that article [i]." Though the Biſhop has not the merit of ſaying this with a profeſſed deſign, like Father Simon, *pour appuyer la Tradition,* yet the Church of Rome has not the leſs obligation to him for aſſigning ſo much virtue to this their powerful aſſiſtant, which has conveyed to them all they want; and indeed moſt of what they have. But if the *traditional* doctrine of a future ſtate prevailed amongſt the Jews, in the time of Moſes, and that he would truſt to the ſame conveyance,

[h] Monſ. Simon avoit dit, *pour appuyer la Tradition,* que la reſurrection des corps ne peut ſe demontrer par le Vieux Teſtament—ces expreſſions plus claires de la reſurrection & du ſiecle à venir, qui ſe trouvent dans le *ſecond Livre Maccabees,* ſont une preuve evidente que les Juifs avoient une Tradition touchant la Reſurrection, dont il n'eſt fait aucune mention dans les anciens livres de l'Ecriture. Les Proteſtans & les Sociniens qui ne reçoivent point les *Maccabees* ne pourront pas la prouver ſolidement par le Vieux Teſtament. *Pere Simon, Reponſe au Sentimens de quelques Theologiens de Hollande, &c.* p. 39.

[i] Page 68.

for the safe delivery of it down to the times of Christ, how came it to pass that he did his best to weaken the efficacy, by studiously contriving to draw men off, as it were, from the Doctrine, and always representing it under the impenetrable cover of temporal rewards and punishments?

2. If a future state obtained by *Tradition*, What occasion was there for the Law of punishing the transgression of the parent upon the children?

3. If it obtained by *Tradition*, How happened it that the Jews are not represented in their History sometimes at least, as acting on the motives, and influenced by the prospect of a future state, and expressing their hopes concerning it like the rest of mankind, who had it by *Tradition*, or otherwise?

4. If it obtained by *Tradition*, How came HEZE-KIAH to say, that *they who go down into the pit cannot hope for the truth :* and DAVID, to represent the dead as going into the place of *silence* and *forgetfulness*, where they were no longer to praise and celebrate the goodness of God? On the contrary are there not passages in the books of SOLOMON and JOB, which plainly shew that no such tradition obtained in their respective times?

5. If it obtained by *Tradition*, What occasion for the administration of an extraordinary Providence under the Law? Or from whence arose the embarras of DAVID and JEREMIAH (not to speak of the disputants in the book of JOB) to account for the prosperity of some wicked Individuals, in the present life? In a word, to the maintainers of this *Tradition* may be very appositely
applied

applied the words of Jesus to the *Traditionists* in general, when he told them, *they made the word of God
of none effect through their traditions.* For certainly, if any thing can render that *word of God*
which *brought life and immortality to light by the Gospel,* of none effect, it is the pretended PRIMÆVAL
TRADITION which the good Bishop so much insists upon.

The learned Prelate indeed obferves, that *the
Jews were possessed of a future state long before the
coming of Christ.* But what is this to the purpose,
if it can be shewn, that the knowledge of it might
be obtained from a quarter very distant from the
old hebrew *Traditions*; and especially if from the
colour and complexion of the Doctrine, it can be
shewn, that it did, in fact, come from a distant
quarter? namely, from their Pagan neighbours;
patched up out of some dark and scattered insinua-
tions of their own Prophets, and varnished over
with the metaphorical expressions employed to
convey them. But not to anticipate what I have
to say on this head in the last volume, I proceed
in the course of my argument.

S E C T. VI.

WHAT is yet of greatest weight, the inspired
writers of the *New Testament* expressly
assure us that the doctrine of a future State of reward and punishment did NOT make part of the
Mosaic Dispensation.

Their evidence may be divided into *two* parts.
In the first, they prove that *temporal* Rewards and
Punishments were the fanction of the Mosaic Dif-
pensation: and in the second, that it had NO
OTHER.

7   I. St.

I. St. PAUL, in his epiftle to Timothy, enforc-
ing, againft certain judaizing Chriftians, the advantages of moral above ritual obfervances, fays;
" Bodily exercife profiteth little; but godlinefs is
" profitable unto all things; having the promife
" of the life that now is, and of that which is to
" come [k]." That is, though numerous ritual obfervances were enjoined by the Law, and fome there
muft needs be under the Gofpel wherever there is
a Chriftian Church, yet they are of little advantage
in comparifon of moral virtue; for that, under
both Religions, the rewards proper to each, were
annexed only to *godlinefs:* that is to fay, under
the Jewifh, the reward of *the life that now is;* under the Chriftian, of that *which is to come.* This
interpretation, which fhews *temporal rewards* to be
foreign to the nature of the Chriftian Œconomy,
I fupport,

1. From other paffages of the fame Writer,
where he exprefsly informs us that Chriftians have
not the promife of the *life that now is.* For to the
Corinthians he fays, fpeaking of the condition of
the followers of CHRIST, *If in this life only we
have hope in* CHRIST, *we are of all men moft miferable* [l]. To underftand the force of which words,
we muft confider, that they were addreffed to Jewifh
Converts tainted with Sadducifm, who argued from
the Mofaic Difpenfation to the Chriftian: And holding that there was no future ftate in the former,
concluded by analogy, that there was none in the
latter. The argument on which they built their
firft Pofition was, that the fanctions of the Law
were temporal rewards and punifhments. Our
Apoftle therefore argues with them, as is his ufual

[k] 1 Tim. iv. 8.   [l] 1 COR. xv. 19.

way, on their own principles. " You deny, ſays
" he, a reſurrection from the dead, or a future
" ſtate of reward and puniſhment. And why?
" Becauſe there is no ſuch doctrine in the Law.
" How do you prove it? Becauſe the ſanctions of
" the Law are temporal rewards and puniſhments.
" Agreed. And now on your own principle I
" confute your concluſion. You own that the
" Jews had an equivalent for future rewards and
" puniſhment, namely the preſent. But Chriſtians
" have no equivalent, So far from that, *they are,*
" with regard to this world only, *of all men moſt*
" *miſerable* ; having therefore no equivalent 'for
" the rewards a future ſtate, they muſt needs be
" entitled to them." This ſhews the ſuperior
force of the Apoſtle's reaſoning. And from hence
it appears not only that Chriſtians HAD NOT, but
that the Jews HAD the promiſe of the Life that now
is.

2. If we underſtand the *promiſe of the life that*
now is to extend to the Chriſtian Diſpenſation, we
deſtroy the ſtrength and integrity of St. Paul's argument. He is here reaſoning againſt judaizing
Chriſtians. So that his buſineſs is to ſhew, that
godlineſs, in every ſtate, and under every Diſpenſation unto which they imagined themſelves bound,
had the advantage of *bodily exerciſe* [m].

The

---

[m] To all this, it hath been ſaid, — " Chriſtians have the
" promiſe of the life that now is, excepting the caſe of per-
" ſecution, Mark x. 30." The words of Jeſus in the Evan-
geliſt are, — *there is no one that hath* LEFT *houſe or brethren, &c.*
for my ſake and the Goſpel's, but he ſhall receive an hundred fold
now in this time, houſes and lands, &c. with perſecutions, and in
the world to come, eternal life. But theſe words evidently allude
to the firſt Followers of Jeſus, while the Church was under an
extraordinary Providence, that is, during the Age of Miracles ;
and

The author of the epistle to the Hebrews speaking of JESUS says: *After the similitude of Melchisedec there ariseth another Priest, who is made not after the* LAW OF A CARNAL COMMANDMENT, *but after the power of an endless life* [n]. The Jewish Religion, called a *carnal commandment*, is here opposed to the christian, called *the power of an endless life.* By *carnal commandment* then must needs be understood a Law promising carnal things, or the things of this life.

II. That the Mosaic Dispensation had ONLY the sanction of *temporal* rewards and punishments, or that it taught not *future*, let us hear St. John; who in the beginning of his Gospel assures us, that *the* LAW *was given by Moses, but that* GRACE *and* TRUTH *came by Jesus Christ* [o]. As certain then as the *Law* did not come by Jesus Christ, so certain is it, according to this Apostle, that *Grace* and *Truth* did not come by Moses. This *Grace* and *Truth* cannot be understood generically; for, the *grace* or favour of God was bestowed on the chosen race, and *truth*, or the revealed will of God, *did come* by Moses. It must therefore be some *species* of *grace* and *truth*, of which the Apostle here predicates; the publication of which species constitutes what is called the Gospel. And this all know to be redemption from death, and restoration to eternal life.

and as that sort of Dispensation is always aided by the course of natural and civil events, we easily see how it would be promoted by LEAVING a country doomed to the most horrid and exterminating destruction. But St. Paul, where he assigns only *the life which is to come* to the followers of the Gospel, is speaking of a different thing, namely of the genius of the Christian Dispensation in general, as it is opposed to Judaism.

[n] Chap. vii. ver. 15, 16.   [o] Chap. i. ver. 17.

Again,

● Again, to this part likewife, let us once more hear the learned Apoftle: *As by one man fin entered into the world, and death by fin; and fo death paffed upon all men, for that all have finned: for until the Law, fin was in the world, but Sin is not imputed where there is no Law. Neverthelefs Death reigned from Adam to Mofes* [p]. It is St. Paul's purpofe to fhew, that *death* came by ADAM through fin, and fo paffed upon all men; and that *life* came by JESUS CHRIST: But having faid that Sin, which brings forth Death, is not imputed where there is no Law, left this fhould feem to contradict what he had faid of Death's paffing upon *all men*, he adds, *neverthelefs death reigned from Adam to Mofes*; taking it for granted that his followers would underftand it muft needs reign from Mofes to CHRIST, as having made *Sin's being* IMPUTED to confift in there being a LAW given. Now I afk how the Apoftle could poffibly fay, *that Death reigned under the* Mofaic Difpenfation, if that People had the knowledge of immortal life to be procured by a Redeemer to come, any more than it can be faid to *reign now* with the fame knowledge of a Redeemer paft; fince we agree that the efficacy of his death extends to all preceding as well as fucceeding Ages? Accordingly in his epiftle to the Corinthians he calls the Jewifh Law, the MINISTRATION OF DEATH, and the MINISTRATION OF CONDEMNATION [q].

2. In his epiftle to the Galatians, he fays,— *Before* FAITH *came, we were kept under the Law, fhut up unto the* FAITH *which fhould. afterwards be revealed* [r]. i. e. we were kept in fubjection to the

[p] ROM. v. 12, & *feq.* [q] 2 COR. iii. 7, & *feq.*
[r] GAL. iii. 23.

Law

Law of Mofes; and, by that means, shut up
and fequeftered from the reft of the Nations, to be
prepared and made ready for the firft reception of
the FAITH, when it fhould in God's appointed time
be revealed unto men. From thefe words therefore
it appears, that till that time, the Jews had no
knowledge of this FAITH.   So much we muft have
concluded tho' he had not faid, as he does afterwards, That till that time, the Jews *were in bon-*
dage under the elements of this world [s].   Now could
men acquainted with the doctrine of *life and im-*
mortality be faid, with any fenfe or propriety, to
be in fuch a ftate of bondage? For though men
in bondage may have an idea of Liberty, yet of
THIS LIBERTY they could have no idea without underftanding, at the fame time, that they were
partakers of its benefits.

3. In his fecond epiftle to Timothy he exprefsly fays, *That* JESUS CHRIST HATH ABOLISHED
DEATH, AND HATH BROUGHT LIFE AND IMMOR-
TALITY TO LIGHT THROUGH THE GOSPEL [t].
But now if *Death* were abolifhed by JESUS CHRIST,
it is certain it had reigned till his coming: and
yet it is as certain, that it could reign no longer
than while the tidings of the Gofpel were kept
back; becaufe we agree that CHRIST's death hath
a retrofpect operation: therefore thofe under the
Law had no knowledge of life and immortality.
Again: *If life and immortality were brought to light*
through the Gofpel, confequently, till the preaching of the Gofpel, it was kept hid and out of
fight [u].   But if taught by Mofes and the Prophets,
it

---

[s] Chap. iv. ver. 3.   [t] 2 TIM. i. 10.

[u] The ferious reader, who confiders all this, will not be a
little furprifed to hear that eminent Scholar and Divine, Dr.
S. Clarke,

it was *not brought to light through the Gospel:*
therefore the generality of thofe under the Law
had no knowledge of a future ftate. But Scripture is ever confiftent, though mens fyftems be
not. And for this reafon we find that *life and
immortality,* which is here faid to be *brought to
light through the Gospel,* is fo often called the
MYSTERY OF THE GOSPEL [x]: that is, a. *myftery*
till

S. Clarke, talk in the following manner, where, after having
fpoken of the doubts and uncertainties of the ancient Philofophers concerning a future ftate, he concludes in thefe words, —
" From all which it appears that notwithftanding all the bright
" arguments and acute conclufions and brave fayings of the
" beft Philofophers, yet *life and immortality* were not FULLY
" and SATISFACTORILY *brought to light* by BARE NATURAL
" REASON." — [*Ev. of nat. and rev. Religion,* p. 146.] — It
would be very ftrange if they had; fince Scripture is fo far
from allowing any part of this difcovery to *natural reafon,* that
it will not admit even the Mofaic Revelation to a fhare, but
referves it all for the *Gospel of* CHRIST: fo that had natural
Religion brought *life and immortality to light,* though not *fully
and fatisfactorily,* the learned Apoftle would be found to have
fpoken much too highly of the prerogatives of the Gofpel.

The truth is, the very learned Writer had two points to
make out, in this famous work; the one was the *evidence of
natural Religion;* and, under that head, he is to fhew, that it
taught life and immortality. His other point was, the *evidence
of revealed Religion,* and there, (to fhew its ufe and neceffity) he
is to demonftrate that bare natural reafon could not difcover life
and immortality. Thus the very method of his demonftration
obliged him, in the former part, to give to natural Religion an
honour which, in the latter part, he was forced to take away:
and to reconcile them with one another, was the purpofe of the
conciliating words above — *yet life and . immortality were not*
FULLY *and* SATISFACTORILY *brought to light by bare natural
reafon:* which indeed does the bufinefs; but it is at the expence
of the learned Apoftle, who fays it was not brought to light at
all, till the preaching of the Gofpel.

[x] EPH. vi. 19. — To this it has been faid, " that the *myftery*
of the Gospel here mentioned, is rather that which is meant by
the

till this promulgation of it by the disciples of Christ : *Which had been hid from ages and from generations, but was then made manifest unto the Saints* [y]. The term was borrowed from those famous *Rites* of Paganism, so named; and is applied with admirable justness. For as the *Mysteries* were communicated only to a few of the wise and great, and kept hid from the populace : so *life and immortality*, as we shall see, was revealed by God, as a special favour, to the holy Patriarchs and Prophets, but kept hid from the body of the Jewish Nation.

4. The Author of the Epistle to the Hebrews says : That THE LAW MADE NOTHING PERFECT, BUT THE BRINGING IN OF A BETTER HOPE DID [z]. Now, that could not be said to be *brought in*, which was there before. And had it been there before, the *Law*, it seems, had been perfect ; and, consequently, would have superseded the use of the *Gospel.* Therefore this *better hope*, namely of immortality in a future state, is not in the Mosaic Dispensation. Let us observe farther, that as the Gospel, by bringing in a *better hope*, made the Law *perfect*, it appears, there was that relation between the *Law* and *Gospel* which is between the beginning and the completion of any matter. From whence these two consequences follow : 1. That the Law wanted something which the Gospel supplied: And what was that something but the doctrine

the word, chap. iii. 3—9. namely the calling in of the Gentiles to be fellow-heirs with the Jews." — For a confutation of this absurd fancy, read — *The free and candid examination of the principles advanced by the Lord Bishop of London*, chap. i. p 24. *& seq.* where the learned and most judicious Author has sufficiently exploded it.

[y] Col. i. 26.   [z] Chap. vii. ver. 19.

of a future State ?   2. That the Law muſt needs
make ſome preparation for that *better hope* which
the Goſpel was to bring in.   What it was, the ſame
writer tells us, namely, That *it had* A SHADOW
[σκιαν] *of good things to come,* but *not the* VERY
IMAGE [εικονα] *of the things*ᵃ.   Hence it is evident
that by this *ſhadow* is meant ſuch a typical repreſentation, ſo faintly delineated, as not to be per-
ceived by vulgar eyes, intent only on a carnal
Diſpenſation.   This was contrived for admirable
purpoſes : For if, inſtead of a *ſhadow* or faint out-
line of a deſign, the Image itſelf, in full relief,
had glaringly held forth the objeᴄt intended, this
objeᴄt, ſo diſtinᴄtly defined, would have drawn the
Jews from that Œconomy to which it was God's
pleaſure they ſhould long continue in ſubjeᴄtion:
And had there been no delineation at all, to become
ſtronger in a clearer light, one illuſtrious evidence
of the Dependency between the two Religions,
had been wanting.

Again, the ſame Writer, to the ſame purpoſe,
ſpeaking of CHRIST ſays, *But now hath he obtained
a more excellent Miniſtry, by how much alſo he is the
Mediator of a* BETTER COVENANT, *which was eſtabliſhed upon* BETTER PROMISES.   *For if the firſt
Covenant had been faultleſs, then ſhould no place have
been found for the Second*ᵇ.   1. We ſee that this
better Covenant was eſtabliſhed by CHRIST, and not
by Moſes.   2. If the firſt Covenant had been faultleſs, that is, had contained *better promiſes,* or
taught the doᴄtrine of a future ſtate, there had
been no room for a Second.

To ſum up all, This admirable writer gives in
the laſt place, the fulleſt evidence to both parts of

ᵃ Chap. x. ver. 1.   ᵇ Chap. viii. ver. 6, 7.

the

the propofition, namely " That temporal rewards and punifhments were the fanction of the Jewifh Difpenfation ; and that it had no other." For in the fecond chapter we find thefe remarkable affertions.

· Ver. 2. *For if the word spoken by Angels was stedfast, and every transgression and disobedience* RECEIVED A JUST RECOMPENSE OF REWARD, *How shall we escape,* &c.

Ver. 5. *For unto the Angels hath he not put in subjection the* WORLD TO COME, *whereof we speak.*

Ver. 14—15. *He* [Chrift] *also himself likewise took part of the · same* [flefh and blood] *that thro' death he might destroy him that had the power of death ; that is, the Devil; and deliver them, who through fear of death were* ALL THEIR LIFE-TIME *subject to bondage.*

Let us lay thefe three texts together.   And we fhall find, 1. from ver. 2. that the fanction of the Law, or *the word spoken by angels,* was of a temporal nature — *every transgression received a just recompence.*   2. From ver. 5. that the Law taught no future ftate—*the world to come not being put in subjection to thefe angels.*   And 3. from ver. 14—15. that the people had not the knowledge of fuch a ftate —*being all their life-time subject to bondage.*   For the Devil is here faid to have *power of death,* as he brought it into the world by the delufion of the FIRST MAN.   Therefore, before *death* can be abolifhed, *He,* who had the power of it, muft be deftroyed.   But his deftruction is the work of the SECOND MAN.   Till his coming therefore, the Jews, as we are here told, *were through fear of death all their life time subject to bondage.*   Chrift then

brought

brought them into *the glorious liberty of the children of God* [c] by setting before them *life and immortality* [d].

To all this, I hope, the reader will not be so inattentive to object, " That what is here produced from the New Testament to prove that the followers of the Law had no future state, contradicts what I have more than once observed, That the later Jewish Prophets had given strong intimations of an approaching Dispensation, with a future state." For the question is concerning a future state's being the Sanction of the LAW, not of later intimations, of its being ready to become the sanction of the GOSPEL.

As inconsiderate would be this other objection, " That my point is to prove that this Dispensation had *no future state of reward and punishment at all*, and my evidence from the New Testament only shews they had not the *christian Doctrine of it*." For to this I answer, 1. That those I argue with, if they hold any difference between the Christian and general Doctrine of a future state of reward and punishment, it is only this, that the Christian Doctrine was *revealed*; the other, a conclusion of natural reason. Now if the Jews had this Doctrine, they must needs have it, as *revealed*; consequently the same with the Christian. 2. That though I myself suppose the natural and the christian Doctrine of a future state of reward and punishment to be very different things; yet I shall

----

[c] ROM. viii. 21.

[d] For the further illustration of this matter, I would recommend to the Reader's serious perusal the first chapter of *the free and candid examination of the Bishop of London's Principles.*

shew,

shew, in due time, that if Mofes were indeed God's Meffenger, and would teach a future ftate, it could be no other than the *Chriftian* Doctrine of it.   But as thofe, I have to do with, may be ready to tell me, that this *due time*, like that of the *Jews' Meffiah*, is either paft or will never come, they will, I fuppofe, readily bear with me while I anticipate the fubject, and in a very few words prove what is here afferted.   Revelation teacheth that mankind loft the free gift of immortal life by the tranfgreffion of Adam; and, from thence, became mortal, and their exiftence confined to this life. Revelation likewife teacheth that the MEAN which Divine Wifdom thought fit to employ in reftoring man from death to his firft ftate of immortality, was *the facrifice of Chrift on the crofs.*   Hence it appears to be a thing impoffible, that any Meffenger from God, any Agent or Inftrument made ufe of for conducting this grand Difpenfation towards its completion, could (were it in his *choice* or in his *office* to promulgate the doctrine of a future State) fpeak of any other but that purchafed by Chrift, and promulged and proclaimed in the Gofpel, fince in fact, on the principles of Revelation, there is no other; and to inculcate another, would be impeaching the veracity of God, and the eternal ftability of his councils.

To conclude, There is one thing which plainly evinceth that if the Jews had the knowledge or belief of a FUTURE STATE of reward and punifhment, they muft have had the knowledge of the REDEMPTION of man by the death and fuffering of Jefus Chrift, likewife.   And it is this, That all the Sacrifices in the Jewifh Ritual regarded only temporal things.   A very competent judge in thefe matters affures us,—Univerfa Judæorum fimul

congefta

congefta Sacrificia ad affequenda hujus vitæ com-
moda omnia facta erant[e]· The confequence is this,
That if the Jewifh religion taught its followers a
future ftate of rewards and punifhments, it either
afforded them no means of attaining future happinefs, or it inftructed them in the doctrine of the
Redemption. To fay the firft, contradicts the nature of all Religion; to fay the latter, makes the
Jewifh ufelefs, and the Chriftian falfe, as contradicting its repeated declarations, that *life and immortality*, or the doctrine of the Redemption, *was
brought to light through the Gospel.*

But what was afked by St. Paul's Adverfaries,
will perhaps be afked by mine, *Is the* LAW *then
against the* PROMISES *of God?* Or does the LAW,
becaufe it had no future ftate, contradict the Gos-
PEL, which hath? The Apoftle's anfwer will ferve
me,—*God forbid: For if there had been a* LAW
*which could have given life, verily righteoufnefs fhould
have been by the* LAW[f]. That is, if the genius of
the *Law* had produced fuch a Difpenfation as was
proper to convey to mankind the free gift of life
and immortality, this gift would have been conveyed by it. All this fhews that the Law was not
contrary to the Gospel, but only that it was not of
fufficient excellence to be the vehicle of God's laft
beft gift to mankind. And it fhews too (and it is
a very fit remark, as the refult from the whole,
with which to conclude this fifth *Book*) that a
future ftate was not the Sanction of the Law of
Mofes, or, in the Apoftle's more emphatic words,
that the *Law did not* (becaufe it could not) *give life.*

Thus, I prefume, it is now proved beyond all
reafonable queftion, THAT THE DOCTRINE OF A

<hr>

[e] Outram de Sacr. p. 305.   [f] GAL. iii. 21.

FUTURE STATE OF REWARD AND PUNISHMENT IS
NOT TO BE FOUND IN, NOR DID MAKE PART OF,
THE MOSAIC DISPENSATION.

It will be afked then, " What were the real fentiments of thefe early Jews concerning the foul?"
Though the queftion be a little out of time, yet
as the anfwer is fhort, I fhall give it here. They
were doubtlefs the fame with thofe of the reft of
mankind, who have thought upon the matter;
that IT SURVIVED THE BODY : But having, from
Mofes's filence and the eftablifhment of another
Sanction, no expectation of future rewards and punifhments, they fimply concluded that *it returned to
him who gave it* [g]. But, as to any interefting fpecu-
lations concerning its ftate of furvivorfhip, 'tis
plain they had none. Indeed how fhould they have
any? when PERSONALITY did not enter into the idea
of this *furvivorfhip*, that being only annexed to the
rewards and punifhments of a future ftate. Hence
it was that thofe ancient Philofophers (almoft all
the theiftical Philofophers of Greece) who confidered the foul as a SUBSTANCE diftinct from the
body, and not a mere QUALITY of it, (for they were
not fuch idiots as to conceive, that *thought* could
refult from any combinations of *matter and motion*)
thofe Philofophers, I fay, who confidered the foul
as a fubftance, and yet difbelieved a future ftate
of rewards and punifhments, denied it all future
perfonality, and held the refufion of it into the
τὸ ἓν, or the foul of the world [h]. And juft fuch
INTERESTING SPECULATIONS concerning it had the
few philofophic Jews of the moft early times, as appears from the book of Ecclefiaftes, which fpeaks
their fentiments. *Who knoweth* (fays this author)

[g] ECCLES. xii. 7.   [h] See Div. Leg. vol. i. b. 3.

the spirit of man that goeth upward, and the spirit of the beast that goeth downward to the earth [i] ? And again: " Then shall the dust return to the earth " as it was, AND THE SPIRIT SHALL RETURN " UNTO GOD WHO GAVE IT [k]." Yet this writer, perfectly conformable to what I have delivered, says, at the same time : *But the dead know not any thing, neither have they* ANY MORE A REWARD, *for the memory of them is forgotten* [l].

And where was the wonder ? that a matter which so little concerned them, namely, the future condition of a portion of etherial Spirit divested of its Personality, should only float idly in the brain, when we reflect that even the knowledge of the FIRST CAUSE OF ALL THINGS, while he made no part of the *National Worship*, was entertained by the Gentiles (as appears from all Antiquity) with the utmost unconcern, neither regulating their notions nor influencing their actions.

But from this uninteresting state, in which the Doctrine, concerning the Soul, remained amongst the early Jews, the SADDUCEES concluded that their Ancestors believed the *extinction* of the soul on death. Hence likewise came some late Revivers of this opinion, of the *extinction of the soul*; tho' maintained under the softer name of its SLEEP between death and the resurrection : For they go upon the Sadducean principle, that the soul is a *quality* only, and not a *substance*.

In support of this opinion, the Revivers of it proceed on the sophism, which Polytheists employ

---

[i] Chap. iii. ver. 21. Vid. *Cleric.* & *Drusium* in loc. [k] Chap. xii. ver. 7. Vid. *Clericum* in loc. [l] Chap. ix. ver. 5.

to

to combat the unity of the Godhead. *All Philosophical arguments* (says the Reviver, after having quoted a number of wonderful things from Scripture, to prove the soul a *quality,* and mortal) *drawn from our notions of matter, and urged against the possibility of life, thought, and agency, being so connected with some portions of it as to constitute a compound Being or Person, are merely grounded on our ignorance* [m]. Just so the Polytheist. "All arguments for the Unity, from metaphysics, are manifestly vain, and merely grounded on our ignorance. You Believers (says he) must be confined to Scripture: Now Scripture assures us, THERE ARE GODS MANY," which, by the way, I think a stronger text, certainly a directer, against the *unity of the Godhead,* than any this learned Writer has produced for the *sleep of the Soul.* But what say Believers to this? They say, that Scripture takes the *unity,* as well as the *existence* of the Deity, for granted; takes them for truths, demonstrable by natural light. Just so it is with regard to that *immaterial substance,* the Soul. Scripture supposes men to be so far informed of the nature of the Soul, by the same light, as to know that it cannot be destroyed by any of those causes which bring about the extinction of the body. Our Dreamers [n] are aware of this, and therefore hold with Unbelievers, that the Soul is *no substance,* but a *quality* only; and so have taken effectual care indeed, that its repose shall not be disturbed in this, which we may emphatically call, the SLEEP OF DEATH. *We can never prove,* (says another of these sleepers [o]) *that the Soul of man is of such a nature*

---

[m] *Considerations on the Theory of Religion,* p. 398. Ed. 3d.

[n] St. Jude's *filthy dreamers* only *defiled the Flesh.* These defile *the Spirit.*   [o] Taylor of Norwich.

that

*that it can and muſt exiſt and live, think, act, enjoy,
&c. ſeparate from, and independent of, the body. All
our preſent experience ſhews the contrary.* The operations of the mind depend CONSTANTLY and INVA-
RIABLY *upon the ſtate of the body, of the brain in particular. If ſome dying perſons have a lively uſe of
their rational faculties to the very laſt, it is becauſe
death has invaded ſome other part, and the brain remains ſound and vigorous* [p]. This is the long-ex-
ploded traſh of *Coward, Toland, Collins,* &c.
And he who can treat us with it at this time of
day, has either never read CLARKE and BAXTER
on the ſubject, (in which, he had been better employed than in writing upon it) or never underſtood them.——So far as to the abſtract truth.
Let us conſider next the practical conſequences.
Convince the philoſophic Libertine that the Soul
is a quality ariſing out of *matter,* and vaniſhing
on the diſſolution of the *form,* and then ſee if
ever you can bring him to believe the Chriſtian
Doctrine of the RESURRECION? While he held
the Soul to be an immaterial ſubſtance, exiſting,
as well in its ſeparation from, as in its conjunction
with, the Body, and he could have no reaſon, ariſing from the principles of true Philoſophy, to
ſtagger in his belief of this revealed Doctrine.——
*Thou fool that which thou ſoweſt is not quickened ex-
cept it die* [q], is good philoſophy as well as good divinity: for if the body, inſtead of its earthly nature
were to have a heavenly, it muſt needs paſs through
death and corruption to qualify it for that change.
But when this *body died,* what occaſion was there
for the *Soul,* which was to ſuffer no change, to
fall aſleep ?

[p] Ib. p. 401.   [q] St. Paul.

But

But their *sleep of the Soul* is mere cant : and this brings me to the last consideration, the sense and consistency of so ridiculous a notion.   They go, as we observed, upon the Sadducean principle, that the Soul is a *quality* of Body, not a *substance* of itself, and so dies with its substratum. Now *sleep*, is a modification of Existence, not of non-existence ; so that though the sleep of a *Substance* hath a meaning, the sleep of a *quality* is nonsense.   And if ever this Soul of theirs re-exerts its faculties, in must be by means of a RE-PRODUCTION, not by a mere AWAKING ; and they may as well talk of the SLEEP of a mushroom turn-ed again into the substance of the dunghill from whence it arose, and from which, not the same, but another mushroom shall, in time, arise.   In a word, neither Unbelievers nor Believers will allow to these *middle men* that a new-existing Soul, which is only a quality resulting from a glorified body, can be identically the same with an annihilated Soul, which had resulted from an earthly body.   But perhaps, as Hudibras had discovered the Recepta-cle of the *ghosts of defunct bodies,* so these gentle-men may have found out the yet subtiler corner, where the *ghosts of defunct qualities* repose.

APPEN-

A P P E N D I X.

A LATE noble and voluminous Author[a], who hath written with more than ordinary fpleen againft THE RELIGION OF HIS COUNTRY, as it is founded in Revelation and eftablifhed by Law, hath attacked with more than ordinary fury the Author of *the Divine Legation of Mofes demonftrated*, and of *the Alliance between Church and State vindicated.*

. I fhall fhortly find a fitter place to examine his reafoning againft the *Alliance.* At prefent let us fee what he has to urge againft the argument of the *Divine Legation*, which is founded on thefe two facts, the *omiffion of the Doctrine of a future State of Rewards and Punifhments.* in the Mofaic Difpenfation ; and the *adminiftration of an extraordinary Providence* in the fame Difpenfation.

His Lordfhip begins with the OMISSION, which he acknowleges : and to evade the force of the argument arifing from it, cafts about for a reafon, independent of the EXTRAORDINARY PROVIDENCE, to account for it.

His firft folution is this, — " MOSES DID NOT " BELIEVE THE IMMORTALITY OF THE SOUL, nor " the rewards and punifhments of another life, " tho' it is poffible he might have learnt thefe

---

[a] L. BOLINGBROKE.

" Doctrines

" Doctrines from the Egyptians, WHO TAUGHT
" THEM VERY EARLY, perhaps as they taught
" that of the Unity of God. When I say, *that*
" *Moses did not believe the immortality of the soul,*
" nor future rewards and punishments, my reason
" is this, that he taught neither, when *he had to*
" *do with a people whom a Theocracy could not re-*
" *strain*; and on whom, therefore, terrors of Pu-
" nishment, *future* as well as present, *eternal* as
" well as temporary, could never be too much
" multiplied, or too strongly inculcated [b]."

This reasoning is altogether worthy of his Lordship. Here we have a DOCTRINE, confessed to
be plausible in itself, and therefore of easy admit-
tance; most alluring to human nature, and therefore embraced by all mankind; of highest account among the Egyptians, and therefore ready
to be embraced by the Israelites, who were fond
of Egyptian notions ; of strongest efficacy on the
minds of an unruly People, and therefore of in-
dispensable use; Yet, all this notwithstanding,
*Moses did not believe it, and, on that account, would
not teach it.*—But then, had MOSES's integrity been
so severe, How came he to write a History which,
my Lord thinks, is, in part at least, a fiction of
his own ? Did he *believe* that ? How came he to
leave the Israelites, as my Lord assures us he did,
in possession of many of the superstitious opinions
of Egypt ? did he *believe* these too ? No, but they
served his purpose; which was, The better governing an unruly People. Well, but his Lordship tells us, the doctrine of a future state served
this purpose best of all; for *having to do with a
People whom a Theocracy could not restrain, terrors of*

[b] Vol. iii. p. 289.

punishment,

punifhment, FUTURE *as well as prefent*, ETERNAL *as well as temporary, could never be too much multiplied, or too ftrongly inculcated.* No matter for that. MOSES, as other men may, on a fudden grows fcrupulous; and fo, together with the maxims of common politics, throws afide the principles of common fenfe; and when he had employed all the other inventions of fraud, he boggles at this, which beft ferved his purpofe; was moft innocent in itfelf; and was moft important in its general, as well as particular ufe.

In his Lordfhip's next Volume, this *Omiffion* comes again upon the ftage; and then we have *another* reafon affigned for MOSES'S conduct in this matter. " MOSES would not teach the Doctrine " of the immortality of the foul, and of a future " ftate, *on account of the many fuperftitions* which " this Doctrine had begot in Egypt, as we muft " believe, or *believe that he knew nothing of it*, or " ASSIGN SOME WHIMSICAL REASON FOR HIS " OMISSION [c]."

We have feen before, that MOSES omitted a future ftate, *becaufe he did not believe it.* This reafon is now out of date; and one or other of the three following is to be affigned; either becaufe it *begot fuperftitions*; or becaufe *he knew nothing of it*; or if you will allow neither of thefe, you muft have recourfe, he tells you, to Warburton's WHIMSICAL REASON, that *the Jews were under an extraordinary Providence.*

Let us take him then, at his word, without expecting however, that he will ftand to it; and

[c] Vol. iv. p. 470.

having

having shewn, his two first reasons not worth a rush, leave the last, established, even on his own concessions.

1. *Moses*, says he, *omitted a future state on account of the many superstitions, which this doctrine had begot in Egypt.* But if the *omission* stands upon this principle, MOSES must have omitted an infinite number of things, which, Lord Bolingbroke says, he borrowed of the Egyptians; part of which, in his Lordship's opinion, were those very superstitions, which this *Doctrine had begot*; such as the notion of TUTELARY DEITIES; and part, what arose out of that notion; in the number of which were *distinction between things clean and unclean*; an *hereditary Priesthood*; *sacerdotal habits*; and *Rites of sacrifice*.

2. However, he has another reason for the omission : MOSES *might know nothing of it*. To which, if I only opposed his Lordship's own words in another place, where (giving us the reasons why MOSES did *know something* of a future state) he observes, there are *certain rites, which seem to allude or have a remote relation to this very doctrine* [d], it might be deemed sufficient. But I will go further, and observe, that, from the very LAWS of MOSES themselves, we have an internal evidence of his knowledge of this doctrine. Amongst the Laws against Gentile Divinations, there is one directed against that species of them, called by the Greeks, NECROMANCY, or *invocation of the dead*; which necessarily implies, in the Lawgiver who forbids it, as well as in the offender who uses it, the *knowledge of a future state*.

[d] Vol. v. p. 239.

3. This

3. This being the fate of his Lordſhip's two reaſons, we are now abandoned by him, and left to follow our own inventions, or to take up with SOME WHIMSICAL REASON FOR THE OMISSION; that is, to allow that, as the Jews were under an *extraordinary* Providence, MOSES in quality of Lawgiver had NO OCCASION for the doctrine of a *future ſtate.*

However, his Lordſhip diſſatisfied, as well he might, with the ſolutions hitherto propoſed, returns again to the charge; and in his *Corona operis,* the book of FRAGMENTS, more openly oppoſes the doctrine of the *Divine Legation;* and enlarges and expatiates upon the reaſon before given for the *omiſſion;* namely, *the many ſuperſtitions this doctrine had begotten in Egypt.*

" ONE CANNOT SEE WITHOUT SURPRIZE (ſays
" his Lordſhip) a doctrine ſo uſeful to ALL Reli-
" gion, and therefore incorporated into ALL the
" Syſtems of Paganiſm, left wholly out of that
" of the JEWS. Many probable reaſons might be
" brought to ſhew, that it was an Egyptian doc-
" trine before the Exode, and this particularly,
" that it was propagated from Egypt, ſo ſoon,
" at leaſt, afterwards, by all thoſe who were in-
" ſtructed like MOSES, in the wiſdom of that Peo-
" ple. He tranſported much of his Wiſdom into
" the ſcheme of Religion and Government, which
" he gave the Iſraelites; and, amongſt other
" things, certain Rites, which may ſeem to al-
" lude, or have a remote relation to, this very
" doctrine. Tho' this doctrine therefore, had
" not been that of ABRAHAM, ISAAC, and JACOB,
" He might have adopted it with as little ſcruple,
" as he did many cuſtoms and inſtitutions merely

" Egyptian. He had to do with a rebellious,
" but a superstitious, people. In the first Charac-
" ter, they made it necessary that he should ne-
" glect nothing which might add weight to his or-
" dinances, and contribute to keep them in awe.
" In the second, their disposition was extremely
" proper to receive such a doctrine, and to be in-
" fluenced by it. *Shall we say that an hypothesis of*
" *future rewards and punishments, was* USELESS
" *among a People who lived under a Theocracy,* and
" that the future Judge of other People, was
" their immediate Judge and King, who resided
" in the midst of them, and who dealed out re-
" wards and punishments on every occasion? Why
" then were so many precautions taken? Why
" was a solemn Covenant made with God, as with
" a temporal Prince? Why were so many pro-
" mises and threatnings of rewards and punish-
" ments, temporal indeed, but future and con-
" tingent, as we find in the book of Deuteronomy,
" most pathetically held out by MOSES? Would
" there have been any more impropriety in hold-
" ing out those of one kind than those of another,
" because the supreme Being, who disposed and
" ordered both, was in a particular manner pre-
" sent amongst them? Would an addition to the
" catalogue of rewards and punishments more re-
" mote, but eternal, and in all respects far greater,
" have had no effect? I think neither of these
" things can be said.

" What shall we say then? How came it to pass,
" this addition was not made? I will mention what
" occurs to me, and shall not be over sollicitous
" about the weight that my reflections may deserve.
" If the doctrines of the immortality of the soul and
" of a future state had been revealed to MOSES,

" that

" that he might teach them to the Ifraelites, he
" would have taught them moft certainly. But he
" did not teach them. They were therefore not
" revealed to him. Why they were not fo reveal-
" ed fome PERT DIVINE OR OTHER WILL BE
" READY TO TELL YOU. For me, I dare not pre-
" fume to guefs. But this, I may prefume to ad-
" vance, that fince thefe Doctrines were not re-
" vealed by God to his fervant MOSES, it is highly
" probable that this Legiflator made a fcruple of
" teaching them to the Ifraelites, how well fo-
" ever inftructed he might be in them himfelf,
" and howfoever ufeful to Government he might
" think them. The fuperftitious and idolatrous
" rites of the Egyptians, like thofe of other
" nations, were founded on the Polytheifm, and
" the Mythology that prevailed, and were fuf-
" fered to prevail, amongft the Vulgar, and
" that made the fum of their Religion. It
" feemed to be a point of policy to direct all
" thefe abfurd opinions and practices to the fer-
" vice of Government, inftead of attempting to
" root them out. But then the great difference
" between rude and ignorant nations and fuch as
" were civilized and learned, like the Egyptians,
" feems to have been this, that the former had
" no other fyftem of Religion than thefe abfurd
" opinions and practices, whereas the latter had
" an *inward* as well as an *outward* Doctrine. There
" is reafon to believe that natural Theology and
" natural Religion had been taught and practifed
" in the ancient Theban Dynafty; and it is pro-
" bable that they continued to be an *inward* doc-
" trine in the reft of Egypt; while Polytheifm,
" Idolatry, and all the MYSTERIES, all the impie-
" ties, and all the follies of Magic, were the *out-*

C c 2   " *ward*

" *ward* doctrine. MOSES might be let into a
" knowledge of both; and under the patronage
" of the Princefs, whofe Foundling he was, he
" might be initiated into thofe *Myfteries*, where
" the fecret doctrine alone was taught, and the
" outward exploded. But we cannot imagine that
" the Children of Ifrael, in general, enjoyed the
" fame privilege, nor that the Mafters were fo
" lavifh, to their Slaves, of a favour fo diftin-
" guifhed, and often fo hard to obtain. No.
" The Children of Ifrael knew nothing more than
" the outfide of the Religion of Egypt, and if the
" doctrine, we fpeak of, was known to them, it
" was known only in the fuperftitious rites, and
" with all the fabulous circumftances in which it
" was dreffed up and prefented to vulgar belief.
" It would have been hard therefore to teach, or
" to renew this Doctrine in the minds of the Ifrael-
" ites, without giving them an occafion the more,
" to recal the polytheiftical fables, and practife the
" idolatrous Rites they had learnt during their
" Captivity. Rites and Ceremonies are often fo
" equivocal, that they may be applied to very dif-
" ferent doctrines. But when they are fo clofely
" connected with one Doctrine that they are not
" applicable to another, to teach the Doctrine is,
" in fome fort, to teach the Rites and Ceremonies,
" and to authorize the fables on which they are
" founded. MOSES therefore being at liberty
" to teach this doctrine of rewards and punifh-
" ments in a future ftate, or not to teach it, might
" very well choofe the latter; tho' he indulged the
" Ifraelites, on account of the hardnefs of their
" hearts, and by the divine permiffion, as it is
" prefumed, in feveral obfervances and cuftoms
" which did not lead directly, tho' even they did

" fo

" fo perhaps in confequence, to the Polytheifm and
" Idolatry of Egypt ª."

What a Babel of bad reafoning has his Lordfhip
here accumulated out of the rubbifh of falfe and
inconfiftent Principles! And all, to infult the
Temple of God and the Fortrefs of Mount Sion.
Sometimes, he reprefents MOSES as a divine Meffenger, and diftinguifhes between what was revealed, and what was not revealed, unto him; and
then, *a future ftate not being revealed to* MOSES *was
the reafon he did not teach it.* Sometimes again, he
confiders him as a mere human Lawgiver, acquiring
all his knowledge of Religion and Politics from the
Egyptians, in whofe *fecret* Learning he had been
intimately inftructed; and then, the reafon of the
omiffion is; *left the Doctrine of a future ftate fhould have
drawn* the *Ifraelites into thofe Egyptian fuperftitions*,
from which, it was MOSES's purpofe to eftrange
them. All thefe inconfiftencies in *Fact* and *Reafoning*, his Lordfhip delivers in the fame breath, and
without the leaft intimation of any change in his
Principles or Opinions.

But let us follow him ftep by ftep, without troub-
ling our heads about his real fentiments. It is
enough, that we confute all he fays, whether under his own, or any affumed Character.

He begins with confeffing, that ONE CANNOT
SEE WITHOUT SURPRIZE, *a doctrine fo ufeful to* ALL
Religions, and therefore incorporated into ALL *the
Syftems of Paganifm, left wholly out of that of the
Jews.*

ª Vol. v. p. 238—9—40—41.

At

At length then it appears, that this OMISSION is no light or trivial matter, which may be accounted for, as he before fuppofed, by MOSES's *difbelief* of the doctrine; his *ignorance* of it; or the *imaginary mifchiefs* it might poffibly produce. We may be allowed then to think it deferved all the pains, the Author of the *Divine Legation of Mofes* has beftowed upon it: whofe WHIMSICAL REASONING, if it ended in a demonftration of the truth of Revealed Religion, is fufficiently attoned for, tho' it were a little out of the common road: for in this cafe the old proverb would hold true, that *the furtheft way about is the neareft way home.*

His Lordfhip proceeds to fhew, in direct oppofition to what he faid before, that MOSES could not be ignorant of the doctrine of a future ftate, becaufe the Egyptians taught it: His knowledge of it, (my Lord tells us) further appears from an *internal* circumftance, *fome of his rites feeming to allude, or to have a remote relation to, this very doctrine.* This I obferve, to his Lordfhip's credit. The remark is juft and accurate. But we are in no want of his *remote relation*; I have fhewn juft above, that the Jewifh Laws againft *Necromancy* neceffarily imply Mofes's knowledge of the Doctrine.

He then goes on to explain the advantages which, humanly fpeaking, the Ifraelites muft have received from this Doctrine, in the temper and circumftances with which they left Egypt. MOSES, fays he, *had to do with a rebellious and a fuperftitious People.* This likewife I obferve to his credit: It has the fame marks of fagacity and truth; and brings us to the very verge of the *Solution,* propofed by the Author of the *Divine Legation*; which

which is, that the Ifraelites were indeed under an EXTRAORDINARY PROVIDENCE, which fupplied all the difadvantages of the OMISSION. Under a *common and unequal* Providence, RELIGION cannot fubfift without the doctrine of a future ftate: for Religion implying a juft retribution of reward and punifhment, which under fuch a Providence is not difpenfed, a future ftate muft needs fubvene, to prevent the whole Edifice from falling into ruin. And thus we account for the *fact*, which his Lordfhip fo amply acknowledges, viz. *that the doctrine of a future ftate was moft ufeful to* ALL *Religions, and therefore incorporated into* ALL *the Religions of Paganifm.* But where an EXTRAORDINARY Providence is adminiftered, good and evil are exactly diftributed; and therefore, in this circumftance, a FUTURE STATE is not neceffary for the fupport of Religion. It is not to be found in the Mofaic Oeconomy; yet this Oeconomy fubfifted for many ages; Religion therefore did not need it; or in other words, it was fupported by an EXTRAORDINARY PROVIDENCE.

This is the argument of the *Divine Legation.* And now, let us confider his Lordfhip's prefent attempt to evade it.

Shall we fay, that an Hypothefis of future rewards and punifhments was ufelefs amongft a people who lived under a THEOCRACY, *and that the future Judge of other People was their immediate Judge and King, who refided in the midft of them, and who dealt out rewards and punifhments on every occafion?* WHY THEN WERE SO MANY PRECAUTIONS *taken?* &c.

Firft, let me obferve, that the PRECAUTIONS here objected to, are intended for an infinuation againft the truth of Mofes's Promife of an *extraordi-*

nary

nary Providence. A kind of SOPHISM which his Lordſhip advances, and only holds in common with the reſt who have written againſt the *Divine Legation:* and which I ſhall here, after much forbearance on my part, expoſe as it deſerves.

MOSES affirms again and again, that his People were under an *extraordinary Providence.* He affirms it indeed; but as it is not a ſelf evident truth, it needs to be proved. Till then, the Unbeliever is at liberty to urge any circumſtance in the Jewiſh Law or Hiſtory, which may ſeem to bring the *reality* of that Providence into queſtion : The ſame liberty too, has the Believer ; if, at leaſt, he can perſuade himſelf to make uſe of it ; as many, ſo profeſſing themſelves, have done both in their Writings and Diſcourſings againſt the *Divine Legation.* Things were in this train, when I undertook the defence of MOSES : And to obviate all objections to the Legiſlator's credit, ariſing from any doubtful or unfavourable circumſtance in the Law or Hiſtory of the Jews concerning this *extraordinary Providence,* I advanced the INTERNAL ARGUMENT of the OMISSION. An argument which neceſſarily inferred " that an extraordinary Providence was in fact adminiſtered in the Jewiſh Republic." What change did this make in the ſtate of the caſe ? A very great one. Unbelievers were now indeed at liberty, and Believers too, if ſo perverſely inclined, to oppoſe, and, as they could, to confute the Argument of the *Divine Legation :* But by no rules of good Logic could they come over again with thoſe ſcripture-difficulties to Moſes's credit, which the argument of the *Divine Legation* had entirely obviated, and which it ſtill continued to exclude, ſo long as it remained unanſwered. For while a demonſtrated truth ſtands good, no difficulties ariſing

2

ſing

sing from it, however inexplicable, can have any weight against that superior evidence. Not to admit this fundamental maxim of common sense, would be to unsettle many a physical and mathematical demonstration, as well as this *moral* one.

I say therefore, as things now stand, To oppose difficulties against the administration of an extraordinary Providence, after that Providence has been proved, and before the proof has been confuted, is the most palpable and barefaced imposition on our understanding. In which however, his Lordship is but one of a hundred: and truly, in this, the least indecent and inconsistent of the hundred; as his declared purpose is to destroy the credit and authority of the Jewish Lawgiver.

I shall not however decline to examine the weight of these objections, tho' they be so vainly and sophistically obtruded.

If there was this EXTRAORDINARY Providence administered, says his Lordship, *Why so many Precautions taken? Why was a solemn covenant made with God as with a temporal Prince? Why were so many promises and threatnings of rewards and punishments, temporal indeed, but future and contingent, as we find in the Book of Deuteronomy, most pathetically held out by Moses?* This difficulty is not hard to be resolved. We find throughout that Book which we Believers are wont to call the *History of Providence*, but which his Lordship is pleased to intitle, *Tales more extravagant than those of Amadis de Gaule*, that God, in his moral Government of the World, always employs human means, as far as those means will go; and never interposes with his *extraordinary Providence*, but when they will go no further. To do
otherwise,

otherwife, would be an unneceffary wafte of Miracles; better fitted to confound our knowledge of NATURE, by obfcuring the harmony of order, in fuch a control of its delegated Powers, than to make manifeft the prefence of its fovereign Lord and Mafter. This method in God's moral Government, all our ideas of Wifdom feem to fupport. Now when He, the great Director of the Univerfe, had decreed to rule the Jewifh People in an extraordinary way, he did not propofe to fuperfede any of the meafures of civil regimen. And this, I hope, will be efteemed a fufficient anfwer to—WHY SO MANY PRECAUTIONS TAKEN, &c. But the Reader will find this argument drawn out more at large, in my remarks on the fame kind of fophiftry employed by Dr. SYKES.

But (fays his Lordfhip) *would the hypothefis of a future ftate have been ufelefs,* &c.? *Would there* (as his Lordfhip goes on) *have been any more impropriety in holding out thofe* [fanctions] *of one kind than thofe of another, becaufe the fupreme Being, who difpofed and ordered both, was in a particular manner prefent amongft them? Would an addition of rewards and punifhments, (more remote, but eternal, and in all refpects far greater) to the catalogue, have had no effect? I think neither of thefe things can be faid.* His Lordfhip totally miftakes the drift of the Argument of the *Divine Legation,* which infers no more, from the fact of the *omiffion,* than this, That the Jewifh Oeconomy, adminiftered by an *extraordinary* Providence, could do without the fervice of the *omitted* Doctrine; not, that that Doctrine, even under fuch a Difpenfation, was *of no ufe,* much lefs that it was IMPROPER. But then one of his Followers, will be ready to fay, " If a *future ftate* was not *improper,* much more if it was of

ufe,

ufe, under an extraordinary difpenfation, How came MOSES not to give it?" I reply, for great and wife ends of Providence vaftly countervailing the ufe of that Doctrine, which, in the laft volume of this work, will be explained at large.

Lord Bolingbroke proceeds next to tell us, what occurs to Him, concerning the REASONS of the *omiffion*; and previoufly affures us, he is *not over folicitous about their weight*. This, I fuppofe, is to make his *Counters* pafs current: For then they become the *money of fools*, as Hobbes expreffes it, when we ceafe to be *folicitous* about their worth; when we try them by their colour, not their weight; their Rhetoric, and not their Logic. However this muft be faid with an exception to the firft, which is altogether logical, and very diverting.

If (fays his Lordfhip) *the doctrine of the immortality of the foul and a future ftate had been revealed to Mofes, that he might teach them to the Ifraelites, he would have taught them moft certainly. But he did not teach them. They were, therefore, not revealed.* It is in mood and figure, you fee; and, I warrant you, defigned to fupply what was wanting in the *Divine Legation:* Tho' as the Author of that book certainly believed, thefe *doctrines were not revealed*, 'tis ten to one but he thought Mofes was not at liberty to teach them: Unlefs you can fuppofe that his Lordfhip, who believed nothing of Revelation, might believe Mofes to be reftrained from teaching what God had not revealed to him; and yet, that the Author of the *Divine Legation*, who held Mofes's pretenfions to be true, might think him at liberty to go beyond his Commiffion. Thus far,

far, then, we may be faid to agree: But this good
underftanding does not laft long.　His Lordfhip's
modefty and my *pertnefs* foon make the breach as
wide as ever. — *Why they were not fo revealed*
(fays his Lordfhip) *fome* PERT DIVINE *or other will
be ready to tell you.　For me, I dare not pretend to
guefs.*　My forwardnefs, and his Lordfhip's back-
wardnefs, are equally well fuited to our refpective
principles.　Should his Lordfhip have guefTed, it
might have brought him to what he moft dreaded,
the divine original of the Jewifh Religion: Had I
forborn to guefs, I had betrayed my caufe, and
left thofe DATA unemployed, which enabled me, I
do not fay to guefs, but to difeover, and to *demon-
firate the Divine Legation of Mofes.*

»However, *This*, his Lordfhip *will prefume to advance, that fince thefe doctrines were not revealed by God
to his fervant* MOSES, *it is highly probable, that the
Legiflator made a fcruple of teaching them to the Ifraelites, howfoever well inftructed he might be in them
himfelf, and howfoever ufeful to Government he might
think them.*

Here, you fee, he perfonates a Believer, who
holds MOSES to be an infpired Lawgiver: But obferve how poorly he fuftains his part! Either Moses did indeed receive the LAW from God, or he
did not.　If he did not, Why are we mocked with
the diftinction between what was revealed, and what
was not revealed, when nothing was revealed? If
MOSES did receive the *Law* from God, Why are we
ftill worfe mocked with the diftinction between
what was revealed, and what was not revealed,
when every thing regarding the Difpenfation muft
needs be revealed; as well, the direction to omit

a Future

a Future State, as the direction to *inculcate the Unity of the Godhead?* Why was all this mockery? the Reader afks. For a very good purpofe : it was to draw us from the TRUE object of our inquiry, which is, What GOD intended by the *omiffion* ; to that FANTASTIC object, which only refpects, what MOSES intended by it. For the intention of GOD fuppofes the miffion and infpiration of a Prophet ; but the intention of MOSES, when confidered in contradiftinction to the intention of God, terminates in the human views of a mere politic Lawgiver; which leads us back again to Infidelity.

But he foon ftrips Mofes of his Miffion, and leaves him to cool, in Querpo, under his civil character as before. And here he confiders, What it was, which, under this character, might induce Mofes to *omit* a future ftate ; and he finds it to be, left this doctrine fhould have hurt the doctrine of the UNITY, which it was his purpofe to inculcate amongft his People, in oppofition to the Egyptian Polytheifm.

Mofes (fays his Lordfhip) *it is highly probable, made a fcruple of teaching thefe Doctrines to the Ifraelites, howfoever well inftructed he might be in them himfelf, and howfoever ufeful to Government he might think them. The People of Egypt, like all other nations, were Polytheifts, but different from all others : there was in Egypt an inward as well as outward Doctrine : Natural Theology and natural Religion were the* INWARD *Doctrine* ; *while Polytheifm, Idolatry, and* ALL THE MYSTERIES, *all the impieties and follies of magic, were the* OUTWARD *Doctrine. Mofes was initiated into thofe Myfteries where the fecret doctrine alone was taught, and the outward exploded.*—For an accurate as well as juft Divider commend me to

his

his Lordſhip. In diſtinguiſhing between the *inward* and *outward* doctrines of the Egyptians, he puts *all the Myſteries* amongſt the *outward:* tho' if they had an *inward*, it muſt neceſſarily be part of thoſe *Myſteries.* But he makes amends preſently, (but his amends to truth is, as it ſhould be, always at the expence of a contradiction) and directly ſays, that Moses LEARNT THE INWARD DOCTRINE IN THE MYSTERIES. Let this paſs: He proceeds— *Moſes had the knowledge of both outward and inward. Not ſo the Iſraelites in general. They knew nothing more than the outſide of the Religion of Egypt. And if a future ſtate was known to them, it was known only in the ſuperſtitious rites, and with all the fabulous circumſtances, in which it was dreſſed up and preſented to the vulgar belief. It would be hard therefore to teach or to renew this doctrine in the minds of the Iſraelites, without giving them an occaſion the more to recal the Polytheiſtical fables, and practiſe the idolatrous rites they had learnt during the Captivity.*

The Children of Iſrael, it ſeems, *knew no more of a future ſtate, than by the ſuperſtitious rites and fabulous circumſtances with which it was dreſſed up and preſented to the public belief.* What then? Moses, he owns, *knew more.* And what hindered Moses from communicating of his knowledge to the People, when he took them under his protection, and gave them a new Law and a new Religion? His Lordſhip gives us to underſtand that this People knew as little of the UNITY; for he tells us, it was amongſt the *inward* Doctrines of the Egyptians: yet this did not hinder Moſes from inſtructing his people in the doctrine of the Unity. What then ſhould hinder his teaching them the *inward* doctrine of a future ſtate, diveſted of its fabulous circumſtances? He had diveſted *Religious worſhip* of the
abſurdities

abfurdities of Demi-Gods and Heroes; What
fhould hinder him from divefting a *future ftate* of
Charon's boat and the Elyfian fields? But the notion of a future ftate would have recalled thofe fabulous circumftances which had been long connected with it. And was not Religious worfhip,
under the idea of a *tutelar Deity*, and a *temporal King*,
much more apt to recal the polythcifm of Egypt?
Yet Mofes ventured upon this inconvenience, for
the fake of great advantages: Why fhould he not
venture on the other, for the fake of greater? for
the doctrine of a future ftate, is, as his Lordfhip
confeffes, even neceffary both to civil and religious
Society. But what does he talk of the danger of
giving entry to the fables and fuperftitions concerning the Soul (fuperftitions, which, tho' learnt
indeed in the Captivity, were common to all the
nations under Polytheifm) when in other places he
affures us, that Mofes indulged the Ifraelites in
the moft characteriftic fuperftitions of Egypt?

However, let us fee how he fupports this profound obfervation. *Rites and Ceremonies* (fays his
Lordfhip) *are often fo equivocal, that they may be applied to very different doctrines. But when they are
fo clofely connected with a doctrine, that they are not
applicable to another, to teach the doctrine, is,* IN
SOME SORT, *to teach the rites and ceremonies.*—*In fome
fort,* is well put in, to foften the deformity of this
inverted logic. His point is to fhew that a fuperftitious Rite, relating to, and dependent on, a
certain Doctrine, will obtrude itfelf whenever that
Doctrine is taught: and his reafoning is only cal-
culated to prove, that where the Rite is practifed,
the Doctrine will foon follow. This may indeed
be true. But then it does not hold in the converfe,
that the Rite follows the Doctrine: becaufe a Principal

cipal may ſtand without its Dependent; but a Dependent can never ſubſiſt without its Principal.

Under cover of theſe groteſque ſhapes, into which his Lordſhip has traveſtied the Jewiſh Law-giver, he concludes, that MOSES *being* AT LIBER-TY *to teach this doctrine of rewards and puniſhments in a future ſtate, or not to teach it, he might very well chuſe the latter*—Yet it was but at the very begin-ning of this paragraph that he tells us, *Moſes was* NOT AT LIBERTY *to teach or not to teach.* His words are theſe, *Since this doctrine was not revealed by God to his ſervant Moſes, it is highly probable that this Legiſlator* MADE A SCRUPLE *of teaching it.* But his Lordſhip very well knows that Stateſmen ſoon get the better of their *ſcruples*; and then, by an-other fetch of political caſuiſtry, find themſelves more at liberty than ever.

I had obſerved above that our noble Diſcourſer, who makes MOSES ſo *ſcrupulous* that he would, on no terms, afford a handle for one ſingle ſuperſtition of Egypt to get footing among his people ; has, on other occaſions, charged him with introducing them in the lump. He was ſenſible that his In-conſiſtency was likely to be detected, and therefore he now attempts to obviate it.—*Tho' he* [Moſes] *indulged the Iſraelites, on account of the hardneſs of their hearts, and by the divine permiſſion, as it is pre-ſumed, in ſeveral obſervations and cuſtoms, which did not* LEAD *directly, tho' even they did ſo perhaps* IN CON-SEQUENCE, *to the Polytheiſm and Idolatry of Egypt.* And could the teaching the doctrine of a future ſtate poſſibly do more than LEAD IN CONSEQUENCE, (as his Lordſhip elegantly expreſſes it) *to the Poly-theiſm and Idolatry of Egypt*, by drawing after it thoſe *ſuperſtitious Rites and fabulous circumſtances* which,

which, he tells us, then attended the popular notion of fuch a State? If, for the *hardnefs of their
hearts*, they were indulged in *feveral obfervances
and cuftoms*, which only *led in confequence* to Polytheifm and Idolatry, Why, for the *fame* hardnefs
of heart, were they not indulged with the doctrine of a future ftate, which did not lead, but by
a very remote confequence, to Polytheifm and Idolatry? Efpecially fince this *hardnefs of heart* would
lefs bear denying them a DOCTRINE fo alluring to
the human mind, than denying them a RITE, to
which habit only and old cuftom had given an
occafional propenfity. Again, thofe Rites indulged to the People, for the *hardnefs of their hearts*,
had, in themfelves, little ufe or tendency to advance the ends of the Jewifh Difpenfation; but
rather retarded them: Whereas a future ftate, by
his Lordfhip's own confeffion, is *moft ufeful to all
Religions, and therefore incorporated into all the Syftems of Paganifm*; and was particularly ufeful to
the Ifraelites, who were, he fays, both a *rebellious*
and a *fuperftitious* People: difpofitions, which not
only made it neceffary to omit nothing that might
inforce obedience, but likewife facilitated the reception and fupported the influence of the doctrine
in queftion.

The Reader has here the whole of his Lordfhip's
boafted Solution of this important Circumftance of
the OMISSION, in the Mofaic Law. And he fees how
vainly this Refolver of doubts labours to elude its
force. Overwhelmed, as it were, with the weight
of fo irrefiftible a Power, after long wriggling to
get free, he at length crawls forth; but fo maimed
and broken, fo impotent and fretful, that all his
remaining ftrength is in his venom. And this, he
now fheds in abundance over the whole Mofaic

Oeconomy. It is pronounced to be a grofs impofture; and this very circumftance of the OMISSION is given as an undoubted proof of the accufation.

—" Can we be furprifed then (fays his Lord-
" fhip) that the Jews afcribed to the all-perfeƈt
" Being, on various occafions, fuch a conduƈt and
" fuch Laws as are inconfiftent with his moft
" obvious perfeƈtions? Can we believe fuch a
" conduƈt and fuch Laws to have been his, on
" the word of the proudeft and moft lying Na-
" tion in the world ? Many other confiderations
" might have their place here. But I fhall con-
" fine myfelf to one; *which I do not remember to*
" *have feen nor heard urged on one fide, nor* ANTI-
" CIPATED *on the other*. To fhew then, the more
" evidently, how ABSURD, as well as IMPIOUS it
" is to afcribe thefe Mofaical Laws to God, let it
" be confidered, that NEITHER the people of
" Ifrael, nor their Legiflator perhaps, KNEW ANY
" THING OF ANOTHER LIFE, wherein the crimes
" committed in this life are to be punifhed. Al-
" tho' he might have learned this Doƈtrine, which
" was not fo much a fecret doƈtrine, as it may be
" prefumed that the Unity of the fupreme God
" was, amongft the Egyptians. Whether he had
" learned both or either, or neither of them in
" thofe fchools, cannot be determined: BUT
" THIS MAY BE ADVANCED WITH ASSURANCE;
" If MOSES knew, that crimes, and therefore Ido-
" latry, one of the greateft, were to be punifhed
" in another life, he deceived the people in the
" Covenant they made, by his intervention, with
" God. If he did not know it, I fay it with
" horror, the confequence, *according to the hypo-*
" *thefis I oppofe*, muft be, that God deceived
" both him and them. In either cafe, a cove-
                                    " nant

" nant or bargain was made, wherein, the con-
" ditions of obedience and difobedience were not
" fully, nor by confequence, fairly ftated. The
" Ifraelites had better things to hope, and worfe
" to fear, than thofe which were exprefied in it:
" and their whole hiftory feems to fhew how much
" need they had of thefe additional motives to
" reftrain them from Polytheifm and Idolatry, and
" to anfwer the affumed Purpofes of divine Provi-
" dence ª."

This argument, *advanced with* fo much *affurance,*
his Lordfhip fays, he does *not remember to have feen,
or heard urged on one fide, nor anticipated on the other.*
A gentle reproof, as we are to underftand it, of
the Author of the *Divine Legation:* for none but
He, I think, could *anticipate* an objection to an
ARGUMENT which none but He had employed.
However, tho' it be now too late to *anticipate,*
we have ftill time enough to anfwer.

Let it be confidered (fays his Lordfhip) *that perhaps
Mofes* KNEW NOTHING *of another life, wherein the
crimes committed in this life are to be punifhed.* —*Confidered* by whom ? Not by his Lordfhip, or his kind
Readers: for his former reafoning, which I will here
again repeat, had brought them to *confider* otherwife.
Thefe are his words: " Many probable reafons might
" be brought to fhew, that this was an Egyptian
" doctrine before the exode; and this particularly,
" that it was propagated from Egypt, fo foon at
" leaft afterwards, by all thofe who were inftruct-
" ed LIKE MOSES, in the wifdom of that People.
" He tranfported much of this wifdom into the
" fcheme of Religion and Government which he

ª Vol. v. p. 194—5.

D d 2 " gave

" gave the Iſraelites ; and, among other things,
" certain Rites, which SEEM TO ALLUDE, OR
" HAVE A REMOTE RELATION TO, THIS DOC-
" TRINE ᵇ." This poſſibly might have recurred to
his Lordſhip, while he was boaſting of his new
and *unanticipated* objection ; and therefore, in the
tricking it up amongſt his FRAGMENTS, to his *per-*
haps, he adds, by a very happy corrective, *altho'*
Moſes might have learnt this Doctrine, which WAS
NOT SO MUCH A SECRET *doctrine, as it may be pre-*
ſumed that the Unity of the ſupreme God was amongſt
the Egyptians. But he had done better to leave
his contradictions uncorrected, and truſt to the
rare ſagacity of his Readers to find them out. He
had ever an ill hand at reconciling matters ; ſo in
the caſe before us, in the very act of covering one
contradiction, he commits another. He is here
ſpeaking of a future ſtate, diveſted of its fabulous
circumſtances ; *Perhaps*, ſays he, MOSES KNEW
NOTHING OF ANOTHER LIFE—*Which was* NOT SO
MUCH A SECRET *doctrine as that of the Unity.*
Now, Reader, turn back a moment, to the long
quotation from his 239th page, and there thou wilt
find, that a future ſtate, diveſted of its fabulous
circumſtances, WAS AS MUCH A SECRET *Doctrine,*
as that of the Unity.—" There is reaſon to believe,
" that natural Theology and natural Religion were
" INWARD doctrines amongſt the Egyptians.
" MOSES might be let into a knowledge of BOTH
" by being initiated into thoſe *Myſteries* where the
" *ſecret* doctrine alone was taught. But we can-
" not imagine, that the Children of Iſrael in
" general enjoyed the ſame privilege. No, *they*
" *knew nothing more than the outſide* of the Egyp-
" tian Religion : and if the *Doctrine we ſpeak of*

ᵇ Vol. v. p. 328—9.

I

" [A FUTURE STATE] was known to them, it was
" known only in the fuperftitious Rites, and with
" all the fabulous circumftances, in which it was
" dreffed up and prefented to vulgar belief."—Is
not this, now, a plain declaration, that a *future
ftate*, divefted of its fabulous circumftances, *was
as much a fecret Doctrine as the doctrine of the Unity?*

But his Lordfhip's contradictions are the leaft of
my concern. It is his prefent Argument I have
now to do with. And this, he fays, he *advances*
WITH ASSURANCE. It is fit he fhould. *Modefty*
would be very ill beftowed on fuch opinions.

He thinks he can reduce thofe who hold no future ftate in the Jewifh Oeconomy, to the neceffity of owning, that MOSES, *or that* GOD *himfelf,
acted unfairly by the Ifraelites.* How fo, You afk?
Becaufe One or Other of them concealed that *ftate.*
And what if they did? Why then they concealed
one of the actual Sanctions of moral conduct, *future punifhment.* But who told him, that this,
which, he confeffes, was no fanction of the *Jewifh
Law,* was yet a Sanction in the moral conduct of
the *Jewifh People?* Who, unlefs the ARTIFICIAL
THEOLOGER? the man he moft defpifes and de-
cries.

And, even in *artifical Theology,* there is nothing
but the CALVINISTICAL tenet of *Original Sin,*
which gives the leaft countenance to fo monftrous
an opinion; every thing in the GOSPEL, every
thing in NATURAL THEOLOGY, exclaims againft
it.

JESUS, indeed, to prove that the departed Ifraelites ftill exifted, quotes the title God was pleafed

D d 3   to

to give himſelf, of *the God of Abraham, Iſaac, and Jacob*; and this, together with their *exiſtence*, proves likewiſe the *happineſs* of their condition: for the relation they are ſaid to ſtand in with God, ſhews them to be of his Kingdom. But we muſt remember, that the queſtion with his Lordſhip is, not of *reward*, but *puniſhment*. Again, JESUS ſpeaks, (indeed in a parable) of the deceaſed *rich man*, as *in a place of torment*. But we muſt remember that the ſcene was laid at a time when the Doctrine of a *future ſtate* was become national. To know our heavenly maſter's ſentiments on the queſtion of *ſubjection to an unknown Sanction*, we ſhould do well to conſider his words, " The ſervant which " knew his Lord's will, and prepared not himſelf, " neither did according to his will, ſhall be beaten " with many ſtripes; but he that knew not, and " did commit things worthy of ſtripes, ſhall be " beaten with few ſtripes[c]." Now the will of a Maſter or Sovereign, declared in his Laws, never includes in it more than the *Sanctions* of thoſe Laws. The Author of the Epiſtle to the *Hebrews* expreſly diſtinguiſhes the ſanction of the Jewiſh law from that of the Goſpel; and makes the difference to conſiſt in this, that the one was of *temporal* puniſhments, and the other of *future*. *He that deſpiſed Moſes's Law* DIED *without mercy under two or three witneſſes. Of how* MUCH SORER PUNISHMENT, *ſuppoſe ye, ſhall he be thought worthy who hath trodden under foot the ſon of God[d]?* Which appeal is without common ſenſe or honeſty, on a ſuppoſition that the apoſtle held the Jews to be ſubject to *future* puniſhments, before that Sanction was promulged amongſt them. From the GOSPEL therefore it cannot be inferred, that the Iſraelites,

---

[c] Luke xii. ver. 47—8.　　　[d] Chap. x. ver. 28—9.

while

while only following the Law of Mofes, in which the fanction of a *future ftate* is not found, were liable or fubject to the punifhments of that ftate.

Let us fee next, Whether NATURAL THEOLOGY, or *natural Religion* (as his Lordfhip is pleafed, for fome reafon or other, to diftinguifh the terms) hath taught us, that a people, living under an *extraordinary Providence* or the immediate government of God, to whom he had given a Law and revealed a Religion, both fupported by *temporal* fanctions only, could be deemed fubject to thofe *future* punifhments, unknown to them, which *natural* Religion before, and *revealed* Religion fince, have difcovered to be due to bad men living under a *common Providence*.

NATURAL RELIGION ftandeth on this Principle, " That the Governor of the Univerfe REWARDS " and PUNISHES moral Agents." The length or fhortnefs of human exiftence comes not primarily into the idea of Religion; not even into that compleat idea of Religion delivered by St. Paul, in his general definition of it. The Religionift, fays he, *muft believe that God is, and that he* IS A RE-WARDER *of thofe who feek him.*

While God exactly diftributed his rewards and punifhments *here*, the light of reafon directed men to look no further for the Sanctions of his Laws. But when it came to be feen, that He was *not always* a Rewarder and a Punifher *here*, men neceffarily concluded, from his moral attributes, that he would be fo, *hereafter:* and confequently, that this life was but a fmall portion of the human duration. Men had not yet fpeculated on the

perma-

permanent nature of the Soul: And when they did fo, that confideration, which, under an *ordinary* Providence came ftrongly in aid of the *moral argument* for another life, had no tendency, under the *extraordinary*, to open to them the profpects of *futurity*: becaufe, tho' they faw the Soul unaffected by thofe caufes which brought the body to deftruction, yet they held it to be equally dependent on the Will of the Creator: Who, amongft the various means of its diffolution, (of which they had no idea) had, for aught they knew, provided one, or more than one, for that purpofe.

In this manner was a FUTURE STATE brought, by natural light, into Religion: and from thenceforth, became a neceffary part of it. But under the Jewifh THEOCRACY, God was an exact Rewarder and Punifher, *here*. Natural light therefore evinced that under fuch an adminiftration, the fubjects of it did not become liable to *future* Punifhments till this fanction was known amongft them.

Thus NATURAL and REVEALED RELIGION fhew, that his Lordfhip calumniated both, when he affirmed, that, *according to the hypothefis he oppofed*, MOSES DECEIVED *the people in the Covenant they made, by his intervention, with God: Or that, if Mofes did not know the doctrine of a future ftate, then* GOD DECEIVED *both him and them.*

Should it be afked, how God will deal with wicked men thus dying under the Mofaic Difpenfation? I will anfwer, in the words of Dr. SAM. CLARKE, on a like occafion. He had demonftrated a felfmoving Subftance to be immaterial, and fo, not perifhable like Bodies. But, as this demonftra-

tion

tion included the Souls of irrational animals, it was
aſked, " How theſe were to be diſpoſed of, when
they had left their reſpective habitations ?" To
which he very properly replies, " Certainly, the
" omnipotent and infinitely wiſe God may, with-
" out any great difficulty, be ſuppoſed to have
" more ways of diſpoſing of his Creatures" [I add,
with perfect juſtice and equity, and with equal
meaſure, to all his creatures as well accountable
as unaccountable] " than we are, at preſent, let in
" to the ſecret of ᵉ." — But if the Author of the
Divine Legation has not promiſed more than he can
perform (as his long delay gives his well-wiſhers
cauſe to ſuſpect and his ill-wiſhers to hope) this
matter will be explained at large, in his account
of the SCRIPTURE DOCTRINE OF THE REDEMPTION,
which, he has told us, is to have a place in his
laſt Volume.

Nothing now remains of this objection but
what relates to the ſanction of *future rewards* :
And I would by no means deprive the faithful
Iſraelites of theſe. His Lordſhip therefore has
this to make his beſt of : and, in his opinion, the beſtowing even of a *reward*, to which
one has no title, is foul dealing ; for he joins it
with *puniſhment*, as if his conſequence, againſt
God's juſtice and goodneſs, might be equally deduced from either of them. — *A covenant* ſays he,
*was made, wherein the conditions of obedience and
diſobedience were not* FULLY, *nor, by conſequence,*
FAIRLY *ſtated. The Iſraelites had* BETTER THINGS
TO HOPE, *and worſe to fear than thoſe which were ex-
preſſed in it.* Tho' it be hard on a generous *Bene-
factor* to be denied the right of giving more than

ᵉ Octavo Tracts againſt Dodwell and Collins, p. 103.

he

he had promifed ; it is ftill harder on the poor *Dependant*, that he is not at liberty to receive more. True it is, that, in this cafe, the conditions are not FULLY ftated ; and therefore, according to his Lordfhip's Logic, BY CONSEQUENCE NOT FAIRLY. To ftrengthen this Confequence, his Lordfhip concludes in thefe words — *And their whole Hiftory feems to fhew how much need they had of thefe additional motives* [future Rewards and Punifhments] *to reftrain them from Polytheifm and Idolatry, and to anfwer the* ASSUMED *purpofes of Divine Providence.*

Whoever puts all thefe things together—" That Mofes was himfelf of the race of Ifrael — was learned in all the wifdom of Egypt — and capable of freeing his People from their Yoke — that he brought them within fight of the promifed Land ; a fertile Country, which they were to conquer and inhabit—that he inftituted a fyftem of Laws, which has been the admiration of the wifeft men of all ages—that he underftood the doctrine of a FUTURE STATE : and, by his knowledge gained in Egypt, was not ignorant of the efficacy of it in general ; and by his full experience of the rebellious and fuperftitious temper of his own People, could not but fee how ufeful it would have been to them in particular." — Whoever, I fay, puts all thefe things together (and all thefe things are amongft his Lordfhip's CONCESSIONS) and at the fame time confiders, that MOSES, throughout his whole fyftem of Law and Religion, is entirely filent concerning a future ftate of Rewards and Punifhments, will, I believe, conclude, that there was fomething more in the OMISSION than Lord Bo-LINGBROKE could fathom, or, at leaft, was willing to difcover.

But

But let us turn from Moses's conduct, (which will be elsewhere confidered at large) to his Lord-ship's, which is our prefent bufinefs.

1. Firft, he gives us his conjectures, to account for the *Omiſſion*, exclufive of Moses's *Divine Legation :* but, as if diſſatisfied with them himfelf (which he well might be, for they deftroy one an-other)

2. He next attempts, You fee, to prove, that the *Legation* could not be *divine,* from this very circumftance of the *omiſſion.*

3. But now he will go further, and demonftrate that an EXTRAORDINARY PROVIDENCE, fuch a one as is reprefented by Mofes, and which, the Author of the *Divine Legation* has proved, from the circumftance of the OMISSION, was actually adminiftered in the Jewifh Republic, could not poffibly be adminiftered, without deftroying *free will*; without *making Virtue fervile* ; and without *relaxing univerfal benevolence.*

4. And laftly, to make all fure, he fhuts up the account by fhewing, that an *extraordinary* Providence could anfwer no reafonable end or purpofe.

In his firft and laft order of evafions, he feems to be alone ; but in the fecond and third, he had the pleafure of feeing, many an orthodox Writer againft the Divine Legation, in CONFEDERACY with him, to ufe his Lordfhip's language, when he fpeaks of the good underftanding between DIVINES, and ATHEISTS.

I have examined his firft and fecond order. The third and fourth remain to be confidered ; it is the laft refuge of his infidelity.

1. His

1. His principal objection to the adminiſtration of an extraordinary Providence, ſuch as MOSES promiſed to his people, on the part of GOD, is, that it would DESTROY FREE-WILL. But here let me obſerve, that he affects to diſguiſe the immediate Object of his attack; and, in arguing againſt an *extraordinary Providence*, chuſes to conſider it in the general, as the Point riſes out of an imaginary diſpute between Himſelf and the Divines; who, he pretends, are diſſatisfied with the preſent order of things, and require, as the terms of their acquieſcence in God's government, the adminiſtration of an *equal Providence, here.* But, this obliquity in diſguiſing the true object of his attack, not being of itſelf ſufficient to embarras the queſtion, he further ſupports it by a prevarication: for it is not true, that Divines are diſſatisfied with the preſent order of things, or that they require a better. All the ground they ever gave his Lordſhip for imputing this ſcandal to them, being only their aſſertion, " That if the preſent ſtate be the whole of Man's exiſtence, then the juſtice of God would have more exactly diſpenſed good and evil *here:* but, as he has not done ſo, it follows, that there will be a ſtate of Rewards and Puniſhments *hereafter.*"

This premiſed, I proceed to his firſt objection,— " In good earneſt (ſays his Lordſhip) is a ſyſtem " of particular providences, in which the ſupreme " Being, or his Angels, like his Miniſters to re- " ward, and his Executioners to puniſh, are con- " ſtantly employed in the affairs of mankind, " much more reaſonable?" [than the *Gods* of EPICURUS or the *morals* of POLEMO] " Would the " JUSTICE of God be more MANIFEST in ſuch a " ſtate of things than in the preſent? I ſee no room

" room for MERIT on the part of Man, nor for
" JUSTICE on the part of God, in such a state [f]."

His Lordship asks, *whether the Justice of God
would be more manifest* in such a state of things,
where good is constantly dispensed to the virtuous,
and evil to the wicked, *than in the present*, where
good and evil happen indifferently to all men? If
his Lordship, by *the present state of things*, includes the rectification of them in a future state,
I answer, that the *justice of God would not be more
manifest*, but equally and fully manifest in either
case. If his Lordship does not include this rectification in a future state, then I answer his question by another: Would the Justice of the Civil
Magistrate be more manifest, where he exactly dis-
penses rewards to good men, and punishment to
evil, than where he suffers the Cunning and the
Powerful to carve for themselves?

But *he sees no room for merit on the part of Man,
nor Justice on the part of God.* If he does not see,
it is his own fault. It is owing to his prevaricat-
ing both with himself and his Reader; to the turning his view from the Scripture-representation of an
equal Providence, to the iniquities of Calvinistical
election, and to the partialities of Fanatics concerning the favoured workings of the Spirit; and
to his giving these to the reader, in its stead.
How dextrously does he slide *Enthusiasm* and *Pre-
destination* into the Scripture-doctrine of an equal
Providence!—*If some men were* DETERMINED TO
GOODNESS *by the secret workings of the spirit*, &c.
Yes indeed, if you will be so kind to allow him,
that under an equal Providence, the Will is over-
ruled, he will be able to shew you, there is an end

[f] Vol. v. p. 425—6.

of

of all merit and demerit. . But this fubftituting ARTIFICIAL THEOLOGY (as he calls it when he is in an humour to abufe it) in the place of bible-theology, is his ufual leger-de-main. So again,— *I can conceive ftill lefs, that individual Creatures before they have done either good or evil, nay, before their actual exiftence, can be the objects of predilection or. averfion, of love or hatred, to God.* Who, of the Gofpel-Divines, againft whom he is here writing, would have him *conceive* any thing of this at all? It is the ARTIFICIAL THEOLOGER, the depraver, as he fays, of the Gofpel, who would draw him into fo abfurd a fyftem. But what has this exploded *Theology*, that abounds only in human inventions, to do with the extraordinary Providence, reprefented in holy Writ! To fay, that this Providence takes away man's merit and God's juftice, is confounding all our ideas of right and wrong. Is it not the higheft merit of a rational creature to comply with that motive which has moft real weight? And is not God's juftice then moft manifeft when the order of things prefent feweft difficulties and obfcurites in our contemplation of it? His Lordfhip was plainly in thefe fentiments,. when, arguing againft God's compliance with the Jewifh *hardnefs of heart*, he thought it more becoming the Mafter of the Univerfe, to bend the perverfe ftiffnefs of their Wills: and, when, arguing againft a *future ftate* from the prefent good order of things, he will fhew, he fays, AGAINST DIVINES AND ATHEISTS IN CONJUNCTION, that there is little or no irregularity in the prefent difpenfations of Providence; at leaft, not fo much as the World commonly imagine. And why was this paradox advanced, but from a confcioufnefs that the more exact the prefent adminiftration of God's providence appeared, the more manifeft it made

made his Juftice ? But now his Lordfhip's followers may be apt to fay, that their Mafter has here
done no more, indeed fcarce fo much, at leaft not
in fo exprefs terms, as a celebrated Prelate, in one
of his *difcourfes* at the *Temple*; who tells us, " That
" an immediate and vifible interpofition of Pro-
" vidence in Behalf of the righteous, and for
" the punifhment of the wicked, would INTER-
" FERE WITH THE FREEDOM OF MORAL AGENTS,
" AND NOT LEAVE ROOM FOR THEIR TRYAL [s]."
But they who object this to us, have not confidered the nature of moral differences. For, as another learned Prelate well obferves, *A little experience may convince us, that the fame thing, at different
times, is not the fame* [h]. Now if *different times* may
make fuch alterations in identity, what muft *different men* do ? The *thing faid* being by all candid
interpretation to be regulated on the *purpofe of faying*.

2. Lord Bolingbroke's fecond objeÆtion againft
an equal Providence is, that it would MAKE VIR-
TUE, SERVILE.——" If the Good, befides the
" enjoyment of all that happinefs which is infepa-
" rable from Virtue, were exempted from all
" kinds of evil, and if the Wicked, befides all
" thofe evils which are infeparable from Vice,
" and thofe which happen to all men in the or-
" dinary courfe of events, were expofed to others
" that the hand of God inflicted on them in an
" extraordinary manner, fuch Good men would
" have VERY LITTLE MERIT; they would have,
" while they continued to be good, no other
" merit than that of children who are cajoled into

_____

[s] Vol. ii. p. 258—9.   [h] *Scripture vindicated from the
misrepresentations of the Bp. of Bangor, j. 165.*

" their

" their duty; or than that of Galley-flaves who
" ply at the oar, becaufe they hear and fee and
" fear the lafh of the boatfwain [i]."

If the perfection of a rational Creature confift
in acting according to reafon: and if his merit
rifes in proportion as he advances in perfection;
How can that ftate which beft fecures him from
acting irrationally, leffen or take away his merit?
Are the actions of the Deity of lefs worth for his
moral incapacity of being unjuft or malignant?
The motive which induces to right action is indeed
more or lefs *excellent* according to the dignity or
nature of the Agent: But the queftion here is not
concerning the *excellence*, but the *power* of the motive to turn ACTION into PASSION; which is the only
way I can conceive of deftroying *merit* in the fubject. Now I hold, that this fancy, That motives
exterior to the Being on which they work, are
able to turn an Agent to a Patient, is one of the
greateft of *Phyfical* abfurdities; and therefore
commonly goes about difguifed, in the garb of
Metaphyfics. For while AGENCY remains, MERIT
fubfifts: the degrees of which do not depend on the
lefs or greater force which the motives have on the
affections, but on the more or lefs reafon of the
choice. In a word, there is no other way of taking
away the merit and demerit of human actions,
than by taking away agency, and making MAN paf-
five, or, in other terms, A MACHINE.

But, to expofe in a more popular way the futility of this reafoning, it will be fufficient to obferve,
that the objection holds equally againft all religious Sanctions whatfoever. And fo indeed it was

[i] Vol. v. p. 428.

fairly

fairly urged by Lord Shaftſbury: who pretended that every motive regarding SELF, tended to ſervilize Virtue. Without doubt, one ſort, juſt as much as another; a *future ſtate*, juſt as well as an *equal Providence*. Nay, if we were to appreciate matters very nicely, it would ſeem, that *a future ſtate without an equal providence* (for they are alway to be conſidered ſeparately, as they belong to different Diſpenſations) would more ſtrongly incline the Will, than *an equal providence without a future ſtate:* as the value of *future* above *preſent* good is in this caſe, immenſely great. But the human mind being ſo conſtituted, that the *diſtance* of *good* takes off proportionably from its influence, this brings the force of the two ſanctions nearer to an equality; which at length proves but this, That the objection to the *merit of Virtue* holds againſt all religious ſanctions whatſoever. In the uſe of which objection, Lord Shaftſbury was not only more ingenuous, as he urged it againſt them *all*, but more conſiſtent, as he urged it on his doctrine of a perfect *diſintereſtedneſs* in our nature; whereas Lord Bolingbroke is amongſt thoſe who hold, that *ſelf-love* and *ſocial*, tho' coincident, are two eſſential principles in the human frame.

" That two conſiſtent motions act the Soul,
" And one regards ITSELF, and one the WHOLE.

But we might go further, and retort upon both theſe noble Adverſaries of Religion, that the charge of *making virtue ſervile* affects all *moral*, as well as *religious* ſanctions; as well that, whoſe exiſtence they allow, as thoſe, which they would perſuade us to be viſionary; both theſe illuſtrious Patrons of infidelity acknowledging that moral ſanction which ariſes from *God's making the practice of virtue our* INTEREST *as well as duty*[a]. Now interest and *servility* is, it seems, the same thing, with these generous Spirits, as it was with the good old woman, Joinville speaks of, amongst the Enthusiasts of Syria, who carried about a pan of live-coals in one hand, and a dish of cold water in the other, to burn up Paradise and to extinguish Hell, that men might be brought to serve God dispassionately, without hope or fear.—So near a-kin are Fanaticism and Free-thinking, that their nature betrays them even when they strive most to hide their common parentage.

His Lordship's third cavil to an equal Providence is, that it would RELAX GENERAL BENEVOLENCE.

——" But would there not be, at the same
" time, some further defects in this scheme? I
" think there would. It seems to me, that these
" good men being thus distinguished by particular
" providences, in their favour, from the rest of
" mankind, might be apt either not to contract,
" or to LOSE THAT GENERAL BENEVOLENCE,
" which is a fundamental Principle of the Law of
" Nature, and that PUBLIC SPIRIT, which is the
" life and soul of Society. God has made the
" practice of morality our interest, as well as our
" duty. But men who found themselves con-
" stantly protected from the evils that fell on
" others, might grow insensibly to think them-
" selves unconcerned in the common fate: and if
" they relaxed in their zeal for the Public good,
" they would relax in their virtue; for public
" good is the object of Virtue. They might do

[a] Vol. v. p. 429.

" worse,

" worfe, fpiritual pride might infect them. They
" might become in their own imaginations the
" little Flock, or the chofen Sheep. Others have
" been fo by the mere force of Enthufiafm, with-
" out any fuch inducements. as thofe which we
" affume, in the fame cafe; and experience has
" fhewn, that there are no Wolves like thefe
" Sheep [b]."

The *cafe affumed*, to which his Lordfhip objects,
and againft which he pretends to argue, is that of
an *equal Providence which exactly diftributes good to
Virtue, and to Vice, evil.* Now the prefent objection to fuch a ftate is, an' pleafe you, that this
favourable diftinction of good, to the virtuous man,
would be apt to *deftroy his general benevolence and
public fpirit.* Thefe, in his Lordfhip's account, and
fo in mine too, are the moft fublime of all Virtues;
and therefore, it is agreed, they will be moft highly
rewarded: But the tendency of this *favourable diftinction*, if you will believe him, may prove *the
lofs of general benevolence and public fpirit.* As
much as this fhocks common fenfe, his Lordfhip
has his reafon. *God has made the practice of morality our* INTEREST *as well as duty.* But *men, who
find themfelves conftantly protected from the evils that
fall on others, might grow infenfibly to think themfelves
unconcerned in the common fate.*

God has made the practice of morality our INTEREST
as well as duty. Without doubt he has. But does
it not continue to be our *intereft*, under an equal,
as well as under an unequal Providence? Nay, is
it not more evidently and invariably fo, in the
abfence of thofe inequalities which hinder our

[b] Vol. v. p. 429.

feeing

feeing clearly, and feeling conftantly, that *the practice of morality is our* INTEREST *as well as duty.*

—*But men, who found themfelves conftantly protected from the evils that fall on others, might grow infenfibly to think themfelves unconcerned in the* COMMON FATE. What are thofe *evils*, under an equal Providence, which *fall on others*, and from which the good man is *protected?* Are they not the punifhments inflicted on the wicked? And how is the good man protected from them? Is it not by his perfeverance in Virtue? It is therefore impoffible he fhould grow unconcerned to thofe evils which his Lordfhip calls the *common fate*, when he fees his *intereft* and his duty fo clofely connected, that there is no way of avoiding thofe evils but by perfevering in virtue. But the name of *common fate*, which he gives unto them, detects his prevarication. He pretends to reafon againft an equal Providence, yet flurs in upon us, in its ftead, a *Providence which only protects good men*; or rather *one certain fpecies of good men*; *and leaves all other to their* COMMON FATE. But admit it poffible for the good man to *relax in his benevolence, and to grow infenfible to the common fate:* there is, in *the ftate here affumed,* a fpeedy means of bringing him to himfelf; and that is, his being no longer *protected from the evils that fall on others:* for when men *relax in their benevolence*, his Lordfhip tells you, *they relax in their virtue:* and, give me leave to tell his Lordfhip, that when men relax in their virtue, an equal Providence relaxes in its protection; or, to fpeak more properly, the rewards of virtue are abated in proportion.

However, *fpiritual pride* (he fays) *might infect the virtuous, thus protected:* And this he will prove *a fortiori*, from the cafe of ENTHUSIASTS; who only
imagine

imagine they have this protection, and have it not. Now, what if we fhould fay, it is this very *enthufiaftic fpirit* itfelf, and not the vifions of *Protection* it is apt to raife, which is the true caufe of *fpiritual pride?* ENTHUSIASM is that temper of mind, in which the imagination has got the better of the judgment. In this difordered ftate of things, Enthufiafm, when it happens to be turned upon religious matters, becomes FANATICISM : and this, in its extreme, begets the fancy of our being the peculiar favorites of Heaven. Now, every one fees, that SPIRITUAL PRIDE is the *caufe*, and not the *effect* of the diforder. For what but fpiritual pride fpringing out of prefumptive holinefs, could bring the Fanatic to fancy himfelf exalted above the common condition of the Faithful? It is true, when he is got thus far, the folly which brought him hither, may carry him further; and then, all to come will be indeed the effect of his diforder. But fuppofe it were not the enthufiaftic Spirit, but the vifions of protection, it is apt to raife, which is the caufe of fpiritual pride; Is there no difference between a *vifion* and a *reality?* Fancy may occafion thofe diforders which Fact may remove. This, I perfuade myfelf, is the cafe here : The real communication of Grace purifies thofe paffions, and exalts them into virtues, which, the ftrong delufion of fuch a ftate only renders more grofs and violent. And here it may be worth while to take notice, that his Lordfhip, in this objection to an extraordinary Providence, from the hurt it does to general benevolence, feems to have had the *Jewifh People* in his eye ; who in the latter ages of their Republic, were commonly charged, and perhaps not altogether unjuftly, with want of benevolence to the reft of mankind: a fact, which tho' it makes no-

thing

thing for his purpose, makes very much for mine, as it furnishes me with an example to support what is here said of Fanaticism; an infirmity pretty general amongst the Jews of those Ages. They had outlived their extraordinary Providence; but not the memory, nor even the effects of it; nay, the warmer tempers were hardly brought to think it had ceased. This filled them with spiritual pride, as the elect of God; a disposition which, it is confessed, tends readily to destroy or to *relax* general benevolence. But what now are the natural consequences, which the actual administration of an equal Providence would have on the human mind? In this case, as in the other, a warm temper, whose object was Religion, would be obnoxious to the common weakness of our nature, and too apt to disgrace itself by spiritual pride: but as this is one of the vices which an equal Providence is always at hand to punish, the cure would be direct and speedy. The recovered Votary, we will now suppose to be received again into the number of the Good; and to find himself in the *little flock and chosen sheep*, as they are nick-named by this noble Writer. Well, but his danger is not yet over; the sense of this high prerogative of humanity might revive, in a warm temper, the still unmortified seeds of spiritual pride. Admit this to be the case; what follows? His pride revives indeed, but it is only to be again humbled: for punishment is still closely attendant on vice and folly. At length, this holy discipline, the necessary consequence of an equal Providence, effectually does its work; it purifies the mind from low and selfish partialities, and adorns the Will with general benevolence, public spirit, and love of all its fellow creatures.

What

What then could fupport his Lordfhip in fo perverfe a judgment concerning the ftate and condition of good men under an equal Providence?
That which fupports all his other infults on Religion; his fophiftical change of the queftion. He
objects to an equal Providence (which, Religionifts
pretend, hath been adminiftred during one period
of the Difpenfation of Grace) where good men
are conftantly rewarded, and wicked men as conftantly punifhed; and he takes the matter of his
objection from the fanatical idea of a *favoured elect*,
(which never exifted but in over-heated brains)
where reward and punifhment are diftributed, not
on the proportions of merit and de-merit, but on
the diabolic dreams of certain eternal decrees of
election and reprobation, unrelated to any human
principle of juftice.

But now, Reader, keep the queftion fteddily
in your eye, and his Lordfhip's reafoning in this
paragraph difclofes fuch a complication of abfurdities as will aftonifh you. You fee an equal
Providence, which, in and through the very act of
rewarding benevolence, public fpirit, and humi-
lity, becomes inftrumental in producing, in thofe
fo rewarded, felfifhnefs, neglect of the public, and
fpiritual pride. ——

His Lordfhip's laft objection to an extraordinary
Providence is, that it would NOT ANSWER ITS
END.

" I will conclude this head (fays he) by ob-
" ferving, that we have *example* as well as *reafon*
" for us, when we reject the hypothefis of parti-
" cular Providences. God was the king of the
" Jewifh

" Jewiſh People. His preſence reſided amongſt
" them, and his juſtice was manifeſted daily in re-
" warding and puniſhing by unequivocal, ſignal,
" and miraculous interpoſitions of his power.
" The effect of all was this, the People rebelled
" at one time and repented at another. Particular
" Providences, directed by God himſelf immedi-
" ately, upon the ſpot, if I may ſay ſo, had par-
" ticular temporal effects only, none general nor
" laſting : and the People were ſo little ſatisfied
" with this ſyſtem of Government that they de-
" poſed the ſupreme Being, and inſiſted to have
" another King, and to be governed like their
" neighbours ᶜ."

In ſupport of this laſt objection, the Reader ſees,
his Lordſhip was forced to throw off the maſk, and
fairly to tell us what he aimed at ; that is to ſay, to
diſcredit the extraordinary Providence mentioned
by Moſes. An equal Providence, ſays he, will
not anſwer its *end*. What is its end ? Here, his
prevarications bring us, as uſual, to our diſtinc-
tions.— When this Providence is adminiſtered for
the ſake of *Particulars*, its firſt end is to diſcipline
us in virtue, and keep us in our duty : When adminiſtred for the ſake of a *Community*, its firſt end
is to ſupport the Inſtitution it had erected. Now
his Lordſhip, proceeding from reaſon to example,
gives us this of the Jewiſh Republic, to prove
that an equal or extraordinary Providence does not
anſwer one or other or both theſe ends,

But it is unlucky for him, that here, where he
employs the example, he cannot forbear, any

ᶜ Vol. v. p. 430.

more

more than in numberlefs other places of his writings, to tell us that he believes nothing of the matter. — *How long this Theocracy may be faid to have continued* (fays he) *I am quite unconcerned to know, and fhould be forry to mifpend my time in inquiring.* The example then is unreal, and only brought as an argument *ad hominem*. But, the misfortune is, that no laws of good reafoning will admit fuch an argument *ad hominem* on this queftion, *Of the* EFFECTS *of a* REAL *extraordinary Providence*; becaufe the nature of the effects of a REAL Providence can never be difcovered by the effects of a PRETENDED one. To fay the truth, his Lordfhip is at prefent out of luck. For had he indeed believed the extraordinary Providence of the Jews to be *real*, his own reprefentation of the cafe would, on his own principles, have proved it but *pretended*. For 'tis a principle with him, that where the means do not produce the end, fuch means (all pretences notwithftanding) are but human inventions. It is thus he argues againft the Divinity of the Chriftian Religion; which he concludes to be an impofture from its not having effected that lafting reformation of manners, which he fuppofes was its principal defign to accomplifh.

So far as to the CHOICE of his example. He manages no better in the APPLICATION of it.

We have diftinguifhed, concerning the *ends* of an extraordinary Providence. Let us fuppofe now, that his Lordfhip takes the principal end of the Jewifh Theocracy to be the reformation of *Particulars*. He refers to their hiftory, and pretends to fhew they were not reformed. Now whatever other confequences may attend this fuppofed Fact,

the

the moſt obvious and glaring is this, That his
Lordſhip, in procceding from *reaſon* to *example*,
has given us ſuch an example as overturns or ſuper-
ſedes all his reaſoning.   According to his reaſoning, an extraordinary Providence would tye virtue
and good manners ſo faſt down upon every Individual, that his very Will would be forced, and
the merit of doing what he had not in his power
to forbear, abſolutely deſtroyed.   The Reader
would now perhaps expeƈt his example ſhould confirm this pretended faƈt ? Juſt otherwiſe. His example ſhews his faƈt to be a fiƈtion, and that men
remained as bad as ever.

But I have no need of taking any artificial advantage of his Lordſhip's bad reaſoning. For,
when we ſee it ſo conſtantly oppoſed to truth, it is
far from being an additional diſcredit to it, that
it is as conſtantly oppoſed to it ſelf.

The truth indeed is, that the great and principal
end of the JEWISH THEOCRACY, was to keep that
People a ſeparate nation, under their own Law and
Religion, till the coming of the MESSIAH ; and
to prepare things for his reception by preſerving
amongſt them the doƈtrine of the UNITY. Now,
to judge whether the Theocracy or extraordinary
Providence effeƈted its end, we have only to conſider, Whether this people, to the coming of
Chriſt, did continue a diſtinƈt Nation ſeparated
from all the other tribes of Mankind, and diſtinguiſhed from them, by the worſhip of the one true
God.   And on enquiry, we ſhall find, they not only did continue thus diſtinƈt and diſtinguiſhed, but
have ſo continued ever ſince. A Circumſtance
which having no example amongſt any other People;

7

ple, is fufficient to convince us, that there muft have been fome amazing power in that Theocracy, which could go on operating for fo many ages after the extraordinary adminiftration of it had ceafed. Let us conclude therefore, that his Lord-fhip having nothing to urge againft the due efficacy of this extraordinary Providence, but that, *the people rebelled at one time and repented at another, and that this Providence had only temporary effects*, is the moft ample confeffion of his defeat.

The End of the FOURTH VOLUME.

E R R A T A.